MW00988157

Postmodern Apologetics?

John D. Caputo, *series editor*

PERSPECTIVES IN
CONTINENTAL
PHILOSOPHY

CHRISTINA M. GSCHWANDTNER

Postmodern Apologetics?

Arguments for God in Contemporary Philosophy

FORDHAM UNIVERSITY PRESS

New York ■ 2013

Library of Congress Cataloging-in-Publication Data is available from the publisher.

Printed in the United States of America

15 14 13   5 4 3 2 1

First edition

for JanElle and Kara

Contents

Abbreviations

Martin Heidegger

BT   *Being and Time*. Translated by Joan Stambaugh. Albany: SUNY Press, 1996.

BW   *Basic Writings*. Edited by David Farrell Krell. San Francisco: HarperCollins, 1993.

DT   *Discourse on Thinking*. Translated by John M. Anderson and E. Hans Freund. New York: Harper & Row, 1966.

ID   *Identity and Difference*. Translated by Joan Stambaugh. New York: Harper & Row, 1969. [For the essay "The Onto-theo-logical Constitution of Metaphysics," also reprinted in *The Religious*, edited by John D. Caputo. Oxford: Blackwell Publishers, 2003: 67–76.]

PR   *The Phenomenology of Religious Life*. Translated by Matthias Fritsch and Jennifer Anna Goscetti-Ferencei. Bloomington: Indiana University Press, 2004.

PT   "Phenomenology and Theology." In *The Religious*, edited by John D. Caputo. Oxford: Blackwell Publishers, 2003: 49–65.

Emmanuel Lévinas

BPW   *Basic Philosophical Writings*. Bloomington: Indiana University Press, 1996.

GDT   *God, Death, and Time*. Translated by Bettina Bergo. Stanford, Calif.: Stanford University Press, 2000.

OB   *Otherwise Than Being or Beyond Essence*. Translated by Alphonso Lingis. Pittsburgh: Duquesne University Press, 1981.

TI   *Totality and Infinity: An Essay in Exteriority*. Translated by Alphonso Lingis. Pittsburgh: Duquesne University Press, 1969.

Jacques Derrida

AR   *Acts of Religion*. Edited by Gil Anidjar. London/New York: Routledge, 2002.

CF   *Circumfession*. In *Jacques Derrida*, edited by Geoffrey Bennington. Chicago: University of Chicago Press, 1993.

DNT   *Derrida and Negative Theology*. Edited by Harold Coward and Toby Foshay. Albany: SUNY Press, 1992. [For the essays "Of an Apocalyptic Tone Newly Adopted in Philosophy" and "How to Avoid Speaking: Denials."]

GD   *The Gift of Death*. Translated by David Willis. Chicago: University of Chicago Press, 1995.

ON   *On the Name*. Edited by Thomas Dutoit. Stanford, Calif.: Stanford University Press, 1995.

Paul Ricoeur

CC   *Critique and Conviction: Conversations with François Azouvi and Marc de Launay*. Translated by Kathleen Blamey. New York: Columbia University Press, 1988.

CR   *The Course of Recognition*. Translated by David Pellauer. Chicago: University of Chicago Press, 2005.

FS   *Figuring the Sacred: Religion, Narrative and Imagination*. Edited by Mark I. Wallace. Translated by David Pellauer. Minneapolis: Fortress Press, 1997.

LD   *Living Up to Death*. Translated by David Pellauer. Chicago: University of Chicago Press, 2009.

OA	*Oneself as Another*. Translated by Kathleen Blamey. Chicago: University of Chicago Press, 1992.
RB	"Religious Belief: The Difficult Path of the Religious." In *Passion for the Possible: Thinking with Paul Ricoeur*, edited by Brian Treanor and Henry Isaac Venema. New York: Fordham University Press, 2010.
SE	*The Symbolism of Evil*. Translated by Emerson Buchanan. New York: Harper & Row, 1967.
TA	*From Text to Action: Essays in Hermeneutics II*. Translated by Kathleen Blamey and John B. Thompson. Evanston, Ill.: Northwestern University Press, 2007.

Jean-Luc Marion

BG	*Being Given: Toward a Phenomenology of Givenness*. Translated by Jeffrey L. Kosky. Stanford, Calif.: Stanford University Press, 2002.
CQ	*Cartesian Questions: Method and Metaphysics*. Chicago: University of Chicago Press, 1999.
GWB	*God Without Being*. Translated by Thomas A. Carlson. Chicago: University of Chicago Press, 1991.
VR	*The Visible and the Revealed*. New York: Fordham University Press, 2008.

Michel Henry

I	*Incarnation: Une philosophie de la chair*. Paris: Seuil, 2000.
IT	*I Am the Truth: Toward a Philosophy of Christianity*. Translated by Susan Emanuel. Stanford, Calif.: Stanford University Press, 2003.
MP	*Material Phenomenology*. Translated by Scott Davidson. New York: Fordham University Press, 2008.
WC	*Words of Christ*. Translated by Christina M. Gschwandtner. Grand Rapids, Mich.: William B. Eerdmans Publishing Company, 2012.

Jean-Louis Chrétien

AS   *The Ark of Speech*. Translated by Andrew Brown. London/
      New York: Routledge, 2004.

CR   *The Call and the Response*. Translated by Anne A. Davenport.
      New York: Fordham University Press, 2004.

HH   *Hand to Hand: Listening to the Work of Art*. Translated by
      Stephen E. Lewis. New York: Fordham University Press, 2003.

R   *Répondre: Figures de la réponse et de la responsabilité*. Paris:
      Presses Universitaires de France, 2007.

UU   *The Unforgettable and the Unhoped For*. Translated by Jeffrey
      Bloechl. New York: Fordham University Press, 2002.

Jean-Yves Lacoste

EA   *Experience and the Absolute: Disputed Questions on the Humanity
      of Man*. Translated by Mark Raftery-Skeban. New York:
      Fordham University Press, 2004.

PD   *La Phénoménalité de Dieu: Neuf études*. Paris: Cerf, 2008.

PP   *Présence et parousie*. Paris: Ad Solem, 2006.

Emmanuel Falque

DCA   *Dieu, la chair et l'autre: D'Irénée à Duns Scot*. Paris: Presses
      Universitaires de France, 2008.

MP   *The Metamorphosis of Finitude: An Essay on Birth and
      Resurrection*. Translated by George Hughes. New York:
      Fordham University Press, 2012.

NA   *Les noces de l'agneau: Essai philosophique sur le corps et
      l'eucharistie*. Paris: Cerf, 2011.

PG   *Le passeur de Gethsémani: Angoisse, souffrance et mort. Lecture
      existentielle et phénoménologique*. Paris: Cerf, 1999.

Merold Westphal

GGD   *God, Guilt and Death: An Existential Phenomenology of Religion*.
      Bloomington: Indiana University Press, 1984.

KC   *Kierkegaard's Critique of Reason and Society*. Macon, Ga.: Mercer
      University Press, 1987.

OO	*Overcoming Onto-Theology: Toward a Postmodern Christian Faith.* New York: Fordham University Press, 2001.
SF	*Suspicion and Faith: The Religious Uses of Modern Atheism.* Grand Rapids, Mich.: William B. Eerdmans Publishing Company, 1993. [Reprinted by Fordham University Press, 1998.]
TS	*Transcendence and Self-Transcendence: On God and the Soul.* Bloomington: Indiana University Press, 2004.
WW	*Whose Community? Which Interpretation? Philosophical Hermeneutics for the Church.* Grand Rapids, Mich.: Baker Academic, 2009.

John D. Caputo

DH	*Demythologizing Heidegger.* Bloomington: Indiana University Press, 1993.
MRH	*More Radical Hermeneutics: On Not Knowing Who We Are.* Bloomington: Indiana University Press, 2000.
OR	*On Religion.* London/New York: Routledge, 2001.
PTD	*The Prayers and Tears of Jacques Derrida: Religion Without Religion.* Bloomington: Indiana University Press, 1997.
RH	*Radical Hermeneutics: Repetition, Deconstruction, and the Hermeneutic Project.* Bloomington: Indiana University Press, 1987.
WG	*The Weakness of God: A Theology of the Event.* Bloomington: Indiana University Press, 2006.
WWJD	*What Would Jesus Deconstruct? The Good News of Postmodernism for the Church.* Grand Rapids, Mich.: Baker Academic, 2007.

Richard Kearney

A	*Anatheism: Returning to God After God.* New York: Columbia University Press, 2010.
AF	*After God: Richard Kearney and the Religious Turn in Continental Philosophy.* New York: Fordham University Press, 2006. [For the essays "Epiphanies of the Everyday: Toward a Micro-Eschatology," "Enabling God," and "In Place of a Response."]

GMB   *The God Who May Be: A Hermeneutics of Religion.*
       Bloomington: Indiana University Press, 2001.
SGM   *Strangers, Gods and Monsters: Interpreting Otherness.* London/
       New York: Routledge, 2003.

Preface

Postmodern Apologetics? Both of these words tend to be loaded and, at times, hotly contested. Both have negative connotations, at least in some circles. And, in fact, they seem diametrically opposed to each other. Is not *apologetics* a militant defense of traditional Christianity, associated with forced baptisms, mass conversions, and screaming demagogues? And is not *postmodernism* an equally militant rejection of any such belief, in favor of other beliefs or no particular beliefs at all, either complete and utter relativism that rejects all values and virtues or a meaningless term thought up by some doomsayers who thought the modern age was over when, really, we are still in the middle of it? If "apologetics" stands for blind and dogmatic faith and "postmodern" for the complete rejection and even suppression of faith, how could the two possibly meet? Yet obviously, both descriptions are caricatures.

The introduction explores the history of apologetics in more detail, so let me define it simply in terms of the subtitle: "Apologetics" is used here to characterize the ways in which contemporary philosophy articulates the coherence and value of religious experience and belief in God. Quite a few contemporary thinkers have begun anew to examine the question of whether it is possible to have an experience of the divine and what such an experience might look like. And my central argument is that they do indeed engage in arguments for the validity, coherence, and meaningfulness of such thinking about religious experience. Thus, they are, at least in some minimalist sense, apologetic projects: projects in defense of God or

Christian faith. (A couple among them do actually go further and occasionally make statements about Christianity having the *best* or even *only* account of an experience of the divine. That would be a much stronger, and probably more problematic, apologetic claim.)

Yet, in all cases, these "apologetic projects," if they may be called such, are qualified by the term "postmodern." The meaning of that term will also emerge more fully in the course of the discussion, but I take it loosely to refer to what comes after the modern and is sufficiently different from or even opposed to it, to require a separate term. More specifically, I use it roughly synonymous with what has come to be called "continental" philosophy (as opposed to "analytical" philosophy), usually including twentieth- and twenty-first-century French and German thinkers, often occupied with such philosophical occupations as existentialism, phenomenology, hermeneutics, and deconstruction (although there are others). The thinkers treated here are primarily French, or deeply influenced by French thinkers, and are all phenomenological and, to some extent, hermeneutic thinkers. Perhaps a more correct (and less contentious but also less interesting) title would have been "Phenomenological Apologetics" rather than "Postmodern Apologetics."

This book, then, has essentially two purposes: On the one hand, it is an introduction to major thinkers in what is beginning to be called the field of "Continental Philosophy of Religion," written for students and any other interested "lay person." Thus, I aim above all to present the arguments here as clearly and non-technically as possible, which is also why I have tried to keep the notes and extensive engagement with secondary sources to a minimum. A section with suggestions for "further reading" is provided at the end of the book. On the other hand, the book also sustains an argument that the philosophies treated in Part I prepare and those in Part II sustain an apologetic argument for Christianity. Part III deals with the most recent American appropriations of and responses to the French thinkers treated in Part II.

To set the scene, the introduction provides a brief and rather sweeping survey of what an apologetic endeavor used to look like and shows how such arguments grew to be generally considered unsuccessful and even invalid. In Europe, by the early (and certainly the middle) of the twentieth century, religion seemed to be at the very least outmoded, if not actually dead. Most philosophers were no longer interested in religious questions and, for much of the twentieth century, religion was largely a philosophical taboo. This has dramatically changed in the late twentieth and early twenty-first century and now quite a few, primarily French, philosophers are again talking about God and religion. The introduction lays out this history of apologetics and the demise of the project of "natural theology." It also introduces the shift toward renewed thinking about God and religious experience in the endeavors of "phenomenology" and "hermeneutics." It explains what these endeavors are and how they might prove useful for thinking about God, while also qualifying what sort of thinking that might turn out to be. (This survey is by its very nature very introductory and those familiar with this history and with the fields of phenomenology and hermeneutics may want to start with Chapter 1 instead.)

Part I lays the groundwork for the arguments in Part II. Chapter 1 discusses Martin Heidegger who is an absolutely essential figure for all the thinkers treated in the second and third parts of the book. None of the contemporary "religious" phenomenologies would be possible or coherent without Heidegger's thinking. Of course, this chapter cannot survey Heidegger's entire philosophy, but it explains certain fundamental concepts that are assumed by all the later thinkers, such as the notion of "ontological difference" and of metaphysics as "onto-theo-logy." It deals with Heidegger's contention that theology is an "ontic" science that is absolutely distinct from phenomenology or philosophy as an "ontological" thinking, as put forth in his early essay "Phenomenology and Theology." It also considers the significance of Heidegger's language of Being and his claim that the term has no place in a "theology," especially as the status of ontological language becomes significant for several of the later thinkers. The chapter concludes with a discussion of Heidegger's notion of truth as *aletheia* and some of his late writings on the holy, the gods, and the Fourfold.

Chapter 2 treats the philosophy of Emmanuel Lévinas. Against the claim of some commentators, it argues that Lévinas is not a theological thinker and that his philosophy does not provide an argument for Jewish belief (or for Christian belief, for that matter). Unlike what might be said of the later thinkers, Lévinas does not provide a defense for God and is not even really interested in religious experience or religious phenomena. Even his writings about the infinite and God are directed toward and placed in service of his ethical concern for the human other. Yet, Lévinas's philosophy, even far more explicitly than Heidegger's, makes the later thinking possible through his heavy use of biblical terminology, his strong emphasis on transcendence and otherness, and also by his critique of onto-theo-logy.

Chapter 3 considers certain aspects of the philosophy of Jacques Derrida. Although Derrida claimed that he "rightly passes for an atheist," he has written extensively on religion and has explicitly engaged some of the other thinkers treated here. Derrida is not a religious thinker and does not provide arguments for religious belief, yet he certainly figures prominently, especially in the American discussion of the other French thinkers. I discuss his arguments that "différance" is not a type of negative theology and consider his writings on the name of God and on khōra. The chapter also examines some of his more recent writings on the gift, forgiveness, hospitality, and the role of religion in politics. As in the case of Heidegger, this chapter obviously deals with only some of Derrida's extensive writings, namely those that are most influential for the larger discussion of religion and the divine.

Part II considers the more explicitly "apologetic" thinkers. It begins with Paul Ricoeur, focusing especially on his work on religious hermeneutics. It does not treat all of Ricoeur's extensive work and certainly does not argue that all of it is religiously motivated, as Ricoeur was always very careful to distinguish his philosophical from his religious projects. Yet the texts in which he is concerned with Scripture or an interpretation of religious experience do indeed make an argument for religious language as meaningful and true. The chapter explores his notion of religious truth as manifestation, as a source of meaning, and as an invitation to transformation. It also shows how his interpretation of religious texts leads him to define religious language as poetic, polyphonic, and excessive. The chapter hence suggests that even the more heavily phenomenological thinkers remain indebted to Ricoeur's religious hermeneutics, especially in the way in which he defines the "truth" of religious experience.

Chapter 5 explores Jean-Luc Marion's religious phenomenology and his desire to safeguard God's name from idolatry and univocity. It outlines Marion's project, focusing in particular on his proposal of a phenomenology of givenness, the possibility of saturated phenomena, and an erotic reduction that leads to the possibility of an alternative type of knowledge, grounded in the heart instead of the mind. It shows how his philosophy proposes to introduce new religious phenomena into the realm of philosophy and to argue for their coherence, validity, and appeal.

Chapter 6 treats Michel Henry's phenomenology of immanence and affectivity, which especially in his final works takes on an explicitly religious character and becomes closely identified with a particular interpretation of Christianity. Drawing a stark contrast between the "Truth" of Christianity and the "truth" of the world, he contends that Christianity provides access to a phenomenology of immanence that is able to overcome certain problems in the phenomenological project by speaking of the immediacy of Life as the origin of all affectivity. According to Henry, it is through Christ that we participate in the divine life of God as self-affection and is the only way in which we can become authentic persons. He also provides a trenchant critique of contemporary culture and the truths of science and technology.

Chapter 7 is concerned with Jean-Louis Chrétien's phenomenology. Chrétien attempts to recover something more originary and more primordial than traditional philosophy, something that escapes its obsession with presence and evidence. In so doing, he draws on biblical texts and poetic sources in order to open up a dimension of experience that is hidden and beyond "normal" experience, something situated at the extremes of experience and thought. He shows how we are always already responding to a prior "call," whether this is the call of beauty, of other humans, of nature, or even of God. Chrétien opens the path for an exploration of spirituality, of prayer, and of religious experiences of hope and memory. Religious and mystical thought receive new (philosophical) life and justification in Chrétien's analyses, whether in uncovering a religious dimension of the call-response structure, in analyzing the human voice as a response of praise to the world, or by highlighting the physicality and need for embodiment in religious experience.

Jean-Yves Lacoste's phenomenology of liturgy is the subject of Chapter 8. Closely following and at times vigorously criticizing Heidegger's philosophy, Lacoste has developed a phenomenological analysis of prayer and liturgy as our "being-before-God," which he suggests goes beyond Heidegger's "being-in-the-world." He also attempts a recovery of "presence" as a useful phenomenological term by focusing on the mystery of the Eucharist. For him, liturgical experience and presence are always also closely linked to the expectation of the *parousia*. Like Chrétien, Lacoste is very interested in phenomenologies of prayer and of the body. He also emphasizes the communal aspect of religious faith far more than some of the other thinkers.

Chapter 9 examines the writings of Emmanuel Falque, current dean of the faculty of philosophy at the Institut catholique in Paris and a new voice in this emerging field. Falque is particularly interested in questions of the body, examining themes of corporeality and resurrection, flesh and Eucharist. He draws explicitly on liturgical and theological texts for his phenomenological analysis, but also interacts with the work of several other thinkers examined in this volume. Part II ends with a preliminary conclusion that brings the various claims of these thinkers together and argues more fully that they are all on some level engaged in an apologetic project, although this apologetic differs from the modern one associated with natural theology.

Part III considers the reception of these thinkers more specifically in the North American context, focusing on the three thinkers that have contributed most to this contemporary conversation: Merold Westphal, John D. Caputo, and Richard Kearney. The chapters in this part examine their work but focus especially on the ways in which they appropriate the various French thinkers and often modify their ideas. Chapter 11 contends that Merold Westphal's philosophical project is best understood as a postmodern version of faith. In his work on hermeneutics and phenomenology, Westphal argues that postmodern thinking not only criticizes Christian faith, but if taken seriously, can serve to enrich and enliven it. I examine Westphal's work under three foci: his argument for a postmodern faith, his thinking about a "postmodern self," and his vision of a God freed from the shackles of onto-theo-logical restrictions.

In Chapter 12, I approach John D. Caputo's work as an argument for postmodern hope. Caputo is most well known for his interpretations of Jacques Derrida, yet his writings range from his early engagements with Heidegger's work to his most recent discussions of Malabou and Žižek. The chapter explicates his writings on Heidegger and Derrida in some detail, since they have been so influential in the contemporary discussion. It goes on to consider his proposal for a "radical" hermeneutic project that would rethink issues of faith, ethics, and scientific knowledge. It concludes by examining his more recent proposals for a "theology of the event" or a theology of "perhaps," while arguing that the figure of hope is at the heart of all of Caputo's work.

Finally, Chapter 13 engages the work of Richard Kearney and asserts that it is best understood as a kind of postmodern charity. Kearney's deeply hermeneutic work seeks to articulate a God of possibility and promise who is incarnated in our care for the poor and marginalized. The themes of hospitality and welcome to the stranger are central to Kearney's work. The chapter sets forth his proposal for a God of "loving possibility" and his micro-eschatological "anatheistic retrieval," which makes it possible to think about God "after God" and to find the divine in the "littlest things" of mundane reality. The book concludes by considering the similarities and parallels between these various projects and wondering what this may mean for speaking of the divine and religious experience today.

The philosophers discussed here are obviously a selection only. There are many other contemporary thinkers, even French thinkers, who speak about God, faith, or religion. Among these, one might mention Julia Kristeva, Luce Irigaray, Gianno Vattimo, Slavoj Žižek, Jean Greisch, Jean-Luc Nancy, Alain Badiou, and Claude Romano. Many of them are important thinkers and the fact that they are not discussed here does not mean I dismiss their arguments or find them irrelevant. Yet they do not appear to be engaged in any particularly "apologetic" project. Rather, they are often using religious themes for other (for example, psychoanalytic, social, or political) purposes. They do not engage religion, or specifically Christianity, for its own sake in the way in which the thinkers treated in Parts II and III of this book do. Finally, the reader will notice very quickly that most arguments (and examples) are concerned with various versions of *Christian* belief or thinking and the "God" referred to is usually (although at times a fairly untraditional version of) the Christian God (with the exception of Lévinas and to some extent Derrida). My exposition and analysis of the various arguments will then also be primarily (if not exclusively) in a Christian register. Some of the phenomenological and hermeneutic arguments may well apply also to other religious traditions and may certainly be able to do productive work there (and these traditions might have more convincing examples of religious experience), but it would be far beyond the bounds of this project to venture into these directions.

A few concluding comments of a more technical nature: First, I have employed existing English translations whenever possible. When no English translation exists, all translations from languages other than English are my own. Second, all emphases in quotations are in the original, unless indicated otherwise. Third, references to humans or the divine are almost exclusively male in the French writers. While I have sought to be as inclusive as possible in my own writing, I have not altered gender-specific language in direct quotations. Finally, the term "onto-theo-logy," which is central to this discussion and appears in many of the texts, is spelled in a variety of ways. I have generally tried to follow the standard spelling of the author I discuss in the respective chapter (thus employed "onto-theo-logy" in the chapter on Marion, but "onto-theology" in the chapters on Westphal and Kearney). Although the term is not always interpreted in exactly the same fashion by all thinkers, the differences in the use of the hyphen does not itself imply a difference in meaning. (Heidegger himself was not entirely consistent on this point and spelled the term variously "onto-theo-logy," "onto-theology," and "ontotheology.")

Acknowledgments

This book would not have been possible without the assistance of many people. Most obviously, it has profited from the rich thought of the thinkers discussed and, in the case of Westphal, Caputo, Kearney, and Marion, also from generous more direct engagement and encouragement. I thank my colleagues in the philosophy department at the University of Scranton for their support, and especially Tim Casey for reading the Heidegger chapter and Duane Armitage for reading the entire manuscript and making many valuable suggestions (especially in regard to Heidegger). I have also learned much from the students with whom I have discussed the work of these thinkers both inside and outside the classroom, especially Bryne Lewis, Joe Strubeck, Pete Ruane, Joe Quinn, and Bill Woody. I also wish to thank Helen Tartar for her encouragement of young scholars, in general, and for her support of this project, in particular, and for her willingness to read over and provide critique for the Derrida chapter. I am grateful to the readers Jim Faulconer, Jeff McCurry, and Eric Severson for their helpful comments on the initial manuscript. Special thanks to Nancy Rapoport for her excellent copy editing and her patience with my many questions and suggestions.

This book is dedicated to JanElle and Kara, who were not only the first to welcome and befriend this European stranger in the United States, but whose faithful and generous friendship has sustained me over the many years since. Thank you for many late-night conversations about everything from childrearing to matters of God and faith, for putting up with my endless doubts and questions, and for allowing me to be a part of your lives. I am deeply grateful for your friendship.

Postmodern Apologetics?

Introduction

The "Death of God" and the Demise of Natural Theology

As pointed out in the preface, both "postmodern" and "apologetics" are somewhat contentious terms that can mean a whole host of things. This introduction outlines the history of apologetics in the Christian tradition in a very broad and general fashion. It concludes with a very brief introduction to postmodernism and the possibility of something like a "postmodern apologetic."

Early Apologetics

While postmodernism is generally associated with fairly recent thinkers, apologetics has a long and rich history. The term was first used by early Christian communities and individuals ("apologists") who defended themselves against attacks by the larger culture or by particular authorities. At times, "apology" simply meant explaining confusions that had arisen about the Christian faith, defending themselves and their fellow believers against invalid accusations. The Latin word *apologia* did not refer to an "apology" in the English sense of the word, i.e. an admission of wrongdoing and a desire to be forgiven. Rather, it meant a *defense*, whether against actual or merely possible accusation or distortion of the faith. Christians did not "excuse themselves" for their faith, but defended it and themselves against attack. There were several groups that early Christian apologists had to confront. Some of these early apologies were about setting the record straight regarding what it meant to be "Christian," especially by explaining what

Christians did and did not do. For example, several early apologists, such as Minucius Felix, tried to assure their opponents (often with some level of exasperation) that Christians do not fry and eat their babies, that they do not drink blood, and that if their liturgy said that they did that had nothing to do with cannibalism.[1] Soldiers who became Christians had to defend the fact that they would no longer fight. (For early believers, war was thought to be incompatible with Christian faith.) Many apologists tried to explain that Christians were not disloyal to the emperor even if they did not worship him as a god and did not sacrifice to the Roman deities. Some defenses took place in the context of trials: Catherine of Alexandria (early fourth century), who became the patron saint of philosophers for the Western church, is said to have converted multiple "pagan" philosophers with her reasoned argument on behalf of Christianity before being martyred for her faith. (Her debate with the philosophers, sent to dissuade her from her newfound faith, is pictured on the front cover of this book.) At times, the defense was not directed to legislates and government authorities trying to wipe them out, but instead to competing religious beliefs, such as various Gnostic groups, Jewish faith that was not Christian especially as Christianity became a predominantly non-Jewish sect, and early mystery cults. In all these contexts, Christians had to explain what and in whom they believed in a way that was rational within the context of the time and culture and that made sense to their various audiences. As all these early adversaries or interlocutors were at least on some level religious (even "pagan" Romans had their deities), few of these apologies or rational explanations ever attempted to convince anyone that there was a god, because everyone believed that. Rather, they would argue about the number and nature of this God (there is only one—though Triune—not several; God is good and loving, not evil; God is the Creator, and so on) and about the character of their practices and liturgies that expressed their belief.[2]

Very early on, Christianity also came in contact with philosophy, especially Stoicism, Platonism, Aristotelianism, and Neoplatonism.[3] Much in these philosophies was appropriated by Christian believers, and even when they disagreed with certain aspects of philosophical thinking, they still adopted many of their methods. Many Eastern Christian writers, for example, tended to think of Plato as inspired by the Holy Spirit long before Christ and talked about the divine logos present within the Greek philosophers in some fashion. In both East and West, particularly devoted and saintly Christians were called "philosophers" and the monastic life was often described as the "philosophic" life.[4] Justin Martyr, one of the first apologists, was also known as "Justin the philosopher." In the West, Boethius not only incorporated many Stoic elements into his thought, but portrayed "Lady Philosophy" as his consolation in his trial, assuring him that fate had no power over him and that God was directing human events.[5] Nemesius, Bishop of Emesa, made a similar argument in the East, drawing extensively on Platonic, Aristotelian, and Stoic philosophy as well as Galen's medical treatises.[6] On issues of natural science, medicine, and other knowledge about the natural world, which we now tend to think of as "science," Christian thinkers generally adopted and propounded whatever Aristotle, Galen, and other early thinkers had said.[7] In the West, much of this learning disappeared with the fall of the West Roman Empire and only slowly emerged again in the course of the Middle Ages often in interactions with Islamic and Byzantine cultures.

The Western Middle Ages were a very different kind of environment from the early Christian centuries in the Roman Empire. The church was becoming far more powerful than it had been in the early centuries and was slowly growing into a large institution. Religion influenced every aspect of people's lives, including the life of the mind. Intellectual culture revived, leading to the founding of the first European universities in the twelfth and thirteenth centuries and to much research, which made possible the later scientific revolution. First in the monasteries and later in the universities, intellectual life became vibrant and organized.[8] There was much discussion, of course, about the nature of God and about many aspects of the Christian life. Often these debates were propelled by earlier literature that had interacted with various types of philosophical thought. Augustine already had left a legacy of Neoplatonism in the West. The translation of the works of the fifth-century Eastern thinker Dionysius the Areopagite also generated much discussion in the West about the nature of God and the possibility of knowing and experiencing the divine. There were other medieval thinkers who developed arguments about God in a variety of ways. Anselm's argument for the existence of God as a being "that than which no greater can be conceived" is another example of these kinds of thought experiments, which were often set within reflections on the spiritual life or in the context of prayer (as is the case for Anselm).[9] None of this thought is really "apologetic" in either the ancient or modern sense of the term, as there was no "secular" culture against which the medieval thinkers had to defend themselves. All their reflection happened within the context of a culture suffused with religion in every aspect of personal, social, and public life.

At the height of this development in Western thinking came Thomas Aquinas. What made him so important was the almost simultaneous reintroduction of Aristotelian thought into the West. Three great ancient cultures came together here: Eastern Byzantine, Islamic, and Western Catholic, all suffused and often connected by Judaism via trade and translation (although anti-Semitism was also always a reality in all three of these cultures). Aristotle began to be translated and read at a rapid pace, and Aquinas not only commented meticulously on almost every passage he received of Aristotle's writings, but incorporated the Greek philosopher's thought fully into his own system of Christian truth. Aquinas was an intellectual architect, unparalleled in his success at organizing and presenting Christian faith in the most coherent and convincing manner of the time. From the very beginning of his great work *Summa Theologiae* (a "summation" or "summary" of theology), he wonders what "knowledge" we can have of God and whether theology is a "science" (i.e., an organized and structured way of theoretical thinking in Aristotle's sense).[10] Aquinas suggests that although we may not be able to know God's essence intimately in this life, much knowledge about God and divine things can be attained through practicing rigorously our natural reason without obvious recourse to Christian revelation. This he calls "natural theology" (as opposed to "revealed theology," which is accessible only through revelation). One must remember that Aquinas's conversation partners (even in the *Summa Contra Gentiles* speaking to "pagans") were never atheists in the contemporary sense of the term. Everybody in medieval Europe (including Jews, Muslims, and other minorities) believed in God, and in fact almost all of them believed in a single supreme God and hence shared a monotheistic faith. Therefore, when Aquinas outlined his famous five proofs for the existence of God, no one actually doubted God's existence as such or had to be convinced of it by proof. This is probably also why Aquinas could conclude each proof so easily by saying: "And this is what everyone calls God" (whether speaking of the first cause or what gives ultimate reason and beauty to the universe). Aquinas was reconciling his Christian faith to the "secular" knowledge about the natural world to which he was exposed and doing it brilliantly (Thomists today still continue this tradition), but he was doing it at a time and in an environment where things were still relatively homogenous. Basic theological principles were generally assumed and although interpretation of them differed, such diversity of interpretation took place within an overall coherent Christian worldview. Basic natural principles were also agreed upon and all research was fueled by the insights gained through the writings of Aristotle (which, at the time, were not regarded as contradictory to the Christian spirit). To bring these two together in a natural theology that would explore truths of faith (such as the existence of God, the reality of evil, the need for a Creator and Redeemer, the ethical behavior expected in the Christian life, and so forth) with the tools of natural reason was not an impossible and not even a particularly contentious endeavor (although Aquinas's writings were briefly placed on the Index of forbidden books and one did have to pay some attention to the religious authorities when setting forth one's beliefs). Thus, while *revealed theology* assumed matters one could know and have access to only through faith in revelation (such as the doctrine of the Trinity or of the incarnation, although such truths were few for Aquinas), *natural theology* investigated the matters (both divine and human) that one might understand and access through the use of reason. For many thinkers, Aquinas included, that field was vast indeed, because, after all, reason is given to us by God and thus its employment would ultimately also lead us to the divine.

The Demise of Natural Theology

This began to change slowly in modernity with the emergence and growth of nation states and the various developments in art, economy, science, and industry. The scientific revolution did not erase belief in God—all early scientists were devout believers in the Christian God (including Isaac Newton who rejected the idea of the Trinity but did not therefore stop believing in a divinity that moved the spheres)—but it certainly changed the conception people had of the natural world and of what it meant that God "created" the world.[11] The major challenge to Christian faith came much later. The Reformation and especially the religious wars that followed tore the coherence (and to some extent also the credibility) of the Christian worldview apart. It also led to an increasing questioning of ecclesial authorities of various colors and shapes. The devotion to the new art, sculpture, architecture, painting, and literature—including translation and writing in the vernacular—contributed to this development by re-directing the otherworldly perspective of the Middle Ages to a celebration of beauty, of the human body, of nature, and of life here and now. And although the usual portrayal of Galileo's challenge to church authorities is, for the most part, a caricature of what actually took place,[12] the new science and the ways of thinking accompanying it did increasingly present a challenge to the more monolithic Christian worldview of earlier times. Why?

First, because the new science focused on meticulous research and independent thought. In and of themselves, these were nothing new: Much meticulous research had been and continued to be done in the monasteries and religiously oriented universities.[13] Yet although there was still a general sense in which research was ultimately to God's glory or in service to God, it no longer always coincided with a religious vocation. Kepler, who wanted to "think God's thoughts after him," had initially considered becoming a priest but finally decided that investigating the mystery of the universe scientifically gave him closer access to the divine and he pursued his research with unparalleled rigor. Many new inventions (such as the telescope, the clock, and especially the printing press) made research and its speedy communication possible on an unprecedented scale and pace. And although religious authorities often sponsored such research, their influence was at times also seen as a hindrance to the independence valued by the critical spirit. Nicolaus Copernicus, Johannes Kepler, Galileo Galilei, René Descartes, Francis Bacon, Edmund Hailey, and many others advanced knowledge about the natural world significantly. Their research found its culmination in the work of Isaac Newton, who combined all the available knowledge and insight into one coherent and overwhelmingly convincing system of the natural world. Even this move to questions of knowledge (epistemology) from questions about reality (ontology or metaphysics) that is advocated most profoundly by Descartes is an important shift in emphasis as it focuses not so much on what is already "out there" only waiting to be examined, but instead on the human (usually male) subject who subdues or conquers the object in research or investigation. Thus, research did not replace questions about God or even at first seem to threaten them in any sense, but it did constitute an important shift in emphasis from an investigation into how the *divine* spirit had ordered the world to what the *human* spirit could discover and know about nature.

Again, although Newton himself or his system was certainly not seen as any threat to Christian faith, but often as in service to it or at least confirming the Creator's majesty in putting the universe together so mathematically, the role God played in this system had become much smaller. In Newton's universe, everything is predictable, calculable, perfectly rational, entirely coherent, and well-ordered. God put together this universe and maintains it in working order, but beyond that there is not really much work to be done for the divine. Following Newton, many thinkers began to question the viability of miracles. Miracles came to be defined as anything that was "unnatural" or "supernatural," i.e., anything that broke or at least defied the natural laws Newton had established as ordering and determining the whole universe. (This constituted a new conception of miracles. As the universe had never before been portrayed as a mechanical system run by natural and predetermined laws, miracles also were not conceived as "exceptions" to such a system.) And slowly but surely miracles became increasingly more "unnatural" and less convincing and more difficult to prove to the point where David Hume argues that they really do not occur at all.[14]

The accomplishments of reason in Newton and natural science, but also in many other areas, such as the arts and literatures, seemed incredibly impressive to a great many people. In particular, mathematical reason and logic, which had accomplished so much in the discovery of the universe, appeared to precede it and be at its very foundation. Increasingly, scholars, including many prominent theologians such as Marin de Mersenne, argued that God also must employ reason, logic, and math in exactly the same fashion we do. The very construction of the universe seemed to prove this. God was eminently rational, the greatest mathematician and geometer. In fact, geometry, math, and logic were really superior to God. God could not have acted otherwise, could not accomplish a self-contradiction, could not cause two plus two not to be four, or create a square circle. These basic principles were called the "eternal truths" and they were thought to precede, or at least be equal to, God. (They are "eternal" because they co-exist eternally with the divine.) God would (and could) not do anything illogical or irrational. Human reason thus (although finite) was basically on a par with God and could discover most things about the divine and the universe it had fashioned.[15]

This celebration of reason reached its height in the Enlightenment, especially in the philosophy of Immanuel Kant who suggested that the right slogan for the Enlightenment was to have the courage to use one's own reason and not to submit to anyone else's authority or influence, whether religious or secular.[16] Think for yourself! It was Kant who put the nail in the coffin of natural theology, arguing essentially that religion was only possible "within the limits of reason alone," that it was an entirely rational affair, and that the only useful concern of religion was ethics.[17] The God hypothesis could not be proven, but was necessary to motivate moral behavior and for it to be rewarded. Kant therefore systematically demolished all "proofs" that had been given for God's existence, showing that God's existence could never be proven or disproved by human reasoning.[18] In his critical project, Kant outlined what reason can and cannot do in the attempt to provide a revolution for philosophical thinking in the way Copernicus did for scientific thought. Reason for Kant has both theoretical and practical application. *Theoretical* reason or understanding answers the question of what we might know. Kant is quite clear that we cannot know anything about the existence of God or of anything that is beyond the categories and concepts of our mind, which filters and interprets all experience. We can have understanding of *phenomena*, of how things appear to us, but not of the *noumena*, namely of how things are in and of themselves. *Practical* reason is essentially concerned with action, especially moral action. For morality, God's existence must be assumed, although it cannot be theoretically proven.[19] The role of religion for any rational thinking then becomes limited to ethics. This far more limited role for God and religion will finally be challenged even further by Friedrich Nietzsche and other thinkers.

Many people had, in fact, attempted to harmonize the new science with traditional Christian beliefs. It was argued, for example, that only a wise and loving Creator could have fashioned such a perfect universe. One famous argument, put forward by William Pailey, used the example of God as a watchmaker: If one were to walk along the beach and find an intricately fashioned watch, one would immediately recognize that this watch could not have come about by chance but must be the result of intelligent design. Thus, the order and beauty of the natural universe clearly exhibited the hand of its Creator, the watchmaker. This argument became considerably less convincing after Charles Darwin showed that apparent order and adjustment can actually be the result of chance and adaptation and need not be the result of rational design. Others joined Darwin in demolishing any coherent notion of natural theology.[20] Various political revolutions evidenced that not all governmental authority was directly given by God. Karl Marx argued that economic and political exploitation could not be justified by divine design and that God was not the driving force behind capitalism but instead the idea employed to justify exploitation and suppression of the masses. In fact, economic and social history could be sufficiently explained by their own moving factors (such as economic oppression, alienation, and class struggle) instead of religious reasons. Ludwig Feuerbach contended that religious belief could be explained through various social and cultural factors that make it necessary to project an all-powerful authority figure, which then becomes defined as divine. Thus, "God" is merely a reflection or projection of our own desires and needs. Sigmund Freud, finally, demonstrated that we are deeply motivated by unconscious drives, desires, and fears. Thus, what had previously been thought of as "sin" was re-defined as "disease."[21]

Theology was also doing its own questioning. Much work had been accomplished in the area of biblical research. Some Latin texts were shown to be falsely translated or to rely on forged documents and various interpretations competed for the new translations into the various vernacular languages. Many theologians and biblical scholars, such as Friedrich Schleiermacher, applied the new methods of literary research to the biblical texts (which had also happened in various ways in the past but its results did not seem as threatening to earlier audiences[22]). These thinkers paid attention to the original context, arguing about sources and questioning whether certain texts had actually been written by the authors to whom they were traditionally attributed. Thus, biblical research generally concluded that the texts of the New Testament had arisen within and out of the experience of the early churches and were not necessarily eyewitness accounts by actual disciples of Christ. Many texts of the Old Testament were shown to be late compilations of earlier fragments of texts. (For example, the famous Wellhausen theory argued that the Pentateuch, the first five books of the Bible, were not actually composed by Moses but by at least five different authors or groups of authors who had very different emphases and concerns and lived at different times.) Even other texts of the tradition were shown to have been written much later than originally thought, such as the highly influential works of Dionysius the Areopagite (now for that reason often called Pseudo-Dionysius). Scripture seemed no longer simply the authoritative word of God given directly into human hands, but rather a very human document riddled by many human errors, and very particular to the time and space in which it was written. Much biblical research is still grappling with the repercussions of all this. The contemporary philosophical discipline of hermeneutics, which will play a large role in several of the philosophies examined in this book, is rooted in this activity of examination and interpretation of texts.

Friedrich Nietzsche finally attacked the link between religion and morality by announcing what has become known as "the death of God." The most famous articulation of this is the parable of the madman in *The Joyful Wisdom*. (The title *Die fröhliche Wissenschaft* is also sometimes translated as *The Gay Science*.) A man is portrayed as running into the marketplace in broad daylight with a lantern, screaming that he is searching for God. When people laugh at him, he announces that "we" have killed God and warns about the implications of such a terrifying act:

> Whither is God? . . . I shall tell you. We have killed him—you and I. All of us are his murderers. But how have we done this? How were we able to drink up the sea? Who gave us the sponge to wipe away the entire horizon? What did we do when we unchained the earth from its sun? Whither is it moving now? Whither are we moving now? Away from all suns? Are we not plunging continually? . . . Are we not straying as through an infinite nothing? Do we not feel the breath of empty space? Has it not become colder? Is not night and more night coming on all the while?

The "madman" concludes by wondering: "How shall we, murderers of all murderers, comfort ourselves? What was holiest and most powerful of all that the world has yet owned has bled to death under our knives? . . . Is not the greatness of this deed too great for us? Must not we ourselves become gods simply to seem worthy of it?"[23] Nietzsche certainly does not mince words on the weighty implications of this announcement. The central consequence is that there is no further grounding for moral values and that morality must be created anew by us as we take charge of our own lives. Nietzsche, drawing out the implications of Kant's thinking, identifies Christianity with a particular grounding for moral values. He considers it a quasi-Platonic system where truth and values are located in another reality. Nietzsche defines Christianity as the "extremest thinkable form of corruption," a form of *ressentiment* (resentment) that keeps the masses satisfied and the strong down by glorifying suffering itself and advocating humility.[24] Nietzsche predicts what becomes true subsequently: Belief in God has effectively died. God is no longer a convincing hypothesis. A coherent worldview like that of Christian Platonism is no longer available. Nor can we ground one universal system of moral values, like that of Kant, in an overarching reason, religious or not. All values must be revalued and recreated without the security of belief.[25]

Postmodernism

Postmodernism is, to a large extent, the result of this recognition that there is no longer a coherent worldview or ultimate (metaphysical) ground of values, beliefs, and truth. Jean-François Lyotard, who coined the term *postmodernism*, defines it as a "disbelief in metanarratives."[26] Postmodernism no longer subscribes to one single, coherent worldview, one story about all of reality (i.e., a meta-narrative), but instead advocates telling "little," local stories (*petits récits*). Postmodernism has also been defined as "antifoundationalism," i.e., as a challenge to the modern project, associated especially with Descartes, of finding a certain and indubitable grounding and foundation for truth, on which all other knowledge may be based. Many people now tend to think of ethics as shaped and defined by particular cultures or even as being merely personal opinion or preference. There is no absolute truth that might tell us what is right and wrong in all cases. Very often, even philosophical "postmodern" thought is assumed to be complete relativism or even nihilism and thus seems threatening to many people. The philosophy of deconstruction, associated with Jacques Derrida, is often read as utter relativism or as a desire to destroy all beliefs or commitments. That is a serious misreading, not only of Derrida, but also more generally of postmodern philosophy, which is by and large very concerned with questions of justice and even truth. But postmodern philosophy certainly approaches these questions in a very different way than ancient, medieval, and even (maybe especially) modern thought. John D. Caputo characterizes the postmodern in characteristically gripping fashion:

> All of that [the developments that produced postmodernism] effectively put a lot of what the Enlightenment was trying to sell us on the run, and good riddance. Good riddance to the idea of pure worldless and solipsistic subjects, to the ideal of pure presuppositionless science, to a pure prelinguistic world, to pure objects, to pure consciousness, and to pure reason. Give us some good old-fashioned impure thoughts! The world is a lot more complicated than the moderns think, a lot messier, less well-programmed, less rule-governed, more open-ended and open-textured. . . . the collective idea that human thinking turns on the ability to move among shifting perspectives, vocabularies, and paradigms, we call the *postmodern turn.*[27]

He also emphasizes that "Postmodernism is thus not relativism or skepticism, as its uncomprehending critics almost daily charge, but minutely close attention to detail, a sense for the complexity and multiplicity of things, for close readings, for detailed histories, for sensitivity to differences."[28] Postmodernism, then, challenges the idea that there is one overall coherent version of the Truth, that access to such Truth is through (disembodied and abstract) rationality, and that it is possible to get to some objective position from which to see the world in a neutral fashion. Instead it stresses the importance of listening to many different voices and perspectives, especially those oppressed or marginalized by authorities of whatever sort. It also recognizes that we always speak from within a particular (historical, cultural, economic, political, and so forth) context and that truth is thus always embodied and particular.

Where does all this leave us today? It leaves us with an intellectual society and culture that is predominantly secular, often agnostic, if not atheistic. This is true of much of European culture and it is certainly true of American intellectual life, although that is often confined to academic (or predominantly urban) settings and does not always penetrate the rest of the culture. For most of the twentieth century, the assumption was that intellectuals did not require the "God hypothesis" and that they could do without religious experience of any sort (which was often derided as hype, "enthusiasm," or superstition, if not the source of all bigotry and prejudice).[29] Instead, intellectuals were informed about the truths of science, even if the Einsteinian universe is not quite as transparently coherent and well-organized as the Newtonian one. Science, in fact, has become the paradigm for truth, and truth tends to mean only statements of fact that can be verified through repeated observation and experimentation.

Contemporary intellectuals have little trouble acknowledging that life has evolved from simpler life forms, that the universe formed through an initial blast of energy and continues expanding while creating stars and planets in the course of its evolution. To think that some sort of divinity might have something to do with this process or might possibly even have interrupted and influenced it, or even worse might have become incarnate at the peculiar evolutionary stage of a human being, living on some puny little planet in this vast universe, or that this God might be influenced by the prayers or liturgical gestures of these insignificant beings—all these have become quite unthinkable for many today.

What does all that mean for "thinking" or philosophizing about God today? It means that we have a much harder and very different task before us. Perhaps for the first time in history society no longer subscribes to one common and coherent belief system. Hence, a defense of God cannot proceed from a shared starting point or even assume agreement about basic beliefs or presuppositions. Yet, in order to convince someone, one must talk to him or her in a language that is at least on some level comprehensible. One version of contemporary philosophy of religion attempts this by appealing to the paradigms of modernity or science and defending new proofs for God's existence.[30] On the one hand, analytical philosophers criticize Kant's dismissal of these proofs and try to show (often by using logical parameters) that they are indeed quite coherent. On the other hand, many thinkers accept the contemporary scientific and philosophical worldview, but seek to demonstrate that Christian belief at the very least is not incompatible with it and possibly even provides the best explanation for it.[31] Much philosophy of religion therefore attempts to show the coherence of Christian faith in light of secular culture's "knowledge" about science (and science taken in its widest sense: as natural science, but also as knowledge about human thinking, feeling, and acting, as insights regarding the emergence and behavior of cultures, thus including the social sciences). These philosophies consequently assume that "truth" is indeed defined along scientific parameters, that it means verification and certainty, established by evidence and experiments. In many ways such philosophy continues the "modern" experiment and does not subscribe to postmodernism.

Yet a very different way of talking about faith and God has recently emerged in European philosophy. In 1991, French philosopher Dominique Janicaud was asked to give a report about the status of contemporary French philosophy. He argued, apparently quite appalled by his own discovery, that French phenomenology had been subverted by what he called a "theological turn."[32] Theology had "highjacked" philosophy, especially in the work of philosophers Emmanuel Lévinas, Jean-Luc Marion, and Michel Henry. Janicaud deplored this move and called for a "minimalist" phenomenology (of the sort conducted by Maurice Merleau-Ponty) that would be radically atheistic (or at the very least agnostic) and exclude all discussion of God or religion from philosophy. Phenomenology is concerned with faithful examination of the phenomena, he contended, and God could never become such a phenomenon to be examined. Any religious faith or its phenomena are not a concern of philosophy. Janicaud's label has stuck and the "theological turn" has become a way of defining an increasingly vibrant discourse in contemporary (primarily French) philosophy. Even thinkers not included in the group of thinkers Janicaud condemned and certainly not committed to a particular religious affiliation, such as Jacques Derrida or Jean-Luc Nancy, have begun talking about religion. The various representatives of this discourse are the subject of this book's discussion of contemporary philosophy's new reflection on God. Before we talk about any of the individual representatives of this conversation, however, a brief introduction to the kind of language and philosophy in which they engage and which they assume, namely the language and method of hermeneutics and phenomenology, is required.

Phenomenology and Hermeneutics

What is phenomenology? And how can it enable talk about God? To a large extent, the latter question will be answered differently by the various thinkers discussed in this book. Still, at least a brief answer to both questions is in order here. Phenomenology concerns the examination of phenomena or, in its most popular slogan, constitutes a "return to the things themselves." Edmund Husserl, usually considered the founder of phenomenology as a philosophical project, conceived phenomenology as a philosophical investigation that would be rigorous in its method and would be able to verify its insights without recourse to either psychology or (natural) science. In fact, philosophical phenomenology is prior to and more fundamental than either of these investigations. Phenomenology is a return to the phenomena, to things as they appear to our consciousness. Phenomenology in Husserl's sense sets aside any concern with the existence of these phenomena ("out there") in order to focus entirely on their appearance. This setting aside (or "putting in parentheses") is called a *reduction* or *epoché*.[33] According to Husserl, in focusing on the appearance of phenomena in this way, we can reach their essences and give evidence for them. Such evidence is possible by the close connection (in fact, simultaneous appearance) of phenomena (called *noema*) and their modes of appearing or their phenomenality (called *noesis*). One of Husserl's central insights is the close connection between the phenomenon and its reception (what is referred to as "intuition" and "intention"). We intuit or experience phenomena, but we always also intend them. Intention provides us with what is often not given by the phenomenon itself (such as the "back side" of a large object, which we cannot see or "intuit" when we stand in front of it, but which we automatically provide in consciousness or "intend" due to our previous experience with such objects). Consciousness synthesizes various intuitions through intentionality and thus provides for a coherent experience. Through this process we are able to grasp the meaning, or "signification," of the phenomenon and to provide evidence for it.

Husserl is primarily concerned with "normal" and fairly simple objects, which we encounter on a day-to-day basis. Increasingly, however, phenomenological thinkers in the generation following Husserl (such as Heidegger, Lévinas, Derrida, Merleau-Ponty, and Henry) become interested in investigating other phenomena that are far more complicated and much less obvious. These lead to investigations of the phenomena of the human flesh (which Husserl had already distinguished from an experience of the human body), experiences of moods or dreams or our encounter with art and music, and especially the experience of other people who surely are not identical to objects. Increasingly, these investigations are taken as permission to examine even more radical phenomena, such as an experience of the divine. These contemporary philosophers are thus concerned with very different questions than traditional (either early or modern) apologetic projects. Their emphasis is on showing that it is possible to describe a religious experience phenomenologically and that such depiction is meaningful. Most of them are quite critical of any attempt to "prove" God's existence or at least set it aside as a concern not relevant to phenomenology (which is not really about demonstrating the existence of anything, including the world in which we find ourselves, but about describing our experience of this world and what we encounter within it). Their defense of faith, if it is such a defense, is about showing that such experiences can be examined and described phenomenologically in meaningful fashion.

The discipline of hermeneutics also plays an important role in the contemporary conversation. Philosophical hermeneutics arose out of the earlier practices of religious and legal hermeneutics, which sought to interpret biblical and legal texts respectively and to communicate their meaning to the relevant audiences (the preacher or priest to the religious community, the lawyer or judge to the court). Hermeneutics is primarily a theory of interpretation: How might we understand *today* what the text meant *then*? Increasingly, however, hermeneutics came to be no longer just about understanding what the original author might have meant but about the various ways of appropriating and reading texts today. Contemporary hermeneutics recognizes that we can never fully know what the original author meant and also contends that this is not the only thing worth knowing, but that many other aspects of interpretation matter. Central to the method of interpreting is what is known as the "hermeneutic circle": a back-and-forth between the particulars of the text and the larger context, understanding the whole in terms of the parts and gaining a richer comprehension of the parts by looking at the whole. This "circle" can refer to the move between one term or sentence in light of the entire text, one text in light of the larger corpus of the writer, one author and his or her texts in light of the historical and cultural context of the time, and so forth. A similar back and forth is always at work between the reader and the text (both the original audience and the contemporary reader). And while hermeneutics always remains deeply devoted to the text and its interpretation, it also increasingly becomes applied to life and action. Already in Heidegger, hermeneutics refers to the "facticity" of life, the concrete life lived and to be interpreted within its particular context and the larger world. Heidegger also contends that we "project" ourselves into the future by imagining our future possibilities, which then become the hermeneutic context in which we act out these possibilities. Ricoeur, one of the thinkers examined in this book, is particularly interested in this movement between text and action. (In fact, the title of one of his major works on interpretation is *From Text to Action*.)

Hermeneutics plays a role in the contemporary discussion because of this basic recognition that texts and actions, indeed all of life, require interpretation. Religious language, whether drawn from the biblical text or from the religious tradition, is also always in need of such interpretation. And, indeed, several thinkers explicitly reflect on the nature of religious language. What is its status in relation to other languages? What does it mean? What does it accomplish? And even when hermeneutics is not an explicit topic within their writings or even rejected as a method (as happens, for example, in Michel Henry's work), it is still operative in terms of the choices made about the texts and images employed to illustrate or advance the argument. And it is, of course, always present in the readers' interpretations and evaluations of the respective projects and proposals about the divine and religious experience.

These are, then, some of the questions about God and religious experience asked by contemporary phenomenological and hermeneutic thinkers and they are consequently also the questions that will occupy us in our examination of their work:

What does it mean to have an experience of the divine? What does such an experience look like? Can it be confirmed or falsified?

What language is used to speak of such an experience? How must we interpret it? How can we describe or even communicate it?

What effect does religious experience have on the human subject or on consciousness? Is the human recipient transformed by phenomenal experience of the divine and if so, how?

Can we move "from text to action"? Can one interpret or gain truth from religious actions (instead of just texts such as the Scriptures)? And what sort of "truth" is this?

PART I

Preparations

Martin Heidegger and Onto-theo-logy

There has been much speculation about the religious influences on Heidegger's thought and on the religious potential of his work. Several theologians, such as Rudolf Bultmann, Karl Rahner, and Paul Tillich, were inspired by his philosophy and used it extensively in their own writings. Janicaud himself makes Heidegger to some extent responsible for the religious turn, while drawing on other aspects of Heidegger's thought for his desire to keep philosophy pure and safe from theological contamination.[1] Heidegger's corpus is vast indeed and I will make no attempt to treat it in its entirety here. Rather, I will focus on the aspects of Heidegger's work that are of particular import for our topic, either because they have been extensively used by other thinkers, are assumed by them as basic, or because they are the ones most heavily criticized by some of the thinkers discussed later. Some very basic things have to be said, however, about his phenomenology to set the stage. (Those familiar with his work may want to skip the next few paragraphs.)

Heidegger's thought, from beginning to end, is concerned with the question of Being (*Sein*), which he considers to be the primary question of philosophy, although it has been neglected for much of philosophy's history. Heidegger's method of philosophical investigation is phenomenology, which he defines as a return to the things themselves, a permission to allow phenomena to manifest themselves as they appear to us most authentically in our everyday living within the world. Early on, Heidegger's locus for investigating Being and its history is through an investigation of what he calls *Dasein*: human being, the one being for whom Being is an issue, the being we are and whose own being (or existing) is closest to us, but often forgotten or ignored. Especially in his major work *Being and Time*, Dasein is thought to permit some sort of access to Being as such: Dasein is the space (or one of the places) where Being might manifest itself. Yet Being is (as Aristotle, a philosopher very important for Heidegger, said) "spoken of in many ways" and Heidegger is particularly concerned to ensure that the meaning of Being would not be reduced to only one version or interpretation thereof. According to Heidegger, this is precisely what has happened in the history of philosophy: Being has been described in one particular mode of being (for example, as the "forms" or Ideas, as actuality, as substance, as Reason, or as the will to power) while other modes have been ignored. Such monolithic definitions of Being, although they are certainly revelatory in some fashion, also cover over much by ignoring the many other manifestations of Being. We must therefore both "deconstruct" the history of philosophy and learn from it: deconstruct its limited definitions, overcome its desire to reduce the meaning of Being, and learn from the truth that has indeed been revealed in its various manifestations in some fashion. This "destruction" or "overcoming" of metaphysics is one essential component of almost all contemporary projects. None of the thinkers writing in Heidegger's wake intend to return to metaphysics as we knew it previous to Heidegger. They practice their own versions of overcoming or replacing metaphysics in various registers.

One of Heidegger's most important insights into the nature of metaphysics is what is called the "onto-theo-logical constitution" of metaphysics. (His essay on that topic will be examined in more detail in the third section of this chapter.) Metaphysics, Heidegger contends, is historically constituted as an "ontology" (a history of being) and always also as a "theology." This means that the various modes of being that metaphysics acknowledges are generally grounded in a "highest being" or a divine being. This supreme being tends to be called "God" and is something like a first cause or even an uncaused cause, the *causa sui*. This is not the God to whom Christians (or others) pray, but it is the philosophical concept of the divine, which grounds all other entities within the world, believed to be created by this supreme being. Ontological and theological grounding are thus always wrapped up with each other, and the history of metaphysics is defined by this intermingling and mutual grounding. The highest being must not necessarily even be called "God," strictly speaking, but it has the connotations of a divine being by providing the ultimate ground and cause for all other existence.[2] In this mutual metaphysical implication, something else happens: The difference between the mode of being of particular beings (or entities) and that of the supreme being often collapses and subsequently becomes forgotten. Even more important, the mode of being of all beings (including the supreme being) becomes indistinguishable from Being as such. The very Being of beings is no longer thought. These various differences and distinctions are referred to as the *ontological difference*, which has several connotations in Heidegger's thought. Ontological difference is covered over or ignored in the history of metaphysics and Being, as such, is forgotten. Heidegger wants to make us aware of these various ontological differences at stake, especially the most fundamental one: the difference between particular beings and Being as such. In subsequent thinkers, onto-theo-logy becomes the shorthand way of talking about all these various problems in the history of philosophy, but especially of the implication of God into the history of philosophy. And in the thinkers most critical of the contemporary turn to theology, one at times has the impression that any mention of God within philosophy is, by definition, onto-theo-logical (and therefore to be rejected). Thus we must be entirely silent about God in philosophy. It is precisely this assumption that many of the authors treated here try to combat.

The concern with Being in its various modes and the connection (or not) between beings and God (or even Being and God) is important to most of the contemporary thinkers, especially Marion, Lacoste, and Kearney. Heidegger himself always disassociated his thought of "Being" from any concept of "God." This is most evident in a famous comment Heidegger made in a seminar conversation in Zürich, where he was asked about precisely this connection (which apparently happened quite frequently and greatly exasperated Heidegger, forcing him to reiterate repeatedly that "Being" did not mean "God," was not equal to God, and, in fact, had very little to do with God). Heidegger said in this interview that if he ever were to write a theology (which he occasionally felt inclined to do), the word "Being" would not appear in it.[3] God has nothing to do with "Being." At another point in the seminars, he reiterates this even more fully:

> One could not be more reserved than I before every attempt to employ Being to think theologically in what God is God. Of Being, there is nothing to expect here. I believe that Being can never be thought as the ground and essence of God, but that nevertheless the experience of God and of his manifestedness, to the extent that the latter can indeed meet man, flashes in the dimension of Being, which in no way signifies that Being might be regarded as a possible predicate for God.[4]

This distinction between God and "Being" is also made in other places in Heidegger's work. I will here examine three particularly important texts: his early essay "Phenomenology and Theology," his essay "The Onto-theo-logical Constitution of Metaphysics," and his lectures "Phenomenology of Religious Life." I will conclude by briefly saying something about his notion of truth as *aletheia* and his late writings on the "holy" and the "fourfold," which return to the topic of the divine but in a very different (and considerably less explicitly Christian) fashion.

"Phenomenology and Theology"

"Phenomenology and Theology" is one of Heidegger's earliest articles (a lecture first given in 1927) and more or less contemporaneous with *Being and Time*. It assumes much of what is laid out in that larger work. Heidegger contends within the lecture that there is a fundamental distinction between the two disciplines of the title, indeed that they are "absolutely different" from each other. The usual distinction between the two as more or less equivalent disciplines, theology dealing with "faith" and philosophy with "reason," is false. Instead, phenomenology is an ontological science, which deals with Being as such in the most fundamental fashion, while theology is one of the many ontic sciences, which treat particular aspects of the concrete being-in-the-world of individual beings. Theology is thus similar in character to biology, chemistry, or geometry. That is, positive sciences consider particular entities, such as numbers or plants or various modes of Dasein's specific being. Philosophy, as phenomenology, is the only discipline that deals with Being as such and is thus prior (and superior) to all the other sciences. Heidegger concludes that "theology is a positive science, and as such, therefore, is absolutely different from philosophy" (PT, 50). Heidegger goes on to examine first the "positive" and then the "scientific" character of theology, while giving some pointers of how theology as a science might consequently relate to philosophy.

Heidegger first demolishes the traditional assumption that theology is grounded in revelation and examines its truths. It is not the science of "God," as its name might lead us to expect. Instead, theology concerns the particular mode of human Dasein as a believing being. Faith is one possible existential mode of being of human Dasein, or, in Heidegger's terms: "Faith is the believing-understanding mode of existing in the history revealed, i.e., occurring, with the Crucified" (PT, 53). Theology, then, is concerned with the Christianness of human beings, which is most decidedly not a universal (or the most fundamental) mode of being of Dasein. Theology can be scientific as it investigates the historical interpretations "faithfulness" or "Christianness" has assumed in the history of theology, in particular those displayed in the New Testament. It does not itself give rise to faith, but actually "renders it more difficult" by examining its particular manifestations (PT, 55). It does not constitute and should not compose its own system nor should it assume a particular philosophical system, as has often been the case in the past, although it can be systematic in its scientific rigor. Furthermore, theology also must use its own internal standards of evidence, instead of assuming those of a different science, which are foreign to its own discourse. Theology must be concerned with action, with the action of faith; it is thus a practical science. "Theology is not speculative knowledge of God," but "is founded primarily by faith" (PT, 56, 57).

Philosophy can be helpful in a very limited fashion for the theological enterprise. It can neither lead to faith nor analyze faith. Yet it can provide certain concepts that connect the particular ontic character of theology to the more general ontological character of all experience as investigated by phenomenology. Thus, the theological (ontic) concept of sin, so Heidegger's example, might point us to the pre-Christian ontological category of guilt, which is a more general, more original, and more basic experience of Dasein. Heidegger contends that this does not limit theology, does not make it dependent upon philosophy (the phenomenological concept of guilt does not "found" the theological concept of sin), and does not specify its content. Rather, it "is determinate in one respect, in that it formally indicates the ontological character of *that* region of being in which the concept of sin as a *concept of existence* must necessarily maintain itself" (PT, 59). The radical separation between philosophy and theology allows theology to refocus itself on its own "creedal character" and the proper source of its own statement in the Scriptures and the actions of faith. Heidegger rejects any notion of Christian philosophy and any sense in which philosophy might possibly be dependent upon theology in any way. Therefore, there is also no phenomenological theology, as phenomenology functions as the method for philosophy only and cannot be applied to the positive sciences (such as theology, math, or psychology). Heidegger concludes that "there is no such thing as a Christian philosophy; that is an absolute 'square circle.' . . . Phenomenology is always only the name for the procedure of ontology, a procedure that essentially distinguishes itself from that of all other, positive sciences" (PT, 60).

Several conclusions can be drawn from this. On the one hand, Heidegger seems to forbid strictly any conflation or even conversation between philosophy and theology. He also appears to make it impossible to apply phenomenological insights to theology or to consider questions of faith, of God, or of the possibility of religious experience, within philosophy. The two disciplines are radically separated. On the other hand,

Heidegger calls theology back to focus on its own sources and methods instead of appropriating those of philosophy. To some extent, Heidegger's distinctions may have a purifying function. Theology is informed by its own creedal character. Theology arises out of the actions of believers as they live out their faith in their mode of being as people of faith. Theology is not speculation about the existence of God, does not seek to ascertain God's nature, but instead describes faithfully the way in which Christians experience life within the world of faith. These are all themes that are either presupposed or will be taken up by other thinkers. In fact, the very different character of these new "postmodern apologetic" projects may depend on this re-direction of the focus of theology. All of them do indeed analyze and describe the actions and words that arise out of faith or the life believers live, instead of engaging in arguments about abstract propositions about the divine. They do not speculate about God's existence (an activity rejected almost unanimously), but they describe the life of faith as it actually takes place. Thus, Lacoste analyzes human liturgical being-before-God, Chrétien depicts the prayerful response to the call, Marion the dazzling dimension of spiritual experience, Henry the intimate experiences of suffering and joy that flow directly out of the divine life, Falque the corporeality and "animality" of the Eucharist, and even Ricoeur continually seeks to return to the primary experiences of faith which he sees explicated most clearly in the Scriptures read by the community of the faithful. While many of these thinkers will argue that Heidegger's distinctions between theology and phenomenology in this early essay are too sharp, and they go on to appropriate phenomenological method and tools extensively for describing the experience of faith, in many ways their focus on the life of faith instead of on doctrinal propositions is, at the very least, consistent with Heidegger's suggestions here, if not actually dependent upon it.

The Facticity of Religious Life

What is interesting, however, is that Heidegger's very early lectures on the *Phenomenology of Religious Life*, which have only recently become available and therefore have not had a great impact on the discussion, actually do consider phenomenology of enormous significance for an analysis of religion.[5] Especially in the second part of his "Introduction to the Phenomenology of Religion," lectures given in the winter of 1920–21, Heidegger conducts a thoroughly phenomenological analysis of religious life as found in several of Paul's letters (Galatians, and 1. and 2. Thessalonians; there are also some remarks about Ephesians). There is no hint here yet that the experience of religion is confined only to an ontic domain and is not relevant to the ontological structures of existence. In fact, much of the terminology later employed in *Being and Time* to speak of the ontological being of Dasein is here used to depict Paul's experience or that of his audience. Thus, although these lectures played little if any role in the use of phenomenology to speak of religious phenomena and certainly their appropriation of phenomenological terminology for a depiction of religious life was soon rejected by Heidegger, they may indicate that at least at one point in Heidegger's path such an application was possible and that it may indeed be recovered by other thinkers.

In his analysis of Paul's letter to the Galatians, Heidegger seeks to explicate "the fundamental religious experience" and its "connection to all original religious phenomena" (*PR*, 51). He outlines two basic determinations, which are guiding phenomenological explications for him: "1. Primordial Christian religiosity is in primordial Christian life experiences and is itself such. 2. Factical life experience is historical. Christian religiosity lives temporality as such" (*PR*, 55). Heidegger will indeed spend quite a bit of time in the lectures outlining Christian facticity, historical experience, and temporality. He seeks to understand Paul in the context of his communal world, describing him as a wandering preacher who has a relationship with the communities to which he writes. We must understand Paul's concrete situation in order to be able to appreciate what he writes and approach it phenomenologically. This situation, Heidegger suggests in a close reading of the text, is that of a special relationship with his audience: "These passages emphasize that for Paul the Thessalonians are there because he and they are linked to each other in their having-become" (*PR*, 65). Here Heidegger seems to employ what is called in other texts a "hermeneutics of facticity," which stresses the importance of the context in which we find ourselves for any understanding of our being and relations with the world. The recognition that we always already find ourselves within particular circumstances that shape our interpretation of any new experience is an important element of hermeneutics. Knowledge is always contextual. Heidegger argues in the lectures that "this knowledge is entirely different from any other knowledge and memory" because "it arises only out of the situational context of Christian life experience" (*PR*, 65). This kind of knowledge Heidegger defines as the starting point for theology. Thus, like the later article that distinguishes theology from phenomenology by stressing its context of the experience of faith, here that very context enables a phenomenological analysis. By accepting a connection with God, the believer is transformed before God (*PR*, 66). A "Christian life experience" (*PR*, 71) emerges out of this particular context and is worked out in believers' lives. Heidegger points out that this life experience, as outlined by Paul, is in contrast to that of the world and challenges it. While the world promises "peace and security" (as in the second letter to the Thessalonians on which Heidegger is commenting), the Christian experience is aware of the insecurity and distress of life. It is a more authentic way of being in the world. There are important parallels here to Heidegger's later explication of "anxiety" as central to the being of Dasein and its search for "authenticity." Heidegger rejects objective historical constructions of Paul's situation in favor of this deeper phenomenological analysis that tries to penetrate into Paul's actual experience in his concrete situatedness.

Heidegger also draws more general conclusions about the Christian life from this analysis of Paul. Christian religiosity is defined by temporality and by living in a world shared with others and historically determined by various relations. He says that "Christian factical life experience is historically determined by its emergence with the proclamation that hits the people in a moment, and then is unceasingly also alive in the enactment of life. Further, this life experience determines, for its part, the relations which are found in it" (PR, 83). Heidegger analyzes this life-world of the early Christian communities in quite a bit of detail. The Christian lives within the world in terms of facticity and temporality. This Christian facticity is an enactment of the Christian religious experience. Heidegger concludes that "the Christian is conscious that this facticity cannot be won out of his own strength, but rather originates from God—the phenomenon of the effects of grace." He judges "an explication of these complexes" as "very important," as it is a phenomenon also deeply and fundamentally experienced by Augustine and Luther (PR, 87). He rejects the idea that Christians could find a "foothold" in God as blasphemous, but instead emphasizes the Christian experience of the world as determinative, which is an experience of the world as given by God. This description is thus rich in phenomenological categories and descriptions that Heidegger will only shortly afterwards (especially in Being and Time) apply to the fundamental experience of Dasein: its facticity, its being-in-the-world which is shared with others, its temporality and historicity, its being toward death (no longer before God or in expectation of the parousia, an important theme in both letters to the Thessalonians). The parallels between the two accounts are striking indeed.

Finally, it is also interesting that Heidegger is thoroughly dismissive in these lectures of any endeavor to examine God in terms of the "concept of validity." He calls this "the pinnacle of error" (PR, 73). He explicitly rejects theoretical proof and dismisses the idea that "dogma as detached content of doctrine in an objective, epistemological emphasis could ever have been guiding for Christian religiosity" (*PR*, 79). He concludes the lectures by emphasizing that "real philosophy of religion arises not from preconceived concepts of philosophy and religion. Rather, the possibility of its philosophical understanding arises out of a certain religiosity—for us, the Christian religiosity" (*PR*, 89). Instead, a philosophy of religion must begin with a real relationship to history and a phenomenological analysis of the peculiar historical situation that is being examined. Meaning emerges not out of an objective account of a distant historical past, but from a phenomenological engagement with the historical situation as a living present. This is precisely the kind of rejection of philosophical categories of rationality for religion in favor of a phenomenological examination of religious experience that characterizes the thinking of all the philosophers examined in this book. Although these lectures themselves surely cannot have opened the path to such thinking, as their publication came much too late, and despite the fact that they seem comparatively insignificant in Heidegger's thought as a whole, even on the topic of God and religion, they still show the phenomenological possibilities for an exploration of religiosity, whether in the letters of Paul or in other concrete religious experience. And they also briefly point to the problematic nature of traditional philosophical thought about God. The reason why this thought is so problematic is addressed in his lecture on "The Onto-theo-logical Constitution of Metaphysics."

"The Onto-theo-logical Constitution of Metaphysics"

As already briefly outlined, Heidegger shows that metaphysics is characterized by what he calls an onto-theo-logical structure. He gave his now famous lecture on "The Onto-theo-logical Constitution of Metaphysics" as the final lecture of a seminar on Hegel's *Science of Logic* in February 1957 and it was published with another lecture under the title *Identity and Difference*. In this piece, he reiterates that metaphysics is marked by an oblivion of Being and especially by forgetting the difference between Being and beings (*ID*, 50–51). At various times in history, the thinking about or forgetting of Being took on different shapes and a "step back" would assume an investigation of these various epochs, but certainly not a return to any particular one of them. The history of ontology determines the being (or the beingness/existence) of beings or entities by founding them on a supreme or divine being. This being is usually called God; thus, metaphysics also tends to be theological in character: "If thinking (*Wissenschaft*) must begin with God, then it is the thinking (*Wissenschaft*) about

God: theology" (*ID*, 54; trans. modified). Heidegger suggests that "Western metaphysics, however, since its beginning with the Greeks has eminently been both ontology and theology . . . to those who can read, this means: metaphysics is onto-theo-logy" (*ID*, 54). Heidegger shows this in particular for the philosophies of Leibniz and Hegel in which the divine, or some notion of it, functions as ultimate grounding, as principle of sufficient reason. Ontology and theology make common cause, to their own detriment. Heidegger warns: "Someone who has experienced theology in his own roots, both the theology of the Christian faith and that of philosophy, would today rather remain silent about God when he is speaking in the realm of thinking. For the onto-theo-logical character of metaphysics has become questionable for thinking, not because of any kind of atheism, but from the experience of a thinking which has discerned in onto-theo-logy the still unthought unity of the essential nature of metaphysics" (*ID*, 54–55). Thus, Heidegger recognizes a kind of philosophical theology at work in the philosophical tradition itself that has become closely tied to metaphysical reflection about Being. This connection is problematic and the new kind of thinking Heidegger advocates should separate itself from any such theological reflection.

He continues by examining how the deity managed to enter the history of philosophy: "What is the origin of the onto-theo-logical essential constitution of metaphysics?" (*ID*, 56). Heidegger shows how, especially in regard to Hegel, Being is thought as ground of all being: "The Being of beings reveals itself as the ground that gives itself ground and accounts for itself" (*ID*, 57). Metaphysics, which encompasses all beings and their existence, grounds them in a Highest being. Being as such (*Sein*), the supreme being (i.e., God or the *causa sui*), and all other beings (or entities in the world) become wrapped up with each other in a reciprocal relationship of providing grounding for each other and justifying each other: "The Being of beings is thus thought of in advance as the grounding ground. Therefore all metaphysics is at bottom, and from the ground up, what grounds, what gives account of the ground, what is called to account by the ground, and finally what calls the ground to account" (*ID*, 58). Here, Heidegger separates both ontology and theology (but the philosophical theology he has just outlined, not an account of the experience of faith) from other disciplines such as biology or cosmology, for which they provide the more fundamental grounding. Ontology and theology give the other disciplines their *logic*; thus, metaphysics is "onto-theo-logic" (*ID*, 59). This kind of metaphysical thinking provides both first and final cause and thus represents the Being of beings as *causa sui* (self-caused cause). Heidegger maintains that *causa sui* is "the metaphysical concept of

God," namely what grounds all other being (*ID*, 60). He makes very clear that the ontological and the theological grounding of metaphysics are not two separate things that happen to have occurred together. Rather, they always belong intricately together. The supreme being is always thought in conjunction with the being or existence of all other beings; the two cannot be separated from each other. The very difference between them becomes forgotten and thus is another instance of "ontological difference." We can never get back to a point where "Being" and "beings" can be thought separately from each other. To make the "step back" that Heidegger advocates, namely to think the history of metaphysics anew, is to face this difference. Such a thinking, however, requires an openness to what is usually veiled or covered over.

The first "proper name" Heidegger gives to the "All-Highest" One who unifies all things and grounds them in the thinking of being is Zeus (*ID*, 69), thus again making it very clear that he is speaking of a *concept* of the divine and not an experience of God in faith. What Heidegger calls "perdurance," which is how the difference is manifested, "is a circling, the circling of Being and beings around each other," as they ground each other reciprocally (*ID*, 69). Not only does Being provide the ground of existence for beings, but beings also account for Being. Even this very process of grounding or of causation is a type of being. Heidegger mentions Leibniz as an example of this onto-theo-logical structure of reciprocal grounding, which neglects to think difference, because difference itself is used to speak of beings and thus becomes invisible. He summarizes: "When metaphysics thinks of beings with respect to the ground that is common to beings as such, then it is logic as onto-logic. When metaphysics thinks of beings as such as a whole, that is, with respect to the highest being which accounts for everything, then it is logic as theo-logic" (*ID*, 70–71). The difference between them cannot be considered within metaphysics itself. And then Heidegger makes a final comment about the supreme being or the "god" of *causa sui* that is thus wrapped up in this constitution of metaphysics. These have become probably the most-quoted words in the whole lecture: "This is the right name for the god of philosophy. Man can neither pray nor sacrifice to this god. Before the *causa sui*, man can neither fall to his knees in awe nor can he play music or dance before this god" (*ID*, 72). The "god" so essential for the grounding of beings for most of the history of metaphysics is not a religious God, not the God of piety, not a God to be worshipped. Heidegger makes no claims about the God of faith at all in this lecture. The theology at work in metaphysics is a philosophical theology, very different from the analysis of the life of faith mentioned in the first and second sections of this chapter. This frequently has been read (by thinkers such as Janicaud) to mean that any renewed thinking about theology within philosophy is condemned to failure, because it immediately becomes part of the onto-theo-logical structure characterizing the whole history of metaphysics. We must thus be silent about God within philosophy.

Yet Heidegger goes on to suggest that "the god-less thinking which must abandon the god of philosophy, god as *causa sui*, is thus perhaps closer to the divine God. Here this means only: god-less thinking is more open to Him than onto-theo-logic would like to admit" (*ID*, 72). For many thinkers, especially the ones discussed in the rest of this book, this presents tantalizing possibilities. Possibly, the "death" of the god of philosophy, the god of *causa sui* or even the god that grounds all values whom Nietzsche's madman seeks and recognizes as having been killed, is an event to be celebrated rather than bemoaned. Maybe Heidegger's "deconstruction" of metaphysics and his retrieval of the question of Being may open a different way of speaking about the divine, namely the kind of divine to whom one may pray or before whom one might want to dance and who would not be tied to metaphysical thinking as the ground of all beings? Heidegger seems to suggest as much in this brief comment. This new thinking about God or the divine, if such thinking is to be possible, would need to avoid very carefully falling back into any kind of onto-theo-logy. Thus, many of the contemporary projects (Lévinas and Marion most obviously, but most of the others as well) explicitly try to think "beyond" or "otherwise" than Being/being. God must be thought "without" Being or not as ground. Or, as Marion will insist, we must find a way to "overcome" ontological difference and think God "beyond" or "without" it. Near the very end of the lecture, Heidegger wonders whether the language of Western philosophy is capable of thinking without being tied to its traditional metaphysical nature. He suggests that we must find "other possibilities of utterance" or maybe even "a telling silence" (*ID*, 73). Heidegger does not seem confident that Western language will be able to free itself from its ties to metaphysics. This problem will return again and again in Lévinas and other thinkers, as they seek to find language for expressing the absolute or the infinite or the other without such metaphysical constrictions.

Truth as *Aletheia* and Meditative Thinking

Already, *Being and Time* had included a reflection on truth, a topic Heidegger also later explores in other essays, such as "On the Essence of Truth" and "The End of Philosophy and the Task of Thinking."[6] In both

Being and Time and "On the Essence of Truth," Heidegger reviews the presumed link between truth and being in much of philosophical history and the ways in which truth has been defined as a logical proposition, as correspondence to facts or agreement and accordance with a particular state of affairs. This is what we might today call scientific or technical truth. Even in this kind of truth, Heidegger emphasizes the *relationship* that is established between the statement of a fact and its correspondence to reality. Furthermore, in order to be confirmed as truth a being must show itself as such and be discovered (*BT*, 201). *Aletheia*, the Greek word for truth, Heidegger points out, means "unveiling" or "unconcealment," revealing what was previously covered up or hidden (*lethe*). Heidegger shows the connection between this meaning of truth as discovery and human existence: "Being true as discovering is a manner of being of Da-sein. What makes this discovering itself possible must necessarily be called 'true' in a still more primordial sense. *The existential and ontological foundations of discovering itself first show the most primordial phenomenon of truth*" (*BT*, 202–3). This kind of truth is thus central to what it means to be human. The human way of being in the world, which consists of an "attunement" to and openness to the world, shows that this meaning of truth is primordial. We are "untrue," when we fall prey to simple assimilation to the larger crowd and close ourselves off to the recognition of our own facticity or "thrownness." To live authentically or truly is to live in discovery instead of concealment. This is closely connected to Heidegger's hermeneutic analysis of facticity, the recognition of human beings as "thrown" into the world and thus finding themselves within a particular world and its concrete structures and context, including other beings, as well as his analysis of Dasein's "projection" toward the future and the realization of Dasein's own finitude and eventual death. Other hermeneutic thinkers will continue to think truth in light of its connection to the opening of a world and human dwelling within it.

Heidegger recognizes that this understanding of truth is not the one prevalent today. In fact, in "The End of Philosophy" he will associate the forgetting of *aletheia* as unconcealment with the beginnings of metaphysics as onto-theo-logy (*BW*, 446). In these earlier texts, however, Heidegger insists that "disclosedness is an essential kind of being of Da-sein" (*BT*, 208). In fact, truth can be discovered only through Dasein's disclosing of it: "*All truth is relative to the being of Da-sein*" (*BT*, 208). This does not mean that truth is arbitrary, but that it is essentially related to Dasein's discovery and unveiling of it. In "The Essence of Truth," Heidegger is less concerned with Dasein's relationship to truth, although he reiterates even more strongly that "'truth' is not a feature of correct propositions that are asserted of an 'object' by a human 'subject' and then 'are valid' somewhere, in what sphere we know not; rather, truth is disclosure of beings through which an openness essentially unfolds" (*BW*, 127). In this text, Heidegger focuses closely on the relationship between truth and freedom. Beings or entities can only be shown forth in truth and can only fully disclose themselves if the human being lets them be freely. By manipulating or coercing beings, we cover them up or conceal them and thus hinder their disclosure. Concealment is "untruth" and yet this untruth belongs essentially to truth, as uncovering or unconcealing are necessarily connected to concealment.[7] Heidegger concludes here that "the essence of truth is not the empty 'generality' of an 'abstract' universality but rather that which, self-concealing, is unique in the remitting history of the disclosure of the 'meaning' of what we call Being" (*BW*, 137).

In "The Origin of the Work of Art," Heidegger articulates truth as unconcealment again and suggests that it is unveiled in the "clearing" of beings, where beings both become present and withdraw (*BW*, 177–78). Truth "happens" in the work of art as a kind of revelation. Works of art "make unconcealment as such happen in regard to beings as a whole" (*BW*, 181). Beauty and creation allow truth to stand forth, or, as Heidegger says at the very end of this essay: "Art is the setting-into-work of truth . . . art lets truth originate" (*BW*, 202). Art originates truth because it brings forth something new: "The establishing of truth in the work is the bringing forth of a being such as never was before and will never come to be again" (*BW*, 187). Marion will later analyze art in terms of a seeing of the "unseen" that brings what was invisible (or previously unseen) into phenomenality. Great artists see what no one else has seen and thus add to the realm of phenomenality by introducing new phenomena within it and making them visible to us. Similarly, Chrétien speaks of art as what shows forth beauty where we both experience the truth of the world and bear witness to it or try to shelter its fragility. These analyses of art are profoundly influenced by Heidegger's reflections on truth and art, although they seek to bypass his reliance on art as a being or as a revelation of Being.

Heidegger later explores this further by making a distinction between calculative and meditative ways of thinking.[8] He argues that while we are becoming increasingly better at calculative thinking, which is closely associated with technology and rushes from one thing to the next, we are simultaneously increasingly neglecting meditative thinking. Meditative thinking is a deeper and slower and far more difficult thinking that confronts us with the most fundamental questions about ourselves and existence: The human being "is a *thinking*, that is, a *meditating* being" (*DT*, 47). It is also the kind of thinking that allows for creativity (and thus allows truth to be revealed) because it is rooted and grounded in concrete contexts, while calculative thinking is disembodied and not tied to any place. Indeed, in "The End of Philosophy," he suggests that defining truth in terms of calculation or correctness is due to missing the essential connection between *a-letheia* as un-concealment and *lethe* as concealment (*BW*, 448). In the "Memorial Address," Heidegger warns that if we were to cease thinking meditatively at all we would have forgotten the very essence of what it means to be human, which would be a far greater danger even than the outbreak of a third world war with atomic weapons. He says:

> This assertion is valid in the sense that the approaching tide of technological revolution in the atomic age could so captivate, bewitch, dazzle, and beguile man that calculative thinking may some day come to be accepted and practiced as the only way of thinking . . . then man would have denied and thrown away his own special nature—that he is a meditative being. Therefore, the issue is the saving of man's essential nature. Therefore, the issue is keeping meditative thinking alive. (*DT*, 56)

Meditative thinking, like the earlier explanation of truth, is about openness to the mystery of Being and about a free relation to it that allows it to reveal itself. The term he employs to speak of this openness and "releasement" in regard to technology is *Gelassenheit* ["letting-be"], a term he has appropriated from the medieval mystics (especially Meister Eckhart).

This distinction between objective truth and truth as unconcealment or between calculative and meditative thinking will inform many of the later thinkers and will be an important part of the hermeneutic element in contemporary philosophy. Ricoeur makes distinctions between truth as verification and truth as manifestation, associating the first with scientific thought and the second with poetic thought, which is very close if not identical to Heidegger's own distinctions. Henry draws an even starker division between the "truth of the world," which he associates with Galilean science, and the "Truth of Christianity," which is about manifestation and self-affection. Marion will speak of a truth of the mind and juxtapose it to a truth of the heart or the will. One kind of truth is known abstractly and theoretically, while the other is known through being encountered in love. Chrétien and Lacoste make similar distinctions at certain points, but will carry further the connection between truth and art or creativity in particular. Even the thinkers who do not explicitly speak of two types of truth or two ways of thinking, presuppose Heidegger's notion of truth as unconcealment or revelation and assume that even in this revelation much is covered over that must still be unveiled.

The Holy and the Fourfold

As the brief examination of the "Memorial Address" in the last section has already shown, mystical and poetic language becomes more prominent in Heidegger's later writings and may imply a greater affinity with speaking of the divine or spiritual experience. Although Heidegger does not draw the distinctions between philosophy and theology quite so starkly anymore (he does not actually speak of theology at all at this point), his relation to religious language or the topic of God is still highly ambivalent. In the "Letter on Humanism" Heidegger challenges the need to retain a term such as "humanism" while maintaining that his rejection of terms such as "values" and "humanism" neither means that his "philosophy teaches an irresponsible and destructive 'nihilism,'" nor that his reflections on Nietzsche's word on the death of God imply that his (or Nietzsche's) philosophy is godless (*BW*, 249). Heidegger reiterates in this letter his contention that to speak of God as the highest being or the ground of all values is to refer to a philosophical concept that is not helpful to the life of faith or to the history of philosophy. The rejection of such a concept does not imply anything about the existence of God: "With the existential determination of the essence of man, therefore, nothing is decided about the 'existence of God' or his 'non-being,' no more than about the possibility or impossibility of gods" (*BW*, 252–53). His philosophy does not make any claims about God; it is neither atheistic nor theistic, but is indifferent to the very question (which in examining the "existence" of God as "supreme being" is essentially a metaphysical one). For Heidegger, the question of Being and of human Dasein is far more pressing than any decision about the divine: "But the holy, which alone is the essential sphere of divinity, which in turn alone affords a dimension for the gods and for God, comes to radiate only when Being itself beforehand and after extensive preparation has been illuminated and is experienced in its truth" (*BW*, 242). It is not possible even to open the question of the existence or nature of God, before one has understood (or at least sufficiently investigated) the "being" of human beings. Thus, Heidegger hopes to leave the question open. Yet he does point out that his investigations may make possible a new thinking about the divine via the holy: "Only from the truth of Being can the essence of the holy be thought. Only from the essence of the holy is the essence of divinity to be thought. Only in the light of the essence of divinity can it be thought or said what the word 'God' is to signify." This is not a project that can currently be undertaken because "how can man at the present stage of world history ask at all seriously and rigorously whether the god nears or withdraws, when he has above all neglected to think into the dimension in which alone that question can be asked?" (*BW*, 253). This leaves open the hope that it might become possible to do so in the future, as Dasein opens itself to an experience of the holy.

These references to the "holy" or the "gods" or a "last god" reoccur in Heidegger's final writings with increasing frequency, but are seldom spelled out in any detail. Usually they amount to brief allusions instead of full discussions. The only theme that receives fuller attention is the notion of the "fourfold" (*Geviert*). The fourfold refers to the connection between earth and sky (or heaven), divinities and mortals. The four are closely connected and one cannot be thought without the other. In his essay "Building, Dwelling, Thinking," where Heidegger examines the relations between building and dwelling and the way thinking can arise in these connections, he articulates the idea of the fourfold as the space in which we dwell as mortals on the earth, under the sky, before the divinities and other people: "But 'on the earth' already means 'under the sky.' Both of these also mean 'remaining before the divinities' and include a 'belonging to men's being with one another.' By a *primal* oneness the four—earth and sky, divinities and mortals—belong together in one" (*BW*, 351). The fourfold, then, expresses an originary experience of our belonging to the ground and to the larger context in which it rests. The divinities belong inextricably to earth and sky and are not something over and against them: "The divinities are the beckoning messengers of the godhead. Out of the holy sway of the godhead, the god appears in his presence or withdraws into his concealment" (*BW*, 351). Human beings dwell within this fourfold and yet also protect or safeguard it. "Saving" here is an essential activity of humans, not of the gods. In relation to the gods that means: "Mortals dwell in that they await the divinities as divinities. In hope they hold up to the divinities what is unhoped for. They wait for intimations of their coming and do not mistake the signs of their absence. They do not make their gods for themselves and do not worship idols. In the very depth of misfortune they wait for the weal that has been withdrawn" (*BW*, 352). To dwell and thus to keep the fourfold "safe" is to "let things be," to nurture them instead of exploiting them. In what follows, Heidegger envisions the divinities as what we give thanks to, what receives our gratitude. The relation between "thinking" and "thanking" is something Heidegger also explores in other contexts and which Chrétien, Lacoste, and Marion will pick up and develop.[9] In all these reflections, the divinities certainly do not refer to the metaphysical definitions of the supreme being that characterize the onto-theo-logical constitution examined earlier. Rather, they are intimately connected to things, maybe even presenting their immortal face in some fashion. The fourfold is very much connected to place and things. Good building and dwelling allows the players in the fourfold to become one and to be sheltered together.

Several thinkers have argued that this theme of the holy or of the gods, which becomes more prominent in Heidegger's final writings, does not refer to any sort of traditional notion of God, especially not a Christian one. Even Heidegger's enigmatic claim in the *Spiegel* interview (which was published shortly after Heidegger's death) that "only a god can now save us" does not refer to the Christian or maybe a religious sort of God.[10] Richard Kearney maintains that the "god" Heidegger evokes, or to whom he may even attribute some salvific function, is the god of the poets.[11] Although Heidegger's language "is deeply resonant with the religious language of Christian eschatology," it does no more than hint at the possible hovering of "some kind of deity . . . in the vicinity."[12] In a later text, Kearney criticizes Heidegger's position quite strongly:

> For Heidegger, Judeo-Christian faith—indeed the philosophy and practice of religion in general—has exhausted the possibilities of God and left us with an empty space. And Heidegger seems to suggest that it is from this very emptiness and dereliction—from the very void of being where gods are absent—that the new gods will arise. But only, of course, for the cognoscenti who are awestruck enough to hearken. Ours is, whether we like it or not, an "atheistic" age. And one gets the impression that if we do not begin from that phenomenological given, we cannot even begin to listen to the voice of the "last God." Heidegger's "last God" is not destined for *homo religiosus* in the ordinary sense, but for a very select number of votaries bound to an esoteric truth and bold enough to withstand the shock waves of its irruption.[13]

John D. Caputo, on whom Kearney partially relies for his analysis, criticizes Heidegger's notion of the holy and the gods even more forcefully:

> The god that emerges in Heidegger's late writing is a profoundly poetic god, a woodland god arising from a poetic experience of the earth as something sacred and deserving of reverence. This is a cosmo-poetic god, not the ethico-religious God of the Hebrew and Christian scriptures, not a God of the suffering, of mercy and justice and flesh laid low. It has nothing to do with the God whom Jesus called *abba* or with biblical words of healing and mercy, with the widow, the orphan, or the stranger. Indeed, Heidegger's later writings are

more suggestive of a certain Buddhism, a certain meditative, silent world reverencing, than of Judaism or Christianity and the emancipatory power of biblical justice.[14]

This interpretation of Heidegger hence seeks to establish a fundamental distinction between these "later gods" and a more ethical (Jewish or Christian) God, which they associate with the thinking of Lévinas and even Derrida.

Ben Vedder makes a similar argument in more detail and applies it especially to the notion of the fourfold. He argues that the "holy" is "nature" for Heidegger and is superior to any particular "god."[15] The holy or the whole is earlier and more primordial than the gods. Only the poets can name the appearing or coming of the holy. The gods instead are included in the fourfold, which also includes mortals, heaven, and earth. Vedder claims that "the fourfold functions as a counterparadigm to ontotheological thinking and its anthropocentric and subjectivistic forms" (220). All four of the terms are intricately related to each other and cannot be thought without the others. Vedder argues that the fourfold is experienced as a historical event and that it has nothing to do with the Christian god. The holy refers to the fourfold as a whole. He maintains: "The holy has to appear as that in which human being can find its wholeness. The holy is not god, the godhead, the highest entity of metaphysics, or the divine grace. It is an ontological phenomenon that is expressed in the thinking of being" (236). Vedder finds that although one could still talk about this in certain theological terms, it would have to be a non-ontotheological theology and not one that introduced a "God" as an entity (225). A Heideggerian "theology" would be "poetic": Theology becomes the task of the poet. The poet is able to listen for the word of the holy and name it. Vedder concludes that this turns theology into a kind of poetry, which attunes itself to the gods and finds the right words to praise them: "*Theologia* is the song that is sung by the poet" (278).

Benjamin Crowe instead sees considerably more continuity between Heidegger's early and late writings on phenomenology of religion.[16] He claims that Heidegger's early work on religion emerges out of his interaction with the particular theological climate of the time and that this is similarly true of his later work. Even Heidegger's later work has profoundly religious implications. The "revolution" Heidegger envisions for European life is still characterized by religious experience, although now no longer grounded solely in analyses of "primitive Christianity" (Paul's letters) but taking into account the Greeks and Hölderlin (101). Crowe thinks that especially Caputo's reading of Heidegger's "abandonment of Christianity" in his later work is exaggerated and "drastically misrepresents Heidegger's work" (102). Instead, he interprets Heidegger's use of "the holy" as a significant part of a phenomenology of religion that seeks to understand human being-in-the-world and its particular manifestation in "mythical Dasein." Crowe contends that "for Heidegger, the 'holy' is *the* crucial term in the 'understanding of being' that lies at the very core of 'being-in-the-world'" (109). It is "not a principle from which concepts of particular deities are derived" but instead "is Heidegger's term for the objective side of an understanding of being that anchors the intelligibility of religious concepts and practices" (115). This sense of the sacred is something that must be recovered in the contemporary world for real change to become possible. A search for the gods does not equate with poetry or nature mysticism but rather refers to religious practices that search for meaning before the wholly other (128–30). He concludes:

> Heidegger addresses the situation of the present age head on. He suggests that, in the first instance, room be made for the "holy" and for the epiphanies of the divine. He also suggests that the practices whose meaning is grounded in religion be preserved and nurtured, even in the face of growing meaninglessness. Above all, Heidegger suggests that cultural crisis cannot be met with the erection of a new "table of values," but rather with the reinvigoration of the tradition and the criticism of the present age. This, in the end, is the central message of Heidegger's phenomenology of religion from start to finish. (134)

Thus, Heidegger may well have a "phenomenology of religion," although he certainly is not involved in any sort of defense of Christian faith, however conceived. As Crowe, drawing on Westphal, says: "Heidegger's primary concern is with the *meaning* of religious life rather than with the *justification* of religious beliefs" (135). In this regard, Heidegger is absolutely fundamental for everything that follows. He provides the phenomenological context in which all subsequent thinking is conducted, even when aspects of his thought are challenged. His early claim that philosophy and theology are radically separate and operate in different spheres is consistently confronted. His insistence that metaphysics is onto-theo-logically constituted is assumed as a given and any renewed thought about God is argued to be other than onto-theo-logical. Perhaps most important, his notion of truth as *aletheia* becomes a way of speaking about truth in a different way and of positing a truth alternative to that of the natural sciences, a truth that might be equally valid in its own way but functions within a different hermeneutic circle as calculative thinking and therefore has its own methods and criteria.

2

Emmanuel Lévinas and the Infinite

Lévinas was one of the first thinkers to introduce phenomenology into France. Originally Lithuanian Jewish, he emigrated to France as a young student. He was educated in Straßburg and spent a formative year (1928–29) with Husserl and Heidegger in Freiburg. Husserl had retired but was still teaching, and Heidegger had just published *Being and Time*. Students flocked to his lectures. Lévinas talks about this experience in *Ethics and Infinity*, an interview with Philippe Nemo and broadcast on French radio, describing the excitement of Heidegger's initial lectures and the tremendous impact of *Being and Time*, which he calls "one of the most beautiful books in the history of philosophy" (he is far less impressed with Heidegger's later philosophy).[1] Although Lévinas later became quite critical of Heidegger and Husserl, he is also deeply influenced by their thought. When Husserl came to Paris to give his famous lectures that became the *Cartesian Meditations*, Lévinas translated for him and helped translate and edit the text for the French publication.

As a naturalized French citizen and a soldier in the French army, Lévinas was imprisoned in a prisoner of war camp and survived the war. All of his extended family perished; only his wife and young daughter survived in hiding. The Shoah is rarely mentioned in Lévinas's work and he seldom refers to it explicitly, although his second major work, *Otherwise Than Being*, is dedicated to the victims of the Holocaust.[2] In some ways his philosophy may indeed at least partially be regarded as a response to the atrocities of the Shoah and especially of Heidegger's failure in regard to it, although one should take care not to reduce his thought to a mere response to the Holocaust. Furthermore, although Lévinas was indeed involved in the Jewish communities in Paris and taught for years at the École Normale Israélite, he consistently sought to distance his philosophical work and writings from his Jewish faith, his Talmudic lectures, and his involvement in the Jewish community in France.[3] Lévinas always insisted that his religious commitments and his philosophical thought were separate and had little to do with each other, especially in the face of various claims that his philosophy was but a veiled religious project and despite the fact that his philosophy is indeed sprinkled liberally with religious terminology and imagery. This chapter seeks to show that Lévinas was right to deny that his philosophy was merely an invitation to Jewish (or Christian) faith. In fact, it argues that Lévinas makes every attempt in his philosophy to "secularize" his faith and to appropriate any religious insights for purely philosophical purposes and ends. Lévinas does not lead the attentive reader toward faith, but in many ways he actually leads away from it. Yet one certainly must admit that Lévinas's philosophy in a more general sense does clear the path for the thinkers who succeed him and are deeply influenced by him: Marion and Kearney especially, but also Derrida, Henry, Chrétien, and even Ricoeur (who was also often quite critical of him). In more than one respect, their philosophies and thoughts about God would have been impossible without Lévinas's philosophy of the other.

This chapter begins with a brief summary of Lévinas's critique of Husserl's and Heidegger's thought and then goes on to outline Lévinas's own project of alterity and infinity. It will explicate what Lévinas means when he calls ethics "first philosophy" and explain what he says about the "other" and what he means by the "face." I will then examine in what sense (if any) Lévinas speaks about God or guides us toward (religious) transcendence and look at some of the heavily religious terminology he employs in his thought. The chapter will conclude by showing in what ways Lévinas made a "theological turn" in French phenomenology possible and how he might have enabled the more recent "apologetic" projects.

Critique of Phenomenology

There are several ways in which Lévinas is critical of Husserlian phenomenology and Heideggerian Dasein philosophy, although he also appropriates and even applauds much of their thought. Several of Lévinas's early writings are on Husserl and phenomenology. His earliest essays (many of which were collected into the volume *Discovering Existence with Husserl and Heidegger*—the English translation is missing a couple of the essays on Heidegger and also does not include him in the title) and his first book, *The Theory of Intuition in Husserl's Phenomenology* (1930), are concerned with Husserl's philosophy. Lévinas agrees with Husserl that phenomenology opens a new and unique way of access to the things themselves. He employs Husserl's terminology of intuition and intentionality. Like Husserl, he is interested in how consciousness approaches what (or whom) it is conscious of. Yet while Husserl's greatest aim is to provide evidence for the perceptions of consciousness and to present and understand them in the greatest clarity, to provide signification for them and assign meaning to them, one could say that Lévinas's intent is almost diametrically opposed to this search for clarity and evidence. It is not that Lévinas exults in obscurity and ambiguity for its own sake. Rather, he senses something essentially *unethical* about this approach of consciousness to everything and everyone that stands outside of it or is apprehended by it. Instead of eliminating the difference and enigma of the other, Lévinas seeks to uphold them. Yet he does not try to eliminate phenomenology. Lévinas is quite insistent at times that his thought is still phenomenological.

In his early essay *Time and the Other* Lévinas first explicitly explores the idea of alterity. He proceeds from the solitude of existing to the encounter with something strange or other. His first exploration of this other is in terms of insomnia: the eerie experience of lying awake at night and feeling the presence of an anonymous absence. There is something "there" and yet not there. One might hear a strange noise, sense an impersonal presence, although it cannot be identified and remains anonymous. This is a first interruption of consciousness by something utterly strange and different. Lévinas refers to it as the *il y a* (literally "it has here" without an identified object, usually translated as "there is"[4]). This encounter with the other is not yet ethical (as it will be in most of Lévinas's later philosophy) and it does not fully rupture the self. Encounter of the other is here more an encounter with an anonymous presence (mediated through time) rather than with a human other, although this experience is already quite unsettling. The *il y a* and the experience of insomnia disorient me and confront me with a strangeness I cannot control or fully comprehend. In *Existence and Existents*, Lévinas continues this argument by pointing out the strangeness even of the very experience of existence. The whole essay is a critique of Heidegger's conviction that existence is the primordial experience. He interacts with several of Heidegger's themes: being, the world, death, and time. Lévinas suggests that the philosophical tradition is characterized by a kind of solipsism because it always speaks of a single subject, facing only him- or herself. Instead, Lévinas explores a "face-to-face" relation, here again put primarily in terms of time.

Alterity and Infinity

Lévinas's first major work, *Totality and Infinity*, first published in 1961, outlines much more fully the difference between the phenomenology of which he is critical and his own project. He depicts traditional philosophy as concerned with "totality." Lévinas argues that the major problem in Western philosophy is that it has closed off all access to the other and instead reduces all difference to sameness. Even phenomenology, although it emphasizes the essential relationship between consciousness and the objects of consciousness, between the activity of perceiving and what is being perceived, still attempts to grasp and comprehend as fully as possible what appears to consciousness as a phenomenon. The goal of phenomenology, as that of most of philosophy, is comprehension or knowledge, evidence and understanding. Lévinas claims that Western philosophy (including phenomenology) has always been obsessed with light, presence, and the self. Philosophy attempts to enlighten, to bring to light, to make present, to understand fully, to lay out plainly, to grasp. Knowledge is a kind of power that gives the subject possession and control of the known. I—as the conscious subject—am in charge and assimilate the known to myself. Lévinas finds that this desire to comprehend another person or subject matter fully and to reduce something to complete evidence or appearance implies that what is other or different becomes assimilated to my own understanding and therefore reduced to me—it becomes a version of myself. What was dark becomes light; what was hidden becomes uncovered and exposed to full view. In becoming exposed, grasped, laid out and comprehended, the phenomenon loses its alterity (otherness) or difference from consciousness and instead becomes a part of it. This process of assimilation and full comprehension is particularly detrimental when the other, the phenomenon that faces me, is not an object or a machine, but a human being.

What is other or different or strange or incomprehensible is scary, unsettling, and fearful. The stranger has always been a threat on some level.[5] So what do we do when something or someone is "strange" or "different"? Either we destroy: try to eliminate the scary stranger, to wipe out anything that induces fear. Or we assimilate, comprehend (encompass), make like us—so the stranger really becomes merely another version of the self. Lévinas calls this "reducing the other to the same," something he thinks the entire tradition has done consistently. Even phenomenology, despite all its careful attention to the "things themselves" and how they show themselves to us, does the same kind of thing by trying to assimilate everything to consciousness, making it known and clear and visible to the knower (to the "I"). Lévinas thinks that this process of "grasping" and of "assimilating" or "comprehending" is deeply unethical. Instead, Lévinas suggests, we must be open to utter alterity, complete difference. We must allow the other to remain other and thus always strange and unsettling. The "I" does this by realizing that the other interrupts me and startles me without my taking the initiative, that the other is always already there, has always preceded me (the dimension of temporality as "diachrony" is extremely important in Lévinas, although it cannot be explored in detail here). In fact, for Lévinas, the "I" only become a self by responding to the other.

Lévinas insists that while I might be able to grasp and fully comprehend an object, I should not do so with another person because in doing so I would reduce the other precisely to an object I can grasp and manipulate. Lévinas himself, then, wants to make space in his thinking—in phenomenological thinking—for real difference. For Lévinas, that is a profoundly ethical task, from beginning to end. Perhaps his most famous claim is that "ethics is first philosophy."[6] He is not saying that ethics is somehow temporally or historically first, but rather that "ethics is *better* than being" and certainly that it does not derive from ontology. It is unethical to reduce the other to a mere version of myself, comprehending the other in my terms, grasping (literally and metaphorically) the other in my control. To attempt to do so is to treat the other as an object to be exposed to light and to be examined at my will and pleasure. It is unethical to extrapolate from my experience of myself and simply assume that the other is and feels exactly like me. Lévinas therefore seeks to unsettle the history of philosophy (or of "ontology") and to open it up to the alterity and difference of the other.[7] Philosophical history, according to Lévinas, tends to "totality" in being closed to the infinity of the other and attempting to enclose this infinite difference in a totality of sameness (thus his title *Totality and Infinity*).

Yet Lévinas tries to accomplish this openness to alterity *within* phenomenology. His descriptions of insomnia, the anonymous *il y a* ("there is"), or later of the face, the feminine, and so forth, are phenomenological in character. Lévinas is attempting to formulate the phenomenological experience of an absolute alterity, something that cannot be seen or grasped by consciousness. Thus, one must instead examine and depict the *impact* this phenomenon makes on consciousness instead of describing the phenomenon itself, because it is so "other" that it defies description (or rather, to describe it would reduce its alterity to sameness). Lévinas describes this impact of alterity in terms of shock, interruption, being unsettled and surprised. He often refers to the phenomenon as an "enigma." Later, he will employ the language of the "trace": Although we cannot experience the phenomenon itself, we can experience and depict the traces it has left after having always already passed before us. Although we cannot "constitute" or "intend" the other in Husserl's sense, we can still engage in the kind of patient and careful description that is a hallmark of the phenomenological method. Lévinas will occasionally speak of this as "counter-intentionality": Intentionality proceeds from the other toward me instead of the reverse. I can feel myself envisioned and interrupted by the other instead of treating the other as an object I envision or intend.

The Other and the Face

The other comes to me, Lévinas claims, as the "face."[8] I do not "see" the face, but hear it. Lévinas is not talking about a physical face where I could describe the color of the eyes or the shape of the mouth and nose. The face speaks to me. In general, the auditory sense is much more important to Lévinas than the visual one. He explicitly tries to recover the emphasis on "hearing" in the Jewish tradition against the emphasis on "seeing" in the Greek and Christian one. The face has one basic message: "Thou shalt not kill!" It therefore orders and begs at the same time. Lévinas always insists on what he calls the "asymmetry" of this order that proceeds from the other. On the one hand, the face speaks from a "height": The other is infinitely above me and prior to me. The injunction of the face comes as an order or a command. On the other hand, the face is also vulnerable and exposed. Lévinas occasionally points out that the face is the only part of the body we do not clothe: It is naked, easily destroyed or ignored. He does not claim that I would be completely unable to kill the other or to destroy the face (although even when I do so I have not actually gained a real victory because at the very moment at which I eliminate the other, he or she has also escaped my control). Rather, he says that I "should" not kill, that it is unethical to do so, and that this call to respond to the other in peace is more primordial than the state of war. In order to express this vulnerability of the other, Lévinas increasingly employs the biblical language of care for the neighbor, for "the widow, the orphan, and the stranger." These are the three groups who represent the weakest and most vulnerable elements of society, those who have no real status and are almost entirely dependent on the pity or charity of others. The Jewish tradition has a strong sense of obligation to these vulnerable groups. Lévinas seeks to universalize or translate this obligation to any needy person who requires my help.

My obligation to the other, however, does not really establish a relationship between us, because such a relationship would always be on *my* terms: It immediately has connotations of assimilation and control. There certainly is an encounter with the other, but this encounter proceeds from the other; it is more like a sudden interruption: Lévinas uses imagery from a simple surprise knock at the door to the "trauma" of an explosion. He is most emphatic that he is not advocating the establishment of a symmetrical or reciprocal relationship, maybe on the model of Buber's "I-Thou" relation.[9] Anything that would assimilate the other to me and make him or her tame and comprehensible is a violation of the ethical encounter, a reduction of the other to the same. Drawing on Isaiah's overwhelming encounter with the divine who calls him to fulfill a mission to the people (Isaiah 6:1–9), Lévinas suggests that the appropriate response to the other's call to me is: "here I am." In French ("*me voici*"), this response is in the accusative and at times Lévinas employs this expression as a summary for his philosophy: While most of traditional philosophy speaks of the subject in the first person, in the nominative and as the main subject, Lévinas wants to speak of the self in the accusative, "accused" and displaced by the other. Instead of "grasping" and "comprehending" the other, I am put in question by this encounter and called upon to respond. In his later work, Lévinas depicts this response as a complete self-emptying on behalf of the other, sharing "the last piece of bread out of one's own mouth."[10]

By interrupting me and demanding not to be killed, the other addresses me directly and awakens my responsibility. I become a self only through this address and call of the other. I become unique, become an individuated self, not because I can think (Descartes) or because I have a rational soul (Aristotle) or because I am a *Dasein* experiencing my world and aware of my finitude (Heidegger). I am uniquely myself because the other has singled me out and demanded my assistance. It is my responsibility for the other that distinguishes me from the crowd and turns me into a self. In his later work, Lévinas carries this even further by claiming that I have a responsibility even for the other's responsibility, that in some way I become "hostage" to the other by "substituting" for the other, taking the other's place (see the discussion of the "hostage" in the next section). For Lévinas, this is always an asymmetrical relationship: The other claims this from me, but I have no right to claim anything similar of the other. Often, Lévinas puts this in terms of a quote from Dostoevsky's *The Brothers Karamazov*: "Each of us is guilty before everyone, for everyone and for every thing, and I more than the others."

Substitution and Justice

In "Violence and Metaphysics," an early essay written in response to Lévinas's work *Totality and Infinity*, Derrida argues that Lévinas's philosophy may possibly be subject to the same kind of violence it tries to circumvent.[11] He claims that the infinity of the other might also become violent and thus re-institute the war it tries to prevent. He is also insistent that it is impossible to escape metaphysics, that even this radical language of alterity is still speaking philosophically. Derrida rightly recognizes that Lévinas does not appeal to theology or Jewish mysticism but that his thought is based on "a *recourse to experience itself*" (83). Yet he wonders about how an absolute encounter could be described when there can be no appearance and when it is complete rupture. "Asymmetry, non-light, and commandment then would be violence and injustice themselves," Derrida contends, unless God is present: "God alone keeps Lévinas's world from being a world of the pure and worst violence" (107). Despite this reference to God, Derrida recognizes that Lévinas does not engage in theology here, that "the face of God disappears forever in showing itself" (108). Derrida's questions are primarily questions about language: How can one speak of the other without violence and reduction? How would one express the irreducible? Derrida claims that Lévinas does not recognize sufficiently that "discourse is originally violent" (116). And ultimately Lévinas engages in self-contradiction on this point of language: "Lévinas *in fact* speaks of the infinitely other, but by refusing to acknowledge an intentional modification of the ego—which would be a violent and totalitarian act for him—he deprives himself of the very foundation and possibility of his own language" (125). Not to recognize the violence of discourse becomes a worse kind of violence. And a similar violence attaches itself to Lévinas's desire to "do without the verb *to be*" (147).[12] Derrida concludes that "not to philosophize" still is "to philosophize" (152).

Lévinas is actually very aware of the inadequacy of traditional philosophical language for his project. He consistently refers to the need for philosophy to speak "Greek" and realizes quite acutely that even his own thought could never escape these philosophical restrictions. In his later work, he often distinguishes between what he calls the "saying" and the "said" (a theme that can also be found in *Totality and Infinity* but is not as prominent there). The "saying" refers to what is at the verbal or even preverbal level, what cannot be expressed, what may precede even thought itself. The "said" is the language into which the "saying" immediately becomes solidified when it is expressed in statements and especially in writing. Philosophical propositions are the quintessential form of the "said," but all language quickly loses its fluidity and is obligated to refer to objects and reality. One might say that to some extent "saying" and "said" recover Heidegger's distinctions between meditative and calculative language, although "saying" clearly does not map onto *aletheia* in terms of its activity of unveiling and uncovering (one often has the impression that it is more about a desire to remain hidden and concealed, although Heidegger and Lévinas agree that concealing and unconcealing are closely connected to each other). Lévinas identifies his use of "Jewish" biblical imagery and terminology precisely as a way to hold the "saying" open longer. Traditional philosophical terminology hardens much more quickly into a "said" because these terms are already loaded with centuries of meaning from which it is nearly impossible to free them. The biblical imagery thus can unsettle this static discourse and remind us of something more primordial, precisely because it is so surprising and unfamiliar to the philosophical context.

To some extent, in response to Derrida's objections (although in no way a concession), Lévinas's language for the ethical obligation to the other becomes even more intense and extreme in his second major work, *Otherwise Than Being or Beyond Essence*.[13] He radicalizes his earlier analyses: While in his earlier work *Totality and Infinity* (especially in the account of enjoyment) the self gives to the other out of the abundance of its own resources, in *Otherwise Than Being*, the self is itself in a position of need. Care for the other hence becomes a much more excessive demand, which may entail extreme suffering or even death for me. He explicates this in extreme terms that describe this obligation as a kind of violence, in which I am "torn from myself": "But giving has meaning only as a tearing from oneself despite oneself, and not only *without* me. And to be torn from oneself despite oneself has meaning only as a being torn from the complacency in oneself characteristic of enjoyment, snatching the bread from one's own mouth. Only a subject that eats can be for-the-other, or can signify. Signification, the one-for-the-other, has meaning only among beings of flesh and blood" (*OB*, 74). Instead of giving out of the abundance of my own resources as I enjoy them complacently, the self is now depicted as itself in real physical distress but nevertheless called upon to give. I am to share my last piece of bread, to prevent the other's starvation by sacrificing my own life. I am called to be completely "for the other." Lévinas goes on to explicate this in terms of total vulnerability and exposedness to the other to the point where I am responsible for the other's death: "It is as though I were responsible for his mortality, and guilty for surviving" (*OB*, 91).

He speaks of the ethical encounter now as a kind of *substitution*, where I take the place of the other even to the point of death. Substitution does not mean that I could "replace" the other or stand in his or her shoes. Rather, it refers to the fullest self-sacrifice, one that gives one's own life in place of that of the other. Lévinas argues that ethical alterity requires not only that I am responsible for the other in need, but also that I am responsible for the very responsibility of the other to the point of becoming the other's hostage. Lévinas employs the metaphor of maternity to illustrate this: The maternal womb is taken over by the other, feeds the other, without having any choice in the matter or even actively giving itself to the other. He thus radicalizes the asymmetry he had already outlined in *Totality and Infinity*. The self is completely obligated to the other but can claim no such reciprocal obligation from the other on its own behalf. And Lévinas insists that this unconditional self-offering is the very condition for any "pity, compassion, pardon and proximity—even the little there is, even the simple 'After you, sir.' The unconditionality of being hostage is not the limit case of solidarity, but the condition for all solidarity" (*OB*, 117). If my response to the other were based on a theoretical equality, a tit-for-tat, a sort of reciprocal contract, it would quickly degenerate into an economic exchange where I do the minimum required for the contract. Ethics instead by its very nature does not assign value in terms of calculation or exchange. Its very possibility depends on unconditionality and infinite generosity.

Lévinas was asked over and over again how such an extreme dedication to the other can be justified and whether the other is not also responsible for us. Must the relation not be symmetrical for it to be ethical? Lévinas rigorously denies this, but he does concede that our lives as they are lived in a world of varying relationships are even more complicated. We always already find ourselves within a social setting where there is more than one "other." Lévinas calls this "the third" to show that there is not merely an encounter between two, but that a third always enters immediately. I am obligated not only to the other who faces me, but other others also have claims on me. I cannot meet all of these claims at the same time and thus must negotiate and compromise. Sometimes I have to speak on behalf of a whole group that is being treated unjustly and in that case the group might include me (and therefore I am in a sense also asking for justice for myself). Lévinas refers to this situation of "the third" as the relation of justice (or occasionally of "morality" as distinguished from ethics). Only in the context of justice may I expect anything from others. The ethical relation, instead, is always asymmetrical and characterized by absolute obligation. This ethical relation is primary, indeed primordial, and all social and public relations are secondary and parasitic upon it. Politics (or the relation of "justice"), for Lévinas, is a kind of concession where ethics has always already failed, where we are no longer attentive to absolute transcendence and yet always haunted and interrupted by the ethical encounter, by the call to responsibility. Yet even justice is only possible because of the higher obligation of ethics that precedes it and makes it possible through the promise of uncompromising peace.

The Role of "God" in Lévinas

Dominique Janicaud speaks of Lévinas's philosophy as a theological highjacking. In Lévinas's thought, "phenomenology has been taken hostage by a theology that does not want to say its name."[14] He claims that Lévinas is not attentive to experience in the way phenomenologists ought to be, but instead introduces a violent transcendence that crashes in from elsewhere but cannot be examined or justified phenomenologically. And certainly Janicaud is not the only one who feels uncomfortable with Lévinas's liberal use of religious terminology and his strong appeal to an apparently utterly transcendent and mysterious "other." Yet is it really Lévinas's goal to "open a perspective onto the greater glory of the infinite" and "swerve" into ontotheology?[15] To speak of "absolute otherness," "complete transcendence," or "infinity" does seem to refer to "God" or the divine. That, however, does not necessarily follow for Lévinas. Alterity, infinity, otherness, even transcendence are first and primarily about the human other, the stranger, the one most vulnerable. This does not mean that Lévinas never mentions or never speaks of God. He does. But his talk about God is always in the service of his philosophical project of speaking of the human other. Several aspects of his thinking make this clear.[16]

First of all, Lévinas is quite clear that we cannot have direct access to God. In fact he does not even seem to think that we can have something like "faith in" God. One cannot say "I believe in God" because the divine cannot become the subject of a proposition or thesis (*GDT*, 200). Acting in "the name of God" is not about believing in God:

> The Infinite is not "in front of" me; I express it, but precisely by giving a sign of the giving of signs, of the "for-the-other" in which I am dis-interested: here I am (*me voici*)! The accusative here is remarkable: here I am, under your eyes, at your service, your obedient servant. In the name of God. But this is without thematization; the sentence in which God gets mixed in with words is not "I believe in God." The religious discourse that precedes all religious discourse is

not dialogue. It is the "here I am" said to a neighbor to whom I am given over, by which I announce peace, that is, my responsibility for the other. (*BPW*, 146)

God is not a term that invites belief but a word that directs us to the other. We do not believe in God or have relationship or dialogue with the divine. Rather, the Infinite always directs us toward the human other and places us in service to the other.

Lévinas usually does not even use the term "God" but more often speaks of the "infinite" or of "illeity" (from the French third person singular *il*—which can mean both "he" and "it"). He is quite clear that he is not referring to the "personal" God of religion with whom one might have a relationship. Rather, God is the "trace of illeity," what has always already passed and cannot be identified. The divine has only left a trace and we are always too late. The trace indicates the utter absence and obscure alterity of God. Direct relationship between God and the self is not possible. Lévinas goes out of his way to emphasize the obscurity of this trace and speaks of it as the *absolutely Absent*.[17] No relation or signification is possible. The trace of illeity indicates absolute alterity that escapes any kind of revelation or appearance and is completely without measure. Lévinas describes it, instead, as the "origin" of the face, of the alterity of the other: "It is in the trace of the Other that the face shines . . . The face is, in and of itself, visitation and transcendence. But the face, fully open, can at the same time be in itself, because it is in the trace of illeity. Illeity is the origin of alterity . . ." To be in the image of God for Lévinas implies to stand "in the trace of the divine." One cannot pursue the trace toward God, but must walk toward the others who are held in this trace.[18]

Hence, Lévinas's primary concern is always our encounter with the human neighbor. This is particularly evident in one of the series of Lévinas's final lectures at the Sorbonne, the ones collected in *God, Death and Time* under the title "God and Onto-Theo-logy." He formulates his task in these lectures most explicitly as that of hearing a "God not contaminated by being" which seems to indicate a theological concern or at least one focused on the divine: "One attempts here to formulate notions which have no meaning except in their relation with the other. And one searches an access to a non-ontological notion of God, beginning from a certain dis-inter-estedness; one searches an escape from ontology beginning with the relation with the other in its difference which makes objectivity impossible" (*GDT*, 180). This seems to imply that he is primarily interested in developing a non-ontological way of speaking about God. Yet although he reiterates this repeatedly as the main theme of the lectures, in fact they say very little about the divine. Continually and almost obsessively Lévinas returns to the theme of the human other and our responsibility to the face. He formulates the notion of God most explicitly as that of the Cartesian "infinite in us" and speaks of it as the aim of our desires, as an inner desire to search to fill a void at the core of our being. Yet this desire for the infinite cannot be fulfilled for Lévinas. Rather, we are continually returned to the face of the other that we encounter in the way of this desire. The (human) other for whom we are responsible stands in the trace of the divine and in some sense blocks access to it.

We hear the word "God" only as a certain witness of the other of something beyond itself, thus in a sense an other beyond the other. Lévinas circumscribes the only context in which any non-ontological notion of God is possible: "That which we call God can only take meaning starting from the relations with others. It is only beginning from these relations that God can 'manifest' himself" (GDT, 185, see also 194). Although here something like a manifestation of God seems possible, at other times Lévinas denies that any such manifestation could ever take place. As we attempt to approach God, we simply encounter our obligation to the human other. To find access to a language that might speak of God, one must get beyond ontology and place the question of God within the context of the relation with the other. "God" will not appear or manifest the divine outside of the ethical language that Lévinas has outlined. "God" only makes sense, only is given meaning in my relation to the other, my response to the other and openness to the neighbor. I never meet God but only the other person. Whenever I might suppose that I have had a glimpse of God's glory, really I have only encountered the concrete face of the other, which is not usually a pleasant or welcome sight. While I may have desire for the divine infinite, I am always continually turned toward the weak and vulnerable human stranger whom I do not desire. "Holiness" is only possible "if the desirable commands me to the undesirable *par excellence*: to the *other person* . . . The referral to the other is an awakening to nearness, which is responsibility for the neighbor to the point of substitution, which is the enucleation of the transcendental subject" (GDT, 223). Holiness is precisely that call to become the other's hostage, to substitute for the other to the point of complete self-sacrifice.

Even in other articles, Lévinas emphasizes repeatedly that the divine cannot be named, is never manifested, and cannot be defined. An analysis similar to that in the lectures can be found in the article "God and Philosophy"[19] (included as a chapter in *Of God Who Comes to Mind* and also translated in the collection *Basic Philosophical Writings*). Lévinas insists again in this article that traditional thought about God in terms of Being has limited and restricted God. Far from drawing theological conclusions from this, however, he speaks of God in terms of a desire for the infinite within us, a desire that is different or transcendent. This transcendence "is ethics," is "a responsibility for the Other (*Autrui*), a subjection to the other (*autrui*)" (*BPW*, 140). He summarizes his concern in a manner very similar to the lectures: "In this ethical reversal, in this reference of the Desirable to the Nondesirable, in this strange mission that orders the approach to the other (*autrui*), God is drawn out of objectivity, presence, and being. He is neither an object nor an interlocutor. His absolute remoteness, his transcendence, turns into my responsibility—nonerotic par excellence—for the other (*autrui*)" (*BPW*, 141). All God-talk is ultimately about ethics, leads me toward the suffering neighbor for whom I am responsible. The cries "addressed to God" are those of "the nakedness of someone forsaken" who calls me to "my responsibility in spite of myself" (*BPW*, 143). Although Lévinas's essay begins with God and even employs that term in the title, it is essentially an essay about my responsibility to the human other. All apparently religious subjects and allusions in Lévinas guide us back to that overriding ethical theme. Any testimony to the Infinite must be one of ethical responsibility: "The subject as hostage has been neither the experience nor the proof of the Infinite, but a witness borne of the Infinite, a modality of this glory, a testimony that no disclosure has preceded" (*BPW*, 144). God is not the one toward whom I am turned or whom I should aim to reach, but rather I express the Infinite in my concern for the neighbor, in my complete self-sacrifice.[20] It is the human other who matters, not God.

Furthermore, even when Lévinas does speak of the divine, his language for God is highly ambivalent. In his early works, especially in *Totality and Infinity*, the infinite actually refers to the face of the other, and only in his later works does it more clearly designate something or someone divine. In both cases, he appeals to the terminology of an "idea" of the infinite, recalling Descartes's reference to this idea within him that could not stem from himself. In *Totality and Infinity* the Infinite is what the "I think" "can nowise contain and from which it is separated by a relation called the 'idea of infinity'" (*TI*, 48). This, so Lévinas, is an "exceptional" idea unlike any other, because we cannot account for it. Lévinas here identifies "the infinite, the transcendent, the Stranger" with each other. In this early work the Infinite functions solely as a term designating otherness, transcendence, alterity, or difference. It is what cannot be contained. In later sections of *Totality and Infinity*, the infinite becomes identified almost entirely with the face: "The idea of infinity, the infinitely more contained in the less, is concretely produced in the form of a relation with the face. And the idea of infinity alone maintains the exteriority of the other with respect to the same, despite this relation" (*TI*, 196). There is no mention of God here; in fact, several times Lévinas explicitly rejects the appeal to God in Descartes's notion of the infinite.

In *Otherwise Than Being*, however, the infinite no longer designates the ethical relation per se. The infinite is not identical to the neighbor or to the face, but precedes them in diachronic fashion. It is within the trace of the infinite that we encounter the neighbor. My responsibility to the neighbor is in some sense already grounded in what Lévinas calls "the glory of the infinite": "The more I answer the more I am responsible; the more I approach the neighbor with which I am encharged the further away I am. This debit which increases is infinity as an infinition of the infinite, as glory" (*OB*, 93). Here also, the response to the other is the primary focus. Lévinas speaks of it as

> a witness to the Infinite, but a witness that does not thematize what it bears witness of, and whose truth is not the truth of representation, is not evidence. There is witness, a unique structure, an exception to the rule of being, irreducible to representation, only of the Infinite. The Infinite does not appear to him that bears witness to it. On the contrary the witness belongs to the glory of the Infinite. It is by the voice of the witness that the glory of the Infinite is glorified. (*OB*, 146)

The Infinite, who here does seem to be equated with the divine (as it is in most of Lévinas's later works), does not appear and is not thematized, but rather serves only as witness to the responsibility for the other. Although not identical, both of these ways of talking about the Infinite serve the same purpose. Thought about God, for Lévinas, always serves not as an end in itself but as a means of illustrating or making possible an encounter with alterity that allows for the ethical approach of the neighbor. Talk about God helps us articulate the utter otherness of the human other. The reverse movement (from humans to God) is not only not possible but also not of primary interest to him.

This becomes even clearer when one considers how Lévinas speaks of God as the "other." The term is so "other" that it is in danger of being confused with an utterly indeterminate transcendence that appears to sustain next to no connection with a religious notion of the divine. Lévinas claims that "God is not simply the 'first other (*autrui*),' the other (*autrui*) par excellence, or the 'absolutely other (*autrui*),' but other than the other (*autre qu'autrui*), other otherwise, other with an alterity prior to the alterity of the other (*autrui*), prior to the ethical bond with the other (*autrui*) and different from every neighbor, transcendent to the point of absence, to the point of a possible confusion with the stirring of the *there is*" (*BPW*, 141). God is so absent, so utterly other, so transcendent, that thought about the divine becomes almost indistinguishable from thought about nothing or terrifying absence.

Religious belief, then, is impossible for Lévinas, at least within the realm of his philosophical project. God cannot be reached. The divine cannot even be thematized in philosophy. There is nothing we could say about the infinite directly. And certainly something like "religious experience" would make very little sense within Lévinas's philosophy. Any desire to "experience" God directly would constitute a denial of the call of the suffering neighbor to whom I ought to respond instead. We can, then, say nothing about belief in God and can have no relationship with the divine but must focus entirely on our ethical obligation to the neighbor.

Yet Lévinas never completely abandons language of the divine. Why? Why speak of God if one cannot speak of God? Why bring God into the relationship with the other, if "God" has no sense without the other, if every encounter in the trace of God is really only an encounter with the human neighbor? It seems that "God" is employed by Lévinas as a term for the most extreme otherness, which is so absolutely different that it remains irreducible. This irreducibility is able to hold open the alterity of the other. The name of "God" in Lévinas functions as the only word that cannot be reduced, that always escapes our grasp and therefore as the only term that holds open infinite transcendence and utter alterity. I can reduce the (human) other, can refuse to respond to the other's call, can turn my back on the responsibility that I will always owe to the other. I can ignore the neighbor if I so desire, can live alone in my world appropriating all its goods for myself, can stay outside of ethics. Yet, while the face of the neighbor can be "reduced to the same" and can even be murdered, this is impossible to do with God. One cannot ever get enough of a grasp on God to hold the divine. The idea of God stands for the "noncontained par excellence" because it can never become "contemporary," "correlate," "co-present," "comprehended."[21] Thus, God is the otherness behind the other that always reiterates my responsibility even as I try to evade or subvert it. God is the third, the illeity that stands outside my relation to the other and continually reminds me of my obligation.[22]

It is precisely this notion of God that prevents the collapse of ethics for Lévinas. I can reduce or even kill the other, but I cannot reduce God. The word "God" is unique, says Lévinas, "in that it is the only word which is not extinguished or blown out or whose saying is not absorbed. It is only a word and yet it turns upside down semantics. Glory encloses itself in a word, it makes itself being but always already undoes its dwelling. Immediately unsaid, this word does not marry itself to grammatical categories" (*GDT*, 204). Thus, the word "God" (or maybe the name of God) stands for the sort of transcendence and alterity that can never be entirely erased. The rationality of transcendence cannot be reduced to the rationality of philosophy, and in fact, can never even enter within it. The thought of God always ruptures the sense of the self and reminds it of something beyond it. The infinite cannot be welcomed, cannot be received, but we are put in question by it, traumatized by it, sent toward the other. The only thing that appears in the space of rupture is the face of the other. The infinite affects thought only by devastating it, by calling it outside of itself, by awakening it. The infinite can never be welcomed or received. It does not manifest itself. Yet it refers to a desire without hunger and without end [*sans faim et aussi sans fin*], which alone makes something like (non-erotic) love possible (*GDT*, 221). This utterly separate transcendence, however, although desired and desirable (as the "good" beyond being), can never be desired directly but only sends us again toward the other, the neighbor, whom we do not desire. Ethics is beyond ontology, precisely because it is concerned with the good, because it is "better" than being (*GDT*, 224). Lévinas, then, rejects the language of ontology because it reduces ethics, not because it is inadequate for theology. Although that may also be the case, it is not what Lévinas wishes to emphasize.

The terminology of "glory," a term Lévinas employs more heavily in his later work, makes a similar point. He speaks of this idea as a glory that figures only in a distance or in an abyss that can never be bridged (*GDT*, 162), alluding to some of the overwhelming epiphanies of the divine glory in the Hebrew Scriptures. Such glory overwhelms any attempt to comprehend it. The divine cannot be closed down in a "said," because it is never fully thematized, never comes to language (*GDT*, 191). One must speak of it and bear witness to it, but such speaking is not philosophy and cannot become the topic of a discourse. The infinite always recedes from view, regardless of how much one attempts to approach it. There can be no model of transcendence. God will never approach, can never be named. God does not become present because nothing is capable of holding the infinite. God has always already passed and hardly left a trace.

Thought about God functions positively in Lévinas only when it is thought about infinity that leads to openness to the other. To be "struck by the *in* of infinity" is not to have a religious experience, but rather to awaken "subjectivity to the proximity of the other" (*BPW*, 142). Lévinas says this more clearly in an interview with Richard Kearney. He explains:

> The word of God speaks through the glory of the face and calls for an ethical conversion or reversal of our nature. What we call "lay morality," that is, humanistic concern for our fellow human beings, already speaks the voice of God. But the moral priority of the other over myself could not come to be if it were not motivated by something beyond nature. The ethical situation is a human situation, beyond human nature, in which the idea of God comes to mind. In this respect, we could say that God is the other who turns our nature inside out, who calls our ontological will-to-be into question.[23]

The word "God" for Lévinas consequently functions as the term that founds, confirms, and maintains my ethical obligation, my continual responsibility for the other that precedes even my birth and comes to me from an infinite distance. Lévinas is thus always ultimately concerned with ethics or my relation to the human other, rather than theology or my relation with God. The religious imagery and terminology that he employs (widow, orphan and stranger; testimony and prophecy; call and election; holiness and glory) are always used in the service of ethics, subordinated to the concern for the human neighbor. There is no "theological turn" in Lévinas. Rather, there is a philosophical turn: Lévinas employs the religious imagery but empties it of its theological connotations or its context of faith and instead employs it for purely philosophical ends. And yet Lévinas does contribute to the more explicitly theological projects of later thinkers. How does he do so?

Impact of Lévinas's Thought

Lévinas is so important, first of all, because his phenomenology profoundly influences all French thinkers after him: The work of Marion, Henry, and Lacoste, and even that of Derrida, would be unthinkable without him. Yet Lévinas also opens opportunities for these later thinkers because he changes the thrust of phenomenology radically and opens it in directions that are not present in Husserl or Heidegger. Even in Husserl, phenomenology stresses the relation between knower and known, between consciousness and what one is conscious of, between noesis and noema, between intention and intuition. Knowledge for Husserl is always knowledge *of* something. But consciousness assimilates and constitutes this "other" one attempts to know or of which consciousness is conscious. Husserl's most important goal is to provide evidence, to get to "truth." And one gets to such truth or evidence through the constitution of objects and through the comprehension of consciousness. Evidence, clarity, and light are of the highest priority. Consciousness or the self is completely in charge. For Heidegger, the question of Being includes an important dimension of obscurity, of concealing, of what is unapparent. This obscurity can never be erased or entirely uncovered. Yet Heidegger is interested in it for the sake of what it reveals. And the one who engages in this process of revealing is Dasein. Human being is clearly at the center for Heidegger and he speaks of it as a "Lichtung" (a clearing or, literally, a "lighting") for Being and Truth. Even *aletheia* itself, truth, for Heidegger is about uncovering, revealing, bringing to light. In Lévinas's view, Heidegger's philosophy is profoundly unethical. Neither Husserl nor Heidegger, according to Lévinas, leaves any room for real alterity. No "other" can appear (and certainly not remain other) in traditional phenomenology, but phenomenology is all about the self enlightening everything else and assimilating it to itself. Instead, Lévinas attempts to explore phenomenologically, what it might mean for the other to "appear"—not by becoming "present" and "comprehensible" but by making an impact that can be felt and experienced (phenomenologically) and yet remain truly other and different. Thus, Lévinas makes a space in phenomenology for "infinity" or "alterity" or even for "transcendence," not as such but in its impact upon us. By emphasizing otherness and alterity so strongly and by employing language like "infinity" and "transcendence," Lévinas makes it possible to explore in phenomenology what does not present itself to consciousness as an object, but might in fact never be reducible to comprehension.

Furthermore, Lévinas is also one of the first to take the implications of Heidegger's description of metaphysics as "onto-theo-logy" seriously, to think philosophy in a different mode, and to do so in a rigorous fashion. Indeed, that is one of the reasons why he is so difficult to read; he attempts to write in a language that subverts philosophy from within. He therefore suggests that we might have to speak of God as "different" from Being, or even as "beyond" Being in some fashion. Lévinas is the first to challenge Heidegger in this way and to envision the possibility of something "beyond" or outside of Being, something or someone entirely without relation to Being or manifestation.[24] Many of the contemporary thinkers, especially Marion, will similarly avoid ontological language and attempt to find a way to depict more primordial phenomenological experiences that might be impossible to express in terms of simple appearance or manifestation of objects or entities.

Finally, by employing such explicitly religious terminology, Lévinas makes it possible for other thinkers to use examples from the Scriptures or even appropriate religious language without being immediately dismissed.

In a sense, he forces access for such language in philosophical discourse, even if many thinkers continue to remain uncomfortable with it. The very fact that Lévinas uses such terms as "infinity," "absolute alterity," and "transcendence" opens a certain space for the divine, gives these terms again a certain legitimacy in philosophy (and maybe precisely because Lévinas himself does *not* apply them to God). French philosophy after Lévinas becomes obsessed with the other to the point where the term has become a veritable cliché. Maybe precisely by evacuating such language of its religious content, by using "glory," "prophecy," "witness," and "care for widow and orphan," in such a purely phenomenological sense, he enables others to employ religious language without immediately assuming that any such endeavor would be inherently theological.

Perhaps most important, Lévinas is one of the first to speak of a reversal of intentionality and to envision a self that is not a self-sufficient subject. Much of his later work is concerned with working out what it might mean for the self to be accused, responsible, obligated, guilty, even hostage to another prior to any action or decision taken by the self. In fact, for Lévinas, the self only becomes an individuated, particular self via this responsibility toward the other, through the other's call to and claim upon the self. While this reversal or unsettling of the subject is not the primary or only focus of the work of the later thinkers, it certainly is an important aspect for many of them, including Ricoeur, Marion, Henry, Chrétien, Lacoste, Falque, and Kearney. It also makes it possible to think about what it might mean for this less autonomous and powerful self to become vulnerable and receptive in the face of something or someone divine (although again that is not part of Lévinas's own philosophical reflections or intentions).

3

Jacques Derrida and "Religion Without Religion"

Jacques Derrida's writings are extensive and few of them have any direct bearing on the subject of religion. Yet, especially since the publication of Kevin Hart's *The Trespass of the Sign*,[1] Hent de Vries's *Philosophy and the Turn to Religion*,[2] and John D. Caputo's *The Prayers and Tears of Jacques Derrida*,[3] as well as Derrida's repeated participation in the popular *Religion and Postmodernism* conferences at Villanova University (also initiated and hosted by Caputo),[4] some of Derrida's writing has exercised great influence on the growing conversation that seeks to conduct discussion about religion in a postmodern environment. The interpretation of Derrida in this context has been strongly colored by John Caputo's presentation of Derrida's thought in many of his works and countless addresses and conversations at conferences. Much of this can be summarized by the phrase "religion without religion," which Derrida uses occasionally and Caputo frequently. But it is also encapsulated by the repeated affirmation "*Oui. oui.* Yes. yes." which appears often in Derrida's work and which Caputo interprets as a summary of deconstruction as a whole, as a quasi-messianic hope (although without messiah, just as its "religion" is without religion, i.e. without commitment to any particular tradition).[5] This chapter will thus in no way be a summary of or introduction to Derrida's large and difficult corpus. Rather, it will present how certain aspects of Derrida's philosophy have become very influential for the work of the other thinkers treated in this book and especially for their reception in the English-speaking (especially North American) context. Marion, in particular, has been frequently read almost solely in light of his engagement with Derrida at the first *Religion and Postmodernism* conference in 1997 on "God, the Gift, and Postmodernism." Thus, the question of the gift and its undecidability has often become the primary context in which Marion's work is discussed (which, as the chapter on his thought will show, is a rather limited and unhelpful way to approach Marion's work). Similarly, Chrétien, Lacoste, and even Lévinas have often been read in light of and in the context of this popularity of Derrida. Needless to say, they are, of course, also influenced to some extent by Derrida's thought, and Marion is at times explicitly responding to it. And to the extent that Caputo's version of Derrida has opened the conversation on "postmodernism and religion," it has also opened a place for the reception of these other, much more explicitly religious, thinkers.

Différance and Negative Theology

One of Derrida's earliest references to theology occurs in his early address "Différance" (included in the English translation of *Speech and Phenomena*).[6] In a single paragraph in this lengthy text, he acknowledges that the difference and deferral that he is outlining in this address might remind listeners of the deferring moves of "negative theology," although he hastens to assure his audience that différance is not negative theology and should not be confused with it. He says:

> Thus, the detours, phrases, and syntax that I shall often have to resort to will resemble—will sometimes be practically indiscernible from—those of negative theology. Already we had to note *that* differance *is not*, does not exist, and is not any sort of being-present (*on*). And we will have to point out everything *that* it *is not*, and, consequently, that is has neither existence nor essence. It belongs to no category of being, present or absent. And yet what is thus denoted as differance is not theological, not even in the most negative order of negative theology. (134)

While negative theology ultimately always refers to some sort of "supraessential reality," even if beyond any categories, and thus a superior divine being, différance is "irreducible to any ontological or theological—onto-theological—reappropriation, but it opens up the very space in which onto-theology—philosophy—produces its system and its history. It thus encompasses and irrevocably surpasses onto-theology or philosophy" (134–35). Différance does not refer to a master discourse but to a constant deferral of meaning, pointing to the differences and distinctions always operative in the play of meaning. It is not itself a concept or a word or realm. Rather it refers both to the indecidability of meaning itself and to the multivalency and complexity of meanings. It is neither primordial nor eschatological (another way in which it is different from theological discourse). It does not point to a being who might originate it (145). There is no further reference to theology in the rest of the essay which is mostly concerned with semiotic and linguistic questions. Yet by distinguishing différance from negative theology and, indeed, by referring to theology in the first place, their supposed similarity became occasion for much discussion about the two. The volume *Derrida and Negative Theology* examines Derrida's closeness to this tradition of theological thinking.[7] It includes Derrida's essays "Of an Apocalyptic Tone Newly Adopted in Philosophy" and "How to Avoid Speaking: Denials" as a preface and Derrida wrote as a post-script his essay *Sauf le nom*, which was later included in the collection *On the Name* (together with the essays "Passion" and "Khōra"). *"Sauf" le nom* can mean not only "except" or "without" the name, but also "save" or "protect" the name.

While "Of an Apocalyptic Tone" does not engage religious questions explicitly (except for a brief discussion of John's Apocalypse at the end of the text[8]), "How to Avoid Speaking: Denials" is far more fully about negative theology and to some extent even about Derrida's own religious heritage, his Jewish and Arabic/Islamic background about which he precisely "avoids speaking" in the text by focusing instead on Greek, Christian, and Heideggerian paradigms for negative theology.[9] Derrida opens his lengthy address "How to Avoid Speaking," originally delivered in Jerusalem, with the intent to speak of the relationship of his work to "negative theology." He admits a "family resemblance" between différance and negative theology. Both are discourses that seem "to return in a regular and insistent manner to this rhetoric of negative determination, endlessly multiplying the defenses and the apophatic warnings" and both refuse to fit into dualistic categories of sensible/intelligible, positive/negative, inside/outside, superior/inferior, active/passive, present/absent, and so forth. They exceed "the order and the structure of predicative discourse" (*DNT*, 74). He insists again that he does not write negative theology because there is no final authority attributed to a name in his work and because there is no final move to "hyperessentiality," to some final divine being beyond Being (*DNT*, 77).[10] Yet he also admits a certain fascination with the infinite deferrals of various "negative" theological discourses and expresses the need to speak of their relationship more clearly and more fully (*DNT*, 82). Reflections on avoiding speaking, avoiding finally saying anything, and on the secret accompany his discussion throughout.

Jacques Derrida and "Religion Without Religion" ■ *61*

He spends the most time discussing Greek (Platonic and Neoplatonic), Christian, and Heideggerian places or paradigms for apophatic speech. In the first section, he contrasts the Platonic "good beyond Being" and the khōra of the *Timaeus* and shows their influence on Christian mysticism. He argues again that a hyperbole of the good remains tied to being in some sense and thus is not neutral: "Ontology remains possible and necessary" (*DNT*, 103). Derrida concludes that "there cannot be an absolutely negative discourse: a *logos* necessarily speaks about something; it cannot avoid speaking of something; it is impossible for it to refer to nothing" (ibid.). Derrida contrasts this to the emptiness of the khōra, which is not a medium or a container or a receptacle: "It does not give place as one would give something, whatever it may be; it neither creates nor produces anything, not even an event insofar as it takes place. It gives no order and makes no promise. It is radically ahistorical, because nothing happens through it and nothing happens to it . . . Khōra is nothing positive or negative. It is impassive, but it is neither passive nor active" (*DNT*, 107). Khōra is not God or the good. As it does not refer to an event or being and does not direct any praise or prayer to a "You," it is not a version of negative theology (*DNT*, 108). Derrida goes on to contrast Christian negative theology, especially that of Dionysius, to the Greek paradigms. He points out that Dionysian discourse is about a transcendent good, not about khōra, in spite of the occasional similarities. Despite their performative dimension, prayer and praise guide us toward an addressee (God), and praise still implies a mode of attribution. Thus there is still a determination at work in this language and even a kind of "politics of initiation or of teaching in general, and of an institutional politics of interpretation" (*DNT*, 113). Derrida reflects extensively on the writings of Dionysius and of Meister Eckhart, showing how these discourses are addressed both to the divine and to the potential reader or the disciple. The prayer itself is already a quotation and referral. A secret manifestation takes place that in its very injunction to silence tries to preserve the divine secret. The "unnaming" of the discourse ultimately does "name" the divine by marking distinctions between appropriate and inappropriate speech.

Derrida concludes his discussion of apophatic speech not with a consideration of the Jewish or Islamic traditions, but instead turns to Heidegger's legacy where negativity enables a kind of transcendence for Dasein. Although Heidegger refuses any possibility of Christian philosophy, Derrida points out that quasi-religious notions of revelation, promise, and the gift are still operative in Heidegger's thinking. The word "Being" is not only said under erasure in some of Heidegger's texts, but it must also be avoided in speech about God. Derrida concludes that "the dimension of

Being discloses the experience of God" in Heidegger despite his attempts to separate them: "But since he recognizes that God announces Himself to experience in this 'dimension of Being,' what difference is there between writing a theology and writing on Being, of Being, as Heidegger never ceases doing? . . . With and without the word *being*, he wrote a theology with and without God" (*DNT*, 128). The address closes with a brief reflection on prayer, wondering whether "pure prayer" (if there were such a thing) would need theology or indeed make it impossible.

It seems, then, that Derrida is interested in the discourse of negative theology because it seeks to hold open discourse at its very limit, because it "deconstructs" sure and affirmative definitions (in this case of the divine). Its process of denial shares certain structural similarities with deconstruction, especially the critique of fixed signifiers and deferral of any ultimate closure of the "name." Yet, Derrida also argues that negative theology is not finally able to defer infinitely, that even its language of praise, which seeks to escape description of the divine, does still make decisions: for God rather than the demonic, for the good rather than for evil or emptiness. Khōra thus is more undecideable than the "good beyond being" or even "God without being."

Khōra and the Name

In *Sauf le nom*, written originally in response to the above-mentioned conference on "Derrida and Negative Theology," Derrida explores negative theology more fully, reflecting especially on the writings of Angelus Silesius, a thinker Heidegger also cites.[11] This essay is conceived as a conversation between a plurality of voices, beginning with the claim that it is necessary to speak in a plurivocal manner, especially in the case of the divine (*ON*, 35). It is not a contentious quarrel, however, but more of a conversation in which one voice interrupts and clarifies another in order to carry the conversation further. He points out that even negative theology itself was often divided and at times even suspected of atheism. Apophaticism pushes language to the limit and yet it also expresses great desire for the divine. Derrida shows that this desire is always equivocal and carries an autobiographical dimension. Its discourse speaks not only to God but also to the disciple and attempts to turn the other toward God. At the same time negative theology is not a clear genre and often includes reflections on death and mortality (*ON*, 44). Derrida points to the ambivalence between the attempt of this theology to exceed language itself and the history or tradition of speaking of the divine, which it paradoxically institutes. Thus, even when it is not naming, when it excepts the name [*sauf le nom*] or is without the name [*sauf le nom*], it still preserves, saves or protects the name [*sauf le nom*]: "Save the name that names nothing that might hold, not even a divinity (*Gottheit*), nothing whose withdrawal . . . does not carry away every phrase that tries to measure itself against him. 'God' 'is' the name of this bottomless collapse, of this endless desertification of language" (*ON*, 55–56). Shortly afterwards, Derrida hints at connection between this "desert" of the divine name and khōra.

He also pursues further his reflection on prayer. Prayer must be thought by praying. It witnesses to the event and yet this event remains in language: "The event remains in and on the mouth, on the tip [*bout*] of the tongue, as is said in English and French, or on the edge of the lips passed over by words that *carry* themselves toward God. They are *carried* [*porté*], both *exported* and *deported*, by a movement of *ference* (transference, reference, difference) toward God" (*ON*, 58). This bearing of language toward God both protects the name and silences it: "They name God, speak of him, speak *him*, speak *to him*, *let him speak in them*, let themselves be carried by him, make (themselves) a reference to just what the name supposes to name beyond itself, the nameable beyond the name, the unnameable nameable" (*ON*, 58). This prayerful speaking of the unnameable is a protection of the name even within a kind of exclusionary gesture: "As if it was necessary both to save the name and to save everything except the name, *save the name* [*sauf le nom*], as if it was necessary to lose the name in order to save what bears the name, or that toward which one goes through the name" (*ON*, 58). This loss is clearly not to be understood as elimination or destruction of the name: "But to lose the name is not to attack it, to destroy it or wound it. On the contrary, to lose the name is quite simply to respect it: as name" (*ON*, 58). One protects the name in saying it and in silencing it: "That is to say, to pronounce it, which comes down to traversing it toward the other, the other whom it names and who bears it. To pronounce it without pronouncing it. To forget it by calling it, by recalling it (to oneself), which comes down to calling or recalling the other" (*ON*, 58). The name has to be deferred, traversed, borne, simultaneously forgotten and recalled. Only thus can it be protected. The name of God is hence linked to the impossible: "it mandates, *it necessitates* doing the impossible, necessitates going (*Geh*, Go!) there where one cannot go" (*ON*, 59). Any writing, especially about the divine, comes after the event and bears its stigmata: Writing is always already wounded by the other (*ON*, 62). Derrida points again to the Greek and Christian paradigms of hyperbolic speech that permeate the Western tradition. No text is pure or uncontaminated by negative theology (*ON*, 69). Not just metaphysics and truth but even such terms as "the gift" or "hospitality" carry theological traces (he will articulate this in much more detail in later discussions on the gift and hospitality). Throughout the text the various voices frequently make careful distinctions between "God" and "the name of God." We have no access to the divine as such, but the name of God does play an important role in our discourses, including political ones (*ON*, 78). Democracy displays aporias similar to negative theology: "Two concurrent desires divide apophatic theology, at the edge of nondesire, around the gulf and chaos of the *Khōra*: the desire to be inclusive of all, thus understood by all (community, *koine*) and the desire to keep or entrust the secret within the very strict limits of those who hear/understand it *right*, as secret, and are then capable or worthy of keeping it" (*ON*, 83–84). He goes on to compare this desire in regard to the secret of the divine to the secret of democracy. This relationship between politics and a (usually veiled) theology is pursued more fully in his more recent works such as *Rogues*.[12]

The essay on khōra does not explicitly mention the divine except in the sense that Plato's *Timaeus*, in which the chora plays an important role, is a sort of creation account. The chora is the quasi-maternal womb or receptacle, the empty void, in which the Platonic demiurge works order and substance. Derrida employs the term more carefully (marking the difference by not employing the definite article, which seems to turn the chora into an entity and by using a different than common transliteration— khōra instead of "the chora," see *ON*, 96). He speaks of the term as an "abyssal chasm" that goes to a similar edge as negative theology (*ON*, 104) yet is distinguished from it. While negative theology is heavily concerned with place and hierarchy, khōra eschews connection to place but rather speaks of a non-place. Although Derrida here is more interested in the ways in which khōra becomes appropriated by the tradition as a never fully articulated generating "other" to philosophy and does not posit it as a competitor to the good (or God) or even in some explicit structural similarity to it, it quickly became part of the debate surrounding undecidability in religion. Especially in the early reception of Marion's work, John Caputo, Thomas Carlson, Robyn Horner, and others all prefer khōra over Marion's saturated phenomenon due to its connotations of emptiness and deferral instead of abundance and bedazzlement. Richard Kearney is one of the few thinkers to have been consistently critical of khōra as a version of the divine name and to call for hermeneutic discernment in its face.[13]

Augustine and Circumfession

Aside from the brief reference to negative theology in "Différance," the first more explicit engagement with religion or faith is probably in Derrida's quasi-autobiographical reflections in *Circumfession* (which are slightly earlier even than *Sauf le nom*).[14] Here Derrida responds to and subverts the text written by Geoffrey Bennington, who attempts to give a more straightforward, explanatory reading of Derrida's work up to that date. Derrida responds by reflections that are posited as a sort of "confession" with frequent references to Augustine and, in fact, extensive quotations from the *Confessions* in the original Latin. They also circle around Derrida's circumcision and the topic of circumcision more generally, as well as the lingering illness and impending death of his mother. In frequent allusions, Derrida plays with certain parallels between Augustine's story and his own: Both were born in Northern Africa, both lived in the "empire" far from home for a large part of their lives (Paris and Rome respectively), and in both cases the concerned mother is dying far from her own home (Nice and Milan respectively). At the same time, Derrida reflects to some extent on the Jewish associations of his childhood. Although his family was not a practicing one, Derrida was circumcised (although it was referred to as "baptism") and suffered the impact of several anti-Semitic measures during World War II (despite being a stellar student he was excluded from school in Algeria and it seems this experience affected him deeply). He speaks of these memories (and their fuzziness) also in several interviews, but *Circumfession* is probably the most thorough engagement with circumcision and confession, indicated even by the title, which runs the two together.

The work defies any straightforward analysis (part of the project is precisely to defy the clear and organized exposition provided by Bennington) but consists of brief journal-like entries, which occasionally even cite earlier journal texts. Many of the more explicitly religious references are actually in the frequent quotations from Augustine's *Confessions* with which Derrida infuses his text. He plays on the reference to God in Augustine's text by speaking of Goeffrey's "theological program," occasionally referring to him as "God" and frequently as "G." where the reference remains more ambivalent. And yet he is addressing not only G. or the reader, but also his mother (whose first name Georgette also begins with that letter), who worries about his faith but dares not ask him directly about it. In response to this concern, Derrida affirms that the "constancy of God" in his life is "called by other names," so that he quite rightly passes "for an atheist" (*CF*, 155). He refers repeatedly to his "prayers and tears" for his children, for his mother, and for himself (this reference becomes the title of Caputo's book). All writing is a kind of confession; one must always ask for pardon for one's writing (*CF*, 48–49). A sudden facial paralysis (caused by Lyme disease) makes him reflect on the possibility of his own death and not just that of his mother who lies dying in a room, not recognizing him and no longer speaking his name. To what extent, he asks, is his discourse a betrayal of his mother as much as an acknowledgment.

In a brief reflection on Yom Kippur, the feast of atonement or of "Great Pardon" (the French name for the Jewish holiday) Derrida affirms that he is confessing to God, indeed has prayed to God all his life (*CF*, 56). Yet these apparently explicit statements are immediately dissimulated by references to Augustine and to his mother. This is also the context in which he refers to his own language as "Christian Latin French" and himself as a "little black and Arab Jew" (*CF*, 58), phrases Caputo will use frequently later when speaking about Derrida. Somewhat later, he calls himself, cryptically, the "last of the eschatologists" and goes on to reject any notion of a meta-language. Confession, always linked to notions of repentance, penitence, contrition, expiation, reconciliation, absolution, even baptism, does not itself provide truth but in Augustine becomes theology in the form of autobiography, addressed as much to his readers as to the God to whom it purportedly seeks to confess (*CF*, 86). Derrida also speaks of himself as "last of the Jews" despite his own break with Judaism and the fact that his sons are not circumcised (*CF*, 154). He comments on this in a later essay: "I introduce myself both as the least Jewish, the most unworthy Jew, the last to deserve the title of authentic Jew, and at the same time, because of all this, by reason of a force of rupture that uproots and universalizes the place [*lieu*], the local, the familial, the communal, the national, and so on, he who plays at playing the role of the most Jewish of all, the last and therefore the only survivor fated to assume the legacy of generations, to save the response or responsibility before the assignation, or before the election, always at risk of taking himself for another, something that belongs to the essence of an experience of election."[15] His religion has always been misunderstood (*CF*, 154) and his prayers remain unrecognized (*CF*, 188). He calls "God" and "death" his "most difficult duties" (*CF*, 172). In fact, he speaks of an "atheist God" as an "other in me" (*CF*, 216), which leads him to found another religion or even to refound "all of them" (*CF*, 222). God is weeping in him and continually haunts him. Conversely, he is also weeping over God's wound, even "de-skinning" himself to the point of blood: "We have just enough breath left to ask for pardon, for the Great Pardon, in the languages of the PaRDeS, for all the evil that my writing is drawn, withdrawn and drawn out from, an eternal skin above not you, but me dreaming of him who dreams of the place of God, burning it up in his prayer and going up toward it like ivy" (*CF*, 143). He describes himself as a prophet waiting for an order from God (*CF*, 257). Occasionally he even speaks of himself in terms of incarnation: "God goes to earth to death in me" (*CF*, 272). This is "a Nothing in which God reminds me of him" (*CF*, 273). In his final reflection he affirms that he has spent his life "inviting calling promising, hoping sighing dreaming, convoking invoking provoking, constituting engendering producing, naming assigning demanding, prescribing commanding sacrificing" (*CF*, 314).

This is the work that most explicitly inspired Caputo's *The Prayers and Tears of Jacques Derrida*, where he seeks to show that these religious themes, which emerge (albeit ambivalently) in *Circumfession*, are not new and strange but can be detected already in Derrida's earlier work. He posits Derrida's prayers and religion as one "without religion," without commitment to or identification with any particular concrete religion. Derrida "rightly passes for an atheist." Yet Derrida's work, so Caputo argues, is imbued with a quasi-religious desire for the "to come," with a quasi-Messianic dimension, which calls for justice, and a quasi-eschatological affirmation and hope.[16] Yet this is only a quasi-"religion" because it is parasitic on the particular religions; Derrida's hope and affirmation (just like the deferral and the naming) are structural not concrete, not filled with content. They speak of the desire and fervor of religion, but at the same time his work is severely critical of the authority, power, and violence wreaked by the particular religious confessions.

The Gift and Forgiveness

The debate surrounding the gift became particularly popular in this context. Especially in the roundtable following Marion's paper at the first Villanova conference on "God, the Gift and Postmodernism," Derrida proclaimed to be very interested in religion and the divine (unlike Marion who repudiated such interest in favor of strictly phenomenological commitments). Both of his works on the gift, *Given Time: Counterfeit Money* and *The Gift of Death*, have certain religious resonances although *The Gift of Death* speaks of religion much more explicitly than the earlier text. Many of the later themes of hospitality and forgiveness emerge already in these works on the gift and remain closely connected to this topic.

The Gift of Death reflects on and responds to the work of Jan Patočka, who distinguishes religious responsibility from the mystery of the sacred, which he associates with the demonic. Patočka presents Christianity as absolutely singular and claims it to be at the root of European democracy. The European self emerges as a dimension of freedom and responsibility that integrates the demonic. Derrida points out that religion and responsibility are always closely linked: "Religion is responsibility or it is nothing at all. Its history derives its sense directly from the idea of a passage to responsibility" (*GD*, 2). Religion becomes a way of making public the "secret" of direct connection to the divine or the demonic. He suggests that "such a passage involves traversing or enduring the test by means of which the ethical conscience will be delivered of the demonic, the mysta-gogic, and the enthusiastic, of the initiatory and the esoteric. In the au-thentic sense of the word, religion comes into being the moment that the experience of responsibility extracts itself from that form of secrecy called demonic mystery" (*GD*, 2–3). The emergence of Europe is hence posited as a "history of responsibility" (*GD*, 4). Derrida shows how, for Patočka, "the history of responsibility is tied to a history of religion" (*GD*, 5), although Derrida himself will go on to be critical of the idea that the responsible self emerges solely through Christianity. More specifically, he argues: "History can be neither a decidable object nor a totality capable of being mastered, precisely because it is tied to *responsibility*, to *faith*, and to the *gift*" (*GD*, 5). It is tied "to *responsibility* in the experience of absolute deci-sions made outside of knowledge or given norms, made therefore through the very ordeal of the undecidable; to religious *faith* through a form of involvement with the other that is a venture into absolute risk, beyond knowledge and certainty; to the *gift* and to the gift of death that puts me into relation with the transcendence of the other, with God as selfless goodness, and that gives me what it gives me through a new experience of death" (*GD*, 5–6). Responsibility, faith and the gift are hence closely con-nected. Derrida concludes this passage: "Responsibility and faith go to-gether, however paradoxical that might seem to some, and both should, in the same movement, exceed mastery and knowledge. The gift of death would be this marriage of responsibility and faith. History depends on such an excessive beginning" (*GD*, 6). Derrida quotes extensively from Patočka's reflections on Plato's *Phaedo* and shows its parallels to Heidegger's analysis of Dasein's "being-toward-death," including the ambivalence between gift and death. Patočka's "messianic eschatology" is a truly political Christian-ity where a transcendent God grounds our responsibility to the other. Derrida establishes a link between Patočka's analysis and the notion of the divine as the *mysterium tremendum*, which he goes on to examine in detail. The themes of secrecy, conversion, and the economy of sacrifice define much of the book.

The second essay, which plays most explicitly on the ambivalent mean-ing of "giving" in the French expression for putting to death ("donner la mort"), also focuses on Patočka. Derrida elaborates on the notion of sacri-fice as it is explicated in the debate between Heidegger and Lévinas over whether one can die for another or in another's place. Even if one were to take the other's place, one still dies one's own death and not that of the other (but only what should or could have been the other's). Derrida questions Patočka's unambivalent talk about God as source and gift of goodness. God is the mysterious and inaccessible source of our responsibility. He is particularly critical of Patočka's conviction that only Christianity gives access to responsibility and shows how responsibility is always linked to notions of guilt: "Guilt is inherent in responsibility because responsibility is always unequal to itself: one is never responsible enough" (GD, 51). This is the case "because one is finite but also because responsibility requires two contradictory movements. It requires one to respond as oneself and as irreplaceable singularity, to answer for what one does, says, gives; but it also requires that, being good and through goodness, one forget or efface the origin of what one gives" (GD, 51). Derrida contrasts this to the analysis of death and guilt in Heidegger and Lévinas (and suggests in that context that both retain traces of Christian thinking).

In the third chapter Derrida reflects extensively on Abraham's "giving" of Isaac (he points out that the word "sacrifice" is mistranslated) and on Kierkegaard's analysis of this story in his *Fear and Trembling*. He notes that Kierkegaard's title is taken from a Pauline passage that enjoins believers to work out their own salvation with "fear and trembling" and links this emphasis on trembling to Otto's popular definition of the divine as the *mysterium tremendum*. The *mysterium tremendum* is a mystery that makes us tremble. It is an experience of a secret that supposedly exceeds seeing and knowing. Does the cause of this trembling lie in the infinite distance or the gift of death or in the disproportion of the responsibility demanded of us? In all these accounts "we fear and tremble before the inaccessible secret of a God who decides for us although we remain responsible, that is, free to decide, to work, to assume our life and our death" (GD, 56). The idea of God as mysterium implies that God is wholly other, totally heterogeneous. Pointing to Abraham's silence in Kierkegaard's analysis, Derrida insists that we do not speak directly with God, there can be no shared discourse between us and the divine (GD, 57–58). Abraham must keep the secret of God's order to put to death what is the most precious to him. In fact, Abraham must speak precisely in order to keep the secret, just as in *Sauf le nom* we must silence the name in order to protect it. Derrida argues that contrary to common perception, responsibility requires secrecy and silence. It is a scandal and a paradox: Responsibility implies both accountability or generality and uniqueness, silence and secrecy (GD, 61).

In order to show this paradox more fully Derrida analyzes Kierkegaard's pseudonymous reflection on Abraham in detail.[17] His analysis shows that the absolute duty of responsibility to which Abraham is called in "giving death" to his son is about absolute responsibility, which always transcends morality. This somewhat lengthy passage is worth citing in full, since it previews Derrida's later accounts of hospitality and forgiveness in important ways:

> The moral of the fable would be morality itself, at the point where morality brings into play the gift of the death that is so given. The absolutes of duty and of responsibility presume that one denounce, refute, and transcend, at the same time, all duty, all responsibility, and every human law. It calls for a betrayal of everything that manifests itself within the order of universal generality, and everything that manifests itself in general, the very order and essence of manifestation; namely, the essence itself, the essence in general to the extent that it is inseparable from presence and from manifestation. Absolute duty demands that one behave in an irresponsible manner (by means of treachery or betrayal), while still recognizing, confirming, and reaffirming the very thing one sacrifices, namely, the order of human ethics and responsibility. In a word, ethics must be sacrificed in the name of duty. It is a duty not to respect, out of duty, ethical duty. One must behave not only in an ethical or responsible manner, but in a nonethical, nonresponsible manner, and one must do that *in the name of* duty, of an infinite duty, *in the name of* absolute duty. And this name which must always be singular is here none other than the name of God as completely other, the nameless name of God, the unpronounceable name of God as other to which I am bound by an absolute, unconditional obligation, by an incomparable, nonnegotiable duty. The other as absolutely other, namely, God, must remain transcendent, hidden, secret, jealous of the love, requests, and commands that he gives and that he asks to be kept secret. Secrecy is essential to the exercise of this absolute responsibility as sacrificial responsibility. (*GD*, 67)

Absolute responsibility goes beyond moral equality and yet can never forget the requirements of morality. My obligation to the beloved stands in direct conflict with my obligation to or responsibility for other others or indeed the wholly and absolute other: God (*GD*, 69). Derrida shows how this plays itself out in our continual responsibility for all others around the world. It is impossible to treat everyone as unique and singular, despite the fact that it continues to be required. To this day, different religious traditions fight over their interpretation of the absolute: "I can respond only to the one (or to the One), that is, to the other, by sacrificing the other to that one. I am responsible to any one (that is to say to any other) only by failing in my responsibility to all the others, to the ethical or political generality" (*GD*, 70). The sacrifice must be made and yet it cannot be justified: "And I can never justify this sacrifice, I must always hold my peace about it. Whether I want to or not, I can never justify the fact that I prefer or sacrifice any one (any other) to the other. I will always be secretive, held to secrecy in respect to this, for I have nothing to say about it" (*GD*, 70). Derrida consistently points to the conflation between the "wholly other" [*tout autre*] and "any other" or "all others" [*tout autre*]: "God, as the wholly other, is to be found everywhere there is something of the wholly other." And he continues: "since each of us, everyone else, each other is infinitely other in its absolute singularity, inaccessible, solitary, transcendent, nonmanifest . . . then what can be said about Abraham's relation to God can be said about my relation to *every other (one) as every (bit) other* [*tout autre comme tout autre*], in particular my relation to my neighbor or loved ones who are as inaccessible to me, as secret and transcendent as Jahweh" (*GD*, 78). He concludes the chapter by emphasizing this undecidability: "Our faith is not assured, because faith can never be, it must never be a certainty. We share with Abraham what cannot be shared, a secret we know nothing about, neither him nor us" (*GD*, 80).

The final chapter with the aforementioned wordplay on the other as its title—*tout autre est tout autre* (every other is wholly other)—takes up the Abraham story again but then moves on to discuss passages about "giving in secret" in Matthew's account of the sermon on the mount. Again Derrida points to the ambivalence of *tout autre*, which can return to God as "wholly other" or to any other as completely different from us. In a critique of Lévinas, he shows that issues of justice, law and politics cannot be disentangled from (religious) issues of responsibility or ethics. The religious is always already wrapped up in the moral, the legal, and the political (*GD*, 86–87). Returning to the question of the secret in Matthew's discussion of "doing good in secret" where only God observes it, Derrida makes a distinction between two types of invisibility: "hiddenness," which is not currently visible but may become so and the "cryptic" or "mysterious," which is inherently invisible and can never become visible. He outlines the "absolute dissymmetry" of God's seeing that always remains invisible to us and yet impels us to responsibility. The sacrifice of the self is thus propelled by the gaze of God (*GD*, 93). Derrida shows in his analysis how the total sacrifice demanded by the Gospel is both outside normal human economy and yet is reinscribed by God into a higher economy of reward and retribution. Although the giving enjoined by the sermon is to be selfless, abundant, and without measure, it ultimately becomes inscribed in a higher economy that will find its reward "in heaven" by "the Father who sees in secret." This is a "highest calculation" that goes beyond justice, a "celestial" instead of a "terrestrial economy" (*GD*, 97). Derrida argues that it is ultimately impossible ever to escape such an economy and yet the religious texts do point to an important "impossible" vision of abundant and selfless giving that enables giving even as it never finally escapes economic considerations. Political concepts ultimately are secularized theological concepts (*GD*, 105). Derrida again makes a clear distinction between "God" and "the name of God":

> We should stop thinking about God as someone, over there, way up there, transcendent, and, what is more—into the bargain, precisely— capable, more than any satellite orbiting in space, of seeing into the most secret of the most interior places. It is perhaps necessary, if we are to follow the traditional Judeo-Christian-Islamic injunction, but also at the risk of turning against that tradition, to think of God and of the name of God without such idolatrous stereotyping or representation. Then we might say: God is the name of the possibility I have of keeping a secret that is visible from the interior but not from the exterior . . . God is in me, he is the absolute "me" or "self," he is that structure of invisible interiority that is called, in Kierkegaard's sense, subjectivity. (*GD*, 108–09)

God is made manifest through the desire for the secret: "That is the history of God and of the name of God as the history of secrecy, a history that is at the same time secret and without any secrets" (*GD*, 109). The name of God, then, is the call of conscience in me, the name at play in justice and morality. Thus Derrida speaks of religion (or specifically Christianity) in terms of its excess and promise while always pointing to the ways in which it breaks down or undoes itself. The name of God is a name of infinite promise and enables responsibility toward the other, yet this is not about God's existence, which always remains undecidable.

Derrida carries these reflections further in several lectures on forgiveness.[18] For-give-ness also includes the connotation of "giving" or "gift" (in French, *par-don* or *par-donner*). In his introductory lecture to this course (reprinted as keynote address in *Questioning God*) he interacts with Vladimir Jankélévitch's two essays on forgiveness, which establish a contradiction between the excess of forgiveness demanded in the earlier essay [*Le Pardon*] and the firm rejection of forgiveness as impossible or even immoral in light of the horrors of the Holocaust ["L'imprescriptible"]. He explicitly links the gift with forgiveness. Both display similar aporias, both have temporal dimensions (forgiveness is usually associated with the past, the gift with the present), and both are closely connected. For example, I can never give enough or appropriately, even for my gifts I must always ask for forgiveness. Derrida wonders about some of the assumptions or claims Jankélévitch makes in his discussion—for example, whether collective pardon is possible, whether forgiveness must always be granted face to face, whether forgiveness has to be requested before it can be granted, and about who ultimately grants forgiveness. Although the irrationality of evil and the omnipotence of love can indeed not be reconciled as Jankélévitch claims (26), Derrida distances himself from Jankélévitch's assertion that forgiveness for Germans is immoral and from the quasi-equation of forgiving and forgetting in Jankélévitch's treatment. Like the gift, Derrida suggests, forgiveness is always infinite and unconditional and thus ultimately impossible. We can truly only forgive the unforgiveable since what can be simply excused really does not require forgiveness (30). He makes a more careful distinction between the unforgiveable and the imprescriptible or inexpiable (suggesting that Jankélévitch collapses the two). Reflecting on the exchange of letters between Jankélévitch and a young German who asked him for forgiveness in response to his text, Derrida stresses the work of mourning that is always necessary for forgiveness. Ultimately, forgiveness is "reserved for God" (44) because only God's name can stand in for other names; God is the "absolute substitute" (46). Forgiveness is a passage to the limit: "Absolutely unconditional forgiveness" is necessary in order to think "the essence of forgiveness, if there is such a thing" (45). Forgiveness is the "impossible truth of the impossible gift" (48). This impossibility, however, does not exonerate us from responsibility, but rather expresses its requirement more strongly. One always already betrays others in action and speech. Derrida concludes by stressing that forgiveness is not about knowledge (70).

Hos(ti)pitality and Justice

Many of Derrida's later works are deeply influenced by Lévinas's thought of the other. Maybe the most beautiful and moving illustration of this is Derrida's address "Adieu" at Lévinas's funeral in 1995. Derrida interprets Lévinas's thought as an extended reflection on the many dimensions of hospitality, including its more problematic connotations of "hostage" and "enemy." The French term "le hôte" can mean both host and guest and Derrida frequently plays with this ambivalence. Furthermore, in several languages, the terms for guest, friend, and enemy are closely associated or even identical (such as *hostis* in Latin from which the French and English terms for hospitality, hostility, and hostage are all derived). Derrida shows how, in Lévinas, the impact of the other on the self moves from the self being the host of the other in Lévinas's early works (such as *Totality and Infinity*) to that of being hostage to the other in Lévinas's later oeuvre (especially *Otherwise Than Being*), suggesting that the two are not as far apart as may seem to be the case at first glance.

Derrida's writings on the topic of hospitality are closely linked to his discussions of the gift and of forgiveness.[19] He explores the impossibility of hospitality, on the one hand, as the complete openness to any other, any stranger who might come in and require anything of me, might even kill me and, on the other hand, the need to have a home and certain things at one's disposal (even a certain space to oneself) in order to give to the other, to be able to practice true hospitality. Both are necessary, yet they seem to contradict each other. True hospitality, like the true gift, is thus impossible and yet is the impossible for which we are to strive. (To say that something is impossible shows something structural about it in Derrida's view; it does not mean that we ought to abandon it, should give no gifts or not practice hospitality or friendship.) Especially in his 1997 lectures, some of which were published as *Of Hospitality* and others under the title "Hostipitality" in *Acts of Religion*, Derrida frequently reflects on religion in conjunction with hospitality. The line between hospitality and hostility is particularly fine (and maybe most frequently transgressed) in religion. All religions, especially the Abrahamic ones, counsel hospitality to the other, especially the stranger. Indeed they make it a fundamental requirement in one's dealing with others. Yet probably nowhere is hostility so frequent and so extreme, as clashes of various fundamentalism around the world show.

In the "Hostipitality" lecture Derrida refers to the hospitality of Abraham, which is hospitality to a stranger. This other is unknown and surprises us. Violence always remains a real possibility and yet without such open generosity there is "no welcome of the other as other" (*AR*, 361). Pure hospitality is always concerned with the unforeseeable stranger: "If I welcome only what I welcome, what I am ready to welcome, and that I recognize in advance because I expect the coming of the guest as invited, there is no hospitality" (*AR*, 362). We welcome the other as we do the Messiah; indeed, any stranger could be the Messiah. The other is not a close or comfortable "fellow," possibly not even human (*AR*, 363). (Here, Derrida only hints at this possibility of hospitality to animals. He explores this topic much more fully in his posthumously published lectures *The Animal That Therefore I Am*.)

In this context, Derrida reflects extensively on Islamic practices of hospitality as mediated through the French Roman Catholic scholar Louis Massignon who speaks of Islam as a culture of hospitality. Derrida quotes extensively from Massignon, including his reflections on Abraham's and Lot's hospitality to the angelic strangers, a story that has significance in all three Abrahamic traditions. Derrida draws many parallels between the work of Lévinas and that of Massignon, seeing both deeply characterized by the theme of hospitality to the stranger, including such notions as substitution, hostage, expiation, and solidarity (*AR*, 376). In the second lecture, Derrida goes on to link hospitality to the notion of forgiveness. Forgiving is the "supreme gift and hospitality par excellence" (*AR*, 380). He reiterates that forgiveness must be infinite and unconditional, employing a Jewish story about Yom Kippur, the day of atonement or of "Great Pardon." Here also he insists that forgiveness must "forgive the unforgiveable" and that, like the gift and hospitality, it is the "possibility of the impossible" (*AR*, 385–86). In this context, he establishes a further link with the question of justice, which always fails in the face of forgiveness. Forgiveness or justice cannot be prescribed; they always transcend the law.

In an earlier essay examined in more detail at the end of this chapter, Derrida speaks of justice in terms of a "messianicity without messianism": "This would be the opening to the future or to the coming of the other as the advent of justice, but without horizon of expectation and without prophetic prefiguration" (*AR*, 56). He refers to the messianic as a "general structure of experience" concerned with the coming of the other and justice, which does not refer to any particular religion or "determinate revelation." And yet this messianicity is not an issue of knowledge but of faith: "This justice, which I distinguish from right, alone allows the hope, beyond all 'messianisms,' of a universalizable culture of singularities, a culture in which the abstract possibility of the impossible translation could nevertheless be announced. This justice inscribes itself in advance in the promise, in the act of faith or in the appeal to faith that inhabits every act of language and every address to the other" (*AR*, 56).

In the final lectures on hospitality, Derrida focuses especially on the theme of the stranger or foreigner. Again he highlights Islam's hospitality to strangers, including those of other religions, while explaining that it was a conditional hospitality that had to recognize the inherent superiority of Islam. He evokes the Song of Song's love for the foreigner, which speaks of an "ageless hospitality, or a hospitality of all ages, a hospitality which could only survive itself before its time" (*AR*, 407). Even love requires forgiveness and again highlights its impossible character. Hospitality always assumes the logic of substitution. This notion of substitution, he suggests, brings together his reflections on hospitality, on Abraham, on the stranger, and on death or mourning (*AR*, 414). This is not the substitution of equivalence, of one object for another, "no general equivalence, no common currency, which would ensure this exchange as two comparable values." It is not even sufficient to speak of substitution solely (as

Lévinas does) in terms of "irreplaceability, of singularity and unicity," but the self who substitutes must be aware of itself: "This self, this ipseity, is the condition of ethical substitution as compassion, sacrifice, expiation" (*AR*, 419–20). Hospitality, compassion, sacrifice, substitution are all linked with each other and with the question of what it means to be human. Derrida here also foreshadows again his reflections on the animal and its implications for how we speak of the human (*AR*, 420).

Derrida's later work, then, repeatedly returns to religious topics and illustrations, frequently using examples from Jewish and Christian scriptures, especially in his discussions of the gift, hospitality and forgiveness. Although he often points to the ambivalent nature of these examples, as in his discussion of Matthew's "seeing in secret" that amounts to re-inscription in a higher "heavenly economy," he also recognizes the ways in which religious languages have privileged such themes as hospitality and forgiveness. Despite all the cruelty and violence perpetrated in the name of religion— and Derrida does not hesitate to point to these and warn us of them—the religions have also held open the promise of the impossible: generous giving, compassionate hospitality, forgiveness of the unforgiveable. These terms and experiences thus always carry religious resonances and traces.

Faith and Politics

Yet at the same time as these more "positive" treatments, Derrida also does not hesitate to point to some of the more problematic legacies of religion. In a 1996 text that grew out of a conference on Capri, for which Derrida originally proposed the topic of religion, Derrida reflects explicitly on the question of "Faith and Knowledge." The subtitle "The Two Sources of 'Religion' at the Limits of Reason Alone" evokes Kant's *Religion Within the Limits of Reason Alone* on which Derrida comments repeatedly in the text.[20] He begins by doubting whether we can speak of religion in the singular and whether it is possible to discuss it in the abstract. He previews that his concern will be also with evil and with the connections of religion to the political and to technology, what he calls the evil of "abstraction." Derrida points out that language and nation play an important role in religion and any notions of revelation, including the recent "return of religion" through various sorts of fundamentalisms (although Derrida warns of any simplistic assumptions about these terms, especially in conjunction with Islam). The name of religion and of God is always performed in many different ways and is deployed as a "pledge of faith" that appeals to the other (*AR*, 46). Even phenomenology and hermeneutics are in some sense grounded in the religious connotations of light and of the interpretation of religious texts. Derrida makes clear that none of the participants in the discussion are professional theologians, yet all are interested in philosophy's influence on democracy and the state, seeking to free this "public place" from "religious dogmatism, orthodoxy or authority (that is, from a certain rule of the *doxa* or of belief, which, however, does not mean from all faith)" (*AR*, 47). In this context Derrida links his own discourse on negative theology to the history of democracy (*AR*, 48, also 99). He points out that the terms religion, faith, and theology are not identical to each other and that these terms, and equally the concept of reason, are inscribed in a history.[21] He also shows that Kant distinguishes between religion in the form of cult (which he rejects) and the rational religion of morality and thereby uncovers an important dialectic. Kant's privileging of the moral religion of Christianity over all other faiths points to an important dimension Derrida will call "globalatinization," namely "this strange alliance of Christianity, as the experience of the death of God, and tele-technoscientific capitalism" (*AR*, 52).

To a large extent, the text circulates around the connection between religion and salvation in the etymological link between "the holy, the sacred, the safe and sound, the unscathed, the immune" (*AR*, 42, 70). And these terms are already connected to economic and political questions, in which religion will emerge to be deeply complicit: "[K]nowledge and faith, technoscience ('capitalist' and fiduciary) and belief, credit, trustworthiness, the act of faith will always have made common cause, bound to one another by the band of their opposition" (*AR*, 43). Based on this etymological connection, he distinguishes between two "sources" of religion: on the one hand, belief or faith, which is connected to the fiduciary or credit and fidelity, and, on the other hand, the experience of holiness or sacredness. Although religion can combine both emphases, they need not be connected and do refer to separate experiences. The rest of the text to a large extent explores these two aspects of religion. Derrida therefore points to a certain "mystical foundation of authority," which shows that even science and certain political practices and "tele-technological performance" are rooted in belief and trust of some sort. "Universal rationality" and "political democracy" can never be fully dissociated from their origins in religious traditions or what Derrida calls their "anthropo-theological horizon" (*AR*, 57). To this Derrida contrasts the Platonic chora as the borderline place of finitude and nothing, which would be "the name for place, a place name, and a rather singular one at that, for that spacing which, not allowing itself to be dominated by any theological, ontological or anthropological instance . . . does not even announce itself as 'beyond being' in accordance with a path of negation, a *via negativa*," but "it says the immemoriality of a desert in the desert of which it is neither a threshold nor a mourning" (*AR*, 58, 59). Derrida posits a sort of indecision or vacillation between these two that might lead us to a new kind of "tolerance" (*AR*, 59). Yet even the concept of tolerance, he admits, is rooted in a "sort of Christian domesticity" and was circulated "in the name of the Christian faith" (*AR*, 59). Instead Derrida proposes a tolerance that might be rooted in a respect for "the distance of infinite alterity as singularity" (*AR*, 60). Yet even this respect would retain a link to religion.

In an extensive Post-Scriptum to the earlier more impromptu reflections, Derrida takes up again explicitly the question of religion and connects it to his earlier thinking about protecting the name. Here he questions whether it is possible to speak of religion religiously or whether speaking in its name does not rather promote a tendency to violence: "One must in any case take into account, if possible in an areligious, or even irreligious manner, what religion at present might *be*, as well as what is *said* and *done*, what *is happening* at this very moment, in the world, in history, *in its name*" (*AR*, 61). He points to the ways in which expressions of religion including wars waged in the name of religion have become "cyberspatialized or cyberspaced" (*AR*, 62). Many Western initiatives conducted in the name of democracy are in some way "wars of religion" (*AR*, 63). Religion cannot be clearly separated, according to Derrida, from "concepts of ethics, of the juridical, of the political and of the economic" (*AR*, 63). He suggests that "the fundamental concepts that often permit us to isolate or to *pretend* to isolate the *political* . . . remain religious or in any case theologico-political" (*AR*, 63). Democracy and the many ethical, economic, and juridical concepts associated with it cannot be separated from their religious heritage, which still deeply influences and shapes them.

Derrida also links again the notion of religion and of responsibility, which for him is rooted in the Latin character of Western religion. God is still "the witness as 'nameable-unnameable,' present-absent witness of every oath and every possible pledge" as sacrament and testament (*AR*, 65). The supposed oppositions between reason and religion or science and religion or even modernity and religion are false and naive, because they hide "how the imperturbable and interminable development of critical and technoscientific reason, far from opposing religion, bears, supports and supposes it . . . religion and reason have the same source" (*AR*, 65–66). These connections speak of "globalatinization," which "circulates like an English word that has been to Rome and taken a detour to the United States." Religion becomes appropriated in "strictly capitalist," "politico-military," or "hyper-imperialist" ways, which continue to be deeply religious and employ religious terminology.

Derrida insists repeatedly that he is not speaking of religion per se but of the "return of the religious" today. He shows how often religious calls for peace are a way of "pursuing war by other means" (*AR*, 79). Our contemporary culture is a "juridico-theologico-political culture," which attempts to impose globalatinization in the name of peace (*AR*, 79). The capitalistic economy, which is closely connected to "technoscientific performance," is based on a quasi-religious faith and fiduciary trust. Religious violence spreads death, employs the tools of rape, and embraces technology in a dangerous fashion. There is, then, "no incompatibility, in the said 'return of the religious,' between the 'fundamentalisms,' the 'integrisms,' or their 'politics' and, on the other hand, rationality, which is to say, the tele-techno-capitalistico-scientific fiduciarity, in all its mediatic and globalizing dimensions" (*AR*, 81). Religion and rationality in their various contemporary guises are closely connected; religion is intimately linked with tele-technoscience.[22] This is, for Derrida, about a "universal structure of religiosity" in contemporary culture (*AR*, 86). Derrida shows the ambivalent fashion in which religion upholds the dignity of life and yet is linked to sacrifice and death. The "religiosity of religion" is about:

> The excess above and beyond the living, whose life only has absolute value by being worth more than life, more than itself-this, in short, is what opens the space of death that is linked to the automaton (exemplarily "phallic"), to technics, the machine, the prosthesis: in a word, to the dimensions of the auto-immune and self-sacrificial supplementarity, to this death-drive that is silently at work in every community, every *auto-co-immunity*, constituting it as such in its iterability, its heritage, its spectral tradition. (*AR*, 87)

Religion and violence are closely linked, not only in practice but also in their inherent sacrificial logic. The fervent belief in democracy expressed in patriotism and various aspects of national language and citizenship is similarly deeply rooted in religious structures, as are seemingly opposing calls for universality, cosmopolitanism, and ecumenism (*AR*, 92). The two "sources" of the logic of religion (fiduciarity/faith/trust/credit and safe/sound/immune/holy/sacred) ultimately reflect and presuppose each other (*AR*, 93). Derrida ends the discussion by cryptically referring to several of his previous discussions of religion, including language, khōra, the name, cinders, and the gift of death: "The auto-immunity of religion can only indemnify itself without assignable end. On the bottom without bottom of an always virgin impassibility, *chora* of tomorrow in languages we no longer know or do not yet speak. This place is unique, it is the One without name. It *makes way, perhaps*, but without the slightest generosity, neither divine nor human. The dispersion of ashes is not even promised there, nor death given" (*AR*, 100).[23]

Derrida and Religion

Derrida, then, especially in his late work, is concerned with the impossible and what is "to come," with a messianic dimension that, however, always remains in the future as a promise while inspiring us to work toward it. Hence it is not a telos but a call. The "impossible" is the structural dimension of the gift, of justice, of hospitality, and of forgiveness, maybe even of democracy. They all require a kind of impossible excess and abundance or transgressing of boundaries while always simultaneously succumbing to economy and exchange in everyday life. Yet a promise holds them open as an impossible that enables and crosses the possible. Thus, every gift, even as it re-enters economic exchange, harbors the promise of gratuitous generosity. Every word of forgiveness as it relativizes the unforgiveable, still speaks a word of hope in horror; every act of hospitality even as it is limited by needs and available resources still whispers of an open and unlimited welcome. Yet in this very openness, deconstruction also harbors dangers. The stranger knocking on the door may be a vulnerable and needy orphan or a violent terrorist. Deconstruction holds open the undecidability of this situation. There are no objective or neutral external parameters that would allow us to decide between the possibilities. And yet one must decide and thus always does so with tremendous risk.

At the same time, in Derrida's analysis of religion, whether the "heavenly economy" in *The Gift of Death* or the globalatinization in "Faith and Knowledge," the link between religion and politics or religion and capitalism or technoscience is also deeply troubling. Although Derrida makes many fairly positive comments about the ways in which the name of God can function to hold open the possibility of the impossible and the ways in which hospitality, gift, and forgiveness carry promises precisely through their religious heritage, he certainly cannot be interpreted to endorse religion wholeheartedly or to argue for firmer adherence to any particular faith. While Derrida consistently acknowledges the ways in which we are shaped by the Western religious heritage and is quite clear that we can never escape the complicity of religion and politics even in our democracies, this surely cannot be construed as an affirmation of faith or of Christianity in any straightforward manner. Overall, Derrida is certainly more critical of religion than apologetic on its behalf. Even in his more positive treatments of hospitality, forgiveness, and the gift where religious themes are evident in his analysis, he tries to free these notions from their religious connotations. Hugh Rayment-Pickard says that "Derrida's theology is *only* theology in *so far as* it traverses a zone *formerly constituted* as theological."[24] In no way are his treatments explicitly Christian treatments of these topics, even when he takes recourse to biblical texts. His more direct discussions of negative theology also show this. Although he admits a certain apophatic structure of language in general, even explicit mystical theology is about the *name* of God. It does not give us direct access to the divine. The name of God can serve as an inspiration for hospitality and forgiveness, or even as a reminder of responsibility and obligation, but it does not make possible any sort of direct access to God.

And yet Derrida's reflections do matter for the current discussion. On the one hand they are important because they have influenced many of the debates explicitly, especially in regard to the notion of the gift. Many read the contemporary sources with Derrida's discussions and texts in mind. And, of course, the various thinkers discussed here are also all influenced by Derrida to a smaller or larger extent. Even when they do not explicitly refer to him, they are certainly aware of his writings and his critiques of religion. On the other hand, Derrida's work has become particularly important for the North American appropriation of the other thinkers. Especially John D. Caputo and Richard Kearney, but also many other contemporary thinkers not explicitly discussed here, read Marion, Henry, Chrétien, and Lacoste after and to some extent through Derrida. Papers on Derrida are still more prominent at many philosophy conferences with religious themes than presentations on Marion, Henry, or any of the other thinkers (except perhaps Ricoeur). Thus, while Derrida himself can be considered a "religious" thinker only in a highly ambivalent fashion, his work continues to have important implications for any thinking about religion today.

PART II

Expositions

4

Paul Ricoeur: A God of Poetry and Superabundance

Ricoeur was one of the most prolific French philosophers in his long life, authoring over thirty books on a great variety of topics. He was born in 1913 and died in Paris in 2005, having taught for many years in Straßburg, Paris, and Chicago. Ricoeur is known primarily as a hermeneutic thinker, although his hermeneutic work always also refers to and assumes phenomenology and interacts with various other philosophical approaches. In fact, in many ways a possible conversation between various philosophical traditions, approaches, and discourses could be said to be a distinctive mark of Ricoeur's philosophy. Richard Kearney suggests that the theme of "translation," in the widest sense of that term, characterizes Ricoeur's thought from beginning to end.[1] Ricoeur was always eager to fuel conversation and attempt translation and mediation between extremes and to pay attention to the value and truths in a great variety of apparently antagonistic positions and thinkers. Although religion (or specifically Christianity) is certainly not the central focus of his writing or teaching and he usually rigorously separates his more religious reflections from his other philosophical work, an interest in and concern with religion are visible at every stage of his philosophical journey.[2] This extends from his early writings on myth and fallenness, over his reflections on biblical hermeneutics and a Christian concept of history, to his final writings on justice, faithfulness, and forgiveness. More than any of the other thinkers discussed in this book (including perhaps even Lévinas and Derrida), Ricoeur was always very careful to uphold a strict demarcation between his thought and writing on religious topics and his philosophical hermeneutics.[3] Given the magnitude of Ricoeur's published work, this cannot possibly be an introduction to Ricoeur's thought as a whole. This chapter will focus instead on those works that specifically address religious topics and will mention others as appropriate. It will begin with a short review of Ricoeur's early work on myth and symbolism, then discuss his writings on biblical hermeneutics, briefly consider the religious or theological themes in some of his later writings, and conclude with an evaluation of the "apologetic" character (if any) of his work.[4] I will argue that although Ricoeur is always careful to separate theological and philosophical interests in his work, he does suggest that Christianity can provide particular insights to which we cannot have access otherwise.

Myth and Symbolism of Evil

Ricoeur's early work focuses on the fallibility of the human will. His writings on the symbolism of evil appear within that context. He analyzes various myths of fallenness and investigates how they convey a truth about the human condition. In fact, this is a topic that can be said to occupy Ricoeur throughout his career, as much of his work on narrative and, of course, especially *Oneself as Another* (1990) and *The Course of Recognition* (2004), deal with the topic of the human self in various ways. Even in this early text on *The Symbolism of Evil*, Ricoeur's great familiarity with the Hebrew and Christian traditions, especially his thorough knowledge of Scripture, is very obvious. Ricoeur sees the biblical texts as contributing essential insights about the human condition. The myth of the fall says something about who we are that no other myth says in quite the same fashion. This assertion about the particular contribution of Christian thought is one we will encounter repeatedly in Ricoeur, although he does not always defend it in great detail.

Ricoeur first examines what he calls "primary symbols" for evil: defilement, sin, and guilt. All three are at work in the biblical narrative and in subsequent doctrines that arose out of these narratives. (Ricoeur also deals with other myths that contain symbolism of evil—he distinguishes four basic types—but the others will not concern us here.) As in much of his later work, Ricoeur brings together hermeneutic and phenomenological approaches in this volume. Beyond the specific investigation of evil, he contends that myth and symbol can be retrieved hermeneutically and that by engaging in a wager of openness to the narratives and their original meaning as well as in philosophical analysis, we can return to a second naïveté. In this way, the symbols are again filled with meaning for us, even if we cannot simply go back to the original innocence that made no distinction between myth and history. Philosophy can learn from myth: "The symbol gives: a philosophy instructed by myths arises at a certain moment in reflection, and, beyond philosophical reflection, it wishes to answer to a certain situation of modern culture" (*SE*, 348). We will encounter repeatedly this claim that scientific and "meaning-filled" (often identified with the religious) approaches have been separated and must be brought together in a new way for the contemporary person. Here it is expressed in the admission that we can no longer take the Adamic myth literally as "history." The question of whether something "literally happened" did not pose itself in the same way when myth and history were not yet separated. Today, we must acknowledge the scientific approach to truth in history. Yet that should not close us to other ways of approaching the material, different ways of thinking about and defining truth that are just as significant, and perhaps even more important, than the scientific one. We will return to this point later in the chapter.

In his work on symbolism, as is true also for his essays in hermeneutics and other writings, Ricoeur is quite insistent on the need to recognize that there is "no philosophy without presuppositions" but that we must always admit and honestly inhabit our starting point.[5] This is what has been called the hermeneutic circle and Ricoeur embraces that circle wholeheartedly, wagering that in doing so (and thus circling between "text and action" or "presupposition" and "life" or "belief" and "reality") the wager will be filled with meaning and both challenge and confirm all aspects of the circular move:

> I wager that I shall have a better understanding of man and of the bond between the being of man and the being of all beings if I follow the *indication* of symbolic thought. That wager then becomes the task of *verifying* my wager and saturating it, so to speak, with intelligibility. In return, the task transforms my wager: in betting *on* the significance of the symbolic world, I bet at the same time *that* my wager will be restored to me in power of reflection, in the element of coherent discourse. (*SE*, 355)

The philosophical wager begins with faith, analyzes it and thus fills it with coherence.

Yet this is not a neat or uncomplicated synthesis that merely confirms its own presuppositions. Ricoeur (much more thoroughly than we can examine here) was himself a "master of suspicion" (as he calls Marx, Nietzsche, and Freud whom he studied in detail and on whom he wrote extensively). He always sought to uncover incoherence and dissonance and to acknowledge all aspects of an issue, in particular those most antithetical to an easy solution. In regard to symbols, he insists that "the world of symbols is not a tranquil and reconciled world; every symbol is iconoclastic in comparison with some other symbol, just as every symbol, left to itself, tends to thicken, to become solidified in an idolatry" (*SE*, 354). This is not something we should bemoan as a return of primordial chaos. Rather, it is an evidence of life and what he will later call "the fullness of language." Complexity, dissonance, and multiplicity are signs of life, authenticity, and meaning. Any examination of language, symbols, or texts, for Ricoeur, returns to an examination of life: "The task, then, is, starting from the symbols, to elaborate existential concepts—that is to say, not only structures of reflection but structures of existence, insofar as existence is the being of man" (*SE*, 356–57). Or, in his even more well-known phrase, which serves as the title to the conclusion, the symbol always "gives rise to thought."

Manifestation and Poetic Discourse

Ricoeur emphasizes the wager of the hermeneutic circle in particular when examining Scripture or issues of faith. He insists that it is not dishonest to start within the community of faith and then examine its texts and beliefs philosophically. Belief can lead to understanding and understanding enriches faith. Belief also always requires interpretation. And yet the biblical texts and the community of faith out of which they arose, and for whom they are authoritative, are worth examining, because they do indeed provide a specific kind of truth and meaning. Ricoeur speaks of this again in terms of the wager: Biblical texts are located within and arise out of a community of faith. They are thus given meaning by and within this community that believes in them. By examining them with their own criteria, we can come to "test" their claims and fill them with meaning. The hermeneutic circle thus confirms the truth of the biblical discourse by its constant back and forth movement between text and action.

Ricoeur focuses primarily on biblical discourse. He is far more hesitant to engage in theology. Repeatedly, he makes a distinction between several "levels" of discourse: The discourse of faith (especially the one found in the Bible as the original expression of various Jewish and Christian communities) is the most immediate and the closest to the primary expressions of living faith. Dogma and creeds, as a second level discourse, are built on this primary level. Theological doctrine, finally, is a third-level discourse and is most removed from the life of faith.[6] As in his more general philosophical work, Ricoeur is then most interested in the texts that are closest to life, in this case the biblical texts.

In an early article on "Philosophy and Religious Language," Ricoeur outlines three assumptions underlying his work on religion: First, religious faith is articulated in discourse. Religious experience "comes to language" (*FS*, 35). Second, "this kind of discourse is not senseless, . . . it is worthwhile to analyze it, because something is said that is not said by other kinds of discourse—ordinary, scientific, or poetic" (*FS*, 35). Third, this discourse makes truth claims that must be understood on their own terms. Ricoeur here draws a distinction between two types of truth: truth as verification and truth as manifestation.[7] He suggests that biblical speech is true in a different way from that of the discourse of science. These texts do not wish to "verify" or "describe," but rather they manifest or reveal. Ricoeur calls this type of truth "poetry." Poetry is not a genre in this context, but "a function of discourse."[8] Poetry does not mean whimsical fantasy. Instead, it refers to a type of truth that is revelatory of a particular way of being in the world. It does not describe a state of affairs, but instead it invites the reader (or listener) into a type of world that it lays out and reveals. In his essays on hermeneutics, Ricoeur speaks of this as "the world of the text": the kind of world that is imagined by a text and developed through the text and the imagination of the readers who are thus invited to enter into this world and inhabit it in some way. This kind of world is not, strictly speaking, "real" in the sense that it describes a state of affairs. Rather, it projects a different kind of world that can indeed become real when we take it up and live it out. In regard to the biblical texts, this means that a particular way of being in the world is unfolded before the reader, that this new being reveals something about the world, something that is communal and cosmic and not merely individual, and that this being is a rupture of our ordinary world (*FS*, 43–45). The biblical world is one that challenges our preconceptions and assumptions about the world and instead calls us to a new type of being. The biblical texts invite or even challenge us to think about the world as it should be, not as it presently is. Through biblical poetry, we are enabled to envision ourselves differently and to imagine another way of being. Hence, this poetry has an inherently ethical function: The world it envisions is one of hope for peace and justice. This is indeed about truth, but it is a truth that confronts and challenges us to make it real instead of a truth that can be verified as corresponding to a particular state of affairs. Later, he will speak of biblical discourse as a different, "nonphilosophical" "manner of thinking," a kind of thinking that is not primarily about acquisition of knowledge (*CC*, 149). In this context, he expresses the fear that the challenge of the poetic biblical language may one day no longer be heard in our age of increasing secularization and religious multiplicity: "The small voice of Biblical writings is lost in the incredible clamor of all the signals exchanged. But the fate of the Biblical word is that of all poetic voices. Will they be heard at the level of public discourse? My hope is that there will always be poets and ears to listen to them. The minority fate of a strong word is not only that of the Biblical word" (*CC*, 169).

Ricoeur does imply that this religious truth is not merely arbitrary. It is not only the community of faith that is interested in it. Rather, something important about the human condition is said in these texts. A world is opened for us to inhabit in a way that is not quite true of any other narratives or other poetic texts. We are challenged to ethical and just behavior in a way in which other "poetry" might not challenge us (and certainly science does not). Ricoeur also clearly gives legitimacy to religious discourse. Manifestation is indeed a type of truth and the "truth" of "verification" cannot rule over, control, or dismiss it. It has its own criteria of truth that are just as valid as those of other discourses. There is no master-discourse (not even the scientific or philosophical one) that would allow us to judge all other discourses and reject some out of hand. Religious discourse thus has a validity and justification. It speaks truth, it transforms the world, it even challenges false versions of the self. The religious wager is filled with meaning in its enactment.

Biblical Polyphony and Limit-Expressions

The most distinctive characteristic of the biblical discourse is, of course, the "God-reference" in it. Ricoeur examines the biblical texts in great detail and uncovers the particular type of "God-talk" within them. Although he speaks of biblical discourse in general as poetic, he also acknowledges the different genres of discourse employed within the biblical canon. Scripture contains narrative, prophecy, laws, prayers, and hymns, as well as wisdom discourses. These various genres name God in different, often even conflicting, ways.[9] While narrative, for example, speaks of God as the main actor in a historical drama concerned with liberation (hence it speaks *about* God who is put in the third person as an actor in the story), in prophecy it is God who becomes the one speaking behind and through the prophet (in the first person). The content of this prophetic "naming" is not the reassuring narrative of redemption, but often contains accusation and judgment. Similarly, the psalm or hymn addresses God in a personal "you," while wisdom literature tends to "universalize" and depersonalize any naming of God. These various ways of speaking of God are not necessarily easily compatible. Ricoeur calls it "biblical polyphony" and insists that the multiple voices heard here are important and should not be homogenized into a single univocal voice. God is named in many ways and this naming is therefore complex and multi-faceted. God is not only the name that brings the various discourses together but "also the index of their incompleteness. It is their common goal, which escapes each of them" (*FS*, 228).[10] God is thus beyond the discourse as a whole and cannot be captured by it (or by any of the particular genres).

This language of the biblical discourse in general is characterized by a kind of excess or by what Ricoeur names "limit-expressions." Limit-expressions are terms that portray life "at the limit": They are excessive and often present extreme situations and demands. They cannot be said to "correspond" to the world in any factual sense. This is particularly obvious in the parables, which often portray extreme conditions that are not to be taken at face value. The parables speak of a different kind of world and a different way of being in that world. They challenge us to behave in a new way, to live according to the extravagant and abundant generosity of the kingdom. What Ricoeur sees specifically in the parables, he often also says about Jesus's message more generally.[11] Christ's call for his disciples to abandon everything, to "hate" their relatives, to rip out their eyes or cut off their hands, are not meant to be taken literally, but rather to portray the radical demands of the kingdom in superlative and excessive fashion. Jesus himself is portrayed in excessive terms and calls for a radical re-orientation of social and political life. Ricoeur speaks of this as a logic of superabundance in contrast to our more common logic of equivalence or proportionality. He sees a similar logic at work in Paul's talk about the abundance of salvation. Throughout, Ricoeur is always eager to preserve the balance and paradoxical relationship between the logic of superabundance expressed in love (or mercy) and the logic of equivalence expressed by justice. Neither should be subordinated to the other, yet each destabilizes and challenges the other.[12]

Biblical discourse therefore unsettles us and summons us to become different. This analysis supplements Ricoeur's other investigations into the nature of the human subject, especially in *Oneself as Another* and *Course of Recognition*. The article that constituted the final address of the Gifford Lectures is instructive in this regard. (These lectures became *Oneself as Another* minus the final two lectures, which had a religious theme.) In this lecture, Ricoeur envisions a "summoned self" who responds to various types of "calls": the prophetic vocation, the summon to imitate Christ, the Augustinian notion of the inner teacher, and the testimony of conscience (*FS*, 262–76). The prophet is addressed by God, his or her self "decentered" and "unsettled," and sent on a mission to proclaim the divine word. Similarly, the later "Christian" versions of such a divine address (*imitatio*

Christi, Augustine's notion of the "inner teacher," and the voice of conscience) imply a dialogue with the divine that calls the self for an often uncomfortable mission. This article then again emphasizes how biblical discourse and thinking can dislocate and have an impact on more general human experience. It shows the importance of unsettling self-identity and summoning the self to a different vision of the world (*FS*, 273). Limit-expressions have something important to say to us and are not to be rejected. The challenge to our world and the new world they represent is essential and must be heard. We are not to ignore their message. Ricoeur is certainly not concerned with "proving" God's existence according to scientific criteria or even with imposing a Christian version of morality or justice on everyone. But he is also not willing to dismiss the real meaning and challenge to our common ways of being that the biblical discourses present.

While his earlier articles on biblical hermeneutics often focus on the form and function of that discourse in general, one of his final books, *Thinking Biblically*, is a more clearly exegetical study of specific biblical texts. His essays on Genesis 2–3, Exodus 20:13, Ezekiel 37:1–14, Psalm 22, Song of Songs, and Exodus 3:14 are written in response to biblical scholar André LaCocque's more explicitly exegetical studies of the same texts. (They collaborated on this volume, which also includes two additional essays by LaCocque.) The most distinctive characteristic in these reflections is Ricoeur's insistence on the importance of the "history of reception" of these texts. Ricoeur neither rejects the insights of contemporary biblical criticism nor returns to a (now naive) traditional reading of the texts. Yet he shows that meaning and insight are gained from not merely dismissing more traditional readings, but by having them interact with the more contemporary ones. "Sparks of meaning" are created at these "points of friction" between what seem, at first glance, to be utterly incompatible readings. He also tries to mediate fruitfully between various philosophical analyses of God's relation to "being," grounded in a reading of Exodus 3:14 where God is proclaimed as "I am," a text often read in a metaphysical fashion as proclaiming an identification between God and being. Ricoeur thinks that neither such a complete identification nor a complete rejection of such a reading (for example, by Lévinas and Marion) is ultimately very helpful. Each reading must be tempered by the insights gained from the opposing position. The emphasis on the religious community that has read and employed these texts through the centuries is also important. Ricoeur again emphasizes that reading of texts does not happen in a vacuum, but is deeply embedded in the presuppositions of the various communities and individuals whose lives gain meaning from the texts. It both challenges these presuppositions and gives meaning and validation to their faith.

Religious Reverberations in Narrative, Fidelity, and Justice

In many of his more secular works, Ricoeur is also concerned with issues of truth, meaning, and justice. He rarely appeals to the Bible or theological convictions in these texts, but his insights there are certainly not incompatible with what he says about the truth and meaning of biblical discourse and its power to transform action. Ricoeur consistently draws connections between texts and life, as is particularly evident in the title (and content) of one of his major collections of hermeneutic essays *From Text to Action*. In multiple essays and articles in this and other volumes, he argues for this connection between text and life. Action can be subject to hermeneutic analysis (and indeed requires interpretation) in a way very similar to the analysis of texts. This is also one of the central themes of his work on narrative. Narrative arises from life (life *prefigures* narrative), it depicts (or *configures*) life, and finally impacts and shapes our actions (*refigures* life).[13] The narrative self becomes a self through the coherence of its narrative, while continually being challenged by the disruptions, disorder, and challenges of real life. (Ricoeur speaks of this as the interplay of "concordance" and "discordance.") In many ways, what Ricoeur says about narrative more generally mirrors what he has said about the poetic function of the biblical discourse more specifically. Certainly, he does not suggest that the biblical discourse alone has this function. Any great narrative can challenge us in this fashion. The "world of the text" is a more general hermeneutic insight that certainly does not apply only to biblical texts. Any literary text projects its own world, which it invites us to inhabit. And yet it is interesting that these general hermeneutic principles can be applied so seamlessly to the biblical text as well or that insights about biblical poetry can be universalized to speak about narrative discourse more generally.[14] These parallels seem to suggest that the truth of Christianity can indeed inform other sorts of truth in some way or at the very least is not incompatible with them.

In some of Ricoeur's final works, Christian themes make a more explicit (although still quite tentative) appearance. The final book published during his lifetime, *The Course of Recognition*, includes a brief analysis of the Christian notion of agape as a "state of peace" in the search for mutual recognition. Agape goes beyond justice (or is maybe even in contrast to it) by transcending equivalence or comparison (*CR*, 220). Agape is neither friendship (*philia*) nor desire (*eros*), but the "work" of love, which is a work of pardon. In fact, Ricoeur's reflections on agape here recall some of his earlier insights regarding the logic of superabundance present in the Scriptural discourse. Ricoeur also insists that "the discourse of agape is above all else one of praise . . . Love commends itself through the tenderness of its supplication" (*CR*, 222). Agape is related to the gift: "Not being marked by privation, it has only one desire—to give—which is the expression of its generosity" (*CR*, 224). *Memory, History, and Forgetting* also mentions forgiveness as a Christian insight that is not really approached by "forgetting" more generally, although it leaves this at the level of suggestion.[15] *The Just* and *Reflections on the Just* speak of pardon and mercy in Christian terms. In an essay on "Sanction, Rehabilitation, and Pardon," included in *The Just*, Ricoeur suggests that pardon follows a logic that is of a different order, like the third order in Pascal (see the chapter on Marion for more detail on this). Pardon follows the logic of the gift and of superabundance,[16] a term clearly referring to Ricoeur's earlier discussion of the logic of superabundance in the Gospels. Yet Ricoeur does not explore these parallels in the essay. In fact, all of these references are painfully brief and hardly amount to more than a mere suggestion that Christian concepts have valuable insights to offer on these topics without exploring in any detail exactly how they do so.

A draft of a paper on death, titled "Up to Death: Mourning and Cheerfulness" and some fragments reflecting on death were found among Ricoeur's papers after he died. They have been published posthumously under the title *Living Up to Death* and were probably originally written during the time in which Ricoeur's wife passed away (about 1996)[17] and during his own illness and sense of imminent death (2004–5). Ricoeur reflects on the death of the other and the act of mourning that accompanies it. He suggests that we can only envision our own death in terms of the ways we will be missed and mourned by others. He tries to formulate in this meditation the emergence of something "Essential," which he identifies with the religious, although he admits that this identification may well only be possible in the face of death. He says "because dying is transcultural, it is transconfessional, transreligious in this sense: and this insofar as the Essential breaks through the filter of reading 'languages' of reading. This is perhaps the only situation where one can speak of religious experience. Moreover, I am wary of the immediate, the fusional, the intuitive, the mystical" (*LD*, 16). Even here, in these notes not yet intended for publication, Ricoeur is very reticent about the religious and what it might mean, wanting to avoid a "mystical" account of religious experience. Rather, the essential is evident in the compassion of "suffering-with" and thus about our relation to the other (*LD*, 17).

In *Living Up to Death* (as he also does in other places, usually drawing on René Girard's analysis of the scapegoat), Ricoeur strongly rejects a sacrificial theory of atonement that sees Christ as appeasing God's wrath or substituting for us. Redemption is not primarily sacrificial. Rather, it is about service and the gift of life. The "afterlife," then, is in the other, in the community who remembers: "Tie between service and meal. The Last Supper joins dying (oneself) [AND] the service (of the other) in the sharing of the *meal* that joins the man of death to the multitude of survivors reunited in the ecclesia. It is noteworthy that Jesus himself did not *theorize* this relationship and never says *who* he was. Maybe he did not *know*; he *lived* it in the Eucharistic gesture that joins the imminence of death and its afterlife in the community" (*LD*, 55). Thus, as in his earliest texts on biblical interpretation, Ricoeur rejects theological speculation about doctrines in favor of the simple gestures and texts of the community.

Again, Ricoeur is insistent even in this fragmentary and personal text that he is not a Christian philosopher. Instead, he is "on one side, a philosopher, nothing more, even a philosopher without an absolute, concerned about, devoted to, immersed in philosophical anthropology" and "on the other, a Christian who expresses himself philosophically" (*LD*, 69). A Christian for him means "someone who professes a primordial adhesion to the life, the words, the death of Jesus" (*LD*, 69). In the very next fragment, he explores this "reflective adhesion of the figure of Jesus the Christ" further (*LD*, 71). Again, he rebels against any notion of a "sacrificial theory" of atonement. He defines "adhesion" (which he uses throughout in place of "faith") as "someone faithful to a tradition [who] personally commits himself to the asymmetrical relation" (*LD*, 73). *Living Up to Death* also includes some further reflections on biblical criticism and theology. It ends with a short piece on Derrida.

A "Controlled Schizophrenia"

As pointed out in the beginning of this chapter and also evident in the discussion of *Living Up to Death*, Ricoeur was always very vigilant about keeping his philosophical and his more "theological" writings separate. This is particularly obvious in *Oneself with Another*, which was originally presented as the Gifford lectures and ended with two lectures on the "religious" or "biblical" self. Ricoeur justifies his decision not to include these lectures with his "concern to pursue, to the very last line, an autonomous, philosophical discourse" that must "assume the conscious and resolute bracketing of the convictions that bind me to biblical faith" (*OA*, 24). He argues that his entire philosophical work "leads to a type of philosophy from which the actual mention of God is absent and in which the question of God, as a philosophical question, remains in a suspension that could be called agnostic" (*OA*, 24). He wants to preserve philosophy from a "cryptotheological" reading, but also refrain from attributing a "cryptophilosophical function" to biblical faith. Like many others, Jean Greisch has pointed out that the status of this "religious agnosticism" would have to be examined further and that "a philosophical hermeneutics of the self might not be able to do without an analysis of the religious status of the self."[18] As mentioned at the beginning of this chapter, in respect to almost every other topic imaginable Ricoeur was always eager to break down distinctions and to allow for dialogue between opposing positions. It is not entirely convincing, then, that in this one case the boundaries between discourses must be upheld, that reflections on biblical interpretation or topics of faith might not interact with or even influence interpretations of history or the self. To some extent, the watertight division between Ricoeur's strictly philosophical work and his writings on biblical hermeneutics might well be artificial or misleading. One might suggest that the two discourses inform each other much more meaningfully than Ricoeur often admits.[19]

And, in fact, Ricoeur has at times recognized this. During occasional interviews, but especially in the aforementioned series of conversations with François Azouvi and Marc de Launay, entitled *Critique and Conviction*, he admits at the very beginning:

> I should also like to say that we are going to play, in alternation, not only with the broader range but also with comparisons that I have not made previously. I am thinking, for example, of the religious and philosophical domains, which I have staunchly kept separate from one another for reasons I have always sought to justify. But here, in this more open conversation, I shall be more concerned with the problems arising from the interferences, the overlaps of the religious and the philosophical. In writing, I can separate these domains more explicitly and in a more concerted manner; on the other hand, in the exchanges that we are going to have, where the man will speak more than the author, I shall have less justification for cultivating the sort of controlled schizophrenia that has always been my rule of thought. Here the rule of life will overtake the rule of thought. (*CC*, 2)

In this work, Ricoeur speaks much more openly than usual about his personal life, his upbringing, his religious convictions, his friendship with Gabriel Marcel and Mircea Eliade, his ambivalent relationship to Parisian intellectual life (all subjects on which he has usually been extremely reticent), but also about his philosophical commitments and concerns.

One of the final chapters of these conversations is devoted to "Biblical Readings and Meditations." Here, Ricoeur summarizes some of his work on Scriptural discourse but also addresses the question of how his reflection on religion is to be reconciled with his philosophical work. He compares his ambivalence about these two discourses (but also their unity in his person) to having "walked on two legs" (*CC*, 139). It is significant that religion, then, is an entire "leg" for him, more or less equal in value to philosophy, not one among many "legs" that might include his concerns with history, narrative, justice, and others. Apparently, all these are philosophical concerns to which he contrasts the more religiously motivated work. He speaks of the two discourses or genres as having distinct reference points. Their distinction "is absolutely primary" for him. He identifies the philosophical discourse with "critique" and the religious with "conviction," while admitting elements of overlap between them (that is, religious discourse involves critique, while philosophy also has elements of conviction). Here, the theme of community becomes important again: Ricoeur distinguishes the discourses primarily in terms of commitments to different types of community and the reading of different sets of texts, rejecting the term "experience" as being of primary concern. "Each type of reading, and hence of interpretation," he insists, "serves different objectives and begins from presuppositions which are not only separate but often even opposite" (*CC*, 140).

Thus, in these reflections Ricoeur suggests that the stark opposition between theological and philosophical thinking is inadequate and in many ways false; as there are philosophical ways of examining and reading the Biblical texts, so there are also elements of "conviction" within philosophical work. And, in fact, he usually defines his own reading of biblical texts as philosophical, especially in *Thinking Biblically* where his own more "philosophical" interpretation is contrasted with the readings given by the biblical scholar André LaCocque. He emphasizes "canonical reading" of the Scriptures as a mediating approach between historical-critical methods and discourses of faith. Ricoeur insists that even "kerygmatic interpretations," which may seem to oppose philosophical readings the most clearly, are always diverse, multiple, and partial and thus far from monolithic (*CC*, 144). While the "critical attitude" is especially associated with the philosophical task, religion operates within a series of hermeneutic circles that presuppose the community that believes in the claims of the texts and is founded by them. Yet Ricoeur points out that even the movement of critique is problematic, as it presupposes a self-sufficient and powerful subject and does not take seriously the historical condition and thus finitude of our particular situations. Throughout, he acknowledges that some overlap of the two discourses is unavoidable (*CC*, 151). He concludes, regarding his own commitment to the Christian tradition: "If pushed, I would agree to say that a religion is like a language in which one is either born or has been transferred by exile or hospitality; in any event, one feels at home there, which implies a recognition that there are other languages spoken by other people," although he does not want to dismiss the particularity of a religious community as mere chance or descent into utter relativism, where all namings of God by different traditions are thought to be reducible to the same (interchangeable) signifier (*CC*, 145). In *Oneself as Another*, Ricoeur defines faith in very similar terms as "a chance happening transformed into a destiny by means of a choice constantly renewed, in the scrupulous respect of different choices" (*OA*, 25).

These are not the only places where Ricoeur attributes his Christian faith to the chance of his birth in his own concrete and particular context. He does so again in one of the fragments included in *Living Up to Death*, calling it here also "a chance transformed into destiny by continuous choice" (*LD*, 62). His own faith commitment is a conscious affirmation of his particular location and cultural heritage and thus also of his own identity:

> A chance: from birth and more broadly from a cultural heritage. Sometimes I have replied in this way to the objection: "If you were Chinese, there is little chance that you'd be Christian." To be sure, but you are speaking of another me. I cannot choose my ancestors, or my contemporaries. There is, in my origins, a chance element, if I look at things from the outside, and an irreducible situational fact, if I consider them from within. So I am, by birth and heritage. And I accept this. I was born and I was raised in the Christian faith of the Reformed tradition. It is this heritage, confronted repeatedly, at the level of *studying*, by all the adverse or compatible traditions, that I say is transformed into a destiny by a continuous choice. It is this choice that I am summoned to account for, throughout my life, by plausible arguments, that is, ones worthy of being pleaded in a discussion with good-faith protagonists, who are in the same situation as me, incapable of rendering fully rational the roots of their convictions. (*LD*, 62–63)

Here Ricoeur speaks of this continuous choice (and destiny) as an "adhesion" "which includes attachment to a personal figure under which the Infinite, the Most-High, is given to be loved" (*LD*, 64). He insists that this is both relative and absolute. There is no such thing as an "immediate faith" but one is always inscribed into a "hermeneutics of adhesion" (*LD*, 68).

Ricoeur also recalls his early distrust of onto-theo-logical thinking about God and any proofs for God's existence that caused him to remain "agnostic on the plane of philosophy" (*CC*, 150). Here he also acknowledges the cultural situation in France that required distance from religious commitments in order to be taken seriously as a philosopher. Yet, he says, "My two allegiances always escape me, even if at times they nod to one another" (*CC*, 150). In fact, he explores the idea that some of his philosophical thought might be enlarged to include reflections of more theological interest or might have a kind of theological application. He suggests that his thoughts on the self and its otherness may be carried further on the religious plane in a forgetting or giving up of the self. Such a religious reflection on the self might even change the very question of the subject itself: "this shift from the moral to the religious presumes a letting go of all the answers to the question 'Who am I?' and implies, perhaps, renouncing the urgency of the question itself, in any event, renouncing its insistence as well as its obsession" (*CC*, 156).

Near the end of the interview, however, he does actually acknowledge himself to stand at a sort of intersection between the religious and the philosophical dimension:

> In any case, we find ourselves at this intersection without having chosen it. For us it is a given task to make these distinct orders communicate: that of philosophical morality and that of the religious, which also has its own moral dimension, in line with what I called the economy of the gift. This is what I would say today, after having spent decades protecting, sometimes cantankerously, the distinction between the two orders. I believe I am sufficiently advanced in life and in the interpretation of these two traditions to venture out into the places of their intersection. (*CC*, 159)

He lists as possible places of intersection the ideas of compassion or of solicitude and of generosity, returning repeatedly also to the idea of death and the (im)possibility of an afterlife, which connect with the questions of selfhood and memory. In regard to personal resurrection (a topic to which he returns repeatedly in this chapter), he asks: "Where would I now situate myself with respect to this, if I am prepared to accept my heritage as a whole? Do I have the right to filter it, to sift through it: What do I believe deeply?" He responds: "It is enough for the time being for me to know that I belong to a vast tradition, and that men and women also belong to it who have professed with assurance and good faith doctrines from which

I feel myself far removed" (*CC*, 162). Even speculation on the divine name can take on both a theological and a philosophical character: "the critique of the names that are unsuitable for God is at once the philosophical injected into the religious, but also a sort of asceticism internal to the religious that seeks to rid itself of what is unworthy of God" (*CC*, 164). Religion deals with certain "fundamental experiences" of life, with death and creation. And, in fact, in a very early essay included in *History and Truth*, Ricoeur had suggested that "the Christian meaning of history is therefore the hope that secular history is also a part of that meaning which sacred history sets forth, that in the end there is only *one* history, that all history is ultimately sacred."[20] Although such statements are very rare indeed and seem confined to a couple of very early or very late texts, some of which are more informal in nature (such as interviews), they suggest that the two discourses might interact far more fruitfully than Ricoeur usually allows in his more customary reluctance.

In a late article on "Religious Belief," Ricoeur also explores such places of intersection.[21] He takes his own definition of the human as "capable" and expands it to include a possible reception of the religious. Power and impotence intersect for the religious capable person, just as much as for the capable human being in general. The experience of incapacity, religiously interpreted, appears as the problem of evil: I cannot do the good I wish to do; I experience myself as guilty, weak, fallen. Yet despite the human "propensity for evil," our "predisposition to good" is more originary, a point Ricoeur has already emphasized in his early work on evil. Ricoeur grounds belief in the power of religious symbols, the reception of religious texts, and religious practice grounded in the community, but above all in commitment to a "core of goodness": "the religious problematic can be summarized as the extraordinary capacity to make the ordinary person capable of doing the good" (RB, 30). Ricoeur not only addresses the positive contribution of religion to the self, but also highlights its difficulties, which are expressed in the common charge that religion is intolerant and violent. He argues that ultimately such violence is rooted in a "symbolic violence" and not in anything essential to the religious itself. Here also he expresses discomfort with sacrificial theories of atonement, relying again on Girard's analysis of the process of scapegoating as giving rise to sacrifice. Yet he also affirms again the "superabundance" of love that goes beyond the justice of equivalence and proportionality.

Ricoeur suggests that we must give up the idea of a "super-religion" that would contain all the particular religions. Trying to find their common core of truth actually constitutes a temptation of the search for religious truth and erases religious commitment to specific symbols and particular communities. This implies a certain kind of relativism or maybe more a "perspectivism" where the boundaries of other faiths can be approached from within one's own community. Ricoeur conceives such interaction on the model of translation. Just as there is no universal language and we must (and can) learn to translate and approach each other with linguistic hospitality, so religious beliefs can learn to translate and practice the tolerance of hospitality. He formulates this tolerance as follows:

"At the very depth of my own conviction, of my own confession, I recognize that there is a ground which I do not control. I discern in the ground of my adherence a source of inspiration which, by its demand for thought, its strength of practical mobilization, its emotional generosity, exceeds my capacity for reception and comprehension." But then the tolerance that arrives at this peak risks falling down the slope on the other side, that of skepticism: aren't all beliefs worthless? That is to say, do the differences not become indifferent? The difficulty then is to hold myself on the crest where my conviction is at the same time anchored in its soil, like its mother tongue, but open laterally to other beliefs, other convictions, as in the case of foreign languages. It is not easy to hold oneself on this crest . . . (RB, 39)

The address ends with these tentative dots. While Ricoeur almost always managed to hold himself on the crest, the tension is clearly visible in his work.

Of course, these reflections do not ultimately resolve the dichotomies within Ricoeur's discourses or give us a definitive or authoritative answer about his stance on their interpenetration or compatibility. Yet some conclusions can certainly be drawn about ways in which the religious discourse is meaningful philosophically and therefore what place it may have in Ricoeur's philosophy more generally. Throughout, one should keep in mind, however, that Ricoeur never proposes one coherent, overall, monolithic "philosophy," but that he speaks in many different voices and engages in many discourses. His own thinking and writing is also "plurivocal," multiple, and partial, as he insists to be true of the biblical discourses he examines.

First, there are clear parallels between Ricoeur's discourses, in which truth is at stake in various ways. Nowhere does Ricoeur devalue or invalidate more traditional notions of truth. He does not discount the need for verification or correspondence versions of truth, which may well be appropriate on some level. Yet he always limits the extent of their application. In fact, one may say that Ricoeur almost always starts with these notions of truth as certainty and verification and then slowly moves the reader away from their simplistic appeal to pure objectivity. More important, in almost all of his writings, whether they deal with strictly philosophical topics such as the self or history or whether they deal with Scripture and theology, Ricoeur develops an alternative and complementary account of truth that is not simply concerned with facts and states of affairs. This account of truth is characterized by several features: (a) truth is practical: truthfulness is ascertained in consistent action and trustworthiness, (b) truth is communicated and hence communal: not only is it relevant to and grows out of the community (as for history), but even more personal attestation is always fidelity in front of the other and is witnessed by him or her, (c) truth is moral: it is lived before and toward the other and always has a connotation of responsibility, (d) truth is multi-faceted or polyphonic: it speaks in several and often contradictory voices, (e) to some extent truth is thus always elusive: there is no single and no simple account of truth, but in fact it is always changing, unsettled by various hermeneutics of suspicion, and finally (f) truth is transformative: it affects life and challenges it to move in new, different, and better directions. These characteristics of truth are evident in his work on history, his work on the self, his work on narrative texts, and his exploration of the particular nature of biblical truth.

And one might venture to assert that the truth of Scripture is far from as marginal and irrelevant as Ricoeur at times seems to suggest. On some level, he does appear to want to say that the insights from the Scriptural narratives *do* say something important or even fundamental about the human condition and, in fact, that they say something that is *not* said in quite this way (if at all) by other discourses. Even in his earliest texts, Ricoeur claims that religious discourse implies philosophy and makes philosophical statements and truth claims. On the one hand, it is precisely in regard to these texts that he first develops his distinctions between truth as certainty or verification and truth as manifestation or faithfulness. On the other hand, he insists that not only must we recognize that religious language does indeed make these truth claims, but he suggests that its truth claims put in question the criteria of truth of other kinds of discourse (*FS*, 35). Not only may "God-talk" be just as true, just as meaningful, just as verifiable as scientific discourse in its own sphere and manner of discourse, but it may actually serve to question the assumptions and versions of truth of other discourses. Ricoeur always regards as an essential presupposition of his work on biblical hermeneutics, that this truth is "verified" in life (*FS*, 217). He himself connects this to a notion of revelation. Revelation refers to this new world that is proposed and which we must inhabit: "I would go so far as to say that the Bible is revealed to the extent that the new being unfolded there is itself revelatory with respect to the world, to all of reality, including my existence and my history. In other words, revelation, if the expression is meaningful, is a trait of the biblical *world*" (*FS*, 44). Ricoeur clearly feels ambivalent about the term "revelation." In the interview mentioned previously, for example, he says: "In place of revelation, I would rather speak of a situation in which one refers to a constituting imaginary through the resources of religious language, by turn narrative, legislative, hymnic, and perhaps above all, sapiential" (*CC*, 148). And yet these resources of religious language are not negligible, because they and the imaginary they shape tell us something important about the world. They open up a new world within reality and invite us to access it: "What is thus opened up in everyday reality is another reality, the reality of the *possible*" (*FS*, 45).[22]

Religious truth thus does seem to have the ability to question and challenge the truth of other discourses, precisely by envisioning an alternative reality. A task Ricoeur outlines at the beginning of a paper entitled "Hermeneutic of the Idea of Revelation" may well summarize his task regarding faith and reason more generally:

> The way of posing the question which, more than any other, I will seek to overcome is the one that sets in opposition an authoritarian and opaque concept of revelation and a concept of reason which claims to be its own master and transparent to itself. This is why my presentation will be a battle on two fronts: it seeks to recover a concept of revelation and a concept of reason which, without ever coinciding, can at least enter into a living dialectic and together engender something like an understanding of faith.[23]

It is possible, then, that the different genres in his own work function in a similar fashion to the way in which he suggests the different biblical genres function: At times they conflict with each other or even contradict each other, they always point to something beyond them that essentially escapes each individual discourse, and yet meaning emerges through the very conflict and friction created by their interaction with each other.

Ricoeur's claims, then, are certainly much smaller (in the context of his thought as a whole) and less sweeping in scope than those of Henry, Marion, and other later thinkers (as we will see in subsequent chapters). His political, philosophical, and religious situation (he is earlier than they are, prepares the path for them to some extent with his careful and meticulous work; he focuses far more on hermeneutics, on reading and interpreting texts; he is the lone Protestant in a thoroughly Roman Catholic—though secularized—environment and culture) may have a lot to do with that.

Yet they cannot be neglected. Ricoeur does view Christianity as having essential insights that speak of a more general truth and reveal something important about the human condition, including a vision for a better life. His work is apologetic in the sense that it defends the truth of Christian (especially biblical) faith in terms of its ability to give meaning. It is meaningful both in the sense that it gives coherence and validity to religious experience and in the sense that it opens a life before us that is worthwhile to inhabit. Christianity provides a particularly challenging and insightful account of the self and in the limit-experiences of death and mourning can even point to something essential to human existence. Through the tension of its polyphonic discourse, it points to the divine and provides access to a meaningful (albeit not ultimately "rational" or fully coherent) reality.

5

Jean-Luc Marion: A God of Gift and Charity

Jean-Luc Marion (born in 1946) is emerging as an important contemporary French philosopher. Deeply influenced by the philosophies of Husserl, Heidegger, and Lévinas, he has formulated a radical phenomenological project that focuses on the questions of God, religious experience, and the relation between self and other (in terms of a new version of the self and in terms of love). Marion studied at the École Normale Superieur and the Sorbonne and worked closely with both Lévinas and Henry. He is presently teaching at the Institut catholique in Paris, is John Nuveen Professor at the divinity school of the University of Chicago (where he took Paul Ricoeur's place and also holds the Andrew Thomas Greely and Grace McNichols Greeley Chair of Catholic Studies), and is professor emeritus at the Université de la Sorbonne. In the fall of 2008, he was elected to the *Académie française* (one of the highest honors of French intellectual life usually reserved for important literary figures).

Originally trained as a Descartes scholar by the eminent Ferdinand Alquié and having written extensively on Descartes and the late medieval and early modern context in which Descartes worked, Marion first became known in the English-speaking world through his early more theological work *God Without Being* (1991, French 1982). He has since not only published further works on Descartes (*On Descartes' Metaphysical Prism, Cartesian Questions, On the Ego and on God*) and several more theological texts (*Idol and Distance, Prolegomena to Charity, The Crossing of the Visible, The Visible and the Revealed, Le croire pour le voir*), but has also written extensively in contemporary phenomenology (*Reduction and Givenness, Being Given, In Excess, The Erotic Phenomenon, Certitudes négatives*). His notion of the "saturated phenomenon" is increasingly becoming a common term in phenomenological thinking. Together with Henry and Lévinas, Marion was one of the primary targets of Janicaud's attack on French philosophy's "theological turn" and has most often responded to Janicaud on this point. In fact, a second work Janicaud wrote to follow up on *The Theological Turn* (translated as *Phenomenology "Wide Open"*) is concerned much more heavily with Marion's work, arguing for a "minimalist" phenomenology and criticizing what he perceives as Marion's "maximalist" one.[1]

In France, Marion is primarily recognized for his work on Descartes, although his phenomenology is also increasingly gaining recognition especially in light of the recent publications of *The Erotic Phenomenon, Au Lieu de Soi* ("In the Self's Place"; a phenomenological work on Augustine's *Confessions*), and *Certitudes négatives* ("negative certainty" or "negative certitude"). In the English-speaking world, conversely, this work on Descartes is often unknown or disregarded even though it prepares his later phenomenological work in an important fashion.[2] His first two books were on what he calls Descartes's "grey ontology" and his "white theology," respectively.[3] In the first book (and in subsequent ones such as *On Descartes' Metaphysical Prism* and *Cartesian Questions*), Marion formulates a rigorous definition of metaphysics, drawn from Heidegger, but applied to and tested on Descartes's work, whom he regards as absolutely essential for subsequent philosophical thinking on this and other topics. In the second book, Marion examines Descartes's emphasis on the creation of the eternal truths (for example, basic logical and mathematical axioms) and Descartes's refusal to engage in theology (that very refusal emerges as a kind of theological statement). These works thus prepare and support Marion's later arguments about the necessary overcoming of metaphysics and phenomenological language about God and religious experience. The first part of this chapter will lay out these investigations into Cartesian metaphysics and "theology." The second part will examine Marion's well-known reflections on the idol and icon in *God Without Being* and other works. The third part will deal with the idea of the saturated phenomenon and its various philosophical and theological implications and applications. The chapter will conclude with a reflection on the overall apologetic character of Marion's project.

Descartes's Metaphysics and Its Theology

Descartes's Grey Ontology [*L'ontologie grise de Descartes*, 1975] is a close analysis of Descartes's early Latin work *Regulae ad directionem ingenii*

(*Rules for the Direction of the Mind*), which lays out a careful philosophical method for thinking that Descartes hoped would replace the method of instruction in the schools of late medieval scholasticism. Marion argues that the best way to understand this early text is to see it as an appropriation of and argument against Aristotle, although Aristotle himself is not mentioned in the text. Marion develops what he contends is a new definition of metaphysics in Descartes, an argument he continues and supports more fully in *On Descartes' Metaphysical Prism*. In Marion's view, Descartes is the first thinker really to fit the Heideggerian definition of metaphysics as onto-theo-logy. Marion's central argument about Descartes's metaphysical system is that it operates a "grey" ontology, an ontology that is hidden or dissimulated into an epistemology. It is not an explicit ontology in the traditional sense of metaphysics as the science of all beings (including the highest divine being), but Aristotle's metaphysics becomes step by step subverted into an epistemology, where not "being" but the "ego cogito," i.e., the human thinking mind, is central. Descartes is therefore the first to ground all being and entities firmly on a first being, namely the "I think"/ ego cogito. The being of other entities is grounded on and made possible by their becoming thoughts of the ego. The certainty of the thinking mind provides the foundation and grounding for all other beings (they are *cogitata*—things thought by the mind). Furthermore, by thus grounding all other beings, the ego is unable to reflect on its own being as thinking (and cannot ultimately ground its own being). Thus, the ego would have to function not only as the originating cause for all other beings but also as its own cause (*causa sui*). In this early work, Descartes thus develops an onto-theo-logical construction of a metaphysics based on the ego and "forgets" ontological difference, thus fulfilling Heidegger's definition of metaphysics as onto-theo-logically constituted.

Marion continues this argument in *On Descartes' Metaphysical Prism* and *Cartesian Questions: Method and Metaphysics* by pointing out that Descartes's version of metaphysics becomes supplemented by a second onto-theo-logy that is developed in Descartes's later texts, especially the *Meditations*. In this later version, the being of the ego becomes grounded on God as ultimate being (God as *causa sui* and creator of the ego, as "thought of the infinite" that the ego cannot "invent" and a thought greater than the ego that cannot even keep itself in existence from one thought to the next). Descartes's metaphysics is thus "doubled" in its onto-theological structure: two onto-theo-logies crossing each other and attempting to ground each other. Marion employs this basic definition of metaphysics (onto-theo-logy with a *causa sui* grounding and a forgetting of ontological difference) in all his subsequent writings. And when he speaks of "overcoming metaphysics," this is the metaphysics that he thinks necessary to overcome. (This is also why he claims occasionally—especially for Patristic and medieval thinkers such as Dionysius, Augustine, and Aquinas—that they do not engage in metaphysics, properly speaking, or at least that their version of "God" is not subject to metaphysics in this sense.[4]) It is also in this context, especially in *On Descartes' Metaphysical Prism*, that Marion lays out what he perceives as three proofs for God's existence in Descartes's work. He correlates these not only to the two onto-theo-logical systems, but also to the three medieval ways of talking about God (discussed at the end of this and of the next section), while arguing that Descartes's attempt at recovering and appropriating these traditional arguments is ultimately doomed to failure.

The second important point of Marion's work on Descartes emerges in the "white theology" [*La théologie blanche de Descartes*, 1981] and several of the later essays collected in *On the Ego and on God: Further Cartesian Questions*. Marion claims that Descartes vigorously argues against a subjection of God to reason and the increasing tendency to employ univocal language for God. Univocal talk uses the same terminology for both God and human beings and thus assumes there is no essential difference between them. This was happening, for example, with ontological language that was applied in similar fashion to both God and humans (especially by Cardinal Bérulle, a late medieval thinker). God was said to "be" in a similar fashion to the way humans are. The sort of existence God has is not essentially different from that of humans (and all other beings). Something similar happened in the new philosophical and scientific thinking of this time (especially in Galileo, Kepler, and Mersenne). These thinkers consider reason and logic, such as basic arithmetic and geometrical principles, to be eternal and uncreated; thus God is subject to this eternal and unchangeable logic and could not have created these truths or the world that is based on them differently. Descartes argues in several important letters to Mersenne that such a view is heretical and a limitation on God's omnipotence. Instead, God creates the "eternal truths" and they are dependent upon God. God could have chosen to make them otherwise and also to create a different world. As God is not capricious, however, they are not whimsical and unreliable, but God is fully committed to them. (This is a "white" theology because it is erased or "whitened out." "White" also has connotations of purity or innocence here.)

This has important implications for Marion. On the one hand, it is an attempt to preserve God's infinity and otherness and not to make God subject to human logic. In this respect, Marion appropriates Descartes's stance and applauds it. On the other hand, Descartes goes on to develop a notion of analogy (a medieval way of talking about God and human relation to God in a way that Marion thinks is no longer really available to Descartes), which ends up developing the notion of *causa sui* for God (i.e., that God is God's own cause, God eternally causes God's self). Marion contends that Descartes is the first one to employ this term for God, one that was generally rejected as illogical previous to Descartes (and, in fact, with a few exceptions also subsequent to him). This final definition of God emerges within Descartes's proofs for God's existence in the *Meditations*. Marion argues that these are three different proofs (in the Third Meditation God is named "infinite," in the Fifth Meditation God is "omnipotent," and in the Replies to the *Meditations* God is *causa sui*) and that they correspond to the medieval ways of "naming" God, namely a kataphatic (affirmative), an apophatic (negative), and a "hyper-essential" path (one that goes beyond positive and negative description of God; see further description of these at the end of the next section). Yet Descartes amalgamates and confuses these ways and invents the name of *causa sui* for God, a name Marion judges to be both deeply metaphysical and ultimately idolatrous. Marion thus emphasizes in his writings on Descartes that any univocal talk about God is unacceptable and blasphemous because such talk does not preserve God's difference and distance from us and the world. Not only Galileo, Kepler, and Mersenne by affirming the independence of the eternal truths and Bérulle by employing ontological language for God, but also Descartes himself with the *causa sui*, ultimately fall into this trap. Marion argues a very similar point in his more theological work on the idol and the icon.

Idol, Icon, and Distance

Marion is still most well-known for his argument (in *God Without Being*) that God is not subject to "being" and that the traditional ontological language is inadequate for God (does not "attain" to God).[5] Marion draws a distinction between "idolatrous" and "iconic" imagery and language for the divine. An idol is, in fact, a true vision of a God (it is not merely invented or false), but it is one in which the viewer attempts to grasp the divine. The gaze viewing the idol is fascinated, "stopped," and completely held by the divine image presented within it. Yet because this image holds and fills the gaze so completely, "fits" it perfectly, it actually becomes an invisible mirror of the limited conception the viewer has of God. What one "sees" in worshipping the idol is a mirror image of oneself and of one's own vision of the divine. (This happens even when we "idolize" certain "stars"; they often encapsulate what we personally find most worthy of admiration, what we would like to have ourselves, or even how we view ourselves.)

The icon, in contrast, reverses the gaze. The gaze travels through an icon beyond it and thus is not reflected back on itself (but also is not in control of a "finished" vision). Marion claims that when we contemplate or pray before an icon, we find ourselves envisioned by the icon through its inverse perspective (and ultimately become unsettled by God's gaze passing through the icon and toward us). Instead of allowing for a fixed image, the icon becomes a window or a pathway in which gazes (and prayer) can travel back and forth, but which never get fixated on a specific image or concept one could have in one's grasp. We control the idol but, in the icon, control is not possible. Marion analyzes this most clearly in the context of prayer in the final study of *The Crossing of the Visible*, where he speaks of the icon as a corrective to our image-obsessed media culture.[6] In the icon, we do not have to project an image and are not judged in terms of such an image. Instead the icon allows for communion with the one to whom the prayer is directed across the icon while preserving the distance between the two gazes (of the person praying and the one to whom he or she is directing the prayer) exposed to each other in this prayer.

Not only can images or statues serve as "idols" or "icons," but concepts or ideas can also function in this way. The two terms describe different ways of "seeing" and thus can refer just as much to (philosophical) concepts of the divine. Thus, Kant's notion of the "moral God" became an idol whose death Nietzsche announces. The death of this (philosophical) idol is something to be celebrated, as it opens the path toward more "iconic" ways of speaking about the divine.[7] Similarly, the language of "being" has become an idolatrous way of talking about God, which ultimately puts limits on the divine and fixes God in a concept of "God" as supreme being. This idol, a mere mirror image of ourselves, must be uncovered and shown to be inadequate for speaking about God. More iconic ways of talking must be found, meaning that they must ultimately proceed from God and not from us. In *God Without Being*, Marion illustrates this by putting a cross through the term God, "crossing out" the placeholder term "God." We can never adequately name or write about "God"; all such attempts are doomed to become idolatrous at some point or other, to be more about us and our expectations than about God as such.

Marion articulates a very similar argument with the notion of distance in his somewhat earlier work *Idol and Distance*. In order to speak of (or to) God, distance is required. This does not mean that we cannot speak of or to God at all, but it does mean that we can never be in possession of the divine and that any concept of God is ultimately inadequate and in danger of becoming idolatrous. Marion says that distance must be "crossed" (reciprocally) instead of erased. In this work even more clearly than in *God Without Being*, Marion is attempting to overcome "metaphysical" (in the sense given it previously) definitions or ways of thinking about God, responding even more explicitly to the event of the "death of God." (The entire first part of his *Idol and Distance* is a discussion of Nietzsche.) Marion regards the death of God as the death of a concept of God, namely the notion of the "moral God" as the ground of all values. The "death of God" is therefore an event to be celebrated because it frees us from one particular idol of God. Now that this idol is recognized and discarded, we can move on and find new and better ways of talking and thinking about God, new ways of crossing the distance to the divine. In both works, Marion also specifically addresses Heidegger. He thinks of Heidegger (and especially of Heidegger's notion of the ontological difference) as still metaphysical in some sense. Heidegger's writing on theology as an "ontic" endeavor and his notion of the fourfold limit the divine. Instead, God must be thought "beyond being" and beyond ontological difference.[8] God is not merely a being among others, not even the highest or most supreme being. Being is an idol for God, an attempt to define God, but one that ultimately proves limiting, idolatrous, and blasphemous.

Especially in his early work (but not only there), Marion often employs the language of the fifth-century Eastern theologian Dionysius the Areopagite in order to find a better and non-ontological way of speaking of the divine. In *Idol and Distance*, he shows that Dionysius is able to preserve distance and to speak of God non-metaphysically and non-idolatrously better than either Nietzsche or Hölderlin, the other two thinkers discussed in the work. Dionysius does so by "crossing the distance" in prayer or praise, by upholding distance instead of trying to erase it. In the well-known Villanova address on the gift, which was first conceived as a response to Derrida and became the final chapter of *In Excess*, Marion argues that Patristic theology in general escapes ontological and metaphysical language about God. The Fathers, and Dionysius in particular, are not describing or defining God (either positively with kataphatic terminology or negatively with apophatic language), but instead are speaking *to* God in prayer. This language of praise is not descriptive, but performative. Its "saying" is actually a "doing." It does not attempt to define the divine but celebrates God and exposes itself to God in prayer. Such a speaking enables us to be open to the divine (similar to what happens in front of an icon) and to be transformed by God addressing us. Marion calls this the language of "mystical theology" (as opposed to negative theology). It is not merely a "denial" of attributes for the divine or a higher "re-affirmation" but instead goes beyond affirmation and rejection, beyond kataphatic and apophatic language, toward pure praise.

The Saturated Phenomenon and Phenomenality of Revelation

The most important and well-known formulation of these insights is the notion of the saturated phenomenon, which is central to Marion's phenomenological analyses. He has been careful to focus on the implications of this notion for phenomenology (instead of considering its application to theology, which he sees as outside his expertise, although occasionally he suggests its rich potential for application in this area). What does it mean for a phenomenon to be "saturated"? Marion relies on both Husserl and Heidegger here, but of course also goes beyond them (often with implicit help from Lévinas and Henry). Phenomenology is a "return to the things themselves." Hence phenomenology at its best allows the phenomenon to appear from itself, to speak from itself most authentically. Phenomenology frees phenomena to be themselves instead of being mere versions of our projections and expectations. Such freedom becomes possible through Husserl's notion of the phenomenological reduction. Reduction (or the epoché) allows us to set aside (or "bracket") all kinds of assumptions, preconceptions, ulterior motives, or other concerns that might make us fit phenomena into certain paradigms or view them in a particular predetermined fashion. It places limits on all these, so the phenomena can appear most authentically as they actually present themselves to us. They appear as they "give" themselves to us, in their own "givenness" (a term Marion uses to translate *Gegebenheit* or *donation* and which is occasionally challenged by Husserlians as inadequate and already loaded theologically).[9] Marion's phenomenology thus is known as a phenomenology of givenness.

Marion relies heavily on the Husserlian relation between intuition and intention (see the section on phenomenology in the introduction). Intuition is what is given to consciousness by the phenomenon; intention is what consciousness imposes upon the phenomenon. He contends that Husserl was primarily occupied with very basic objects (or even mathematical concepts) that are generally rather poor in phenomenality. These do not provide much in the way of intuition, but we must supplement what is lacking in intuition through our concepts (for example, we never intuit a perfect circle but must intend it in order to identify a shape as circular). Heidegger, conversely, was single-mindedly focused on "beings" or "Being as such." Both of these emphases become necessarily limiting in Marion's view. He argues that we should instead "reduce" more radically by setting aside even these concerns (with "beingness" and "objectness") and by allowing phenomena to give themselves in all their purity and givenness. We would then realize that although there are indeed some phenomena poor in intuition where we are not given much by the phenomenon itself but need to supply a lot through our concepts (intention), there are also phenomena that give lots to intuition and where our concepts always fall short. Such phenomena "saturate" our vision or experience; they are excessive and give "too much," more than we can possibly bear. Consciousness becomes overwhelmed or "blinded" by the excess of givenness and struggles to receive these experiences. Yet even if they cannot be contained in concepts adequately or even at all, these phenomena certainly make an impact on our consciousness. The impact is simply so strong and overwhelming that we cannot bear it or can only give a partial and inadequate account of it. Marion claims that these excessive phenomena convince us to set aside residual phenomenological restrictions, especially those of the horizon and of the constituting ego. Husserl had claimed that phenomena always appear to consciousness within a horizon of meaning. That is to say, we do not encounter phenomena in a vacuum, but are conscious of them as appearing within a larger context. This context makes it possible to identify and experience the phenomenon. For Husserl, this is a fairly active process: The consciousness of the subject "constitutes" the phenomenon within this horizon and thus gives it evidence and coherence. Marion thinks that this process of constitution in which the ego seems to provide almost everything for the appearance of the phenomenon gives the human subject too much power and control and thus restricts the self-givenness of the phenomenon. Similarly, the horizon seems to impose restrictions on the phenomenon: It can only appear within the restrictions of this or that particular horizon. The saturated phenomenon thus goes to the very edge of the phenomenal horizon. It is, so to say, a "limit-experience" at the very boundary of the horizon of consciousness. The saturated phenomenon also destabilizes the constituting subject and turns it into a much less powerful and more receptive version of the self.

Marion gives several examples of such saturated phenomena showing how they subvert Kantian categories of phenomenal intuition: historical events (saturated in terms of quantity), works of art (saturated in terms of quality), the immediacy of our own flesh (saturated in terms of relation), and encounter with the other human, the neighbor (saturated in terms of modality).[10] He concludes that this notion of saturation allows us to deal with far more complex phenomena than traditional (Husserlian or even Heideggerian) phenomenology and that it can also depict how such phenomena are experienced in all their blinding excess. For example, no account of a complex historical event can ever tell the full story. Any account presents one particular perspective that ultimately impoverishes the complexity of the historical event and requires new accounts, other retellings that tell a different part of the story. Similarly, a great work of art cannot be grasped in one glance. A great painting is not understood adequately as an object or as a commodity or as a composition of constituent parts (such as frame, canvas, pigments). Instead, paintings have an effect or impact on us and must always be viewed again.[11] Great paintings are the ones to which we return in order to see them again and again, because they give more than we can possibly grasp in one (or even in many) visit(s).

Marion then goes on to suggest that one might conceive of an absolute limit-experience of such saturation, one that combines all aspects of excess (quantity, quality, relation, modality). Such a supremely saturated and extremely paradoxical phenomenon would be the phenomenon of revelation. Marion insists that he is here only exploring a phenomenological possibility, not making any theological claims (or even any claims that such phenomena actually exist or have really been experienced):

> Phenomenology describes possibilities and never considers the phenomenon of revelation except as a possibility of phenomenality, one that it would formulate in this way: If God were to manifest himself (or manifested himself), he would use a paradox to the second degree. Revelation (of God by himself, *theo*-logical), if it takes place, will assume the phenomenal figure of the phenomenon of revelation, of the paradox of paradoxes, of saturation to the second degree. To be sure *R*evelation (as actuality) is never confounded with *r*evelation (as possible phenomenon). I will scrupulously respect this conceptual difference by its graphic translation. (*BG*, 367)

A phenomenon of revelation or a divine phenomenon (i.e. an experience of God) would be so excessive in every respect that it would overwhelm and "blind" or "bedazzle" intuition entirely. We would have no concepts for it and yet we would feel its impact (for example, blinding light is most certainly experienced even if one cannot look at it at all). Much of Marion's work seeks to describe what such an excessive experience would be like and what its peculiar phenomenological features might be. He insists throughout that this is merely an excessive case of phenomenality and that other saturated phenomena, in fact, are quite common, even banal.[12] We encounter a saturated phenomenon whenever we are seduced by the fragrance of an expensive perfume, when we return to contemplate a great work of art over and over again, when we are swept away by the beauty of a voice singing an aria or the magnificent performance of a concerto. All these are saturated phenomena, phenomena that are rich in intuition and defy concepts or explanation. An experience of the divine would simply be even far more intense in all respects and would be even more impossible to put into words or concepts. All these phenomena are felt by their effects; any description would be utterly inadequate (again language would have to be performative—illocutionary or perlocutionary—instead of descriptive or locutionary).[13]

Marion has also done concrete phenomenological analyses of experiences of saturation. He spends by far the most time on an analysis of love or "the erotic phenomenon." This is a strictly phenomenological analysis, although "love" certainly also is the best word we could find for the divine, as he already suggested in *God Without Being* and *Prolegomena to Charity* (we will return to this in the final section of this chapter). Marion regards the phenomenality of love as a radical challenge to the phenomenality of being. It overcomes metaphysics more successfully than anything else. In *The Erotic Phenomenon*, Marion shows that the experience of love subverts metaphysical conceptions of time and space and displaces our concern with being, as love is more important to us than existence. He engages in careful phenomenological analyses of the flesh, of the beloved other, of the child as the third who emerges from loving union, and of the speech used to talk about love. Love profoundly unsettles the self, the lover who engages in love. This analysis of the self as the lover crowns Marion's argument about a displacement of the self-sufficient Cartesian subject, which he begins in some of his writings on Descartes (especially in *On the Ego and on God*) and explicates in much greater detail in the fifth part of *Being Given* where he develops the notion of a self as "devoted," "given over to," "abandoned," or even "addicted" to the given. If the saturated phenomenon presents itself as a "gift" (established by Part II of *Being Given* in interaction with Derrida's analysis of the gift), the new self is not a subject in charge or control of the phenomenon as an object, but instead becomes the recipient of the gift and devoted to the gift. The lover in *The Erotic Phenomenon* is completely devoted to love and to the beloved, and offers love as a generous gift without expecting any return. Love, for Marion, is entirely selfless, completely committed to the other, and a supreme gift of self-abandon.

This argument is carried further in Marion's more recent work *Au Lieu de Soi*. In this book, Marion applies to the work of Augustine the argument he had already made in several shorter pieces concerning Aquinas and some other medieval thinkers, namely that they are not engaged in metaphysics in the modern (Cartesian) sense of the term. He is careful to show that Augustine does not define God in terms of "Being as such," even if that may appear to be the case in some passages (which he examines in detail). His most fundamental argument in this book, however, concerns the self. He analyzes the language of the Augustinian self as it turns to God in praise and in the mode of confession, thus responding to another instead of establishing itself. He goes on to dispute that the certainty of existence is based on a Cartesian solipsism as a first principle, but instead arises from response and desire (in Augustine this is desire for beatitude). This desire, which plays the role of primary principle, is not "known" in traditional terms. Rather, it is loved. Truth is first of all a matter of love and not of abstract certainty (this is an argument Marion has also sustained in other places and recovers and supports here in far more detail). In this context, he engages in an analysis of the will and its supposed independence of decision, which he judges a myth. Rather, the will operates within an erotic situation of the advance of the lover. Here Marion goes back to many of the analyses he had made in *The Erotic Phenomenon*. He also engages in an analysis of time as the event of creation. Temporality is what enables the gap between ego and self and makes a fall into sin possible. After examining time, Marion goes on to "place" (the "lieu" of the title) and shows the self to be re-"place"-d by another, ultimately by a divine other. We cannot find the place of the essence of the self because it is in the image of the infinite. I can know myself only as loved by another. I become truly myself when I find myself in God.

Most recently, Marion has proposed another term for phenomenology: "negative certainty." In his new book, which uses that expression as its title, he suggests that his phenomenology of givenness has epistemological implications. Instead of providing the sort of indubitable certainty about objects that Descartes advocates in his theory of the subject, saturated phenomena cannot be known in this fashion. Instead, they provide a kind of "negative certainty," inasmuch as we can precisely be "certain" that they remain inherently unknowable. It is not a case of *not yet* having sufficient knowledge but of an element of unknowability that is constitutive of the phenomenon as saturated which will *always remain* essentially unknowable. Marion examines the phenomena of the self, of the divine, and of the event as such rich phenomena, which by definition always escape our knowledge (they are "indefinable," "impossible," and "unforeseeable," respectively). He also provides a new account of the gift (as the "unconditioned"), supplementing it with an analysis of the phenomenon of sacrifice. This negative certainty, then, in Marion's view is a real broadening of our field of knowledge, albeit in an apophatic mode (the parallels to Marion's earlier analysis of negative or mystical theology are striking).

A Theological Highjacking of Phenomenology?

Dominique Janicaud was one of the first, but certainly not the only one, to be critical of Marion's phenomenology.[14] Especially initially, many critics objected to Marion's use of theological imagery, passages of Scripture, and language of "revelation" in his phenomenology. Theologians also felt uncomfortable with his heavy use of Heidegger in his more theologically oriented texts. Much initial criticism, like Janicaud's, amounts to a rejection of any sort of theological terms or concern in phenomenology. Phenomenology should stick strictly to appearances or everyday objects and not engage what is invisible or beyond common experience. To do so would be "metaphysical" because it deals with what goes beyond the physical. (Marion often responded that this is a false and imprecise definition of metaphysics, one that does not take the historical development of the term into account.) The phenomenology of givenness seemed too extreme to many, the saturated phenomenon too overwhelming, the recipient of this phenomenon too passive. Many of these concerns, while not thereby invalidated, no longer apply solely to Marion. Several other thinkers (certainly most of the ones treated in this book, but they are not the only ones) have begun thinking about the ability of phenomenology to deal with "invisible" or "excessive" phenomena, with complex phenomena at the limit of experience. A reconsideration of the Cartesian subject is also central to much contemporary phenomenology. In many ways, the more recent discussions about Marion's phenomenology (and that of others) is no longer about *whether* phenomenology may speak about religious phenomena or even a "divine" phenomenon, but *how* it should do so. Marion himself has also gone back occasionally and shown the potential for this direction in phenomenology in Husserl and other early phenomenological thinkers.[15]

John D. Caputo and other thinkers following his lead have often objected that Marion's talk about God and religion is too determined by his particular religious tradition and ecclesial affiliation to Roman Catholicism.[16] Marion's saturated phenomenon is a specifically Christian version and does not leave much room for other religious experiences. Richard Kearney, as we will see in the final chapter, instead thinks of Marion and Caputo as too indeterminate and too excessive in their talk about God. Their language becomes so negative and so empty that almost anything can stand in for God. Both are missing a hermeneutic process of ensuring that their visions of God and religion are enabling and peaceful instead of disabling, militant and, violent.[17] This argument is carried further in Shane Mackinlay's recent work on Marion, which is particularly critical of the lack of hermeneutics in Marion.[18]

Increasingly, there are also comments about Marion's claims about the self and love. Kevin Hart's edited volume *Counter-Experiences: Reading Jean-Luc Marion*, which grew out of a conference on Marion's *The Erotic Phenomenon*, deals almost entirely with this particular work. Marion is exhorted both to be less worried about the transgression of the line between theology and philosophy (by Emmanuel Falque) and to be more worried about ethics and politics. Marlène Zarader has raised objections to Marion's definition of the self as passive and devoted to the incoming of the phenomenon.[19] Mackinlay makes this argument much more strongly in *Interpreting Excess*, where he argues that the tension between self and phenomenon regularly collapses in favor of the phenomenon that finally becomes a quasi-Cartesian subject in Marion's work while the self remains entirely passive. Marion's work on this topic (especially in light of his recent work on Augustine) continues to inspire discussion and debate.

Sacraments, Saints, and Sacrifice

Marion has throughout emphasized the philosophical character of his work and seldom explicitly engaged in theology. He has vigorously argued against Janicaud's claim that this is a theological project and he constantly emphasizes the more general (secular) nature of the saturated phenomenon. (And indeed his work has important wider implications for phenomenology, which have been suggested above but will not be explored in greater detail here.) Marion is decidedly not doing apologetics in any traditional sense of the term. He is not merely appropriating philosophical language and insights and then "proving" God's existence or various aspects of Christian faith with philosophical tools and within philosophical paradigms. Yet there are indeed several ways in which Marion's work does make an "argument" for Christian faith. Before considering his (few) explicit statements on this, I will briefly explore some of his recent, more heavily theological, articles and then consider to what extent his thought as a whole might be considered "apologetic" and what that term might mean for Marion's work.

Marion has occasionally employed his phenomenological project for what are essentially phenomenological analyses of "theological" or religious phenomena. I will briefly examine three recent examples, namely the phenomenality of the sacrament, of sacrifice, and of sainthood. All three appear together with other such analyses in his most recent works, *Certitudes négatives* and *Le croire pour le voir*.[20] The titles of these books are themselves significant. The first suggests that it might be possible to be "negatively" certain, certain about uncertainty. The second turns upside down the usual assumption that "seeing is believing" in order to imply that sometimes one must believe (*croire*) in order to be able to see (*voir*). This is in some way then also a response to the claim of some critics that they do not "see" anything where Marion sees God or revelation. Marion responds, as he had already suggested in "The Banality of Saturation" that "the fact or the pretense of not seeing does not prove that there is nothing to see. It can simply suggest that there is indeed something to see, but that in order to see it, it is necessary to learn to see otherwise" (*VR*, 124).

The topic of the sacraments, in general, or the Eucharist, in particular, is not new in Marion's work. Already *God Without Being* contains two chapters reflecting on the Eucharist: "Of the Eucharistic Site of Theology" and "The Present and the Gift" (Chapters 5 and 6). In these early pieces, he argues that theology, as speaking (*logos*) about God (*theos*), must proceed from God and be grounded in the Eucharist, which functions as the locus for the hermeneutics of the divine Word (which ultimately refers to Christ). In the Eucharist, we are enabled to cross from "sign" (word) to the referent (the Word himself). The Eucharist is a gift of God's love and not merely the imagination of the assembled community. Any attempt to "grasp" God in the sacrament is idolatrous. *The Crossing of the Visible* concludes with an analysis of icons, the typology of the cross, and of prayer in a sacramental vein. Icons become the locus where divine and human gaze can cross and envision each other in prayer, where each is open and completely vulnerable to the other. More recently Marion has addressed the topic again more explicitly. In his article "The Phenomenality of the Sacrament," he deals with various historical "models of intelligibility" for understanding the phenomenality of the sacrament.[21] These include the language of substance and accidents, of invisible cause with visible effects, and of signifier and signified. Marion suggests that all three share in common the implication that a sacrament gives itself with complete abandon. The peculiar phenomenality of the sacrament is a phenomenality of abandon. The sacrament becomes an icon of Christ, himself the visible icon of the invisible God whom he manifests. God gives Godself wholly in the sacrament. It becomes the intersection where invisible and visible meet in paradoxical fashion and where the Father gives Godself through the Son in the Spirit to the church. This givenness of the sacrament must be received and accepted by us as given in flesh and body. The language of sacrifice is already quite prominent in this piece, as Marion ends on Christ's kenotic self-givenness on the cross. A more recent reflection turns explicitly to the phenomenality of sacrifice.

This appropriation of phenomenology for the topic of sacrifice was first presented as the Lumen Christi Institute lecture at the University of

Chicago in the spring of 2008 under the title "Sketch of a Phenomeno-logical Concept of Sacrifice" and is now included in revised form as Chapter 4 in *Certitudes négatives*. Marion here applies his phenomenology of the gift to the phenomenon of sacrifice. Similar to the gift, the sacrifice escapes the rationality of the (metaphysical) object. Marion rejects violent interpre-tations of sacrifice (such as a suicide-bomber's self-sacrifice); destruction or dispossession are not truly sacrifice. Instead, he suggests, a sacrifice actu-ally enables a gift to appear in visibility. When the gift becomes misappro-priated as a possession it disappears as gift and its gift-status is hidden or even lost. The sacrifice enables the gift to appear again as such, because it no longer lays claim to the gift or attempts to possess it. The sacrifice allows us to "see" differently. It makes possible the response to the given in which the gift (and ultimately even the giver) is able to appear. He illustrates this with the story of Isaac's sacrifice. God's demand of Abraham shows how Abraham had begun to appropriate the gift of Isaac as his own possession. Abraham's willingness to sacrifice Isaac makes visible again Isaac's status as divine gift. God appears as giver of the gift in the sacrifice. The sacrifice "doubles the gift and confirms it." Sacrifice goes beyond the visible gift to givenness itself.

An article on saints and sainthood may serve as a final example.[22] Here Marion argues that sainthood or holiness is invisible and can never be claimed for oneself. And yet it serves as the crux of the paradox of visibil-ity and invisibility, namely as a way of making the invisible visible in some fashion. The article draws on Marion's earlier analyses of visibility and invisibility, especially in respect to art (especially in *The Crossing of the Visible*, Chapter 3 of *In Excess*, and "What We See and What Appears"). Sainthood always runs the danger of self-idolatry, which immediately disqualifies it. Holiness is a limit-experience similar to death. Both can no longer be articulated when they have been experienced. The article culmi-nates in an analysis of Christ as supreme paradox of holiness. Holiness is the hallmark of God's very phenomenality and Christ is the only perfect icon of this invisible holiness, which becomes visible in Christ. This holi-ness (even Christ's) is so overwhelming that it cannot truly be experienced; it is so excessive that we cannot bear its impact. In fact, the experience re-quires a different sort of rationality to understand, one which is invisible and incomprehensible to "normal" rationality. Holiness remains invisible to any but the eyes of faith.

In all three examples, then, the phenomenology of givenness is em-ployed in order to analyze what might be called "theological" phenomena, namely phenomena that have their specific context and appearance within a setting of faith. These phenomena are not proven philosophically, but are taken for granted (any concerns about their existence or appearance in "real life" or "actuality" are set aside). In all three cases, Marion attempts to illuminate a primarily religious phenomenon with categories he has earlier argued apply more generally (to history, to art, to a general experience of the self or the human neighbor, to love). And, in all cases, the analysis culminates in the same paradox: what is originally invisible or unseen now appears in the visible in some fashion. Phenomenological tools are employed in order to speak of an experience of the invisible. Marion does not explicitly argue for religious phenomena; rather he assumes these phenomena and allows them to appear through his analysis and phenomenological description. One could suggest, then, that this constitutes an attempt at giving coherence and rationality (albeit "phenomenological" and not "metaphysical" rationality) to religious phenomena by applying phenomenological description to them. Such a suggestion is given support by Marion's own occasional claims about the proper nature of "apologetics" or "Christian philosophy."

An Invitation to Meet a Loving God

Marion has at times explored the "rationality" of Christian faith. In a couple of brief articles, he explicitly addresses questions of "apologetics" and the possibility of something like "Christian philosophy" (a term he does not particularly like and does not usually employ).[23] Overall, Marion argues that Christianity can make a unique contribution to more general philosophical thinking and that faith has its own peculiar rationality, which gives it coherence, integrity, and validity. In his two most recent books, he posits it even more explicitly as a way to combat the nihilism of our secular culture and give new meaning to our lives.

In an early article on the possibility of something like "Christian philosophy" (retranslated as Chapter 2 of *The Visible and the Revealed*), Marion insists on various unique contributions of Christianity, insights from Christian faith that would not be possible without it. Christian philosophy has a "heuristic" function in that Christianity contributes "phenomena" to the more general philosophical discussion (and it is the task of "Christian philosophy," assuming there is such a thing, to structure and analyze these phenomena rigorously and to introduce them into the wider philosophical discussion). Primary examples for Marion are the Christian concept of history (developed by Augustine), the concept of the person (as hypostasis), and the notion of self-sacrificial love. Indeed, Marion regards love (especially love as charity) as the peculiarly Christian contribution to philosophy. Although one can now engage in a purely secular philosophical or phenomenological analysis of love, originally it entered philosophy through Christianity. He certainly thinks other such (originally Christian) phenomena are possible. Thus, Christianity makes a unique contribution to phenomenality that cannot be replicated in quite the same fashion by anything else.

Furthermore, Marion insists that Christianity has its own particular "logic," a rationality of love that is unlike philosophical (Cartesian) rationality, but therefore no less valid. He often employs Pascal's notion of the three orders to speak of this.[24] The logic of the world is that of the senses, of experience and emotion. The logic of philosophy is that of reason or the mind (for Pascal this logic was supremely expressed by Cartesian philosophy). The logic of love or charity is that of the heart or of the will. Each of these types of logic has its own order and functions within its own realm. Lower orders cannot access the higher ones that are invisible to them. Each realm or logic has its own rules, which make little sense to those of another order. Following Pascal, Marion claims that the "order of charity" (or the logic of Christian faith) is the highest order and therefore can displace and correct the lower orders and is invisible to them. Ultimately, Christian experience and faith therefore are superior to and go beyond worldly (philosophical) logic and reason. This is not something that can be claimed philosophically, however, as philosophy is confined to the second order, the order of reason. Yet this is clearly a contention that Christian faith has a "rationality" or "coherence," even if this is not the rationality of science or even of secular philosophy. It is a rationality of love that has its own methods and ways of reasoning.

More recently, Marion has explored how this erases some of the traditional distinctions between philosophy and theology.[25] Philosophy (at least as phenomenology) no longer aims to constitute itself as a metaphysics or even as a "scientific" project. Similarly, theology has, for the most part, given up defining itself solely in terms of a concern with the "supernatural." Thus, neither can lay claim to an exclusive rationality to which the other discourse has no access. While for a long time both philosophy and theology were obsessed with reaching "the certainty of the sciences," this is no longer the case:

> May we say today that they both failed? It would be better to admit that they both eventually came to the conclusion that neither of them *should* have ever raised this claim, not only because neither of them could sustain it, but, most importantly, because neither of them had anything to *win* by that pretension. Rationality, for both

of them, may appear much more complex and subtle than what the mere paradigm of science would allow us to reach. Exactly as philosophy had no *need* to consider itself as more certain than mathematics and to assume the transcendental role of imposing the conditions of possibility of its rationality and objectivity, theology has no need either to impose its conclusions by formal constraint or to justify its phenomena as if they were and should be objects, according to the rationality of objectivity.[26]

This is precisely the reason why an apologetics of proof and rational argument not only no longer works, but is utterly undesirable. And he concludes the presentation by suggesting something identical to the much earlier address on Christian philosophy as hermeneutic: "In this way, theology and its related field would only provide phenomenology with additional saturated phenomena, among the many others that by itself phenomenology can already list, constitute and contemplate."

Finally, Marion has at times suggested that there might be a different version of apologetics that invites by its inherent appeal instead of attempting to convince through abstract rationality.[27] Again, this apologetics is one of love, which speaks to the heart and will instead of the mind. Depicting the overwhelming love of God is thus an invitation to respond to that love. Marion describes this as an apologetics of vulnerability (or self-emptying, as in the theological term *kenosis*): It reaches out in love and sacrifice, inviting but not compelling a response, awaiting but knowing it can be refused and even ignored. Although *The Erotic Phenomenon* is not a theological work and tries to stay rigorously phenomenological, Marion does hint in a couple of places in the book (especially in introduction and conclusion) that its inspiration is on some level theological and that theology has a fuller knowledge of this love although it requires philosophical tools for explicating it. All human love ultimately has its source in divine love.

One might suggest, then, that Marion's own philosophy does precisely this: provide an alternative rationality that gives coherence to the phenomena of Christian faith, especially the experience of self-sacrificing love. Much of Marion's phenomenology might be regarded as an attempt to provide an open invitation to Christian faith by showing its inherent love, beauty, and vulnerability instead of compelling through any sort of logical deduction. By employing more generally applicable phenomenological analyses to illuminate and elucidate particular religious experiences, he demonstrates such experiences to be coherent within themselves: maybe paradoxical but not simply irrational. And they are also illuminated in all their dazzling splendor: blinding and excessive, yet perfectly vulnerable in their willingness to give themselves entirely to the point of utter abandon. They invite those who experience or "see" them to envision themselves differently, to know themselves as beloved, and to respond with a move of similar loving self-abandon.

6

Michel Henry: A God of Truth and Life

Michel Henry (1922–2002) was one of the early phenomenologists working in France, more or less contemporaneous with Emmanuel Lévinas and Paul Ricoeur. He is most well-known for developing a "material" phenomenology, or, as he later called it, a "phenomenology of the flesh." Many of his early writings are heavily influenced by the philosophy of Karl Marx. Only his more recent (and final) writings are more explicitly religious.[1] Although some hints of these concerns are present in his earlier works (such as an analysis of Meister Eckhart's mysticism in Section III of his major work *The Essence of Manifestation*), they become much more prominent near the end of his life. Henry concluded his work with three books on Christianity: *I Am the Truth: A Philosophy of Christianity*; *Incarnation: A Philosophy of the Flesh*; and *The Words of Christ*, as well as some shorter articles on similar topics. (These are collected in the final volume of a posthumous four-volume collection published under Marion's direction in the *Épiméthée* series.) In these works, Henry develops what he asserts is a distinctly Christian version of Truth, of Life, and of the Self. He sees these insights as opening the way toward a more "real" phenomenology. Henry's latest works are therefore explicitly apologetic. Although he does not defend Christianity as such, he certainly claims emphatically that Christianity provides the only and exclusive access to Truth, Life, and Reality. (He usually capitalizes these terms to distinguish them from what he defines as "the truth of the world" and its conception of life and reality.)

Like Marion (who although much younger than Henry engaged in these issues earlier and therefore precedes him in this discussion), Henry is particularly interested in what might be called a more radical phenomenology. Unlike Marion, however, he puts this in language of radical immanence, not radical transcendence. While Marion emphasizes the distance of the divine, Henry stresses divine immediacy and indeed seeks to erase distance entirely. Henry comments with approval on Marion's insistence on phenomenology's purity and on his definition of a radical basic principle of phenomenology: "as much reduction, so much givenness."[2] Henry affirmed this principle as quite compatible with his own phenomenological project. While much traditional phenomenology (including, for Henry, that of Heidegger) is focused on appearance, Henry finds that a focus on givenness allows for the self-revelation of affectivity. He also sees merit in Marion's emphasis on reduction in a way that is not ontic (14). Appearance becomes reduced to itself and begins to manifest its own givenness. "Appearing" is thus no longer about perception of something separate from us, but about the self-revelation of appearing itself. "Classical phenomenology has never clearly seen that what appears in appearing is first and necessarily appearing itself" (17). Henry applauds Marion's rejection of being as primary and his focus on the appeal, although Henry reads this as an appeal of Life, in which the Living are called to Life and realize themselves as nothing other than it (25).

The Essence of Manifestation was Henry's first major work and already outlined his critique of phenomenology and its radical proposal of immanence and affectivity. He speaks of utter immanence as the invisible, that which is closest to us, yet does not appear as a separate object we might observe. Phenomenology, so he contends, has been too preoccupied with "objects" that appear as things in the world and are thus separate from the "subject" who observes them. Even Heidegger's analysis of human Dasein does not overcome this essential separation between self and observed object or world. Henry instead proposes a phenomenology where consciousness and what it is conscious *of* are not separated, where phenomenality and the phenomenon are identical. He speaks of an invisible that has its own phenomenality and is not just a version of the visible, i.e., what is "not yet" visible or the "underside" of the "nothing." Already in *Essence of Manifestation*, Henry calls this invisible—which cannot be observed as separate and is the very source of phenomenality—"life." Life is experienced immediately in the body, in the self-affectivity of the flesh as it experiences emotions of pain and pleasure. Suffering is not first of all suffering of some external object, but is directly manifested and experienced in the flesh as such. For example, no separation exists between the consciousness of pain and the pain itself. The consciousness or experience of the pain is precisely the pain. The two are one and the same. This is true of all intensely felt emotion and of our very life itself, which is not something separate from us.

Henry's phenomenology has become known as "material phenomenology," which is also the title of a collection of essays where he outlines what distinguishes his own proposal of material phenomenology from Husserl's more traditional version (called "hyletic phenomenology" in the text). Henry engages in a close reading of Husserl's texts to show that Husserl hints at the invisible and the materiality of life, but ultimately does not explicate them. For example:

> Husserl sought to think the movement of life and did so in magnificent terms . . . [Yet] Husserl does not think about the movement of life by starting from the essence of life as something identical to itself; instead, he starts from the only mode of manifestation that he knows: an ek-stasis and the protention of the future. Thereby the movement of life is totally falsified. It is no longer *the drive, which is born from life in its struggle with itself* and from life driven back against itself and overwhelmed by itself. Such a life can no longer maintain itself in the suffering of its suffering of itself; it *aspires to change itself*, to become other. (*MP*, 39)

Instead of life as a "force," Husserl thinks of life as "regard" or gaze of perception. For Henry this is deeply problematic because it misses the essence of life entirely. Consequently, the phenomenological method is unable to analyze the *pathos* of life because this pathos cannot appear as a "perception." Subjectivity becomes objectified as something that can be perceived and placed as separate from our innermost self. It thus also ignores the real living work and the physical pain of the laboring body (*MP*, 99).

Within *Material Phenomenology* Henry also analyzes the experience of the other, an increasingly important topic in contemporary phenomenology. He wonders how it would be possible to "suffer with" the other in Husserl's account in the *Fifth Cartesian Meditation*. Experience of the other, for Husserl, is a kind of perception. Henry sees Husserl's "failure" as twofold: First, the other person is reduced to something like an object of perception. Second, Husserl's view assumes "separate spheres of ownness" that make it impossible to conceive how individual subjectivities may interact with each other. Husserl's notion of the ego is defined "in terms of intentionality, *which is ultimately to say, from a metaphysics of representation*" (*MP*, 117). Henry instead advocates what he calls a "phenomenology of community" in which all members share common access to the reality that makes them what they are: life. They do not do so by consent or via perception, but by virtue of being alive. Henry says, "If it is true that phenomenology does not deal with things but the how of their givenness and thus with pure manifestation as such, this is because the life about which we are speaking is not a thing, a being of a certain kind, given with a set of properties and functions such as mobility, nutrition, excretion, and so on. Life is a how, both a mode of revelation and revelation itself" (*MP*, 119). Life gives itself, as such, and never becomes separated from itself: "No road leads to life except life itself. In life, no road leads outside of itself. By this, we mean that it does not allow what is living to cease living. Life is absolute subjectivity inasmuch as it experiences itself and is nothing other than that experience. It is the pure fact of experiencing itself immediately and without any distance" (*MP*, 120). He contends that community is only possible through sharing in common this original givenness where everyone participates in life together precisely through feeling alive. This does not mean that individuals become indistinguishable as mere expressions of the same life. Rather, Henry shows that it is still possible to speak of individuals within this community of life if we no longer rely on traditional definitions of the ego (as body or independent intentionality), but instead explore the force of self-affectivity. Community arises not "in the world" but "in life."[3] We experience community only as we share in the very pathos of life: "The pathos-with is the broadest form of every conceivable community" (*MP*, 134).[4] *Material Phenomenology* does not explicate this in any sense as Christian or draw on any Christian sources. Yet Henry will later articulate the same account of inter-subjectivity in *I Am the Truth* and *Words of Christ* and there claim that they are only possible in shared access to the divine life in Christ.

Truth

I Am the Truth lays out Henry's "Christian" phenomenology most comprehensively, although he expands on and also qualifies some of its aspects in *Incarnation* and *Words of Christ* (especially the issues of the "flesh" and of Christ as the "word of God"). The status of these works as "Christian" is to some extent ambivalent. As discussed in more detail later, Henry is definitely not engaging in traditional Christian theology and has very little (if anything) positive to say about traditional apologetic endeavors. He also disregards any insights of biblical criticism or biblical scholarship in general and occasionally dismisses such research in rather lapidary fashion.[5] The first sentence of his *I Am the Truth* is: "I do not intend to ask whether Christianity is 'true' or 'false,' or to establish, for example, the former hypothesis" (*IT*, 1). Yet the work is explicitly about Christianity. Its subtitle is "Toward a Philosophy of Christianity" and the main title is a reference to Christ's words from John 14:6 (this is even more striking in the French version, which has a large image of a mosaic of Christ's face on the front cover; similarly, the image of a painting of Christ is on the cover of *Paroles du Christ*). Henry continues in the second sentence of the introduction to lay out what he does intend to do:

> Rather, what will be the question here is what Christianity considers as truth—what kind of truth it offers to people, what it endeavors to communicate to them, not as a theoretical and indifferent truth but as the essential truth that by some mysterious affinity is suitable for them, to the point that it alone is capable of assuring them salvation. We are trying to understand the form of truth that circumscribes the domain of Christianity, the milieu in which it spreads, the air that it breathes, one might say—because there are many sorts of truths, many ways of being true or false. (*IT*, 1)

Henry then forcefully demonstrates what I am calling here a new or different version of apologetics: it is, so to speak, a performance of Christian truth starting from within Christian experience instead of a demonstration of or proof for Christian truth from an allegedly objective (outside) viewpoint. It is a phenomenological explication of truth as it is experienced, not a rational argument that seeks to demonstrate its verity through logical deduction or empirical evidence.

Henry begins *I Am the Truth* by contrasting this "Truth of Christianity" to "the truth of the world," with which it has nothing in common. The truth of the world is deceptive and does not actually provide direct access to truth. It is without meaning or value and certainly without life. The Truth of Christianity, instead, is a thoroughly phenomenological truth in that it does not make a distinction between manifestation and what is manifested. For Christianity, phenomenon and phenomenality are identical. This clearly refers back to the criticism of Husserlian and Heideggerian phenomenology Henry had articulated in *The Essence of Manifestation* and *Material Phenomenology*. The truth of the world is dual in nature: It assumes a separation between "what shows itself and the fact of self-showing" (*IT*, 13). The world is always external to us and its truth different from us, a product of our vision or imagination. Things do not give themselves in their reality, but only as an image or appearance or phenomenon. Henry suggests that any form of truth is passing and transitory, except that of Christianity, which is a pure, eternal, and absolute phenomenological truth (*IT*, 20, 23). Christianity's Truth is manifestation and phenomenality itself. It implies no distance. This Truth of Christianity is itself Life. Later in the work, Henry will come to identify this Truth and Life with God. He makes a strict division between the "truth of the world" (which is that of the science inaugurated by Galileo or of Western philosophy in general) and the "Truth of Christianity" (which is the phenomenology of life and direct experience of the flesh).

Occasionally, Henry seems to suggest that these might simply be two separate and distinct truths. For example, he wonders, "Might we rather say, either to avoid polemics or to remove a real difficulty, that Christianity and biology are not speaking about the same thing, that their discourses do not interfere with each other, that any comparison between them makes no sense?" (*IT*, 36). Henry goes on to reject such a solution, however, as that would posit two different but separate discourses or truths. He insists emphatically that "there is only one Life, that of Christ, which is also that of God and men. . . . What escapes science is that sensible qualities never exist as the simple properties of an object. Before being projected onto that object, they are pure subjective impressions that in fact presuppose sensibility, that invisible essence of Life that is Christian Truth" (*IT*, 37). The Truth of Christianity and that of science are radically different from each other. Science misses life because it has no access to real feeling and pathos. Much of his argument for Christianity, then, actually seems to be an argument against the detrimental influences of science and technology upon our culture.[6] Be that as it may, Christianity is proposed as the source for a far more adequate (in fact the only appropriate) conception of life and affection, one in which we are not separated from our bodies and experiences, from nature or other people: "This phenomenological Life that experiences itself, this actual life that is ours, that inhabits each of our joys and sufferings, desires and fears, and above all the most humble of our sensations, therefore constitutes the great absence in the philosophical and cultural tradition to which we belong" (*IT*, 42). Christianity does not flee reality, in Henry's view, but provides the only authentic access to it.

The Truth of Christianity is self-revelation or, as Henry will call it later, auto-affection. "Christianity is nothing other," he affirms, "than the awe-inspiring and meticulous theory of this givenness of God's self-revelation shared with man" (*IT*, 25). We cannot access divine Revelation through our physical vision or through thought. It does not appear in the world as a phenomenon, but rather is Life revealing itself. According to Henry, it is the only access to life that we have, the only true reality there is, and the only place where we could fully experience love and enjoyment. Henry consequently rejects the "truth of the world" as inadequate and even false because it is always distanced from reality, from the concrete and immediate experience of the flesh in suffering and joy. Instead, in Henry's view, Christianity speaks of an authentic phenomenological experience of reality and is able to establish the sole valid phenomenology of the human person as a "son of God," a participant of the divine life. Although this life is ours as human beings from the beginning, we have rejected and ignored it and must recover this experience through a new birth and salvation in Christ.

Life and Flesh

Henry argues that most of Western thinking, whether scientific or philosophical, has missed the issue of Life and misunderstands what life is. As just mentioned, he sees this as particularly true of Galilean science, but he also criticizes Heidegger's philosophy of Dasein (although he is also informed by it in important ways) as the culmination of philosophy's ignoring of phenomenological life. He therefore proposes what he considers a radical phenomenology of the flesh, where life is understood as self-affection, experiencing oneself as affected. He claims that this direct relationship between consciousness and its self-affectivity has never been discovered or considered seriously in the history of Western philosophical thought. Science, by examining molecules and atoms, has made matters far worse, by reducing life to material particles instead of real experience. Even Heidegger's analysis of "being-in-the-world" still considers life from the outside and does not realize its power of self-revelation. Henry criticizes "diverse ways of slandering life," which he associates with biology and various philosophical approaches. Instead, Henry attempts to construct a "phenomenology of life" which is a phenomenology of the flesh.

This phenomenology of the flesh is not about the visible materiality of the body but about the experience of self-affectivity. While the body refers to our externally visible physicality, the flesh instead designates our inner experience of the body: of our feeling ourselves "touched" and affected. This experience of self-affectivity is expressed in emotion and action. In his view, Western science and philosophy have made an arbitrary and false distinction between life (as visible molecules and biological processes) and the ego exercising power over (or being subject to) these external processes and materials. Science deals only with the body, not the flesh. In Henry's view, instead, Life refers to something internal and invisible (what happens in the flesh): It is what generates me and makes me myself, I participate in it and it makes possible all my experiences. There is an essential passivity to this experience: We "suffer" or undergo Life—that is, it is something that comes to us from the outside because we do not give ourselves our own life and do not generate ourselves. We are affected by Life; we experience our emotions and "passions" as coming to us, as generated *within* ourselves but not *by* ourselves. Humans are not primarily beings in the world, but rather they are generated by "Life" itself. Henry explicates this "Life" (which he equates with "truth" and "reality") as quasi-divine. He links "God" as the source of "Life" with humans as "livings" (or living beings minus the ontological connotations of that expression) who are generated by this Life and live only within it through an analysis of Christ as the "arch-son" who gives access to Life for all other "livings" by being eternally generated in the divine life and thus showing all other sons how to realize their participation in this source of Life. In this context, Henry draws a distinction between "creation" and "generation." While the world is "created," humans are "generated." They participate in Life (and have flesh) not by virtue of their physical birth (no human can actually create or give birth to another human) but only by their participation in the essence of Life (i.e., in God).

Henry emphatically insists that this interpretation of life/flesh is not "world-denying" and that it does not ignore materiality. Instead, it opens up the only proper path to materiality and fleshly reality, a path that has been ignored or denied by scientific and philosophical thought. He judges the usual division established between the real (material, visible) and the imaginary (unreal, invisible) to be artificial and incoherent. For Henry, there is only the one reality of life and the flesh, a concrete (but invisible) materiality, namely that of joy and suffering, of pleasure and pain, thus of our most immediate experiences and actions. One might say that for Henry the world and the body are part and parcel of life itself. It is Western science, instead, that stresses a false reality of "evidence" and "visibility" or "appearance" but is blind to the actions and feelings that underlie it and alone make it possible: "In the field opened by Galilean science, there are material bodies, microphysical particles, molecules, amino acid chains, neurons, and so on, but no Self. In the field opened by modern science, there is no person" (*IT*, 262). In contrast to this emphasis on "material bodies" and "particles," which separates artificially between "soul" and "body" or "materiality" and "consciousness," Henry advocates a more unified view. Only the flesh can grant ipseity (or "selfhood") to the Self. He asserts:

> Because it designates the phenomenological effectuation of the auto-revelation of Life in the ipseity in which each transcendental Self maintains its possibility, because it is nothing other than the phe-

nomenological materiality of revelation of self which makes of each Self a Self, the flesh is linked to it as its most interior phenomenological condition of possibility, to the point where it becomes identical with it. There is no Self without flesh—but no flesh that does not carry in it a Self. (*I*, 178)

Self and flesh are one. This reality of the flesh is one of suffering and affection, constituted by the experiences of joy, sadness, pleasure, pain, and so forth. Our experience of the flesh is a direct experience of material reality. The flesh is so immediate to us that we cannot separate from it.

Incarnation is far more explicitly phenomenological (in a traditional sense) than the other two works, although its central contentions are in line with them. Henry takes on both Husserl and Heidegger in detail and also recovers some insights from Descartes filtered through his own phenomenological reading. He analyzes the phenomenological issues of "appearing," "impression," "life," "image," "visibility," "sensation," "body" and "flesh," appealing to Descartes, Husserl, Merleau-Ponty, and Maine de Biran, but also Irenaeus, Tertullian, and various other Christian thinkers.

The third part of the book, "Phenomenology of the Incarnation: Salvation in the Christian Sense," applies the analyses of the first two parts to the language of sin, life, and salvation, ending with a chapter on the mystical body of Christ. Henry talks about sin as a forgetting of our divine sonship, our source in life, and as a denial of the divine Life that flows in us. The flesh, which is our most intimate subjectivity, shows both our perdition and our salvation. We "sin" when we forget our original givenness of life as the source of our own life and instead become preoccupied with the "things of the world" which are external to us and distract us from our affectivity and our flesh. Instead of realizing that we are "transcendental living Selves," we treat each other as objective bodies, as things in the world that can be manipulated at will. This is why the "Word" (Christ) does not come "into the world" but into flesh, why it becomes incarnate, which means "enfleshed." Again, Henry draws a radical distinction between creation and generation. The world and all within it are created (which we can also only claim when we have realized God as the source of life), but our flesh is generated out of the divine life. This is what it means to be made in the image of God.

Salvation then becomes the recovery of our condition as Sons of Life, our realization of the radical passivity of the Life that generates us and in which we are generated, which is most fundamentally what we are. Salvation is deification, the divinization of our flesh, which is the Life of God. Henry uses the term of the "mystical body" of Christ to designate our experience of the other and our oneness with Christ as the one who communicates the divine life to us and reminds us of our generation within it. Again, Henry is clear that this communal experience of the mystical body does not erase individuality.

Christ, Sin, and Salvation

In *I Am the Truth*, Henry had already dealt with some of these issues. In that earlier treatment he defined sin as a "forgetting" of our divine sonship and an ignoring of the life we have as sons of Life. We are all "sons within the son"—the Arch-Son, Christ. We become a self by realizing the source of our life in God. We lose ourselves when we neglect or forget this source. Here Henry relies primarily on John and Paul to make his case. We only become truly ourselves and, in fact, only communicate with others through Christ. He insists that Christ's injunction "what you do for the least of these you do for me" is "not a metaphor," but to be taken quite literally (*IT*, 17). Our own "ipseity," or selfhood, is only possible in Christ (through the mediation of the divine life). Our very essence is the divine life, which generates us eternally. Christ is the way to Life because he is Life and Truth itself. This Life is one's experience of oneself, precisely what constitutes our innermost selfhood and identity.

Henry is absolutely insistent that there is only one kind of life, the life of God. Thus, insofar as we have life, are alive, are "livings," we have God's life flowing through us (communicated through Christ). Yet why do we so seldom realize this? We tend to forget our condition as sons of Life. Henry claims that we have no clue what we mean when we say "I" or "me" and that philosophy cannot help us with this problem because it solely speaks of the ego. Henry here uses Lévinas's insight that "me" is in the accusative form and claims that it designates our generation from the divine Life. We cannot validly speak of ourselves in the nominative. Yet we can become an "I" that has certain powers that we experience as our own, although they are actually given to us by "transcendental and absolute Life." The ego cannot be the ground of its own being. This "transcendental illusion" of thinking we can ground ourselves causes us to forget our condition as sons, our inherent dependency. This is, in Henry's view, why the Scriptures draw such a stark division between being "of the world" and "being of God." By "caring" about the world and its concerns (a reference both to Heidegger and to Matthew 6:25–34), we forget Life. To forget Life is to forget one's Self. Projecting ourselves into the world, projecting an "image" of ourselves, is to lose the radical immediacy of the self "submerged in itself" (*IT*, 149). Ultimately Henry seems to locate this "forgetting" in birth. We do not "get" our own condition because we have forgotten our selves. Thus, ego and self, as well as Self and Life, become separated from each other. The forgetting happened long before us as an "immemorial" event. Yet "Christianity asserts the possibility that someone may surmount this radical Forgetting and rejoin the absolute Life of God—this Life that preceded the world and its time, eternal Life. Such a possibility signifies nothing other than salvation." Salvation means "to rejoin this absolute Life, which has neither beginning nor end, . . . to unite with it, identify with it, live anew this Life that is not born and does not die—to live like it does, in the way it lives, and not to die" (*IT*, 151). Salvation is rebirth into the divine Life.

This is what Christianity means by being born again: It is a re-discovery of our own life as within the Life of God. Yet we cannot access God through reason. Henry emphatically rejects the traditional proofs for God's existence:

> The fact that access to God cannot be achieved in and through thought, and in rational thought less than any other, renders absurd the very project of demanding proofs for God's existence. Here we come upon one of the great weaknesses of traditional religious philosophy: the ruinous confusion it creates between, on the one hand, the concrete internal possibility of effective access to God, and on the other, the prior establishment of his existence from a rational standpoint. (*IT*, 153)

Proofs for God's existence completely miss the point because the divine can only be accessed through life itself. We come to know God in our hearts. Faith opens us to God. Henry insists that we need to experience a "second birth." We must be born of God. "Salvation consists of carrying God within oneself while being God's son in this new sense"—abiding in God (*IT*, 161). We become "livings" through realizing the divine Life within us. This recognition or realization is given us through the Arch-Son, Christ. Life is our "inner presupposition" but must be recognized by giving up our own autonomy and defeating the ego in the transformation of re-birth into the divine Life.

This leads to the Christian ethic of love and works of mercy (*IT*, 166). One finds oneself precisely by forgetting the self in care for the poor and outcast. Mercy leads to salvation because it reconnects with the life that flows in all of us. Reconnecting with invisible Life, living in the truth, means to reveal God in loving action. Henry suggests that this is what is at the heart of Christ's and Paul's controversies with the Pharisees: a rejection of the laws "of the world" in favor of the law of love. Christian ethic is nothing but a radical exposure to (and of) Life. Life is love, which is why the "highest commandment" is one of love. Loving God, living in God's love, and practicing love means to share in God's life. Thus, interestingly enough, for Henry as for Marion and to some extent also Ricoeur, the crux of the Christian message is love, even if he spends less time than the other two articulating this claim. Love will also be at the heart of God and faith for Lacoste, Falque, and to some extent for Chrétien. And Westphal, Caputo, and Kearney all share this concern for the poor and outcast, a concern that is, of course, also already evident in Lévinas and Derrida.

Word

In *Words of Christ*, as the title suggests, Henry is interested in Christ and in what Christ says about himself as the "Word" of God. The claim of the incarnation is central to this work: What does it mean for Christ to be both human and divine and thus for his words to be both as well? How can we, as humans, hear divine words and understand them? And how would we recognize them as proceeding from God or being divine in some fashion? Henry thus proceeds in several careful steps: First, he examines Christ's words as those of a human being speaking to other humans in their own language and about their own human condition. Already in this first step these words turn out to be rather unsettling in regard to what it means to be human. Then he analyzes Christ's words as those of someone speaking as a human being to humans in their own language, but no longer about them but about himself as the Messiah and Word of God. Third, he considers how Christ's words might differ from human speech: In what sense are they divine? Finally, he wonders how humans would be able to understand these words as coming from God.

In many ways, his treatment relies on his earlier explorations in *I Am the Truth* and *Incarnation*. Yet, in important ways, this work is actually more explicitly Christian than the previous ones: For one, in response to the criticism that his earlier treatment relied too heavily on John's "high Christology" for its claims and thus was too abstract, Henry cites almost entirely from texts from the synoptic Gospels in his final book.[7] Second, many of the more pantheistic-sounding connotations of his earlier treatment of Christ are tempered and qualified and Christ's role as "Arch-Son" of Life and his distinction from the sonship of other humans overall are clarified. Throughout the book, Henry quotes extensively from the scriptures (especially from the synoptic Gospels) for his analysis.

Henry is emphatic that Christianity is not merely "one form of 'spirituality' among others" (*WC*, 20). It does not constitute simply a different or better way of living in the world, but rather, requires a radical break with the world. Christ's words "de-compose" the world and turn upside down common distinctions between the visible and the invisible.[8] Christ severs all natural links with the world and completely reverses its logic and rationality (the Beatitudes serve as one prime example of this). The realm of the invisible (the "kingdom of heaven") replaces the realm of the visible and obvious. Henry even suggests that certain philosophical insights about the invisible stem from Christianity (he cites as examples Descartes, Kant, and Husserl). The most radical reversal concerns again the internal: emotions, desires, feelings, affections. The human condition is supremely expressed in these paradoxical reversals. All reciprocity and "normal" human relations are abolished here as secondary and inauthentic, subject to lies and manipulation. Slowly we recognize through Christ's words that our true being and reality lies in the divine life, that we are "sons of God."

Henry goes on to show how the radical nature of Christ's message begins to raise questions about his identity. Christ not only claims to be the locus in which all humans find themselves generated by the divine life, but as Henry examines in multiple passages, Christ aligns himself with the divine life or claims to have divine knowledge and powers. Christ's message, which so obviously entails a radical change of life—as in the injunction to love one's enemies—also promises the power to make this change. This "power" lies in the communication of the very life of God (which is love itself). Henry does admit that Christ's radical claims, as expressed in the Gospels, demand (then as today) some sort of justification. They are justified first by their radical reversal of all our perceptions and assumptions and by granting the power to live in accordance with them. Second, they are justified by the truth of their origin in God. Ultimately Henry will claim that these words justify themselves. Throughout the Gospels Christ insists that his message is given legitimacy by God. The Pharisees rightly recognize this as blasphemy because Christ identifies himself with God. Christ speaks not the "words of the world," but "the words of Life."

In this context especially, Henry challenges common philosophical and especially phenomenological assumptions about language: Philosophy has usually assumed that one can only talk about what presents itself within the world as an object. In Henry's view, this way of appearing is particular to the "world" and it is by no means the only or even an authentic manner of appearing. Worldly appearing is problematic because it speaks of everything as exterior and different from us. It also makes us "indifferent to it"—we don't really care about it—objectivity cannot assign value. Furthermore, this appearing cannot ground its own existence. All this (externality, indifference, lack of grounding) is also implied by the common referential dimension of language, where we are always talking to someone *about something*. In contrast, the words of life speak directly to us. They are not "about" something. They are not separate from or exterior to us. Furthermore, they unite instead of separating. Christ's words are the words of Truth and Life; they do not deceive.

They are also immediate. In them, suffering is experienced directly and not communicated through images or representation. Henry here appeals to his earlier analyses of the immediacy and self-affection of the flesh. Truth and Life are utterly immediate and immanent. In Christ "saying" and "said" cannot be separated (as Lévinas distinguished them). Christ himself is the word of God and self-reveals the divine Life, which is precisely why this is only possible if it is fueled and suffused with infinite Life. Absolute Life is a Self: Christ. Henry here again distinguishes between generation and creation. The world is created; life is generated (and uncreated). When Genesis is read in light of the Gospel of John, it also reveals these two processes of creation and generation. As the self-revelation of God, Christ is, in fact, God's own self-consciousness and self-knowledge.

Henry concludes his final book by examining the difficulty for humans to hear the divine words, as is evident even in the resistance to Christ's preaching recorded in the Gospels. He employs the parable of the sower, which explicitly refers to the "hearing of the Word" to illustrate the kinds of evils that can intervene and hinder our hearing. Christ's interpretation of the parable shows, however, that the evil really resides in our heart and therefore is ultimately our own responsibility. Although we are radically powerless on our own, we can "hear" by relying on Christ's working in us through our own condition as sons. We do not ground our existence; it is given to us as a gift. Hatred of the Light offered by Christ is the supreme rejection of Life. We can hear Christ's words by recovering our condition as sons of God generated from the divine Life. There is thus no distinction between speaking the word and acting it. Christ's speaking is itself reality and therefore is able to accomplish actions. Ultimately, the hearing of the word is accomplished by being united with it in love, partaking of it, hearing it in one's heart through the Spirit.

The phenomenon of religious experience is validated by doing the word of God and by experiencing its truth within oneself. One lives within the life of God eucharistically: participating in the body and blood of Christ, his flesh being incarnate in us as we identify with his divine Word of Life. Henry cites Christ's words "This is my body" as the ones most powerfully affirmative of the identity between speaking and acting in Christ. He here resumes the eucharistic imagery of the mystical body of Christ that he had already employed at the end of *Incarnation*. To identify with the flesh and body of Christ is to identify with the eternal Word of God and thus with the very Life of God: eternal life.

A Philosophy of Christianity?

Henry insists over and over again that the Christian texts are absolutely unique and the Christian experience identifies the very source of Life and of true phenomenality. It is from this Christian perspective that he criticizes Husserl, Heidegger, Merleau-Ponty, and others. Christianity gives us access to our true self, our true nature, and also provides a useful critique to contemporary culture and its obsession with objects. His critique of this culture and especially its blind belief in the truths of science and the progress of technology are put in the starkest terms:

> In the field opened by modern science, there is no person. . . . On the contrary, the obsolete knowledge of Christianity, a knowledge that is two millennia old, furnishes us not with entirely limited and useless data about humans: today *it alone* can tell us, in the midst of the general mental confusion, what man is . . . Because biology and science in general know nothing about God, they don't know anything about the living transcendental Self drawing its essence from life and without which no person is possible. (*IT*, 262, 264; emphasis mine)

Christianity alone can give us a sense of what it means to be a person. Henry is deeply critical of the "anti-Christian world" in which we are living and of the "scientific reductionism," exacerbated by modern philosophy, which has led us there. In this world, human beings become automatons and robots. Unbridled capitalism creates tremendous economic injustice because it no longer cares about the workers as human beings. The "hyper-development of modern technology" destroys any real work and "sweeps man away from the surface of the earth" (*IT*, 272). We live in a world of simulation and appearances that has lost all access to reality: "This is the marvel—virtual reality—that is going to seduce the inhabitants of the earth, the work of false prophets and false messiahs. They will make extraordinary machines that will do everything men and women do so as to make them believe that they are just machines themselves" (*IT*, 274). Henry employs the language of the biblical book of Revelation to paint these disasters of the contemporary world, which he suggests are an instance of radical evil that is moving toward erasing humanity and life entirely:

> People debased, humiliated, despised and despising themselves, trained in school to despise themselves, to count for nothing—just particles and molecules; admiring everything lesser than themselves and execrating everything that is greater than themselves. Everything worthy of love and adoration. People reduced to simulacra, to idols that feel nothing, to automatons. And replaced by them—by computers and robots. People chased out of their work and their homes, pushed into corners and gutters, huddled on subway benches, sleeping in cardboard boxes. People replaced by abstractions, by economic entities, by profits and money. People treated mathematically, digitally, statistically, counted like animals and counting for much less. People turned away from Life's Truth, caught in all the traps and marvels where this life is denied, ridiculed, mimicked, simulated—absent. People given over to the insensible, become themselves insensible, whose eyes are empty as a fish's. Dazed people, devoted to specters and spectacles that always expose their own invalidity and bankruptcy; devoted to false knowledge, reduced to empty shells, to empty heads—to "brains." People whose emotions and loves are just glandular secretions. People who have been liberated by making them think their sexuality is a natural process, the site and place of their infinite Desire. People whose responsibility and dignity have no definite site anymore. People who in the general degradation will envy the animals. *People* will want to die—but not *Life*. It is not just any god today who is still able to save us, but— when the shadow of death is looming over the world—the One who is Living. (*IT*, 275; trans. modified)

Christianity alone gives us access to this Living One and to true personhood.

This is a forceful argument for Christianity, then, but in a very different sense than traditional apologetics, a project Henry rejects entirely. Instead of arguing *for* Christianity, Henry employs Christianity as the sole and authoritative source for an essentially phenomenological account of the materiality and self-affection of the body. It is primarily in asserting that this phenomenological account is found *only* in Christianity and in using it so heavily as a source of description of this "life" that affects itself, that Henry's thinking ultimately "defends" Christianity. He argues for it not by applying philosophical parameters of truth to the Christian content, but by showing it to be the primary and only adequate source for what he regards as the most fundamental phenomenological issue at the heart of our very existence and of great concern to everyone: access to life and human self-identity. If truly only Christianity gives access to life and if we are all "sons of God" in some fashion and derive all life directly from God and through the divine sonship of which Christ is the exemplar, then Christianity must in some sense be absolutely mandatory for everyone. Henry does not argue that all people must become Christians, but such a conclusion appears to follow smoothly from his account (in fact, in some ways all "livings" are crypto-Christians, sons of the divine life).[9] In order to have access to Life, in order to feel our deepest sufferings and joys, in order to recover our status as divine sons of Life, we must recognize our loss of Life and of the divine and must return and be "saved" through participating in the Life of the Arch-Son. It is quite evident that for Henry there is no other access to Life or Truth (or Reality) but in this way.

Henry makes it abundantly clear that he regards Christianity as unique in this regard. Repeatedly, he insists on its absolutely singular character. He makes it very obvious that he is not engaged in a general phenomenology of religion or of religious experience, but that he is drawing from Christianity for a more general phenomenological project. For example, he claims that "in the realm of thought, it is paradoxically Christianity that brings it [knowledge about humanity]. Among religious beliefs more than two thousand years old, not to mention superstitions, *Christianity is today the only belief that instructs man about himself*" (*IT*, 134; emphasis mine). Christianity alone gives us access to ourselves in face of a culture that seeks to reduce us to automata. Henry also often emphasizes the absolute singularity of Christ. Christ's teaching is unique in the history of religions (*WC*, 44). Certainly this raises all kinds of problematic issues for inter-religious dialogue or for a more general phenomenology of religion, but without a doubt it constitutes a forceful argument for the "Truth" of Christian faith.

Furthermore, Henry repeatedly emphasizes that Christianity, or the "Truth" of "Life," justifies itself and requires no outside proof. The Scriptures need no exterior referent or confirmation because God speaks in them directly and we are able to hear them in our hearts. Although they are not identical with our joy and suffering, they embrace these feelings and our desires and in them we can hear the divine.[10] While normal human language finds credible what corresponds to an exterior reality and rejects what does not seem to do so, it cannot ever justify or prove that reality (nor confirm the correspondence of language to it). Yet Life itself is immediate to our existence and requires no further proof precisely because we live it. We know that we have not given ourselves this life but that it is a gift from the source of life. Thus, our very life is direct proof of the divine life flowing in us. The divine word at work within us both justifies the legitimacy of Christ's words and the validity of the Scriptures (*WC*, 119). The spirit testifies within us to the truth of this word, while evil attempts to convince us otherwise. The phenomenon of religious experience thus testifies to itself and cannot be invalidated. In doing the will of God, one is able to certify the authenticity of the divine word.

In that sense, then, Janicaud is right in perceiving a "theological turn" in Henry's work.[11] Henry clearly maintains that Christianity is "true" and that its Truth, in fact, is the only one giving direct access to fundamental human experience. He justifies his use of religious texts and imagery by arguing that these give access to new domains of experience unknown by traditional philosophy and in so doing enlighten or possibly even invalidate philosophy:

> We are in the presence of a question which we have qualified as decisive, although paradoxically it is never posed by philosophy. If such a question must take on the importance that we present, it is necessary to make this observation: taking under consideration certain fundamental religious themes permits us to discover an immense domain, unknown by the thought that is called rational. Far from opposing itself to a truly free reflection, Christianity would confront traditional philosophy and its canonical corpus with their limits, if not to say with their blindness. (*WC*, 68)

Thus, Christianity gives access to a realm and to phenomena that are completely unknown to (rational) philosophy. Christianity expands and challenges traditional philosophy. It is not a threat to philosophy, but rather points us to an area of inquiry of which philosophy has so far remained unaware and blind. Henry is not giving us a merely personal theological reflection, but he is providing a philosophical argument that explicitly attempts to apply the insights of Christianity to phenomenology. When Henry claims that only Christianity speaks authentically of the materiality of human flesh and of the self-affecting experience of human life in its revelation of all humans as children of the divine life, he is engaged in an apologetic argument. While this argument may not employ philosophy in order to show Christianity's coherence and truth, as more traditional apologetic endeavors did, it employs Christianity in order to show phenomenology's coherence and Truth. Although this may constitute a reversal of traditional apologetic endeavors, it still regards the "Truth" of Christianity as an absolutely essential topic for a philosophical exercise.

7

Jean-Louis Chrétien: A God of Speech and Beauty

Jean-Louis Chrétien's writings are a powerful example of the character of what I have called a new type of apologetics. In no way does he ever engage in anything like proofs for God's existence, evidence for the validity of religious experience, or any consideration of the rational coherence of an idea of the divine. And yet his work is imbued and overflows with Christian imagery and references to Christian sources. Even when he is not addressing explicitly religious themes, his poetic language has the flavor and tonality of Christian mysticism. Chrétien (born in 1952) is one of the youngest of the thinkers treated here, yet he has already published multiple works on quite diverse topics. The books translated into English so far include one on memory (*The Unforgettable and the Unhoped For*), two on speech (*The Call and the Response*; *The Ark of Speech*), and one on art (*Hand to Hand: Listening to the Work of Art*). His other French publications include works on such diverse topics as the promise, how to read the Scriptures, the beauty of painting, the responsibility of response, love, the body, and more reflections on the voice and on speech.[1] Chrétien is a thoroughly phenomenological thinker with fine attunement to our most intimate experiences, yet he is particularly interested in the kinds of phenomena that phenomenology has not traditionally investigated, ones that are at the very limit of phenomenality, especially those connected to aesthetic and spiritual experiences. His writings evoke in the reader a sense of admiration for the beautiful even in experiences of pain and loss. In some ways, he might be likened to Michel Henry (although he is also quite critical of him) in his interest in the human flesh and the intimacy of corporeal experience, including its vulnerability and "woundedness." Yet in other ways he preserves Lévinas's stress on alterity by emphasizing throughout that the call precedes us and that even the experience of touch always implies the other and is thus not an individual and isolated experience.

Overall, one could say that Chrétien is particularly interested in phenomena that are hidden and not obvious and he seeks to describe them faithfully in a way that shows us how their hiddenness is linked to what we often take as more obvious. Thus, he explores the "immemorial," the "unforgettable," and the "unhoped for" (in four essays collected under that title) as much as the "unheard-of" (in *The Ark of Speech*). He often reflects on nakedness and woundedness in places where we might not first look for them (for example, in the voice or in speech). Perhaps the strongest connecting theme in all of his writings is the attention he pays to the many dimensions of the physicality of the voice. Chrétien's philosophy is one of hospitality to the voice. The opening of *The Ark of Speech* captures this well:

> How far does our hospitality go? How far can it go? What can we welcome and gather in, and how? Hospitality is, first and foremost, the hospitality that we give each other, exchanging words and silences, glances and voices. And yet, this conversation cannot take place in a vacuum; it is in the world, this world that we never cease to share—among ourselves but also with other forms of presence, the presence of animals, of vegetables, of things. In our speech, we are equally responsible for them, just as we respond to them. (*AS*, 1)

He continues in this introduction to argue that the word for speech, "parole," comes from the word for parable (*parabola*) and therefore permits the use of (biblical) parables for understanding speech and voice, such as the biblical story of Adam's naming of the animals, which Chrétien interprets as providing an "ark" for them: "Their first guardian, their first safeguard, is that of speech, which shelters their being and their diversity. This is true for more than just the animals. No protective gesture could take responsibility for the least being if the latter had not been taken up into speech" (*AS*, 2). Already here, hospitality is linked to responsibility, an important theme for Chrétien, and it includes responsibility for animals and nature. Such a concern for nature is relatively unique among these thinkers. Chrétien is concerned not just with human corporeality and speech, but with that of all living beings and the world itself.

Chrétien's writing is often performative of this very hospitality to other voices by welcoming many such voices into his own writing and having meaning emerge from a juxtaposition or frequently seamless connecting of them. While beautiful and even inspiring to read, it does at times make it hard to separate Chrétien's own argument from these other voices. In some sense, it may even be unfaithful to his project to do so as it is precisely about showing how all our speaking is already a response to something or someone prior and never a solitary speaking, but always involved in a dialogue and a collective (or "plurivocal"—many-voiced) speaking. Chrétien explores many different phenomena in his writings and much of the thrust of his work is a way of revealing these phenomena and allowing them to speak for themselves and to be experienced, usually through his writing itself. These phenomena, often circulating around themes of beauty and vulnerability, cover a wide range of disciplines. He speaks of the beauty of poetry, painting, and music, frequently analyzing specific works and their authors, creators, or composers. He also examines many religious phenomena, often moving seamlessly from sacred to secular (and the reverse). In his lectures on response and responsibility, for example, Chrétien emphasizes that response and responsibility come in many different modes and then goes on to focus one lecture on poetry, one on tragedy, one on painting and music, and one on contemporary philosophical thought; he ends with one on Christ as the supreme Respondent. Similarly, *Hand to Hand* is an analysis of art, especially painting, but includes a reflection on God as the supreme Creator and God's relationship to human making. This diverse and multivocal nature of Chrétien's writings makes it necessary to cite somewhat more frequently from his work in order to convey something of its poetic tenor. I will discuss briefly several themes in his works and then reflect in conclusion on the ways in which God or religious experience functions in all of these in order to determine in what ways his writings could be said to constitute some sort of "apologetic" for Christian faith.

Voice and Speech

One of Chrétien's earliest works already sketched a phenomenology of the voice. It is characteristically entitled "The Naked Voice" [*La voix nue*], which captures the important sense of vulnerability and physicality that is present in all Chrétien's reflections. Here he begins to develop the idea that our voice is a response to a prior call and that its most essential characteristic is the ability to promise. He also spends much time exploring the physicality of the voice and connecting it to other parts of the body. He explores the phenomena of listening and silence, a secret which he contends philosophy has often erased and covered over in the past. This work tries to recover a phenomenological account of the obscurity of manifestation but also of gift and excess. Another early work reflects on Saint Augustine and the "acts of speech," each of the twenty-three chapters examining a different "act" of speech, such as asking, listening, teaching, rejoicing, singing, weeping, blessing, and so forth. His two most recently published works also focus on the topic of the voice in different ways. *Pour reprendre et perdre haleine* is an extended phenomenological reflection on the breath required for speech and prayer by examining ten "words" employed in the tradition of spirituality, and drawing on poetic, mystical/religious, and philosophical sources. *Reconnaissances philosophiques* also includes several reflections on voice, speech, and word, including essays on Lévinas and Henry. The topic of the voice is a frequent one in Chrétien's writings and is usually closely linked to that of the call or the response, which will be examined next. Thus, the separation between voice and call is rather artificial, as these two always go together for Chrétien.

As mentioned, Chrétien's philosophy may well be defined as that of a hospitality to the voice or to the call and to the response. Both call and response resonate in the voice. For Chrétien, voice is also always closely linked to silence. One cannot be thought without the other. Both speech and silence arise from the "unheard-of" or the impossible, the excess that always escapes me. This emphasis on excess and our deficiency to respond to it will return frequently in Chrétien's writings. Chrétien recognizes voice in many places. Voice is not just about human speech, although that is its most important place for him. Paintings have voices and can also speak silence. Touch has a voice (and the voice also "touches"). He often attributes voice to nature, although he shows how it must become articulated in our speech. Finally, God's voice plays an important role, although certainly not one that would be easy to discern or identify.

Silence, for Chrétien, is an essential human act. Silence is absolutely required for listening and even for true speaking. Without silence, speech becomes mere chatter. Religious silence is a "naked appearance before the Word" and an offering to God. Only in listening to God are we enabled to speak. Out of the fullness of the divine silence, our voices can name and give shelter to the world: "Our voice cannot build the ark of speech, in which everything will be given shelter and received, unless it be in proportion to the hospitality of its silence. It is only by being perpetually translated from silence . . . that our voice can falter and allow itself to be broken, to give itself to what it has to say in such a way that it is not left intact" (*AS*, 74). Silence opens us to the other and thus becomes a "hospitality of silence." This is a bodily and physical attention.

Through speech, we make an "ark" for the world and shelter it within our voice. We shape human life and care for nature through our voice, which is a response to the beauty of the world. According to Chrétien, making the world a home for humankind is "the first and last moral task" (*AS*, 114). It is the human voice that enables such dwelling. He is emphatic that this is not merely a religious task rooted in a conception of the world as creation, but also a philosophical one: "It is not only the faith of the Bible that asserts that we are given the task in our words for responding to the world's beauty and taking responsibility for it. Nor is it merely a religious task. Jerusalem has its gratitude, but Athens has its gratitude too. It is called philosophy. The response that the philosopher makes to the world is to think out its order and beauty." He concludes, "of course, not all gratitude performs a task of philosophical thought, but all true labour of thought is an act of gratitude" (*AS*, 116). Yet Chrétien, at least in this work, focuses more on the religious dimensions, appropriating them philosophically (in other texts he does the reverse). He appeals to insights from the Scriptures or the religious tradition to show something more generally true of the human experience. We must speak of the world in order to become ourselves, precisely because we are physical and earthly creatures. Even a Christian understanding of God emphasizes this in Chrétien's view:

> If we could no longer speak of the world, we would no longer have anything to say, not even about ourselves, since, in describing our exhausted void, as so many people like to do, we are still speaking of the world, of the world's withdrawing. The Holy Bible itself speaks of God only by speaking of the world, of its creation, its history, the human beings who live in it, the animals, the rivers, the mountains and the deserts, the winds and the bushes, of God giving the world and giving himself for the salvation of the world. (*AS*, 120)

As this citation makes clear, any talk about God for Chrétien must always be grounded in the earthly and corporeal context that makes us human. Our creatureliness is expressed through our speaking.

Speech is essentially gratitude. Within speech, we receive the gift of the voice and also return it as we give ourselves. Speech turns us to the other: "The speech most proper to man is thus the speech which is turned to the other, given to the other, a speech of transmigration that crosses boundaries, a speech that is eccentric" (*AS*, 123). Speech also offers up the world. We become witness to the world in our speech: "But if the hymn is vocal, it always has, as well, the scope of an act of witness—the irreplaceable witness of man as such, but also the taking as witness of the entire creation, which itself bears witness in our song. We have to speak on behalf of things, and not only on behalf of one another, as if the world were merely human. Man has a responsibility for creation, a responsibility with which God has entrusted him" (*AS*, 136). Chrétien speaks of speech as an altar for the praise of the world. It is in this offering of the world, this song of praise, that we become truly ourselves, a topic to which we will return.

The Call and the Response also frequently mentions the theme of the voice. In a chapter entitled "The Visible Voice," Chrétien explores the ways in which the voice is not merely an auditory phenomenon, but rather can also be seen and touched: "Visibility reaches its full radiance only through delivering its resonance. Splendor itself is vocal. Not only does the eye listen, it sees truly only by listening. More intimate to the gaze than sight is the fact that it listens" (*CR*, 35). The voice precedes the eyes and articulates the light by which it sees. Here also he interprets the voice as a shelter for suffering and beauty: "To see the suffering and beauty of the visible in the form of voice is to be dedicated to providing it forever with the asylum of our own voice. When the eye listens, we must answer what we hear and answer for what we will hear" (*CR*, 43). In our voice, spirit enters the world. We provide hospitality to it in our speech. By listening to this spirit of the world, we enable others to hear it as well. Listening, voice, speech, call, and response are closely connected here: "I speak by answering, but my response endures only by calling other words that will answer it and, by answering, give me to hear what in my own word and in the voice calling me had earlier found me deaf" (*CR*, 44). Again Chrétien emphasizes that the voice is physical, that is must be incarnated in a body. A disembodied voice is suspect.[2] Even the notion of the "inner voice," as it appears in Augustine, Plutarch, and Kierkegaard, must involve listening, dialogue, and physicality. Chrétien also points out that listening to the voice is an ethical act. To be hospitable to the voice is to enable justice to be served. Analyzing Jean-Pierre de Caussade, he says: "When a man is victimized and humiliated, the divine name of glory is humiliated, and to assist the man back up is to sanctify this same name. The injustice that we witness profanes the divine name of justice, and to fight against injustice is to hear the voice of the Word aggrieved in the event. To answer the voice of events is to speak, but also to act, by letting ourselves be transformed by it" (*CR*, 69). This hospitality to the voice, then, is ethical in character. It is an act of compassion and requires our response to the suffering of the other.

Call and Response

The call might be the most prominent theme in Chrétien and is a topic he mentions in almost all of his writings. His work *The Call and the Response* discusses the call as such, but he also speaks of the call of beauty, the call of God, the call to responsibility, the call in the flesh, the call that precedes prayer, and so forth. In fact, Chrétien himself defines the thrust of his work in terms of his attentiveness to the call: "It is this *excess* of the encounter with things, others, world, and God that is at the center of the project of which this book is a part: this encounter requires, most imperatively, our response, and yet seems at the same time to prohibit it" (*UU*, 121). He goes on to outline several of his works as a response to this encounter (beauty, joy, but also weakness, struggle, testimony to the infinite). Anne Davenport emphasizes the same in her introduction to the translation of *The Call and the Response*. She claims that Chrétien's books "have untiringly aimed at unveiling the phenomenal forms of the religious call-response structure and thus at elaborating a phenomenology within which the core experience of human mystery finds a place" (*CR*, x). She suggests that Chrétien's analyses may well broaden the scope of phenomenology or even challenge some of its assumptions. Chrétien criticizes Heidegger's emphasis on the call as the call of Being and instead shows the call to be one of infinite excess and to have a distinctly religious structure, even when it is not specifically linked to religious phenomena. Davenport thinks that "by restoring the infinite height of the originary call, Chrétien restores the irreducibly religious origin of human speech, which is the same as making it emerge, body and soul, from an infinite creative love" (*CR*, xxi). She also sees Chrétien's writings as performative in character, describing his use of multiple authors and texts as an "innovative approach to philosophy as a fraternal, inclusive, choral event" (*CR*, xxix). Chrétien's goal is "to engage us, namely by creating through speech the conditions for a revelation to reach us, for love to be heard and indeed spoken in the infinite surrender of self-destitution" (*CR*, xx).

In *The Call and the Response*, Chrétien describes the appeal as the origin of speech. Our speech is always a response to a prior call. Even when we refuse to answer, we have responded to the call. And when we seem to be calling forth or appealing, we are actually also responding: "We can only beckon to ourselves what has already turned itself toward us, already manifested itself to us—what calls upon us to call: the full daylight of language is thus already well advanced before the dawn of any call" (*CR*, 5). This is the case whether the event of the beautiful calls us or whether the good or God do the calling. And in answering a call, we find that the answer has already preceded us and that we are held in its embrace (*CR*, 12). Our response becomes a gift that offers itself to the call. Even our very ability to listen and to respond is dependent upon the call. It thus points to an essential vulnerability on our part. We become ourselves only in our response to the call, where our voices join those of others:

> The fact that my very being is the advent of a response shaped by the call's own scission means that there has never been a first instant of response, that I never started to speak in order to answer. Every initiative on my part only perpetuates an immemorial yes, in the rift between two forms of excess. Infinite excess, first of all, of the call over the answer, since the call is of the infinite: by calling me as a person, it calls me not as an isolated and abstract being but calls the totality of the world in space and time along with me, in the inexhaustible chorus of which I am only one voice enduring a perpetual inchoation. (*CR*, 19)

Our responses are always deficient, always incomplete; the call always exceeds them immeasurably. And yet this very vulnerability and insufficiency is what enables and calls forth the response. This inexhaustibility of the call and deficiency of our response, in fact, is what enables us to live, to dwell, and to create: all of our lives become a response to the call.

Chrétien often thinks of the call in a Lévinasian sense. It is the calling to which we must respond *me voici* (here I am): "The call is heard only in the response" (*CR*, 30). Unlike Lévinas, however, Chrétien applies this call to the mission of the church as the mystical body of Christ (a topic he also discusses quite frequently). Thus, the response to the call is a communal one that enables the voice to respond:

> It *is* its identity, or more precisely its ipseity, that by which it replies "Here I am" to the call of the Lord of the world, who by this very call brings it about that he can inhabit this world. We have been chosen in Christ "before the world was made," says the Letter to the Ephesians. This calling is also our mission, that which sends us on a mission to the world. Whether we respond to it or betray it, which is still a mode of response, forms the very heart of our story and its uniqueness. (*AS*, 147).

On another occasion, he speaks of the *me voici* as a more general response to the excess of the gift of self:

> This is about the world, about Being and God, about everything that a person is through being *exposed*. It has to do with everything to which one must respond through the word, that is to say everything, all the way to nothing. It is about what is given to a person, the gift to which one is opened without recourse, about being the only one who can say *Me voici*, here I am, and having said it already, even in silence, by one's face, hands, and entire body. (*UU*, 119–20)

And again even this response of a thoroughly bodily and communal *me voici* on behalf of all, always falls short: "Such a yes, even when proclaimed by all things and by all voices, would still be insufficient." It is "also a promise that keeps us beholden" and "gives us speech only by gripping us by the throat." Our "hymn" of affirmation is "torn and heartrending" and therefore "must remit itself to this promise for safekeeping, entrust itself to it, give itself to it and lose itself, always already, always more, never enough" (*CR*, 32). As evident here again Chrétien always grounds promise and speech in corporeality (the throat) and thereby also exposes its vulnerability. This very vulnerability and loss is partially what keeps the promise "safe"—and it does so precisely by exposing it through our response.[3]

In a recent book on the topic of the response, Chrétien emphasizes its link to responsibility, developing a "phenomenology of response" by analyzing its phenomenality in various different settings.[4] He stresses that response and responsibility go together and are always closely connected to the question or the appeal (or call) that precedes them, which can originate from other humans or from God. Yet even questions I formulate are always a kind of response to a phenomenon I have already encountered before it gives rise to question: "Only the response to an appeal opens the possibility for true questioning" (*R*, 6). Returning to Augustine's *Confessions*, he again points out how beauty responds to and initiates a call. Things and beings of nature, such as trees, also call out to us. Things "nourish our presence, our thought, our speech, they are precious mediators, our guarantors and our respondents, for there is not only emptiness between us, but the world, places, and things" (*R*, 12). Yet it is only the response taken up in responsibility that makes visible the call. This is true even of the call of the divine appeal: "I only hear God's appeal through the response of faith, of revolt, or of confusion" (*R*, 15). Again, response is a bodily experience and a vulnerable one due to the disproportion between call and response. In the second lecture, Chrétien analyzes the singular voice and argues that there is no such thing as a solipsistic speaking. Even responsibility is a speaking to oneself in light of the others and ultimately before others (*R*, 38). Solitary song may also have a polyphonic and choral dimension. Even a monologue (as in Augustine) is a response: "When I am alone, we are two. But when we are two, we are three, because between me and myself, there is always the *Logos*, and here this *Logos* is the divine *Logos*" (*R*, 71). In the third lecture, he analyzes epic and tragedy, while he focuses on poetry, music, and painting in the fourth lecture. The fifth lecture explores the notion of responsibility in philosophy, showing how it begins in response and carries connotations of "answering" within it. The final lectures is entitled "The Respondent stronger than our questions and our offenses" and is an analysis of Christ. In this lecture, he essentially defends a Christian notion of atonement against the many criticisms that have been made of it (i.e., that the notion of satisfaction or of one dying for all is incoherent), including the idea of substitution. And yet even in this defense answers become again questions, which we can only answer within ourselves as we raise new questions (*R*, 237).

Forgetting, Memory, and Hope

The Unforgettable and the Unhoped For collects four essays dealing with the immemorial, forgetting, memory, the unforgettable, the sudden, and the "unhoped for." He begins with a reflection on "the immemorial and recollection" by focusing on Plato's theory of recollection and various readings of it in the history of philosophy (Hegel, Leibniz, Hartmann, Natorp). The immemorial, in Chrétien's interpretation, is what enables us to be human: "The immemorial is what we lived before being human, and in order to finally be human, to be able to be human: what in us overcomes the human and exceeds it is what alone renders us human. There is an immemorial only for us humans and by us" (*UU*, 11–12).[5] He distinguishes the immemorial carefully from simply forgetting something, which is a quite different phenomenological experience. In the second piece he examines more fully "the reserve of forgetting," what is left over or not lost in forgetting. Forgetting is a loss that takes something from us and that affects our relationships with others. For example, he asks: "Is the inflection of cherished voices of those who have died—voices whose diaeresis momentarily disrupts the poet's voice—completely lost even while I continue to hear their resonance at the bottom of my throat? And is the light in their vanished faces extinguished even while its distant rays still reach us, scintillating in the night of our closed eyes?" (*UU*, 41). In forgetting, "I have lost not only what happened or what I did, but a dimension of what I am and can do" (*UU*, 41). In this context, he reflects on Augustine, Nietzsche, Valery, and various other thinkers in order to explore the loss involved in forgetting. Yet this loss is not a deprivation in Chrétien's view, but is what gives us to ourselves and frees us. Forgetting and memory are closely connected, as "without forgetting, there would be nothing that I could remember" (*UU*, 47). Forgetting connects me to the other. Others help me to remember and help to fill what is missing in my memory. Thus, the theme of our relations with others is again central for him. He suggests that "perhaps it is always the other person who is unforgettable" (*UU*, 54). He also insists again on the importance of physicality:

"Incarnate being is by itself power of recalling and remembering, not because the past is inscribed of itself in it in the form of material traces, which are always only present and of the present, but because it alone opens us and relates us to what we can remember. If there is memory only of the past, incarnation is the condition and the place of all memory" (*UU*, 69). Using Kierkegaard, he reflects on the importance of promise and its relation to the other. Here is where remembering connects us to God who is the source of our promises and enables the possibility of pardon or forgiveness.

In his essay on "the unforgettable," Chrétien again emphasizes that forgetting and memory are only possible through the other. He analyzes several Christian writers in order to speak of forgetfulness of self and response to God's memory. God is the one who remembers us: "The unforgettable to which we are faithful would be a place of fear and trembling if we were its only authors and witnesses. Its origin and end are held in the promise of him whose memory we must watch over. God will not forget us. . . . But we are unforgettable for God, for his faithfulness is unwavering" (*UU*, 97). Human faithfulness is thus always enabled by divine faithfulness. Chrétien refers to the stigmata—the marks engraved even on the risen Christ's hands—in order to demonstrate that we are eternally remembered by God. This is our reason for hope. In his final reflection on "the sudden and the unhoped for" Chrétien analyzes various images in Greek tragedy, in particular the story of Alcestis, as an image of what is "unhoped for" (and not merely unexpected). Both Greek tragedy and philosophy cannot really speak of hope, as they have no concept of promise. To this Chrétien contrasts the hope of Christian revelation: "At the point where Revelation permits hope to become hope in God and confidence in God's promise, the unhoped for is charged with a new meaning" (*UU*, 107). He uses the story of Abraham to illustrate this, relying especially on Philo's interpretation of this story. In Philo, hope is closely connected to what it means to be human. It defines us in terms of the promise of our future and again closely connects us to the other. Linking this to his earlier analysis of the gift, he says, "To find without seeking is to let oneself find without having held the initiative. And letting oneself find is endless when it is God who does the finding" (*UU*, 113). An "idolatry of the self" "forgets that the truth given by God, even if given suddenly, needs an eternity to be received, for receiving is also an endless task, and receiving what does not cease is itself ceaseless" (*UU*, 113). It is by receiving ourselves in this way that we truly become ourselves. The "unhoped" for grounds our hope in the future. He sees this as especially true in the promise of the cross. It is interesting that Chrétien here ends again on a decidedly Christian note and even stresses its uniqueness, as most of the rest of the book is relatively straightforward phenomenological analysis without much consideration of Christian thinkers or themes.

Flesh and Touch

Chrétien repeatedly insists on the fleshly and physical character of the voice. The voice must be incarnate (*UU*, 69). Most interestingly, he says as much about the silence and listening of the hand in the making of physical works of art as he says about the physicality of the voice. His most extensive reflection on the body is the untranslated work *Symbolique du corps* [Symbolism of the Body], which is an analysis of the Song of Songs (especially as appropriated by many thinkers in the Christian tradition), organized by reflecting on different parts of the body and linking them to the soul. Chrétien tries to connect a logic and a symbolism of the body in these writers. He reflects both on the individual body or flesh and the more communal sense of the religious community as a body. A similar reflection on the mystical body as a truly corporeal body is also included in his work *Le regard de l'amour* [The Gaze of Love] (see especially Chapter 8 of that book). Throughout, he insists emphatically on the physicality of this "mystical body." To think of this body only, or even primarily, in spiritual terms is to deny the incarnation, to deny Christ's real incarnate body. Christ is incarnate in our physical bodies here and now on this earth.

The most extensive analysis of corporeality translated so far is the final chapter of *The Call and the Response*, which is entitled "Body and Touch." It attempts to develop a phenomenology of touch, grounded in the earlier analysis of the voice. He relies in particular on Aristotle and various readings of Aristotle throughout the tradition, pointing out that Aristotle does not actually explicitly link touch and the hand and does not speak of "fingering." Citing Augustine on touch being "suffused throughout the body," he claims that "this is the reason why touch delivers us into the world without possible return or retreat" (*CR*, 113). While we can choose to avoid other sensory impressions, touch cannot be turned off. In order to avoid touch, we would have to eliminate our bodies entirely. Our bodies connect us intimately to the world, something both Aristotle and Husserl recognized in Chrétien's view. In this context, he is quite critical of the idea of self-affection and the utter immanence of the flesh. Although he does not mention Michel Henry by name, he uses quite a bit of his terminology and thus one may safely conclude that the criticism is indeed directed against Henry. For Chrétien, "self-touch cannot be the truth of touch" (*CR*, 118). Touch is always a response to another. We cannot feel without others and certainly cannot feel ourselves: "We feel only the other, and if we feel ourselves this will be only on the occasion of, and by dependence on, a feeling of the other, not through a reflexivity of the flesh that would be conjectured as its original source. I feel myself only by favor of the other. It is the other who gives me to myself insofar as the return to myself and to my own actions or affections always supposes this other" (*CR*, 120). Chrétien condemns self-affection as a kind of illness.

Touching and sensory delight require the presence of another, although not necessarily that of a human other. Chrétien describes this joy of encounter as follows: "Sensitivity is given to itself only in the profusion of the world, it receives itself through the other and by means of the other. Even self-delight, should it occur, is but the mature blossom of an immeasurably saturated encounter. I experience the joy of seeing, of touching, of hearing, of attentively exercising the diverse possibilities that are mine always by seeing, touching, hearing something other than myself, out in the world" (*CR*, 122). Joy is pure affirmation of the world and of others, which he portrays in beautiful imagery: "The joy of being is of another order than self-sensation and self-enjoyment. Every joy is fueled by a pure yes, rising like flame, without curling back on itself. One never says yes to oneself, which is why one is never truly oneself except in saying yes" (*CR*, 123). This affirmation and yes to the world is intricately linked with love for Chrétien, although this does not refer merely to eros. And again touch is also closely connected to listening and hearing the call, including that of the divine: "To be touched in one's very substance by the Word, beyond all image, is, properly speaking, to listen, to listen with one's whole being, body and soul, without anything in us that escapes hearing and stands outside of it, thanks to the gracious transfiguration accomplished by this very touch. Nor does the ear alone listen; the eye also listens and responds. The possibility of listening, however, ultimately takes root in the totality of the flesh. The flesh listens. And the fact that it listens is what makes it respond" (*CR*, 130). Touch, listening, speaking, and response are again closely linked here. This touch of the divine is as excessive as the call and calls forth our vulnerable and finite response: "When the entire body radiates and burns though this divine touch, it becomes song and word. Yet that which it sings with its entire being, collected whole and gathered up by the Other, is what it cannot say, what infinitely exceeds it—excess to which touch as such is destined, and which in the humblest sensation and least contact here below was already forever unsealed to us" (*CR*, 131). Thus, the call is always corporeal and the response to an appeal involves the entire body as well.

Art and Beauty

Chrétien sees beauty everywhere: in nature, in art, in our voices and bodies themselves. One might say that his very project is one of making this beauty shine forth. It is a theme to which he returns continually. One of his earliest books is called *L'effroi du beau* [The Shock of Beauty] and several of its essays outline how beauty affects us and calls forth our response. Many of Chrétien's more recent writings, however, also focus on beauty. *Reconnaissances philosophiques* examines the topic of beauty in various essays interacting with Kant, Joseph Joubert, and Hans Urs von Balthasar. It also includes an essay on music (reflecting on David's playing before Saul) and one that considers what it may mean for works of art to live, die, and to be reborn or resurrected.[6] In *The Ark of Speech*, Chrétien explores the question of whether beauty says "à-dieu," that is, whether it is offered to or before God. In this context, Chrétien is quite critical of theologian Karl Barth who excludes beauty as a relevant theme for theology and he insists against Barth (and with von Balthasar) that in beauty we respond to God's call. Beauty is an excess that overflows from the divine and thus in our response to God through beauty we draw on its prior source in God's abundant excess. He depicts it as "excessive and surprising": "The flower of beauty, which precedes beauty, is also the flower that beauty offers us, transmits to us, being itself received by that flower, for how could it not call us to what called it to itself, to what gave it to itself and to us, and which is nothing that one could ever, in any way whatsoever, appropriate?" And he continues by linking beauty to God: "To think of God as that which is beyond beauty and gives beauty is to discern that only his excess over and above the beautiful, and over all the formal definitions of the beautiful that we might put forward, makes it possible for there to be a gift of beauty, and for the beauty of creatures itself to be in excess—an excess of itself, which *is* itself in so far as it responds to the call of God" (*AS*, 88). For Chrétien, beauty expresses God's woundedness and suffering. In response, our own speech must become vulnerable and even wounded in order to bear the divine beauty. Beauty calls forth our response because it makes us aware of a prior call. Beauty itself calls us.

Yet beauty is not exclusively painful. Chrétien shows how beauty calls forth gratitude. We must respond to beauty and in doing so we shape the world. Beauty calls forth our responsibility for the world. Here beauty becomes closely linked to speech for Chrétien. It is in speech and in the voice that we respond to beauty and receive the gift of beauty. In fact, by responding thus to the beauty of the world, we speak on behalf of the world and give the world speech. This is the task not just of religious praise but of poetry: "The poet wants the world to concelebrate its praise with him, and he with the world. In this multiple *yes*, which the world bears in it and which we bring to song, men offer the world to each other, make it inhabitable. For a world without poetry is uninhabitable. . . . It is by being sung that the world is properly a world" (*AS*, 131, 132). We are witnesses to the beauty of the world and our gratitude expresses its beauty. By speaking on behalf of things, we are also called to preserve and care for their beauty and to be hospitable to them.[7] In a later text, Chrétien says: "The in-itself of beauty is to be for-the-other, aimed at gathering the other back to itself. What is beautiful is what calls out by manifesting itself and manifests itself by calling out" (*CR*, 9). Beauty calls us back to our origin. It calls forth our response and our listening to its "visible voice." It wounds us, but also brings us to ourselves. We are unsettled and disoriented and thus must find our bearing. This is the case because beauty does not give us a quick or easy answer. It requires silence, listening, attentiveness, and repetition. In our voice we articulate the beauty of the visible: "If beauty is the very voice of things, the face-to-face encounter through which beauty grips us not in its essence a speechless contemplation but a dialogue. Visible beauty becomes properly visible precisely when it speaks to us and we question it. It must speak to us in order for us to see it as beautiful" (*CR*, 35). This response, however, is always polyphonic. Praise, poetry, and art all express beauty in very different ways. Our response to beauty is always insufficient and thus calls forth new voices, new genres, new works of art.

Prayer

Chrétien's reflections on prayer actually bring together many of the themes that have been discussed in this chapter. And it is a topic to which he returns often. A long discussion of prayer is included in *The Ark of Speech*, which is also the piece he presented at the conference organized in response to Janicaud. Yet comments about prayer and even longer reflections on this topic show up in almost all of his works. Prayer is most fundamentally a response to the call. It is the quintessentially religious act because its possibility for speech underlies all other turning toward God, including sacrifice and liturgy. Prayer is dialogue with God, but we learn how to pray only in doing it, as it is really an encounter with the impossible:

> Prayer knows that it does not know how to pray, but it learns this only by praying, it knows it only for as long as it is praying, and is real—like everything about an encounter—only in the impossible. This agonistic dimension is nothing other than the ordeal of transcendence.

For transcendence gives itself only when its distance approaches without ceasing to be distant, and it is encountered only in the ordeal of speech. The second person singular alone can open up the space of such an ordeal. It is only in saying *You* that the I can be completely exposed, in other words laid open to all that it cannot master. (*AS*, 27)

This exposure and vulnerability that is necessary for prayer accounts for its being "wounded speech," which is the title of this particular article on prayer. Prayer gives access to God's suffering; in prayer we actually suffer with the divine. Yet we also realize our own vulnerability and limitations, which render us naked before God: "To have God listening to you is an ordeal, a testing of speech incomparable with any other, for our speech is incomparably stripped bare by it, in all it seeks to hide, to excuse, to justify, to obtain in real terms. Speech appears in the attentive light of silence, the voice is really naked" (*AS*, 27). Prayer exposes our nakedness and makes us utterly vulnerable. Vulnerability and woundedness are always closely connected for Chrétien. In this piece, he examines the differences between vocal and silent prayer, individual and communal or collective prayer, ancient and contemporary versions of prayer, formulary and "free" prayer, often breaking down the supposed distinctions between them (thus he speaks of pre-formulated prayers as actually more free than extemporaneous ones and of individual prayer as always already communal in some sense). Prayer is also always a corporeal experience for Chrétien. It is our bodies that pray.

The voice, however, is also wounded and vulnerable in prayer because it carries within it other voices and offers up prayer for them.[8] In prayer, we give voice to the suffering of other people. Yet Chrétien goes even further than that. Not only does prayer vocalize the woundedness of our fellow human, but it carries all of creation toward God. Prayer offers creation to God, as Chrétien explicates in the piece mentioned previously that asks: "Does Beauty say Adieu?" A-Dieu, as in Lévinas, here means "before-God" or "to God," not simply "good-bye." He calls this offering of beauty to God "a eucharist of speech." (Eucharist originally means "thanksgiving.") As in the earlier discussion of the vulnerable voice, this wounded speech also expresses God's suffering:

Beauty says adieu when the excess of its manifestation calls out, in our own voice which it causes to falter and seizes with urgency, a name higher than all names, which we alone, albeit in fear and trembling, can pronounce. This adieu is an *envoi*: we cannot in God himself contemplate the beauty of things created, for of this beauty we are only the lieutenants and the only mouthpieces. It is our voice that carries to God and into God the adieu of things and of the mute world. If things in all their radiance are charged with a mission to us, we too have the mission of welcoming them, gathering them in, carrying them by means of our voice to a place that they cannot reach of themselves. (*AS*, 98)

Thus, prayer becomes a vehicle for all of creation to return to God. We have a mission, a call, to carry the world bodily before God. We are transformed by this prayer on behalf of all: Not only do we offer beauty up to God, but we ourselves are rendered beautiful in the process. Beauty is always an abundant gift.[9] And this task requires everything of us:

> Yes, beauty can say adieu, but it says adieu only when we offer our own adieu, and all of our voice, so that beauty can break it, and make it all the surer for having been broken, and make it remain trembling, with the trembling of the person who knows that all the sonorities of the song of the world, without a single one being forgotten or left by the wayside, will have to be given by him, in the eternal dawn, to God, who alone made them arise from silence. (*AS*, 110)

Again, hospitality requires our voices to offer themselves on behalf of others, despite the vulnerability and pain this entails.

This praise makes the world "an authentic dwelling place for humankind." By offering the world in praise to God, we actually render it habitable. Praise fuels our labor in and on behalf of the world, inviting us to care for it. Praise is a response to God's creation: "The first of all praises is the praise that God himself utters at his creation. To this silent praise all human words of speech, whether profane or religious, will always be a reply" (*AS*, 115). If we were to refuse to praise, the world would be rendered silent and become uninhabitable. Praise transforms the world into a good dwelling place for all creatures. Near the end of the book, Chrétien returns to this theme and reiterates that we have a responsibility for creation, that the world offers itself in song through us. He refers to St. Francis's "Canticle of the Creatures," but emphasizes that the praise of the creatures requires our voice to become audible: "We can be brothers of the wind and the moon only through this brotherhood founded in the Speech that was itself made flesh . . . it is not enough to sing the world, this song must have meaning, it must say something, it must make sense" (*AS*, 140). Praise is hospitality of speech. Praise "gives voice within itself to the polyphony of the world" (*AS*, 139). Chrétien concludes by suggesting that we become truly ourselves in this praise. As in Lévinas, the self is individuated by responding to the call of the human other; in Chrétien, we become our-selves by responding to the world and expressing its song and offering it to God. He concludes the book by returning to the theme of the Eucharist of speech, uniting our voice to that of the Incarnate Word:

> It is in him and by him alone that the world is gathered and unified so as to be offered to the Father, and in the great variety of the hymns we sing, in their most intimate depths, there is always this hint of tremulousness, suspended, as it were, on the edge of silence, by which the *thank you* wounds a human voice, with a blessed wound, and brings it about that it gives itself, the voice in which all is given. (*AS*, 148)

Chrétien here offers a full phenomenological account for what Marion suggests much more briefly in his reflection on the language of praise in the final chapter of *In Excess*, namely that praise calls and transforms us, addresses us in our offering of the prayer. Chrétien goes far beyond Marion by extending this praise to the whole world, to all of creation, and by embodying it fully.[10]

Religious Imagery and Language

Chrétien repeatedly uses religious examples in his work to illustrate a point. These include religious writers, examples from the Scriptures, theological reflections or references to doctrines, and especially paintings with religious themes (or painters with Christian commitments). Very often these seem to serve simply as examples for the points Chrétien is trying to illustrate. Yet, of course, it says a lot that his points are consistently best illustrated by recourse to the Christian tradition in some form or other. There certainly is a way in which Chrétien appears to imply that the Christian experience (of painting, of prayer, of Scripture) has something significant to say about the human experience, something that is of value, even when not dealing with explicitly "religious" topics, such as the flesh of the body, the intimacy of (erotic) love, the beauty of a painting or a piece of music. And Chrétien does at times address the Janicaudian accusation of "theological turning" more directly. He says in regard to issues of hope, memory and promise, for example, that

> religious and mystical thought and speech have frequently seen and spoken higher, farther, or otherwise than metaphysics in the form that Heidegger has defined for us. And it is necessary to hear their promises. For they are not obsessed and blinded by the human project of

total self-assurance and self-understanding as we truly are (to paraphrase St. Paul), in transparency: they are rooted at each instant in the hearing of an other Word that wounds body and soul, and which they know that, if it wounds completely, could never be completely understood—not even in eternity. This is why religious and mystical thought and speech are necessary for those who would meditate on excess and superabundance, on the force in weakness and the perfection in deficiency. They do more than speak of them: they live them and originate from them. (*UU*, 126)

Thus, religious language is meaningful and true because it gives access to an experience that is not seen as clearly by philosophy. This is the case because these accounts are not as determined by the Cartesian account of subjectivity and Western obsession with the ego. The Christian experience is always already intimately addressed by another and thus it can inform phenomenological accounts in this respect.

Chrétien here does not attempt to "prove" that there is such "an other Word" or give evidence that "religious and mystical thought and speech" are indeed rooted in a real experience, nor does he show that they really "live them and originate from them." He finds it legitimate to seek "the response" for questions to which philosophy "cannot respond in ultimate fashion" "in another source" (*UU*, 128–29). Although he agrees that the distinctions between disciplines should be upheld, he disputes that one could not engage in both and employ insights from one realm for the other.[11] He claims that what distinguishes the two is the fact that theology writes under the inspiration of faith, while philosophy suspends such inspiration, yet both deal in rigorous fashion with ultimate questions: "One is certainly at liberty to say (but one must also demonstrate this) that such questions are badly posed, or that they have no response. It is also possible (and indeed, by saying this one does it) to seek the response in another source, and to examine what light harks back to it" (*UU*, 129). In his introduction to *The Call and the Response*, Chrétien also responds briefly to the allegation of trespassing the boundaries between philosophy and theology. He says that "we cannot simply appoint ourselves to police the presumed clear-cut border between philosophy and theology; we must first, as philosophers, call into question where the border is drawn" (*CR*, 2). To those who wish to ignore the contributions of theology he asks somewhat ironically: "What philosopher would ever elect ignorance as the best counsel and imitate the ostrich as his most advantageous strategy?" (*CR*, 3). For Chrétien, then, the Christian experience provides a rich source for phenomenological reflection, which philosophy ignores only at the peril of its own sterility or poverty. Christian imagery and experience can provide accounts of phenomena that philosophy sees only partially or not at all. These important phenomena lie at the very heart of what it means to be human. We gain a much fuller picture of the human experience if we pay attention to these sources and images.

Chrétien's phenomenology then serves as a powerful example of an apologetics for Christian faith that shows its meaning and significance through an analysis of the Christian experience. Chrétien's depiction of such experience constitutes an argument for its validity and authenticity. By consistently choosing Christian examples for his explorations of beauty, corporeality, and vulnerability, Chrétien shows them to be meaningful and valid phenomenological experiences. While he never argues for their exclusivity or uniqueness, but in fact shows how these biblical or spiritual examples participate in wider human experience and interact with many other aesthetic and poetic sources, his close analyses and careful phenomenological descriptions surely are a way of validating them as meaningful and true experiences that can be conveyed through the tools of phenomenology and thus shown to be valid experiences. His analysis of language and the voice, in particular, reveals a kind of sacred dimension to human speaking while never erasing its vulnerability and corporeality. All creaturely existence and experience are shown to be hallowed in some way through Chrétien's poetic depictions. His defense of Christian faith and experience outlines this task as one of supremely kenotic hospitality: We are called to bear the suffering of the world, including that of non-human creatures, and offer it to God. His poetic phenomenological depictions call us to respond to this call, to "defend" it precisely through our lives in devotion to it.

8

Jean-Yves Lacoste: A God of Liturgy and Parousia

Jean-Yves Lacoste is a French philosopher and theologian, currently affiliated with the University of Cambridge in England. He is chief editor of the *Critical Dictionary of Theology* (2004). Lacoste is strongly influenced by Heidegger, although at times also quite critical of him. His phenomenological interest is focused on liturgy and beauty, although his style of presentation is rather different from that of Chrétien who writes on some similar topics. His books include *Experience and the Absolute: Disputed Questions on the Humanity of Man*, a book on art (*Le Monde et l'absence de l'oeuvre*), and two collections that include many articles on the topics of God and religious experience: *La phénoménalité de Dieu* [The Phenomenality of God] and *Présence et parousie* [Presence and Parousia]. He has also just published a new extensive phenomenological work questioning Heidegger's modes of being, entitled *Être en Danger* [Being in Danger]. *Experience and the Absolute* explores the experience of human being before God or the Absolute. Most fundamentally, it contrasts this liturgical "being-before-God" to Heidegger's "being-in-the-world," arguing that such an examination of human being before the Absolute allows access to a dimension of being not revealed by Heidegger. Lacoste's argument is that this is not only an authentic way of being, but one that reveals important aspects of human Dasein to which Heidegger had no access, precisely because he excluded this aspect of human experience. Lacoste defines liturgy very loosely as any "being-before-God," not necessarily the concrete forms this takes in particular Christian traditions (for example, while worshipping in church), although he draws on them for examples and terminology. He is particularly interested in the ways in which our relation (or attempt at relation) with the Absolute pushes us to certain limit-experiences to which we ordinarily do not have access and which put in question our normal way of Being, challenging us to conceive ourselves differently. Lacoste explores many such limit-experiences, such as those of the nightly vigil, which deprives us of sleep and turns upside down our ordinary relation to time, or the travels of the pilgrim, which suspend relations with place. Liturgy thus subverts our normal relations to time and space by placing us in a non-place and an outside-of-time. We experience ourselves as foreign and as, in some sense, removed from the world, although Lacoste is quick to point out that this is not a world-denying attitude, but one that ultimately comes to affirm the world. The articles collected in the later volumes continue these themes (especially in regard to the topic of liturgy), but they also reflect on questions of truth, knowledge, experience, appearance, and other topics.

Experience and Affection

Lacoste's work is thoroughly phenomenological and deeply grounded in Heidegger's analyses, especially those of *Being and Time*. Although he is fundamentally interested in an analysis of religious experience and the ways in which we "are" before God liturgically, he is very hesitant to employ the term "religious experience." Indeed, he criticizes this terminology, which he associates with Friedrich Schleiermacher's thinking, in the strongest terms, especially when it is interpreted to mean religious feeling. Schleiermacher defined the impulse of religion as a "feeling of ultimate dependence" on the absolute. Lacoste is suspicious of such an embrace of feeling and affectivity as the central core of faith (one wonders whether a criticism of Henry's philosophy of affectivity is also implied here). Religion cannot be reduced to affectivity. God is not merely an object of feeling. God is indeed in some sense someone we can know, but this is a knowledge of experience, not an abstract and purely rational knowledge. Liturgy certainly does not amount to comprehension of God: "No one enters into liturgy without wishing for God to visit him. But no one experiences liturgy without comprehending that God is never there present to consciousness in an entirely obvious way" (*EA*, 63). Nor can liturgy be reduced to consciousness. It always goes beyond it: "If liturgy involved only what lay within the sphere of consciousness, the condescension and the presence of God would have what reaches consciousness and, ultimately, feeling as their measure, and would be susceptible to all the critiques of religious feeling" (*EA*, 63–64). Liturgy should not be defined in terms of consciousness because God always remains absolute and is not experienced by consciousness in any clearly tangible fashion.

Instead, Lacoste employs the method of phenomenology to analyze our experience of being-before-God. Yet this is an experience that differs from those described by Husserl and Heidegger. Lacoste calls it an "irreducible" phenomenon and is concerned with describing how such a phenomenon may appear. He makes a distinction between a description of our experience of a phenomenon and our description of the phenomenon itself. The two are not identical, especially in the case of God and the human other. God is known by faith and the phenomenological reduction would reduce our experience of God to something less than an encounter, as is also true of our experience of other people. Both the experience of the other human and the experience of God are ultimately irreducible. Lacoste finds that

> to attempt to give an account of the type of phenomenon that "I believe in" represents, we discover that in this case reduction is impossible or would disfigure the phenomenon. The right description, in this case as in that of the intersubjective "encounter," requires the transcendent reality of what it describes. Neither the existence of the other nor the existence of God can be put aside: not due to a personal decision or by *petitio principii*, but because to call these existences phenomenologically indispensable to description is merely the right response to their proper mode of phenomenality. (*PD*, 85)

Thus, in the case of an encounter, whether with the divine or a human other, the very phenomenality of the phenomenon requires that it remain irreducible. We cannot "bracket" the question of existence in these cases in the same way in which Husserlian phenomenology asks us to set aside this question in the investigation of phenomena more generally. For God and humans, existence matters. He goes on to show the differences between two types of phenomenality (of God and human other), drawing on and criticizing Lévinas's account of the other.

Lacoste has since examined this question of the possibility of God's phenomenological appearing more specifically, both at the end of *Présence et parousie* and in several chapters of *La phénoménalité de Dieu*. The final chapter of *Présence et parousie* deals with "the appearing of the revealed." Lacoste claims that there are two misinterpretations of phenomenology. The first is that it deals only with the real, only with things that can become objects of consciousness. The second is that there is only one mode of appearing. Instead, he suggests that there are many different kinds of real phenomena and that there are also many ways of appearing. In this context, he examines the appearing of "revelation" (*PP*, 324). This revelation is accessible to anyone who has the eyes to see it. God's appearing bridges the gap between the visible and the invisible, the empirical and the absent, faith and knowledge. God is neither completely hidden nor utterly obvious. God is "known as unknown" but also "unknown as known" (*PP*, 337), both clear and obscure: "The phenomenality particular to the clear-obscure would thus be the major condition of an intelligence of faith (a condition that we posit in our conceptuality, but which is only a theological banality)" (*PP*, 338). Revelation thus has its own phenomenality, which appears in its own time and place.

Lacoste begins his collection on "the phenomenality of God" by arguing that "it is high time to admit that phenomenology is neutral in the debate which opposes philosophy and theology to each other" (*PD*, 9). Like Marion he insists that since phenomenology studies what appears to us, it can put no restrictions or limitations on what kinds of phenomena are allowed to appear or how they are to do so: "Phenomenology is without limits. And that is not its least merit" (*PD*, 11). He suggests that the kinds of objects that are solely specific to a single discipline (i.e. just to philosophy or just to theology) are very rare indeed. When we speak of our experiences of "presence," "anticipation," "promise," and so forth, can we (and must we) not do so both theologically and philosophically? Numbers and God both appear to us, yet their modes of appearing differ and must be described—and both descriptions are phenomenological projects, Lacoste suggests (*PD*, 9). He insists that his method is one of allowing phenomena to appear in whatever mode they give themselves to intuition and also making them appear, that is, putting in the phenomenological work that makes them appear more clearly and more fully (*PD*, 10). (He examines these phenomenological modes in far more detail in his recent more strictly phenomenological work *Être en danger*.) In examining Kierkegaard's *Philosophical Fragments*, Lacoste points out how the boundary line between philosophy and theology has broken down in this text. In another article on Kierkegaard, he emphasizes the same issue. Kierkegaard shows us the importance of love (*PD*, 28). For Kierkegaard we can "think God" in the margins of philosophy precisely by loving (*PD*, 32). This is a theme to which we will return at the end of this chapter, as for Lacoste it characterizes the kind of knowledge we have about God.

In another study, entitled "Perception, Transcendence, Knowledge of God," Lacoste argues that God is not an object that can be discovered through perception, but that phenomenality is larger and that God can be known through affectivity (*PD*, 33). He explains "synthetic perception" and perception of objects in Husserl's phenomenology and tries to introduce a concept of transcendence into Husserl's phenomenology. This transcendence may apply to fragmentary or symbolic concepts, which we cannot perceive comprehensively. Phenomenology is not only about sensorial perception: "Phenomenology is interested in all phenomena, regardless of how they appear" (*PD*, 41). And there are also different modes of phenomenality and different ways of being. He analyzes feeling as a mode of phenomenality, basing his analysis on Scheler. If we want to know whether God or the Absolute have a mode of phenomenality, we must know whether the divine can appear. Although vision of God is usually an eschatological event, Lacoste insists that "we cannot forbid the Absolute to appear and to do so in the realm of affectivity" (*PD*, 47). He insists that there can be no experience of God without love and again criticizes Schleiermacher's phenomenology of religion, which in his view tries to seize and control the Absolute. Again, Lacoste links the possible experience we can have of the divine to a kind of love.

In the earlier text *Experience and the Absolute*, this experience is called liturgical. Lacoste explains that liturgy refers to our entire relation to God, including the spiritual life and prayer. Liturgy overcomes oppositions between interior and exterior, body and soul, individual and communal, this-worldly and other-worldly. This does not mean, however, that God can be reduced to an experience within the world. Rather, liturgy precisely goes beyond this being-in-the-world and its various earthly relations. Lacoste repeatedly contrasts this liturgical experience with the more general Heideggerian experience of being-in-the-world. He defines liturgy "as the resolute deliberate gesture made by those who ordain their being-in-the-world a being-before-God, and who do violence to the former in the name of the latter" (*EA*, 39). He will go on to argue that being-before-God challenges our being-in-the-world and presents a richer and more fully human experience.

Yet such liturgical experience or being is a choice. We do not *have* to encounter the Absolute, if we do not wish to do so. The liturgical experience is available to everyone, but it must be freely chosen. Lacoste speaks of liturgy as an experience that "each and every one of us can attempt to experience provided we accept the existence of a God who does not belong to the transcendental field of experience, and with whom one is not insane enough to wish to maintain an experiential relationship, but with whom it is possible to exist 'face-to-face'" (*EA*, 26). Although we can all enter into this experience, we can also refuse it. We can live as a Dasein in the world without God. We are not destined to choose either atheism or paganism or faith. Although Lacoste recognizes a kind of phenomenological experience of restlessness that may point to a desire for the divine, it is not clearly identifiable as a desire for God. Thus, we must choose to pursue this desire and to open ourselves to the Absolute: "Our exposition to God is thus radically distinct from our opening onto the world in that it speaks to us, not the language of facticity, but the language of an experience of surplus grounded in a divine donation or in an unveiling that we ourselves must undertake" (*EA*, 41). It is precisely this approach or exposition to God that Lacoste seeks to analyze. Like all the previously discussed thinkers, he is less interested in describing or "proving" God than in providing an account for religious experience as it already occurs in "liturgical" relations.

Although this experience is a choice and not shared by everyone, Lacoste argues that it does challenge ordinary experience and shows a deeper dimension of what it means to be human. He concludes the first part of *Experience and the Absolute* by depicting liturgy as making us truly human: "Liturgy, understood in its broadest sense, is the most human mode in which we can exist in the world or on the earth. And it is in the world or on the earth that it responds, once and for all, to the question of the place proper to man: beyond the historial play between world and earth, man has for his true *dwelling place* the *relation* he seals with God or that God seals with him" (*EA*, 98). Similar claims about the unique access liturgy gives to what makes us human conclude the second part:

> Thus the paradoxical joy that is born of humiliation may be the *fundamental mood* of preeschatological experience. The reconciled man, despite what Hegel might say, is still at a distance from his absolute future. And, despite what Nietzsche might say, the disappropriated and humiliated man is not reduced to nothing, and does not reduce himself to nothing, but lives now in the fulfillment of God's promises to come. Man takes hold of what is most proper to him when he chooses to encounter God. This argument can now be made more specific: we can now assert that man says who he is most precisely when he accepts an existence in the image of a God who has taken humiliation upon himself—when he accepts a *kenotic* existence. (*EA*, 194)

Thus liturgical experience, our being-before-God, shows us a deeper and fuller dimension of what it means to be human. We become most ourselves when we stand before God. The liturgical (or kenotic) dimension of being human is its most authentic one.[1] What, then, is this liturgical being like? It is most fundamentally an experience at the limit, an excessive experience that subverts our usual common relationships to time and space.

The Place of Liturgy

The "topology" or "place" of liturgy plays a major role in Lacoste's analysis. He finds that the "topos" of liturgy challenges our habitual conceptions of place and certainly the standard phenomenological descriptions of place, earth, and world. Liturgy takes place in a particular liturgical space. Human liturgical being both confirms and criticizes "topological identity" (*EA*, 26). Liturgical being experiences place as a "dwelling at the limit." Lacoste describes the recluse or hermit as an example for a liturgical way of being that pushes our experience of space to its limits. A hermit lives in reclusion, far away from ordinary living, often in the desert or in a cave. The recluse does not interact with others but uses the space of the cave in order to transcend all attachment to place. The recluse shows that "the relation to the Absolute implies a particular way of disposing of place . . . an ironic subversion of his location . . . The experiential practice of liturgy can open up a space where neither world nor earth is interposed between man and God" (*EA*, 28). A very different experience with a similar result is that of the pilgrim who is not tied to any particular place, but continually wanders from place to place: "No regional particularism, national or otherwise, can define or determine his humanity" (*EA*, 29). The pilgrim is free, not tied to the provincialism of a particular place and ethnicity. Lacoste concludes from these limit-experiences of hermit and pilgrim that "no immanent logic of place is implied in liturgical experience" (*EA*, 32). Lacoste is always careful to emphasize, however, that this is not merely a rejection of attachment to place. It is also an affirmation of the ground because that is the very context where the divine is encountered and it is experienced as contributing to and enabling this encounter. Both critique and affirmation are always present. Ultimately, liturgy "exacerbates our not-being-at-home in the world and is a critique of our relation to the earth" (*EA*, 74).

Even the more "regular" and common space of the church illustrates this. This very space is a liminal place that is unsettled by a "fragile anticipation":

> The church does not thus put itself forward as a space established for definitive existence, and its narthex does not separate the unhappiness of history from the happiness of the eschaton. It puts itself forward as something else: the place of a fragile anticipation. The intervals during which it is our dwelling place, the time of worship or of silent contemplation, bracket the petitions of history and the laws that world and earth impose on us. (*EA*, 36)

In the liturgical space, we exist both in the present experience of history and in anticipation of the future. As the eschaton is anticipated through the liturgy, our normal relations with the world are suspended for the short time of the liturgical event. Liturgical architecture both breaks with the logic of place (it is a kind of "non-place"; we do not live in it), but it also rests on the earth and shows its beauty and significance. Therefore, "liturgical architecture is in tune with another destiny and another rhythm" (*EA*, 36).

Lacoste also links this to our experience of the body. Ecclesial space affirms corporeality. Our relation to the divine engages our bodies. He uses the imagery of the dance to illustrate this. Liturgy consists of bodily gestures and is expressed in the "language of the flesh." In the liturgical dance, "the body symbolically allows worldly or earthly logic to take leave of its inscription in place" (*EA*, 38). In this liturgical dance, we are present before God bodily in a particular time and place. Thus, Lacoste concludes that "it falls to liturgy to do justice to the complexity of the question of place in a way that a phenomenology in which the world and earth constitute the ultimate or the intranscendable par excellence cannot" (*EA*, 39). Liturgy can reveal broader and deeper experiences of space and time, experiences we would miss if we existed merely "in the world."

Lacoste pushes these insights further in *Présence et parousie* where he challenges the standard critiques of presence, which reduce it to objectivity. One might say that the book is a kind of retrieval of presence, where presence becomes a phenomenological event. He argues instead that sacramental presence in particular is not about a place at all, but rather about a kind of non-place. This non-place of the eucharistic celebration is not identical to the eschatological parousia. Lacoste wants to show in this book that the presence of art, for example, gives rise to affection and solicits our freedom. He argues that while Heidegger is primarily interested in human existence in the world, presence is more about the appearance of art or the experience of another human being or anything else that appeals to our affectivity. "Presence is not perceived, it is sensed and welcomed" (*PP*, 13). Affectivity is thus once again contrasted with an experience based in knowledge. While our lack of perception does not "give presence," it is already there to invite our presence. Using the example of eucharistic presence, Lacoste argues that the notion of place here suffers a kind of "extraterritoriality" in respect to the world, to history, and to the earth. The divine "sacramental presence, here and now, puts the atheism of the world, the paganism of the earth, and the violence of history into parentheses" (*PP*, 15). This presence gives rise to the desire for the parousia within us. Presence is thus also closely linked to a new experience of time, which we will examine momentarily.

He is most explicitly concerned with place in Chapter 6 of *Présence et parousie* where he wonders whether faith or liturgy (being-before-God) is a way of being in the world or, rather, being in a different kind of world, which becomes established around its experiences. He begins by outlining Heidegger's analysis of being-in-the-world and the phenomena that can only appear as "aberrant" for Heidegger, but which are, in fact, phenomena of a spiritual life and which he insists are excluded from being-in-the-world only at great danger. Phenomena that put human finitude and existence in question, such as those of liturgy or the phenomenon of hope, cannot appear for Heideggerian facticity. Although the world and human existence reveal themselves in a certain way for Heidegger, this is not the only way in which they can appear. Space and time can be experienced differently, namely liturgically: "The human who prays or who wants to pray only wants to be there for the act of being present to the Absolute" (*PP*, 156). As in the previous analysis of liturgy, the world is put in parentheses. Liturgy gives access to new and different phenomena that cannot appear in a Heideggerian schema and yet are certainly ways of being in the world. In the world, humans exist without God, but that does not mean that humans cannot be present to God. In the presence of liturgy and the experience of hope, being-toward-death is challenged as the final word on what it means to be human. Liturgical experience is "more-than-existing" in the Heideggerian sense, although Lacoste warns us that spiritual existence is not somehow completely separate from "normal" existence. Normal existence can enter into the spiritual life. In fact, the line of demarcation between being-in-the-world and "being-beyond-the-world" cannot be clearly identified. Liturgical being simply exemplifies that the world is larger than being-in-the-world is able to see or experience. The "liturgical possibility" is a "being-beyond-the-world," in which we live not exclusively but additionally and by choice. Lacoste explains: "We can be content with existing. We can also want more—but nothing wants it in our place" (*PP*, 168). Liturgical being opens new possibilities of existence and a vision of the world that are inaccessible to a non-liturgical experience.

Time, Presence, and Parousia

To make a distinction between discussions of place and time in Lacoste's work is somewhat artificial, as the two are closely linked. The "presence" of *Présence et parousie* to some extent refers both to place and to time, although time is the more prominent theme in the explication, especially in its relation to parousia. Yet already in *Experience and the Absolute*, Lacoste speaks of liturgical existence as a new experience of time just as it also challenges our experience of place. Liturgy gives us an experience of time "at the limit." This is especially expressed by the eschatological language of the liturgy. Liturgy speaks of the eschaton, of being in the presence of God, but this is a promise and a desire, not yet a reality: "We desire an eschatological proximity to God. But the liturgies that express this desire do not of course enjoy possession of the eschaton; the Absolute does not make itself present in the world without this presence conforming to the ambiguous modes by which the world manifests it (the world is not the field of theophany but that of the chiaroscuro, the field of a 'kenotic' presence or of the sacraments)" (*EA*, 36). Liturgy always remains ambiguous in its manifestation because the reality that is promised in it never becomes fully present. The sacraments speak of this particularly well and, in *Présence et parousie*, presence will be closely linked to sacramental presence, especially the Eucharist.[2] Liturgy is *"the expectation or desire for Parousia in the certitude of the nonparousiacal presence of God"* (*EA*, 45). Prayer, as he says later, exceeds the normal time of the world and puts it in question (*PP*, 157). Throughout, the presence announced in liturgy or prayer thus is not something we come to possess, but rather this presence suspends our normal relations with the world and our conceptions of it. Instead of opening a new time, it challenges our mundane experiences of time.

The time of liturgy is one of "disinterestedness" in the world. The world still lays claims on us, but while we are before God, time and history do not have the same power over us that they usually do. This does not mean that liturgy is an eternal present without past or future, but its experience of past and future (especially eschatological future) is radically different. Lacoste proposes a diachronic reading of time through the experience of prayer. The person who prays "exists from his own future onward": "The concept of a plenary present is not that of an eternity, and liturgy exercises no power over the eschaton; liturgy can only precariously transmute the worldly reality of divine presence, and welcome it as one would welcome the Parousia. There is, however, no theoretical exaggeration in saying of him who prays that his liturgy's hermeneutic site does not first lie on this side of death, and that, in a certain sense, he has already survived his death" (*EA*, 59). Of course, one cannot prove that there is anything beyond death and yet prayer does go beyond death and exceeds our being here and now. Thus, it frees us from our "being-toward-death" and redefines us as "being-for-life." Lacoste claims that this experience indeed challenges Heidegger's claim that being-toward-death is the most essential definition of human Dasein. Liturgy thinks "beyond our death" by envisioning the possibility of an eschatological existence. It does not prove that such an existence will occur, but it makes it possible "to think an eschatological modality of existence." The logic of liturgy, which is eschatological in character and relies on "a promise and a gift," presents a different kind of logic than that of being-toward-death. While this eschatological dimension that is promised in the liturgy can be ignored, even by the person at prayer, it is an essential part of liturgy. Lacoste insists that

> no intellection of liturgy is possible if we do not recognize in it the clearing in which the Absolute's eschatological claims over us are substituted for the world's historical claims—not, of course, by abolishing the facticity of the world, but by taking possession of the liturgical nonplace and enabling a certain overshadowing of our facticity that does not amount to an act of divertissement. It is in this regard that the *eschaton* is, not the horizon in which the man who prays lives, but already the hidden *present* of our prayers. (*EA*, 61)

This quote summarizes much of Lacoste's argument with Heidegger. Liturgical being challenges Heideggerian facticity, not by annulling it, but by showing another possible dimension beyond it, another way of being. While we never leave the world and continue to perform our prayer within it, liturgy introduces another dimension of reality within our experience that opens us beyond this experience. This way of being (before God) is optional and a gift but it is a real, meaningful, and more profound way of being than that of everyday Dasein.

Again, Lacoste emphasizes that liturgical being is a choice. Liturgy is secondary to being-in-the-world and can always be rejected. It is indeed a regional experience (as Heidegger had claimed in "Phenomenology and Theology"), but its symbolic space at the limit of our existence subverts ordinary being and its relation to the future.[3] Lacoste illustrates this with the "kairos" (the opportune time) of the vigil. In the vigil, the time of liturgy appears as a surplus: "The vigil is time gained, and thus existence gained, and this time is that of a marginal or parenthetic experience" (*EA*, 83). He examines care, restlessness, and patience as concrete phenomenological experiences during the vigil. The vigil opens the person at prayer to God, but makes no promise that God will be encountered. There is attentiveness and expectation, but it is ultimately "a confession of powerlessness" (*EA*, 91). This constitutes a further critique of our being-in-the-world. Liturgy shows that while being-in-the-world is our initial condition, it is neither definitive nor originary. The vigil is an experience of distance and dispossession, which also play important roles in Lacoste's thought.[4]

Liminality and Abnegation

Both in regard to place and time, then, liturgical existence is a liminal experience. The experience of prayer is an experience that "dwells at the limit" (*EA*, 42). Liturgy imposes a "being-at-the-limit" (*EA*, 44). The essence of prayer is praise.[5] Liturgy tries to experience the "proximity or distance of God," but the person at prayer actually "does nothing but prepare the space of a possibility" (*EA*, 46). Liturgy is a nonevent, where we wait for God's veiled presence to manifest itself:

> But the man who prays does not do so in order to prove his existence or the possibility of a mode of existence: he prays, on the one hand, to subordinate what he and world and earth are unveiled as to God's veiled presence, while hoping, on the other hand, that the veiled and omnipresent God will provide proof of his presence. Despite the undeniable importance of a phenomenology of the expectation of God, liturgy must thus appear to us, first of all, as a human power to liberate a space where perhaps nothing can come to pass that, in the sphere of immanence of consciousness, would bear unequivocal witness to God's condescension. (*EA*, 47)

This making oneself present before God and expecting God's presence opens the space of liturgy. It is a liminal experience because God is veiled and never fully comes to presence. Any authentic experience of prayer realizes that the divine always far transcends the person at prayer. Yet, although liturgy pushes us to the limits of experience, it also returns us to the world. Lacoste is emphatic that liturgy is not a denial or rejection of the world, but an affirmation of it: "One enters into liturgy through the passage to the limit traversed by those who recognize in the world a closed region of experience, but who then break through this closure by choosing to subordinate their opening onto the world to their exposition to God" (*EA*, 51). While liturgy suspends the world and its history in some fashion, it also always returns us to it. New possibilities for history and world are imagined in the eschatological dimension of liturgy. The return to the world that takes place at the end of the liturgical experience is not simply a return to everyday existence. We find ourselves, and even the world, radically transformed by this liturgical experience.

The experience of liturgical being indeed has a profound effect on the self. It is a practice of abnegation and poverty and thus essentially kenotic. One example of this is the boredom often experienced in prayer. The time of liturgy is experienced as wasted time: "Although liturgical inexperience need not give rise to boredom, boredom is a constant and useful reminder to us that nonexperience is essential to the liturgical play—and that it can be intolerable to us" (*EA*, 149). Liturgy undoes subjectivity by describing the self primarily in terms of passivity, as a patient waiting before God. This is an experience of abnegation that displaces the modern subject. And yet abnegation also "gives us access to what is most proper to man" (*EA*, 161). We are no longer in possession of ourselves and cannot provide our own grounding. Abnegation has several dimensions. First it designates the "inexperience" of liturgy, where nothing seems to happen because it is suspended between a rejection of the pleasures of the world and the as of yet unfilled expectation of the joy of the eschaton, or at least God's presence. Second, it means the passive availability of the self that is no longer a modern subject.[6] Lacoste describes this as a kind of violence to and negation of this concept of the modern subject. Finally, abnegation shows that the will is involved in this process and chooses to be present, although it simultaneously recognizes that it has no power over the Absolute or its appearing. He concludes that "abnegation wills more than the will to power wills. It does not bring into being; it lets be. But in letting be, it puts itself at the mercy of a God to whom it relates through promises, and who promises more than the immanent reality of 'life'" (*EA*, 166). Thus, like other thinkers, Lacoste puts forward a more passive version of the self, in which we respond to the divine call and become available to it, instead of being an active subject in control of our destiny and of the things around us.

Lacoste therefore thinks of the liturgical self as a "kenotic" self. This self rejects appropriation and chooses dispossession. It separates the link between being-in-the-world and being-toward death by confronting death in light of the promises of Easter, thus emptying it of mastery over death. It exercises dispossession also prior to death. The various examples of asceticism and voluntary poverty in the tradition illustrate this freedom from appropriation as essential to human being.[7] Liturgy encapsulates this kenotic way of poverty and dispossession. Liturgy allows us to move from a philosophical admiration of such an ideal to a practical living of it. Lacoste calls such a self a "being-in-vocation" and demonstrates it with several examples from the Christian tradition, such as that of the "holy fool" or the Kierkegaardian "knight of faith." He argues that "despite the strangeness of these gestures, and even though they are not universally required of everyone who wishes to encounter God, the ascetic does, in fact, act on behalf of everyone and as everyone's proxy" (*EA*, 178). The fool's experience again reveals the relation to the Absolute as that of a limit-experience that goes beyond normal experience toward the eschaton. The liturgical experience, as highlighted by these extreme cases, is ultimately a subversion of being-in-the-world as the most primary and originary experience of the human.

Body and Community

Throughout his work, Lacoste emphasizes corporeality. As pointed out earlier, the body is essential to the liturgical experience. For Lacoste, this insight is particularly centered in the Eucharist. In Chapter 3 of *Présence et parousie*, Lacoste examines "the true and the body," which he subtitles "non-systematic remarks on liturgy and Eucharist." He begins by insisting again that "before being something of which we speak, the mystery is something which we do" (*PP*, 63). Thus, this is also a reflection on the nature of theological language and silence. He examines the grounds of perception and objectivity that allow me to think of myself as a body and to encounter the other. He also examines our experience of the world and Heidegger's notion of facticity. Yet the same body that explores the world and grasps things can also be lifted in thanksgiving during the liturgical act. Lacoste argues that mystery ruptures our ordinary world of perception. Various names can be given to this radical experience (he cites Marion as one example), yet liturgy always consists in rupture. The witness to this experience gives rise to a community that places faith in the testimony. Lacoste insists repeatedly that liturgical words are never singular, but always already communal: "we exist before God in our eucharistic acts" (*PP*, 70). This is not a dissolution of self, but certainly a disappropriation, although it is not one that kills but one that gives life. The Absolute is no longer other but is invited and place is made for peace: "The Absolute who ask us to make place for it always proposes only its peace. The human being who prays is the human reconciled to God. 'Saved,' if one wants" (*PP*, 71–72). Eucharist, self, church, and bodily existence are all linked here (*PP*, 73). The church as a whole, its individual members, and the eucharistic bread are all called *body* of Christ. Even in the eschatological expectation to which the liturgy points and which it desires, bodies are not eliminated. In fact, the Eucharist specifically speaks of this bodily proximity even in regard to the divine. It is the "human body of God given here and now" (*PP*, 73).

Exemplifying this proximity in our lives turns it into an "event of speech." He speaks of liturgical incorporation into the mystery of the Eucharist as a kind of liturgical school that teaches us to speak well of God and of the liturgical event. Lacoste acknowledges that his discourse is about the Eucharist and the liturgy and thus distinct (and distant) from the language of the liturgy itself. And yet all reflection on the *lex orandi* [rule of prayer] must be incorporated again into the liturgical experience. Lacoste outlines how chant has both a relationship with words or speech and is more bodily than they are. Within the liturgy, chant accomplishes "the work of sanctification" (*PP*, 76). In this way, "the liturgical word, in contrast [to our every-day chatter] is a perpetual vocative" (77). It speaks of the most important things, such as life and death, the sacred and the secular, and hospitality. In liturgy we transgress the secular and everyday and are carried beyond it. Sacred and secular intermingle. Being-in-the-world experiences itself as being-before-God. Liturgy uses the words, the bodies, and the things of the world in order to speak of what is beyond the world. It thus constitutes a rupture even with the highest kinds of words uttered in the world (for example, with those of poetry). We participate in the Eucharist within history and yet it is also a pre-eschatological event, a kind of eschatological presence. He defines "parousia" as fullness of presence, while "presence" tends to be partial and provisional. For Lacoste, then, "participation in the Eucharist is the fact of the human as such, body and soul, intellect and affection, aptitude for language and aptitude for silence" (*PP*, 81). As for Chrétien, words and silence are always linked. Liturgy leads to a kind of rich silence where our flesh speaks the promise of life through its participation in the Eucharist: "The flesh destined to die says that it is not its definition to die—the eucharistic word and the eucharistic silence say the desire to live, such as it is raised by the promise of life" (*PP*, 83). Again, Lacoste insists that this interpretation of the Eucharist challenges being-toward-death as the final definition of Dasein.

For Lacoste, not just individual bodies matter, but like Chrétien he always emphasizes the communal dimension as well. Already in *Experience and the Absolute*, Lacoste points out that liturgy is "a plural experience" (*EA*, 157). This is also true of many of his essays, but laid out particularly clearly in "Liturgy and Coaffection," where he examines the experience of prayer by wondering about the "us" that gets together in prayer, by analyzing liturgy as an experience that is not about subjects and objects, and in order to wonder in what sense liturgy is a "coaffective experience" (*PP*, 45). He examines Husserl's notion of the other, which, although it is always plural, allows others to intervene primarily as noematic content (i.e., as projections of our own consciousness). He goes on to analyze Heidegger's "Mitdasein" (being-with-others), which he thinks gets us further than Husserl in that the I does not lodge an intentional gaze on things, but opens a world. Yet even Heidegger does not go far enough in his analysis of being with others. Lacoste does not reject either Husserl's or Heidegger's accounts, but sees them as important explorations of particular human experiences, fruitful each in their own way. And yet he agrees with Lévinas that to take this approach to the other as paradigmatic can become dangerous and violent. Lacoste proposes the liturgical experience of "coram Deo" as an alternative to this monadic existence. It is not about objects and subjects and defies normal versions of intersubjectivity. The things of liturgy (such as candles and icons) "appear" but they do not do so as objects. They are not constituted by consciousness in the way objects are. Rather, they provide a space in which we live liturgically: "Bread, wine, cup, candles, icons, etc. the things which one uses liturgically occupy a space which is not that of geometry but a lived space, and a space which envelops us ourselves" (PP, 51). Again he emphasizes that liturgy is not performed at a distance, but that it involves real body and flesh. And most important here is that liturgy is always a communal experience: "Liturgy thus offers us a pure case of existence as coexistence, of being-there as co-being-there" (PP, 52). To pray with another is a form of concern for the other, just as the things of liturgy are no longer merely things but much more.[8] There is no grasping or representation possible in liturgy. In liturgy we are actors without a spectator. The participation in the liturgy is like that of a drama: "Mystery is something one does, not something one contemplates" (PP, 98). One "exists" in a mode other than being a subject in liturgy. Liturgy is work in common, existence is coexistence. Things become sacraments. Liturgy disqualifies the "everyday" way of being with the figure of cohabitation. It exceeds Heidegger's "being-with-others" because it is a real dwelling with others.

Lacoste here brings together several of his previous insights by showing that the liturgical experience he describes is ultimately communal in character. He reiterates the account provided in *Experience and the Absolute*, that we are in liturgy as a pilgrim in the world, not tied to a particular place, and now extends it to the communal dimension: "Those who pray together undertake an act of communion" (PP, 99). This is a "desire for communion that is not merely a figment of the imagination" (PP, 55, 100). It involves body, memory, affectivity. We participate in it. Liturgy lives a "with" without subject or object. God is not always felt in the heart. Liturgy assumes that we have will, heart, sensibility. The order of manifestation exceeds being-in-the-world. In liturgy, the other is a brother or sister, who is to be "loved without delay" (PP, 59, 102). Existence and life are given liturgically and "shatter the measure of the world" (PP, 103). We have a presentiment of joy, peace, recollection, reconciliation. God is not given in only one way within the condition of the world. In prayer we speak our wish for "a plenary presence of the Absolute at the heart of coaffection" (PP, 103).

Language, Knowledge, and Truth

Finally, Lacoste's account has much to say about language and truth. Liturgy provides us with a new relation to words and the text: "The liturgy makes words un-everyday" (*PP*, 54, 99). Lacoste begins an article on "Philosophy, Theology, and Truth" (in *Présence et parousie*) with several propositions:

> 1. The Christian experience includes the experience of a true language, or at least of a language which pretends to be true. 2. This language is formed at the interior of a form of life, and its formation supposes the accessibility of this form of life. 3. That this language would be true and the corresponding form of life can be appropriated, weighs this language with a requirement of translateability. 4. Before being communicable, the Christian experience thus requires a minimal theory of reference and of signification. 5. Between the truth of words and the totality of an experience there is a necessarily complementary relationship. (*PP*, 85)

These propositions recall much of Ricoeur's insights about religious language. Religious language makes a claim to truth that is confirmed in the kind of life to which it gives rise. Language and experience are in a dialectical relationship with each other. In this particular article, Lacoste seeks to examine these presuppositions and their implications. He wonders about the meaning of truth in this context. Examining both analytical and continental approaches to truth (which tend to posit themselves as exclusive of each other), he points out how both are incapable of dealing with the truth of imagination or religion. Thus, he criticizes a notion of philosophy that is only about philosophy of language and is incapable of dealing with an experience that is communal, that arises from God, that has a common language, and that claims universality (*PP*, 94). This experience, Lacoste suggests, would give rise to a very different theory of language (than either the analytical or the Continental versions).[9] According to Lacoste, "Jesus is Savior" is true "in a world where the language of salvation is an intelligible language" (*PP*, 97). Thus, truth is articulated and shaped within a specific form of life.[10] Lacoste emphasizes that language is organic and linked to subjectivity. We can imagine neither a self without language nor a completely subjective language not linked to the body and to a set of (communal) rules. Lacoste argues that there is no such thing as a "totally other" language of God, but that we use our common human language to speak of the divine. He suggests in closing that what is true matters most to the extent that it responds philosophically or theologically to questions in which humans put themselves in question.

In an article on negative theology or apophasis, which Lacoste calls "silent consciousness" or knowledge, he makes a distinction between two types of knowledge: *connaissance* and *savoir* (*PP*, 120). He thinks of them as two spheres of knowledge, where one is about silent knowledge and the other about knowing language. One is about familiarity, the other about description and explication. He examines Husserlian phenomenology of language and shows that it refuses to deal with the ineffable. Knowing and incomprehensibility always go together. Lacoste examines the tradition that claims that God cannot be known because the divine is incomprehensible. Instead, he argues that God is incomprehensible, precisely because the divine can be known. Lacoste contends that Patristic literature does make a clear distinction between knowing and comprehending. God can be known, but not ultimately comprehended. God is known as mysterious. Yet mystery is linked to liturgy or cult and thus to experience. Thus, the mystery is mystagogically (i.e., liturgically) present in the community and yet always mysteriously absent (*PP*, 130). God's proximity is mediated sacramentally. Liturgy hence does not claim total visibility or coherence, but it is a sacramental experience of the gift of peace. This is not about "religious sentiment" but about living in the element of mystery. Being before God is a kind of knowledge, but not a theoretical or abstract one. It affirms its own incompleteness by distinguishing between the church present and the eschatological reality. The whole human being is bodily turned toward God in the liturgy. The liturgical silence is partial, as it is mixed with the expressive language of praise and prayer. He rejects the idea of a God that would be completely unknowable as folly.[11] Thus, the Absolute can be known both by affect and reason and still remain incomprehensible: "Knowledge of God and the spiritual life are without place in the world" and yet humans can find a place where God can be known and encountered (*PP*, 143). This is a liturgical and eschatological place. Therefore, he says, "theology is accomplished not in negation nor in negation of negation, but in praise, chant or silence, begun in time and continued in eternity" (*PP*, 144). Here, Lacoste seems to disagree with Marion's more forceful rejection of the possibility of gaining any knowledge about the divine, although they agree to a large extent that an experience of God is possible and can be described phenomenologically.

In Chapter 7 of *Présence et parousie*, Lacoste again explores the topic of the language of theology. He reflects here on Marion's question whether the language of theology must also be silent. Must theological discourse be interrupted by periodic silences? After examining the question of suffering, Lacoste suggests that theological language must always be both theoretical and practical and that theology might be "fragmentary and asystematic" (*PP*, 169). He rejects theodicy as a purely theoretical and speculative consideration of "the problem of evil" that disregards the real and concrete suffering of the other by turning suffering into a theoretical problem. The real suffering of the other exhorts us to silence or to "praying with" him or her: "The silence of compassion is not the only case where theology founds itself reduced to silence, but it is an exemplary one" (*PP*, 173). To care for the ill and feed the hungry is an essential part of theology. In this sense, theology is practical because it must be articulated in mercy and compassion.[12] Thus, the "urgency of speaking" and the "urgency of doing" as a community always go together. Humility and compassion are important requirements for theology and they arise out of confession and narrative, not out of reason or certainty.

Already in *Experience and the Absolute*, Lacoste had emphasized that we can speak about God because God's name has already entered into philosophy and liturgical naming presupposes this: "It remains that every attempt we make to improve on how we speak of the Absolute is radically preceded by a veiling that it must presuppose, and which constitutes its horizon. God has been named before I name him" (*EA*, 108). As in Ricoeur, for Lacoste we can speak of God because God has already been spoken of, because there is a history of speaking about God. Yet there is no complete knowledge of God. Prayer and liturgical being always exist in the ambivalent space between knowing and non-knowing. God is always beyond anything we may know, but this not a lack but something essential to the experience:

> The act of presence that constitutes prayer is accomplished after Easter in the element of a knowledge that perhaps leaves room for nonknowledge, but which is not endangered by this nonknowledge. To know is not to understand, and it also belongs to what we should know of God, for our knowledge to be consistent, that God give rise to thought without ever being possible for its reflection on him to come to an end: he must continue to elude our grasp. (*EA*, 141)

Here, the distinction between knowledge and understanding is again important. While we will never be able to *understand* the divine because God always escapes our grasp, we can indeed *know* God. Ultimately, Lacoste will argue that we can only know God in love.

Lacoste shows how even the biblical texts themselves are fragmented and do not give complete answers to our questions. There is no theological system, but rather lots of metaphorical and symbolic narrative. Lacoste rejects the idea of a clear development of doctrine; tradition is always "a continual process that is both hermeneutic and heuristic" (*PP*, 183). Again, he reminds us that "theology does not ask itself whether it is possible to speak of God: it is the inheritor of such a discourse, of which the possibility is obvious" (*PP*, 185). Theology encourages us and helps us to read the biblical texts, but is not the final word about them. Rather, it is the act of listening to the biblical text. This silence also enables prayer: "To read this text is to read before God; hence it is to make one's reading a liturgy, a work of prayer" (*PP*, 187). Lacoste does contend that we can encounter God within theology and insists that this conception of theology does not take from its rigor. Theology therefore is a rigorous discourse of love: "At the revelation of a Loving Sovereign, one doubts whether the only adequate response can be anything but returning love with love. Yet theology may well be speaking of God in loving him. It can say how to deploy the logic of divine love, such as in its self-manifestation and in its transmission from human to human. And that is saying a lot" (*PP*, 191). As in Marion, love has its own logic and theology pursues this logic rigorously. This discourse of love is a way of knowing God and even of communicating knowledge about the divine.

Finally, in an article included in *La phénoménalité de Dieu*, "God Known as Loved: Beyond Faith and Reason," Lacoste draws this out most explicitly. He claims that faith and reason are not opposed to another, but are two types of knowledge. Faith is indeed a kind of knowledge and historically was actually regarded as higher than reason. Lacoste shows the detrimental path this thinking took by identifying the realm of reason with nature and faith with the supernatural. He contends that this masks a more fundamental problem, namely that God wants not only to be known, but to be loved. God appears as love and in order to give rise to love in return. Relying heavily on Kierkegaard for his analysis, Lacoste argues that many objects are visible only when they are loved. While under normal circumstances something has to be known before it can be loved, in the case of God, love comes before knowledge. God is known precisely as loved. Faith and love go together and thus a theology of faith is also a "theory of love" (*PD*, 93). Yet phenomenologically "it would be wise not to imagine the life of the believer as a perpetual act of love responding to a perpetual act of manifestation" (*PD*, 94). Although we can ignore this love or criticize the Scriptures, they are imbued with the logic of love from beginning to end. In Lacoste's view, faith independent of love and hope makes no sense. Similar to Marion, he argues that reason operates by concepts, but that even faith relies on certain types of evidence. To believe means to experience a kind of truth. This truth is experienced through love, in a parallel fashion to the way one "knows" a work of art. Love, then, is a type of knowledge, but knowledge is necessary for it to happen. He concludes: "The name of God has a theological history and nothing can place itself at the end of this history—there where God appears only as love and as being loved—without knowing this history and this history alone allows him to recognize the present Absolute in the form of a servant" (*PD*, 100). Lacoste thus ends, to some extent, where Marion does: Knowledge of God is an alternative knowledge of love. We can experience the divine and give an account of this experience phenomenologically in terms of love.

Lacoste's account is deeply theological, even as it is also profoundly influenced by phenomenology. Lacoste employs phenomenological categories in order to depict our experience before and knowledge of God. He consistently maintains that this "being-before-God," as it is experienced in the liturgical event, is a more profound and deeper account of what it means to be human. Although engaging in liturgy always remains optional, it provides a kind of insight into the human condition that is inaccessible to a purely phenomenological account, such as those of Husserl and Heidegger. Liturgy and prayer push us to the very limits of human experience. They thus enable us to displace our ordinary experiences of space and time, of our bodies and our interactions with others, in a way that leads to greater peace and love by suspending ordinary worldly relations that hold us captive. The kenotic existence of abnegation liberates us from false attachments to places, time, and things and frees us for a more authentic existence. The experience of the Absolute challenges us at the deepest core of our being. Although Lacoste continually stresses that this is an "optional" being and that we are free to reject it, he provides a powerful argument for its authenticity and even necessity. God can indeed be known in love and we can live a life of openness to this love and therefore also to the other. If apologetics means the defense of religious belief and life as meaningful and authentic, Lacoste's work is deeply apologetic.

Emmanuel Falque: A God of Suffering and Resurrection

Emmanuel Falque (born in 1963), along with Jean-Louis Chrétien, belongs to the next generation of French thinkers. He was a student of Jean-Luc Marion and Jean Greisch and is presently dean of the faculty of philosophy at the Institut catholique in Paris. He has degrees in both philosophy and theology and merges the two disciplines far more fully than any of the other thinkers, occasionally even challenging the boundaries between these subject matters as unnecessary and superficial.[1] Falque's work is especially characterized by a phenomenological reading of theological doctrines and thinkers. His dissertation was a phenomenological reading of Bonaventure (*Saint Bonaventure et l'entrée de Dieu en théologie* / "St. Bonaventure and the Entry of God into Theology," published as a book in 2000[2]), followed by a second study in which he reads nine Patristic and medieval theologians for their phenomenological contributions to the topics of God, the flesh, and the other (*Dieu, la chair et l'autre* / "God, the Flesh and the Other," published in Marion's *Épiméthée* series in 2008). He is also author of a three-volume series on suffering, death, resurrection, flesh, and corporeality, where he seeks to push recent phenomenologies of the flesh even further to take full account of our materiality and corporeality in what he calls our "animality." These are also almost always phenomenological analyses of theological themes and doctrines. The first book is identified as an "existential and phenomenological reading" in the subtitle, while the other two are called "philosophical essays" in the respective subtitles. Falque's subject matter, then, is almost exclusively theological and yet he engages in these analyses as a philosopher and argues that they are fully phenomenological treatments. In Falque, "theological phenomenology" reaches its height. This chapter will first examine Falque's methodology that is most clearly articulated in his reading of Patristic and medieval material, especially in *Dieu, la chair et l'autre*. It will then proceed to analyze the most important themes in his trilogy *Le passeur de Gethsémani* ["The Guide to Gethsemane," 1999[3]], *Métamorphose de la finitude* ["Metamorphosis of Finitude," 2004], and *Les Noces de l'agneau* ["The Nuptials of the Lamb," 2011]. As most of these books are not yet available in English, I will provide somewhat more extensive summaries here than for some of the other thinkers in earlier chapters whose works are readily available.

Reading Theology Phenomenologically

Falque begins *Dieu, la chair et l'autre* by articulating his presuppositions and approach to the medieval texts. In the very first sentence, he says, "This book opens with an audacious claim and puts its trust in a wager, namely that it is possible to read the fathers and medievals *philosophically* today, precisely and including theological subjects" (*DCA*, 11). He makes clear that he is not interested in discovering the supposed "roots" of phenomenology in the medievals. Rather, he wants to "put phenomenology itself to work in the theological corpus, in order to show what neither one nor the other has yet seen: the ultimate possibility of describing theology's modes of manifestation phenomenologically, precisely and including *the internal life of the texts of the tradition* that are today to be (re)discovered" (*DCA*, 12). He insists that God, flesh, and other are important themes of contemporary phenomenology that can profit from a reading of the medieval and Patristic texts. In the book itself, he conducts such a phenomenological analysis of Patristic and medieval writings on these topics. Falque anticipates some objections to his practice, namely the idea that God would have to be set aside by the phenomenological epoché or that a phenomenological analysis would distort the theological sources. He suggests, however, that medieval thought can gain a new actuality today by an informed (rather than superficial) "confusion of the genres" of philosophy and theology (*DCA*, 18). He appeals to Heidegger, Marion, and others as examples for such practice. To read the medieval texts phenomenologically means to discover new insights and to do so in a fully phenomenological mode that goes back to the things themselves, in Heidegger's sense. The incarnation itself, which invites us to see and touch, is a profoundly phenomenological event in Falque's view and can lead us to a deeper phenomenological sense of incarnate bodies more generally. Falque insists, however, that his phenomenological reading is not imposed from the outside as a mere method ultimately foreign to the material, but he argues that the texts themselves have a deeply phenomenological character that strikes us as we engage with them (*DCA*, 21). Falque wagers that the "fruits" gained in his phenomenological analysis of the texts will validate and justify such a reading. Instead of forcing the medievals to answer our questions, we can learn how to answer our own questions by seeing how they answered theirs (*DCA*, 26).[4] Falque concludes this initial section by examining again the relationships between philosophy and theology and between philosophy of religion and religious philosophy. He returns to these relations at the end of the book and concludes that his reading has demonstrated that phenomena can be subjected to phenomenological analysis regardless of their domain of origin, including the theological context of medieval texts. The world of theology is just as much the lifeworld of our being-in-the-world. It is not necessary to hold a particular (Christian) faith to profit from phenomenological analyses of the flesh or the other. Phenomenology can indeed serve as method for analysis of what seem like theological subjects and experiences (*DCA*, 476). Philosophical and monastic experience can come together (*DCA*, 478).[5]

God and the Other

After its initial reflection on methodology, *Dieu, la chair, et l'autre* first turns to the topic of God. Falque wonders to what extent medieval thinkers really were "onto-theo-logical" in their thought about God via a close examination of Augustine's *De Trinitate*, the writings of John Scotus Erigena, and Meister Eckhart's mysticism.[6] He points out that the metaphysical backlash against phenomenology's desire to do without metaphysics misunderstands this desire and simply assumes that God can no longer be a subject for philosophy. Yet phenomenology instead provides a different way of talking about the divine, a language that can prove useful for investigating God's "mode of appearing" (*DCA*, 45–46). While the first chapter (on Augustine) shows the tensions between metaphysics and theology, the second chapter (on Erigena) puts forward a more positive account of divine phenomenality as theophany. The third chapter (on Meister Eckhart) concerns the role of phenomenological reduction in talk about God.

Augustine is the first Western thinker to engage Greek philosophy seriously in a theological mode. In Falque's view, Augustine shows a profound and insolvable tension between metaphysics and theology. Augustine's conceptions of the Trinity in terms of relations instead of primarily in terms of substance contradicts Greek philosophical presuppositions, a category that he subsequently "converts" conceptually (*DCA*, 52). In light of Arianism, Augustine tries to find a balance between a definition of God in terms of pure substance and a loss of divine immutability, neither of which are acceptable for him. The language of persons and relations helps Augustine solve this dilemma, although it exposes a tension between received metaphysical definitions and his theological reality. Augustine transforms metaphysical categories in order to express the mystery of faith. In this process "metaphysics is less denied or surpassed than caught and forced to the wall by theology itself" (*DCA*, 60–61). This tension between metaphysics and theology also appears in other places in Augustine's work. Falque shows how Augustine transforms classical schemes of logical attribution, the structure of substance and accidents, and the Platonic relation between image and model. Philosophy must be "silenced" in order to allow God to enter "*theo*-logically into *theo*-logy" (*DCA*, 65). Yet metaphysical models are not simply contradicted by Augustine and the tension between metaphysics and theology cannot ultimately be resolved. Falque suggests that this very tension might prove productive for phenomenology (*DCA*, 67). He is critical of Augustine's attempt to depict theology as being of another "order" than philosophy while continuing to use philosophical categories for expressing this theological mode. Directing veiled criticism at Marion and Lévinas, he distances himself from both an attempt to escape metaphysics entirely and from its transformation into a "theology of the other" (*DCA*, 71). The continued tension between metaphysics and theology is visible in Augustine's return to ontological categories of substance. Instead of evaluating this as a failure, Falque suggests that Augustine's "theologization of metaphysics" has much to teach us (*DCA*, 75). The alternative language, which Falque's treatment seeks to articulate, is dependent upon this tension. Metaphysics is "always already there" (*DCA*, 81). This tension becomes more explicitly phenomenological in the thought of John Scotus Erigena.

Falque contends that Erigena is a phenomenological thinker who seeks to describe God's appearing as a phenomenon. Instead of rejecting a dialogue with metaphysics, such an interaction can lead to a "different phenomenality" and a "new kind of speech" (*DCA*, 87). Falque judges Erigena a more useful conversation partner than Dionysius (on whom Marion focuses) because Erigena continues in dialogue with metaphysics instead of rejecting it for a purely apophatic stance. Erigena speaks of God's theophany by focusing on the incarnation in the flesh. Falque shows how Erigena depicts the phenomenon's appearance into light in terms very similar to Heidegger's. He also defends Erigena against the accusation of pantheism;

instead, Erigena "ontologizes" Dionysian apophaticism. The "nothing" of which Erigena speaks is, as in Heidegger, a mode of being, but also shows that God is not a thing and can never be fully known. God's mode of appearing is different from that of ordinary beings; God is "without being," "without relation," and "without love" in the usual sense of these categories. God's self-manifestation is the very ground of existence for all creatures. The Word bridges the distance between God and creatures. It thus "opens the space for a true *manifestation of God* through which the truth of the divine movement is no longer solely given through its *Essence* in an apophaticism of the Platonic or pseudo-Dionysian sort, but through God's *Appearance* (apparitio) in a theophany of the Scriptural or Erigenian sort" (*DCA*, 123). Yet God as a phenomenon cannot be reduced to a simple or straightforward visible appearance (which, as Falque points out, is also the case for phenomena more generally as Heidegger defines them in his "phenomenology of the unapparent"). "Apparent" and "appearing" cannot be reduced to each other. Falque claims that theophany for Erigena is not merely a "mode" of appearing but belongs to the very "structure" of the divine (*DCA*, 127). God's manifestation prompts and depends upon the human reception and welcome, thus establishing a "third world" in which the human mediates divine manifestation to and for all creatures in a "face-to-face" incarnate encounter. In this a danger remains that the human response will reify or reduce the divine. This danger is addressed by Meister Eckhart's "phenomenological reduction" in the mode of conversion.

Falque stresses the importance of the concept of reduction in phenomenology. The mode of receptivity for phenomena is an important topic for phenomenology and Eckhart analyzes it phenomenologically in terms of a disposition of conversion and detachment. Both Heidegger and Henry make heavy use of Eckhart, although Falque distances himself from their treatments by focusing on Eckhart's notion of religious conversion instead of his apophaticism or idea of *Gelassenheit*. Falque considers Husserl's contention that God's transcendence falls under the knife of the reduction and requires methodological atheism. He shows how Eckhart articulates a process of reduction similar to that of Husserl by relying on biblical figures for a journey into the self that is also able to propose a phenomenological community more viable than Husserl's. He analyzes Eckhart's reading of Mary and Martha in terms of a purely natural attitude exemplified by Mary and a phenomenological attitude reached by Martha who has learned to go beyond physical assurances of the divine presence. Religious detachment becomes a phenomenological reduction to the transcendental ego. The world is suspended, the pure self is discovered, and a new world is constituted—in Eckhart's case the world of God reached via conversion (*DCA*, 161). This is how the divine can be "born" in the self in Eckhart's startling phrase. Falque says: "God is not given *objectively to the exterior*, but is engendered *intentionally in the interior*. This is Eckhart's message which grounds his originality—at least when it is re-read in the light of intentionality" (*DCA*, 165). The ground of the soul and the ground of God become conjoined in a way Falque compares to Ricoeur's notion of "oneself as another" (*DCA*, 170–71). Detachment makes possible a new attachment: "The death of the Christian to the world or his detachment, thus leads him to the birth of God in him or to his own attachment" (*DCA*, 178). Eckhart's notion of "seeing nothing" (like Erigena's or Heidegger's nothing) makes possible a new kind of seeing or manifestation. All things are seen in and as God, which makes possible a notion of phenomenological community. Falque claims that Eckhart is able to resolve Husserl's dilemmas in articulating such a notion and anticipates later thinkers from Lévinas to Derrida. He concludes that "by reading theology, contemporary philosophers also learn what in it is true philosophy" (*DCA*, 190). Yet although Eckhart's "act of conversion" is a kind of "radical operation of reduction," Falque ultimately remains critical of Eckhart's (and Henry's) equation of divine and human, Creator and creature. Difference is not sufficiently articulated. For this we must turn to an analysis of the flesh and corporeality.

The middle part of *Dieu, la chair et l'autre* is devoted to an analysis of the incarnation and our fleshly existence (in Irenaeus, Tertullian, and Bonaventure). This part will be examined in the penultimate section of this chapter when discussing Falque's other writings on corporeality. Let us turn instead to the third part where he discusses Origen, Aquinas, and Duns Scotus on the topic of the other. Against the perception that the problematic of self and other is a modern one, Falque argues again that the early tradition contains "hidden riches." God becomes a "subject" for patristic and medieval thought; consequently, medieval reflections on alterity and even intersubjectivity can be useful today. Thus, this period has much to teach us: about community in Origen, alterity in Aquinas, and singularity in Duns Scotus. Even theological thought about the Trinity already implies a certain conception of community and the importance of the "third" (*DCA*, 351). Falque reassures the reader again that he does not intend to deny the novelty and importance of phenomenology by attributing all its important insights to medieval thinkers:

> Patristic and medieval philosophy is only the occasion for a phenomenology already constituted otherwise, which hence requires only an ultimate verification of its modes of implications . . . One only

discovers and one interrogates the tradition differently because we have *eyes to see* that the tradition does not necessarily give us. Put differently, far from being satisfied here with an application of phenomenology to medieval philosophy, one will recognize that on the contrary medieval philosophy itself is already "pregnant" with phenomenology, even if only the phenomenological attitude as such would make it possible for philosophy to deliver it and to become established. (*DCA*, 353)

Falque argues that the medieval notion of the communion of saints can help us elucidate Husserl's conceptions of intersubjectivity and Heidegger's idea of Dasein as "being-with-others." In the communion of saints, self-definition is wrapped up with and closely connected to one's relation to others, both living and dead. This includes empathy in suffering, the passion of love especially as compassion, and the possibility of deification. Falque puts Origen and Bernard of Clairvaux in conversation on this topic of divine compassion and impassibility and human loving response. He concludes that for both thinkers a common world between divine and human is established where real participation (or "intercorporeality") and community become possible (*DCA*, 373). For Origen, in Falque's view, "being-with" amounts to being incorporated into Christ's flesh. In this communion, our senses are transformed into a spiritual mode and hence sanctified. Thus, the effects of the resurrection are palpable already here on earth. Resurrection is affirmed to be a fleshly transformation, not a disembodied Platonic affair of the soul. Christ's body is united to human bodies through his ecclesial body: the church. Christ establishes a permanent relation with humans. For Falque, therefore, "self-affection and other-affection respond to each other reciprocally in order to constitute a communion of saints and a renewed mode of alterity" (*DCA*, 384). Through this communion, we share a phenomenological world. Selfhood is constituted eschatologically by this community. In Origen, this reaches its height in the notion of apocatastasis (often condemned as heretical): the final reconciliation of all things in God. Falque carries this somewhat insufficient notion of community further with an analysis of Aquinas's angelology, which he suggests provides a more phenomenological account of alterity despite its apparently "confessional" character.

Falque argues that while, for Origen, human and divine are two modes of living in the same world, Aquinas is able to articulate a genuinely phenomenological notion of alterity in his discussion of the nature of angels. He does so by confronting the danger of angelic solipsism in a way that parallels Husserl's attempts to avoid the human ego's solipsism in the

Cartesian Meditations. Traditionally, each angel is thought to be its own horizon (even its own species) and the communication of knowledge and even bodily appearance in particular locations become a problem. Aquinas is able to resolve these issues through a notion of angelic inter-subjectivity that Falque judges more successful than the Husserlian attempt in regard to human egos. Thomas argues that inter-subjectivity is, in a certain sense, "built into" the angelic constitution of self-consciousness through the intelligible ideas communicated by the light of the divine Word (i.e. Christ).[7] Falque suggests that "only such a 'redoubled similarity'—of the angel to God, then of angel to angel—hence comes to ground a community of world among angels, making finally possible an *inter-angelology* by exiting from an angelic solipsism" (*DCA*, 408). Similarly, the difficulty of how to conceive of angels appearing in time and space, if they are truly pure spirits (and thus bodiless), leads Aquinas to propose a shared community between angels and humans. The previous tradition had drawn an absolute distinction between angelic bodies and incarnate bodies (Christ/humans), but failed to articulate the phenomenological nature of these angelic bodies. Aquinas, instead, speaks of angelic corporeality in terms of phenomenological appearance. Like Husserl, he sets aside the question of "what" angelic bodies are and instead focuses on the "how" of their appearance (*DCA*, 415). In this way, Aquinas is able to make sense of an inter-corporeality between humans and angels as the angel assumes a body in order to appear to the human being. This leads to the possibility of a common world shared by angels and humans where the self-consciousness of the angel can be articulated in a way that serves as a "paradigmatic example" for human apperception of the other (*DCA*, 420). This "apperceptive transposition" relies not merely on analogy (as Husserl's does), but angels experience intellectually what humans experience via the senses. Through this parallel experience but in different fashion, it is possible to speak of shared community that preserves real and irreducible alterity. (Falque's goal in this chapter is not to "prove" the existence of angels, but rather to show how Aquinas's medieval treatment of angelic bodies helps us articulate a phenomenological account of community and inter-subjectivity.)

Such alterity also requires a way to establish the real individuation of the other as unique. This, Falque contends, Duns Scotus's notion of *haecceitas* is able to accomplish. Falque suggests that contemporary phenomenology has not managed to articulate true individuation or singularity (despite the fact that Heidegger actually wrote his second thesis on Scotus). Scotus can provide the necessary principle of individuation. By articulating a firm distinction between natural and supernatural, which preserves their difference while making possible their interaction, Scotus arrives at a positive notion of contingency that is our own and singular. Although human being is univocal for Scotus, human existence as well as human knowing are unique and singular. The haecceitas of the human being is half way between that of a stone and that of an angel: While a stone is a completely individuated material substance entertaining no relations of causality with other stones, angels share in a community without material individuation. Humans share communally in the same essence of univocal being and yet are individuals in their specific ways of instantiating that essence in the world (*DCA*, 450). Furthermore, Scotus insists on the particularity of the human soul against the notion of the common intellect (for example, in Averroes). This culminates in an account of love where God loves each human being individually instead of a generic love for humans or for the love humans may generate. Love (as in Marion) requires singularity. In love I love God, self, and other disinterestedly, as God loves the other for his or her own self. Falque concludes with a discussion of angelic singularity in Scotus. For Scotus, "individuality becomes . . . the ultimate reality of being" (*DCA*, 461). The angelic intellect knows the singular directly. Ultimately, the singularity of the other cannot be seized entirely, but is known fully only by God. By knowing and praising God we also are opened to the other's singularity.

Suffering, Finitude, and Death

Le passeur de Gethsémani is subtitled "anguish, suffering and death, an existential and phenomenological reading." Falque points out that these themes have become important phenomenologically, especially in Heidegger's analysis of anxiety and of human finitude (i.e., being-toward-death). He contends in this book that these human experiences of the anguish of death and the suffering of the flesh constitute in some fashion "a metaphysical experience of God" (*PG*, 12). This is possible because, in Christ, God experiences the human condition fully in all dimensions of suffering and death, while humans thereby also have access to experience of the divine. "Passeur" thus has several connotations: It means a "passage" of transition or traversal, but also indicates Christ's preparation of the way for us and guidance across (the basic meaning of *passeur* is "ferryman" or "smuggler"; *Metamorphosis of Finitude* translates it as "guide"), and finally, it is linked to the word for suffering (*pâtir, pâtissant*). Falque begins by considering human finitude in all its dimensions: our anxiety in the face of death and our attempt to escape death. He warns us not to take the subject too lightly: We must acknowledge the real fear of death experienced even by Christ and certainly that of individual Christians as human beings instead of jumping immediately to a salvific message that might alleviate the anguish of death. Only by plumbing the weight and depth of death can we truly ascertain the import of the resurrection. Falque also refuses to reduce the question of death to the doctrine of sin, which he suggests happens far too often. Instead, death is linked to our essential finitude. Christ's "sharing" in the human condition is far more important than some simple "erasure" of death. Finitude, as such, is not sinful. Ideals of absolute perfection must be renounced as impossible. Humans are created good but finite, not perfect. All of who we are is made in the image of God, including our finitude and this applies also to Christ, the "true image" of God. The horizon of finitude and death always already looms before us and threatens to render our life meaningless. Our mortality gives rise to anxiety without having to be perceived as sinful. We must thus face up to our facticity and finitude by facing our death. Falque also warns of escaping the reality of one's own death by focusing on that of the other. One cannot truly die "with" or "for" someone, but must embrace one's own death (i.e., he agrees with Heidegger, that my own death is the one that has ontological significance for me, instead of with Lévinas, that it is the death of the other that really matters). The inescapability of death can lead to despair and hence has an impact on how we live our lives now. Again, he admonishes us not to escape the reality of this despair too quickly by recourse to supposed theological solutions of salvation. We must experience the meaningless of life in light of death in all its depth and dimensions. Meaning can only become possible when it is first suspended in silence, vanity, and anxiety.

After establishing the reality of our anguish in light of death, Falque goes on to consider Christ's experience of this anguish. Anxiety does not refer merely to a psychological fear of dying, but to a certain (metaphysical) attitude toward life in light of death. Both are also present in the account of Christ's struggle in Gethsemane. The fear of death results in a sense of being abandoned and alone, a feeling of sadness and a fear of annihilation or disappearance. The hope of the resurrection cannot be simply read back into this moment in a way that alleviates, and indeed denies, this anguish. Jesus seeks the company of the disciples and feels abandoned by them as they are overcome with sleep. Falque notes that the texts ultimately remain silent about how Christ overcomes this fear and resigns himself to death (PG, 71). It is not a particularly heroic, but an ordinary and "banal" death. Christ's experience, in his view, has a sort of "heuristic power" and import for us: "The awakening of Christ's consciousness before the immanence of this end and the question of meaning it harbors, therefore open already and as in advance toward a new kind of temporality by which Christian eschatology anticipates the totality of the later phenomenological modifications of the ecstases of time" (*PG*, 76). Falque points out that Heidegger himself, in his early readings of Paul, speaks of a religious ecstatic experience of time in which the eschaton is not a simple anticipation of the future, but transforms the present. It is about a "how" of time, not about a "when" (*PG*, 78). Falque argues that Christ's cry of dereliction on the cross similarly anticipates the future in the present and is offered as a "gift of presence." "Past" becomes passage, "present" becomes gift, and "future" refers to possibility "coming to" the self (*PG*, 80). Yet Falque rejects Heidegger's conclusion that the Christian hope for the future eliminates a true experience of suffering and the anguish of death. Rather, he shows how even Heidegger acknowledges that the analysis of anxiety is rooted in a theological progeny. Christ's agony in the garden serves as paradigmatic example for the human anguish of finitude. Falque rejects theological interpretations, which see this anguish as merely symbolic or as purely on our behalf. The story indicates that Christ really experiences an undoing of his own will (not already a victory) and a radical absence of meaning in the cry of dereliction. God here becomes utterly vulnerable and even helpless. The son's "entry into nothingness" is a kenotic act of highest (or rather lowest) degree, a complete self-emptying (*PG*, 95). Falque does acknowledge that Christ as Son is not abandoned by the Father, as some contemporary interpreters suggest, but he insists that this does not diminish his real experience of abandonment and solitude as a human being. Falque concludes that "*the fear of death* [*la peur du décès*] as recoiling before the being-to-the-end of life hence makes place for *the anguish of death* [*l'angoisse du mort*] as a manner of living one's life in the inevitable horizon of the possibility of one's very impossibility" (*PG*, 100).[8] He goes on to examine this Heideggerian definition of death as ontological possibility and his insistence on the "mineness" of death. Falque sees such existential possibility even in Christ's experience. For Christ also, his death functions as a "manner of living" thus previewing a Christian existence, which sees life against the horizon of death (*PG*, 105). This immanent experience of death is not about ontic survival but about a way of organizing one's life against the horizon of an anticipation of death. And while the Son's death is singularly his own, it also stands in relation to his divine filiality and thus to the Father. His life is freely given, an "ultimate possibility of self-sacrifice" and yet not "self-mastery" (*PG*, 113). Falque concludes that Christ hence experiences all the dimensions of death outlined by Heidegger and yet also challenges some of the aspects of Heidegger's thinking, especially the Promethean-like "virility" and the forgetting of the flesh in Heidegger's account.

The final section of the book is devoted to an analysis of the flesh to which Falque will return in much more detail in his most recent book.[9] As his discussion here is closely connected to the analysis of Christ's experience in Gethsemane, it will be briefly discussed here instead of deferring it to the later section on flesh and corporeality. Falque insists again that Christ truly suffers and that this is not immediately relieved through an assurance and consciousness of life. Christ experiences the limitations of his finitude in his own flesh, including burial in the earth. Christ truly lives an earthly existence within the world and suffers in his flesh. He does not escape the corruptibility of his body or the relinquishment of self, including the lack of power of which Lévinas speaks in his account of death. The multiple meanings of the title come again together here: "In suffering this world (*pâtir*) the Son transmits in this to the Father (*passage*) the weight of finitude experienced in his death" (*PG*, 130). The alterity of the Father is encountered in the Son who experiences himself phenomenologically as another (an allusion to both Husserl and Ricoeur). Drawing on other biblical passages (besides the scene in Gethsemane), Falque tries to find a middle way between what he judges to be Marion's total destitution of the self and Henry's completely immanent self-affection. The Son's relation to the Father makes it possible to speak of human and divine alterity and relation as long as Christ's full assumption of our flesh is acknowledged. Falque finds that Heidegger obfuscates real suffering and our fleshly reality by overstressing the intellectual aspects of moods. Falque warns of overemphasizing the salvific nature of suffering, which tends to disguise and sublimate its real pain. Suffering cannot be explained away, it has no real reason or cause, and should not be trivialized. Falque also stresses the importance of touch, appealing to the stories of healing in the Gospels in which Christ either touches or is touched by those who seek relief from suffering. A crossing of flesh takes place here. The miracles also show the importance of bodies and bodily sensation. These enable a shared world (the argument here is very similar to his discussion of Origen and Aquinas in the third part of *Dieu, la chair et l'autre*): "By him [Christ] the totality of internal lived experiences of his body operate at the same time a doubled *passage*—of the human toward God and of the Son toward the Father. What is lived and experienced by the Son in *his* flesh is hence also experienced by the Father (through his uninterrupted communion with the Son)—although in a different manner and a different mode, since not directly fleshly" (*PG*, 155). The point is not an exchange of bodies, but the real experience of the incarnate flesh, which then becomes part of the Divine life. Suffering thus reveals the real truth about human beings in their very vulnerability. Christ's flesh is a vulnerable human flesh. In fact, not even the resurrection erases the wounds of this flesh. Christ's self-giving on the cross finally does make it possible to speak of a "Christian" interpretation of suffering and death. Christ's suffering is a gift inasmuch as it opens the self to the other and thus gives meaning to our suffering (but not inasmuch as it somehow relieves us of it). Suffering is not a "requirement" for "purification" or salvation; it should not be sought out. Although it can become an occasion for purification when it does happen, this does not negate its painful and even absurd character. Suffering cannot ultimately be justified. A full account of incarnation, then, also requires a reflection upon resurrection and re-birth, to which Falque turns in his next work.

Birth and Resurrection

The "metamorphosis," or transfiguration, of finitude is a "philosophical essay on birth and resurrection," which responds to the earlier analyses of suffering and death. Our finitude, so he suggests in the preliminary remarks, is "cracked open" by the possibility of resurrection. Resurrection, one should stress at the outset, for Falque is always about *bodies*, earthly and material bodies, fleshly bodies, animal bodies (as will become even clearer in the following section). He claims that the resurrection is an ontological, not an ontic event; instead of introducing a new or different world, it transforms *this* world. Indeed, Falque is throughout insistent that he is speaking about this reality and not some other removed (spatially or temporally) from our everyday experience: Resurrection becomes "our *manner of being in the world through our bodies* here on earth" (*MF*, xiv). The resurrection "*transforms* the ontological structure of *this* world" (*MF*, 2; trans. modified). Falque stresses again that Christ assumed a fully human condition, which included his birth, passivity, suffering, and finitude. Christ's human facticity is oriented toward death just like ours. His death thus leads to the need to reflect on his birth and ultimately on his resurrection. Falque appeals to the conversation with Nicodemus (John 3) in which Christ speaks of the need for a new birth that will be different from purely natural birth. The first part of the book is devoted to a recapitulation of finitude, the second considers Christ's transformation, and the third part spells out the implications of the resurrection for us. Falque reminds us again that finitude does not equate with "sinfulness" (*MF*, 7) even when it is transformed in its phenomenological ontological content: "Far from disqualifying *finitude* (part I of my argument), resurrection as *metamorphosis* (part II) thus gives meaning to it in the operation of *transfiguration* (part III)" (*MF*, 8). Falque again highlights Heidegger's interpretation of Dasein's experience of its own finitude. Experience is always immanent and is always human. Even experience of God is my human experience, not that of an angel or an animal (*MF*, 15). He notes that religious living and the possibility of religious experience are no longer self-evident today. Falque claims that he appropriates Christ's fully human experience for phenomenological analysis of more general (and ordinary) human experience, including a critique of contemporary conceptions of immanence (*MF*, 19). The incarnation hence serves as his guiding interpretive principle and allows him to develop a phenomenology "of the ordinary human given" despite its theological inspiration. Falque examines the temporal dimension of finitude, which has a clear beginning and is not eternal. Time must be thought from within itself and on its own terms; theological presuppositions about eternity must be set aside. Yet although theological eternity is somehow "a-temporal," he does contend that the weight of temporality is derived from it. Eternity is not some sort of abstract principle, but informs our experience of time. Falque draws on both Augustine's and Heidegger's accounts of temporality in order to establish human finitude in terms of facticity and to combat the idea that this must be a purely atheistic conception. He reiterates Marion's interpretation of the death of God as death of *belief* in God or even the death of Christianity (but not that of God as such) and deals with Merleau-Ponty's suggestion that philosophy and theology are two (incompatible) ways of seeing. Ultimately, Falque suggests that they investigate the same question and he rejects Heidegger's contention that the Christian could not ask this question genuinely because it assumes a suspension of belief. He shows that for Heidegger this is less about the question or the process of questioning than about the one who does the questioning and contends that the same is true for atheism. This experience of "being alone in the world without God" must be taken seriously as a primordial experience.

In the central portion of the book, Falque attempts an ontological analysis of Christ's resurrection, drawing an analogy to Nietzsche's account of Zarathustra and the transfiguration of the "overman." The resurrection is not to be read as a flight from this world but as a renewal of the earthly human condition here and now. It is thus not a rejection of corporeality, quite the opposite. Falque shows how in Paul flesh and spirit are dimensions of the body, which is always open to God. The distinction between mortal and resurrected bodies is a distinction not of substance but of quality: The resurrected body actually appears in a phenomenological fashion. The Christian conception of corporeality, or "new creation," is an affirmation of the original creation; it remains earthly rather than rejecting this life. The resurrected body has a genuinely phenomenological dimension and allows for authentic alterity, for distinction between bodies. Falque goes on to analyze Merleau-Ponty's notion of incarnation and to compare it to the theological doctrine of the incarnation. Christ transforms the weight of our finitude by sharing and experiencing exactly that same finitude in all its weight. And just as Christ is completely human in every way, so we become incorporated fully through him into the divine life. As in the earlier book, he briefly wonders here about the way in which Father and Spirit can be said to participate in the experience of the Son, drawing on theologian Jürgen Moltmann's account. He interprets the Son's suffering as a move toward the Father instead of a "flight from or negation of the Son's passion" (*MF*, 67). Christ's lived fleshly experiences become the lived experiences of the Father's consciousness, which prevents the account from becoming solipsistic. The Father participates in the Son's passion, albeit differently. The divine passion is not simple human suffering, but a compassion that enfolds human suffering and is one with the other in empathy (*MF*, 70–74). The Spirit accomplishes the resurrection of Christ by the Father and thus is the mode of transformation. It is through the Spirit that we gain access to God and are transformed. The resurrection changes everything: human beings, the world, and even God. Through the resurrection, we are incorporated into the divine. It inaugurates a new way of living in the world. Our very finitude is now experienced within God as it is given by the Son to the Father and transformed in the Spirit. This incorporation is still bodily, but according to a different manner of visibility. (Falque hints here already that the Eucharist is central for an understanding of such incorporation, something he will develop in much more detail in the third volume.) We are transformed *within* God instead of God merely coming to us. This does not mean that humans become a fourth person of the Trinity, but rather such transformation happens through their identification with and incorporation into the Son. This is a spiritual, a fleshly, and a dynamic participation.

The final part of the book develops a "phenomenology of the resurrection." This part is written as a mirror image to the first part: A changed world is contrasted to unsurpassable immanence, eternity juxtaposed to time, fleshly rebirth to atheistic humanism.[10] The theological references to "earth" and "heaven," Falque suggests, are not about two geographical or physical locations, but rather, about two ways of living in the world, two manners of relating to God: one that closes in on itself and one that is open to the divine. Earth and heaven are existential categories of lived experience (*MF*, 96). The resurrection is thus not intended to remove us from the earth, but to permeate it with "heaven," to bring the two together. The resurrection hence overcomes the separation introduced between the two through sin. This is not a simplistic anthropomorphism but a truly human way of living in our world. It does not introduce a new or different nature, but a different relation between beings of the world, where the world is seen as filled with meaning. Falque suggests that this makes possible a recovery of presence in contemporary phenomenology, both in a spatial and a temporal sense. He rethinks the relation between time and eternity summarized earlier. The "instant" of salvation (and hence the in-breaking of eternity) is not a different time, but *another way to live the same time* (*MF*, 115). This instant is marked by the "joy of birth," which is a new birth both from above and from below, but concerned with living in this world. Falque distinguishes this joy from philosophical happiness as eudaimonia, or luck. Nor is it a kind of religious ecstasy. This joy of resurrection and birth does not abolish the anguish of suffering and death, but it does mark our daily, ordinary lives. Falque concludes with a reflection on the sexual connotations of knowledge of God as loving *jouissance* (*MF*, 124).[11] Resurrection is a fleshly rebirth, not a purely spiritual experience. A phenomenology of resurrection must culminate in a phenomenology of birth, which leads Falque to an interpretation of baptism, the ecclesial body, and the communion of saints. Must we believe all this? Belief, Falque argues, following Marion, is itself a miracle. And yet, so he insists, his analysis is able to think the fleshly body as open to transformation, which has important phenomenological implications: This flesh is interpreted as the lived reality of the body and thus the body is not treated as an object or a substance. Falque compares this to the phenomenological epoché that sets aside concerns with existence. The transfiguration of the resurrection is a manifestation and consequently phenomenological. The resurrection remains a bodily and fleshly experience. God can be perceived through the senses and Christ is manifested bodily. These concluding claims lead Falque to his most recent work on body and Eucharist.

Flesh, Animality, and Eucharist

The analysis so far has already shown that the topic of the flesh and of corporeality are central to Falque's work. He consistently affirms our bodily nature and the importance of fleshly existence. In *Dieu, la chair, et l'autre*, he develops a robust notion of human flesh through an analysis of Irenaeus, Tertullian, and Bonaventure. In *Les Noces de l'agneau*, he returns to this topic even more fully and devotes almost the entire book to an account of our corporeality, both individual and communal, along with an extensive interpretation of the Eucharist, as "body" of Christ and of the church.

Falque argues that Christian conceptions of the flesh provide insight into what it means to be genuinely human. The "logic" of theology and philosophy come together here (*DCA*, 204). In this section, Falque tries to combat and remedy the tradition's neglect of the flesh. Again, he insists that the reading of the early Christian texts can lead to philosophical insights: regarding the "visibility" of the flesh in Irenaeus's account of Adam, its "solidity" in Tertullian's interpretation of the incarnation, and its "conversion" in Bonaventure's depiction of the relation between divine and human. Falque claims that in Irenaeus God sees himself in Adam as a full human being. Adam makes visible what it means to be human. In Irenaeus's account of creation, God forms Adam's flesh from the earth as a model for the incarnation of the Son. Irenaeus speaks of Son and Spirit as God's "hands" and portrays creation in very physical and material terms where God functions as artist. Falque emphasizes that for Irenaeus it is our flesh that receives the spirit. Christ is the image of God as a fully human person and yet Adam also serves as model for Christ. The image speaks of a double visibility: human for divine and divine for human: "we are already in the image of God through our body and this in the very least inasmuch as 'God made body' in the incarnation will show precisely, and as if retrospectively, that of which we have always already been the image—a divine body, or at the very least one called to be deified" (*DCA*, 242). For Irenaeus, death is not a punishment but a transition to life. Thus, Irenaeus, to some extent, provides an alternative reading of sin and salvation compared with that of most Western authors (especially Augustine).

Falque claims that Tertullian carries these insights further by applying a radically material notion of incarnation to the flesh of Christ, defending it against heretical interpretations that seek to make it less than real. Tertullian focuses the discussion on the physicality of the flesh, both in terms of its reality and its quality, rejecting the Valentinian approach that tries to reduce Christ's flesh to a "soul-like" substance, along with several other heretical Gnostic reductions of the reality of the incarnate flesh. For Tertullian, Christ's flesh does not merely appear as such but has real solidity and experiences a really human birth and death. Falque claims that Tertullian's account has phenomenological value because he speaks of a manifestation of the flesh. Christ's real flesh has profound implications for the salvation of our flesh. Salvation cannot be applied solely to souls. Nor can a schizophrenic distinction between a flesh that is born and flesh that dies be made (as the Gnostic heretic Valentius does). Christ's flesh is just like our real living and dying flesh.

In the third chapter of this section, Falque shows how Bonaventure "philosophically" translates St. Francis's spiritual experience into an account of lived fleshly experience and thereby brings together Irenaeus's focus on the visibility of Adam's flesh as image of Christ and Tertullian's stress on the solidity of Christ's flesh and its implications for our redemption. Falque argues that St. Francis's "Canticle of the creatures" is actually a canticle praising God (instead of being primarily about other "creatures"), in which all earthly creatures come together to recognize God as their Creator. All creatures ultimately depend upon God. Falque focuses on the language employed to describe this experience. The flesh has its own language, just as the Word never appears without a body. Bonaventure develops an account of symbolism that stresses the importance of the senses and affirms "physical" and "spiritual" meanings as intimately connected. Falque illustrates this with what he calls the "limit experience" of St. Francis's stigmata as interpreted by Bonaventure. Here, the flesh of Christ and the flesh of the disciple cross each other and connect intimately. The stigmata show the unity of body and soul in fleshly fashion. Bonaventure thus does not denigrate the flesh but makes it "the leading thread of the economy of salvation" (*DCA*, 343).

Les Noces de l'agneau is Falque's most recent book to date and is explicitly concerned with the topic of the body and the flesh, including a phenomenology of marriage. Throughout the book, Falque seeks to stress our "animality," including the claim that Christ assumes it in all its dimensions. The Eucharist similarly affects and transforms our entire humanity, including an embrace of its animality. The figure of the "lamb" in the title stands for this animality, which is not denied in or excluded by the incarnation. In the course of this discussion, Falque draws a strong (and somewhat troubling[12]) distinction between human animality and what he calls "bestiality," the pure animality of animals that can also be present in humans. This bestiality in humans is a result of sin and is erased in the transformation worked by salvation. Falque also articulates notions of sexual difference grounded in an analysis of eros linked to the Eucharist as a "wedding feast" [*les noces*]. A Christian notion of flesh and body, then, is again interpreted as a full embrace of materiality instead of a rejection of it.

Falque claims that the old distinctions between soul and body have often been recreated on a higher level in the distinctions between flesh and body where flesh designates a phenomenological "experience" devoid of concrete organic materiality (*NA*, 22). He suggests that many phenomenological thinkers ("Husserl, Merleau-Ponty, Lévinas, Jean-Louis Chrétien, Jean-Luc Marion, Jean-Yves Lacoste . . .") in their respective accounts of the flesh have ignored this "organic" dimension of our "animality" that he now seeks to provide (*NA*, 26). In the first part, he examines the "chaos" or "abyss" of our existence in the depths of its concrete biological animality. Hence, to some extent he returns here to the experience of suffering but now considers it in its more profound bodily dimensions. This is a philosophical exercise "at the limit," which examines the "residue" of the body left by the earlier exploration (Falque appeals to Ricoeur here, *NA*, 41). Falque argues that the biological or organic component of the body can be neither reduced to the flesh as a lived experience or to the body as geometrically extended matter, but in fact these standard phenomenological distinctions ignore the concrete reality of blood, flesh, and bones, which cannot be neatly divided into subjective and objective experience. Falque provides a review of the various philosophical connotations of chaos (Greek) or tohu-bohu (Hebrew) as originary experiences of an abyss that retains connotations of passion and uncontrollable biological instincts that come to overwhelm us and are experienced as threatening. He suggests that phenomenology may at times seek too much clarity and identification of these primordial, shadowy experiences. Phenomenology is too concerned with perception and intentionality, even when it seeks to qualify its import (as in various ways in Heidegger, Lévinas, Marion, Chrétien, Henry, and Lacoste). In this way, our experience of chaos as meaninglessness and as uncontrolled passivity is eliminated or contained by the phenomenological exercise, but instead such threatening and troubling experience should be taken seriously. This requires a genuine engagement with the animality of the biological body and its concrete experience of instincts, impulses, appetites, and passions. Falque suggests that the figure of Christ as the "lamb" constitutes precisely such a recognition and embrace of our animal nature, as does the fact that the central sacrament of the Eucharist is a supper and hence affirms the biologically essential activities of eating and drinking. Through the Eucharist, we eat (according to Catholic dogma) the body of Christ and thus share in his animality. The Eucharist in the Paschal lamb is able to lead us from chaos into cosmos, from animality into humanity. Yet Falque insists that this helps us "find the animal in the human" in a way that does not "leave animality (the lamb) in the sacrifice which appears now that of a humanity ('this is my body'), but that the Son assumes it and transforms it precisely by making this animality pass over into humanity recognized by his filiation in the eucharistic bread" (*NA*, 80). Thus, animality remains, but it is now a distinctly *human* animality. Again, Falque reminds us that animality does not equate with sinfulness, as the figure of the sacrificial lamb may well suggest and yet it does embrace the most physical reality of our being. (Falque repeatedly employs the word "meat" for flesh to reinforce this.) At the end of this particular chapter, Falque claims that the Eucharist consequently is not merely an issue of faith but is "credible" with a kind of "universalizable rationality" that is "addressed to everyone" (*NA*, 91). This enables and makes necessary a *philosophical* interpretation of the Eucharist. Falque seeks to provide such an interpretation in terms of eros: The eucharistic body becomes the "eroticized" body; the eucharistic banquet is the wedding supper. Falque relies for this interpretation on past interpretations of the Song of Songs that conceive of God as the divine lover seeking the beloved. Here he criticizes Marion's move to univocity in love, arguing that human and divine love cannot be completely equated (although they are also not utterly distinct as in some other thinkers). In contrast to the earlier works, which focused on the future (anticipation of death and suffering) and the past (the resurrection and birth as finitude), this work focuses on the present, the abiding and remaining in the flesh. This "remaining" makes the earth "habitable" and allows for human dwelling (*NA*, 103–5). Participating in the "body of Christ" remains meaningless unless it is grounded in such a concrete anthropology of the body (*NA*, 110). Falque suggests that the doctrines of transubstantiation and of "real presence" can be recovered and become useful here, as all of humanity is transformed in the eucharistic act.

In the second part of the book, Falque returns to the incarnation to show how Christ assumes our humanity. Humanity is explored in terms of its animality, its organic nature, and its sexuality. Throughout this middle part of the book, he focuses on unity and differentiation, arguing that, even in the erotic union, the fleshly difference of the other must be respected. Falque claims that our animality is not simply an issue of biology or specifically of evolution. Philosophically speaking, the human being must not deny passions and impulses, but embrace his or her animality and transform it into humanity. This animality, which is specific to humans in that they alone are created in the image of God, is characterized by sexual difference. Falque closely engages Derrida's posthumously published text on the animal here arguing that Derrida recognizes that we must face the animal in us in some way (not that he equates "human" and "animal" in any simplistic fashion). While there is already a strong relation between "word" and "flesh" in the biblical accounts, they cannot be reduced to each other. Falque suggests the possibility that the Genesis story of the fall is about Adam and Eve's denial of their particular animality and finitude. Yet this grasping for something other than human actually reduces them not to a supposedly sinful animality, but to "bestiality" (*NA*, 135). Falque analyzes our experience as conscious bodies, which he distinguishes from two extremes: bodies without consciousness (the common hypothesis in regard to animals) and bodiless consciousness (the usual assumption in regard to angels). These extreme cases help differentiate us, but also pose the possible limit-experience for our own existence (namely, that we could fall into pure bestiality or disembodied consciousness). He employs Tertullian (in a similar fashion to the earlier discussion) in order to confirm Christ's real material body. The soul is not something to be separated from the body, but the living breath of the body. And although we belong to the "community of animals," Falque consistently reads this as an inclusion of the animal in the human instead of the reverse. Although all creatures are saved through the incarnation, they are redeemed by and through the human being.[13] Yet Falque also acknowledges that these absolute distinctions between humans and animals have, on the one hand, led us to forget our own animality and, on the other, have often caused us to treat animals as if they were mere machines. Falque likens this forgetting of animality to the forgetting of being (and accuses Heidegger of forgetting pathos and empathy). The worlds of the animal and the human cross just as the worlds of the human and the divine do (*NA*, 171). Our animality actually gives us access to the world. This is even more profoundly the case for what Falque calls a "return to the organic" (the topic of Chapter 5 of the book). Here he seeks to take seriously our materiality, the "what" of our being and not merely the "how" (of animality). Falque insists that the biblical tradition does not deny this "organicity." It also includes a full realization of our mortality, including physical experiences of disintegration and putrefaction. Too often, philosophy has forgotten these bodily realities. Again, Falque appeals to the Eucharist, which is about body and blood, and envisions a sharing of bodies through nourishment. Yet he also makes it clear that he is not talking about a simplistic reduction to organic materials and processes, but that they are always linked to human capabilities and even creativity. At the same time, taking seriously the chaotic nature of the organic provides a much less monolithic and simple vision of the flesh than the accounts provided by Henry and others, which Falque judges too "cosmetic" (*NA*, 197). The reality of the flesh is more than merely a "lived experience" of the body. Falque again focuses on the Eucharist as the real flesh of Christ that can be touched and handled and where Christ is present in person. This gift of Christ's presence (a reference to Marion) makes it possible to live and remain in Christ.[14]

Falque concludes this part of the book with a chapter on sexual differentiation, which he claims provides an account of unity that preserves differentiation. He outlines differences between male and female patterned on the differences between divine and human, by employing the traditional imagery, which depicts the church or humanity as the bride of Christ. He insists that the "otherness" of the erotic flesh must be maintained and that an analysis of the Eucharist can even illuminate sexual difference and erotic experience. Falque criticizes other accounts of sexual difference (especially that of Lévinas), which relegate the female to the interior and depict the masculine in terms of what is exterior. Although he thinks of sexual difference as originary and imperative, he takes great pains to articulate an equal relationship between the two.[15] Falque is quite critical in points of Marion's account of eros and claims that it is not a "saturated" phenomenon, but one "at the limit" whose primary task is differentiation (*NA*, 247). The eucharistic act, he suggests, recapitulates the "erotic act" of marriage (*NA*, 248). In marriage the chaos of our passions is transformed into order and it prefigures the eschatological bridal supper of Revelation. Furthermore, via an analysis of the creation of Eve, Falque claims genuine individuation and singularity for the two partners thus united. In the union of their bodies, the man becomes more truly masculine and the woman more truly feminine (*NA*, 257). Falque concludes with an extensive discussion of desire, which culminates again in a consideration of the role of speech. Desire that arises out of our animality is transformed into mutual love that respects alterity (modeled on the Trinitarian relationships). In desire, one embraces one's own body in a way that requires differentiation. Desire becomes incarnate in the mutual gift of bodies that enables the incarnation of our flesh: "My body *becomes flesh for the other, at the same time that the body of the other also transforms itself into flesh for me*" (*NA*, 274).[16] The church shares in this community of bodies. In taking on our flesh, Christ has experienced our pathos; conjugal union between divine and human becomes possible.

The final part of the book focuses even more explicitly on the Eucharist and is posited as a theological contribution to the discussion of body and flesh by considering how the human becomes incorporated into the divine. Our animal passions, our organic body, and our erotic desire are transformed ("transubstantiated") in the new humanity of the Trinitarian perichoresis (*NA*, 293). Not only does Christ assume our full humanity in all its animality, but he offers this animality "in the eucharistic bread" (*NA*, 195). The mystery of the Eucharist affirms its bodily reality (in the traditional doctrines of transubstantiation and real presence, which Falque suggests thus still have relevance, albeit not in their traditional form). The supposed scandal of "cannibalism" in the Eucharist cannot be dismissed through a purely symbolic interpretation. Falque warns of any reduction that diminishes the reality of the flesh in the Eucharist. Flesh and body must be held together and he asserts again that phenomenology separates them far too often. The Eucharist draws us out of our animality in danger of turning into bestiality and establishes our true humanity, which becomes incorporated into Christ's body. We become truly human when we become body of Christ (*NA*, 324). Falque insists that he is not trying to establish or defend the doctrine of transubstantiation, but to provide an interpretation of the phrase "this is my body" that does not erase its link to organic materiality. Falque quotes extensively from the various Roman Catholic eucharistic liturgies as well as from other ecclesial texts (both medieval and contemporary). Despite all its difficulties, Falque maintains that the doctrine of transubstantiation provides important insights when it is considered as an act of being and an active force (*NA*, 334). In it we are assimilated to God and incorporated into the divine life, which is its "signification" for human intentionality (*NA*, 338). After this discussion, Falque turns to the words of institution, making clear that this is the celebration of a present event and not merely a memory of an occasion in the distant past or a mere future anticipation. The celebration allows us to participate truly in Christ's corporeality, which is a "gift of presence" (*NA*, 347). Finally, Falque considers the practice of eucharistic adoration, which he suggests allows one to see oneself in God (*NA*, 348) in a kind of reversed intentionality. Adoration makes true assimilation possible. The final chapter returns to the question of eros and marriage, now read theologically as the mystical body of the Church. Falque speaks of a "eucharistic ethos" arising out of the gift of the body, illustrated by the Johannine account of the foot-washing, which parallels the last supper accounts in the synoptic Gospels (*NA*, 357). Falque considers the notion of the "viaticum" where the Eucharist is treated as a last rite. He insists again that this is not a transition to some other world but an embrace and affirmation of *this* world. The joy of the eucharistic banquet is grounded in suffering and transforms this life here and now, not to escape from it but to remain in it. The eucharistic logic is a logic of permanence not of flight. The "last supper" [*cène*] does not leave the "scene" [*scène*] of this world. Falque claims that the future of Christianity depends on such a living of the eucharistic reality in all its fidelity to the body and to the flesh (*NA*, 377).

Phenomenology and Theology Again

The religious inspiration in Falque's work is evident throughout, including in his introductions, which generally provide dates for religious feasts (on which the introduction was composed) and thank God or religious leaders for their support and guidance. His work is permeated by frequent quotations from Scripture, liturgical texts, and Vatican documents. Falque clearly sees himself committed to the Roman Catholic tradition in a very explicit fashion and his philosophical work is in its service. This does not mean, however, that his work attempts to "convert" his readers in any overt or covert fashion or that it sets out to prove the rationality or coherence (or indeed the "truth") of Christian or specifically Catholic faith.

Falque suggests in the preface to *Les Noces de l'agneau* that the trilogy as a whole "traces a trajectory of which the itinerary anticipates the end and makes of the human being the privileged place where God comes to encounter us" (*NA*, 11). In this particular book, he explicitly identifies two philosophical parts (Parts I and II) and a theological part (Part III). This suggests that he does perceive clear distinctions between the two disciplines even as he seeks to engage them in greater dialogue.[17] And this dialogue certainly takes place continually in his work. In the second volume of the trilogy, Falque describes his treatment of the resurrection as a "*theological transfiguration* of the *philosophical structure* of the world" (*MF*, xiv; trans. modified). He consistently claims that theology not only has a phenomenological character and thus can be subjected to phenomenological analysis, but also that such an analysis provides important insight to phenomenology. At times, he even seems to suggest that certain theological accounts are more successful in treating phenomenological questions than more strictly phenomenological accounts. And although he employs the terms "theology" and "philosophy" frequently, in a way that would suggest that they refer to different and clearly demarcated domains, in practice they actually flow into and inform each other continually in his work. Biblical passages or theological doctrines provide a frame for the phenomenological analysis; phenomenological tools are employed for analyzing theological texts; theological doctrines are said to have genuinely phenomenological import and are set alongside more mundane experiences. He describes his method at the beginning of *Metamorphosis of Finitude*: "The dialogue with Nicodemus, which serves as a motif through the present work, can be taken to justify the philosophical, and therefore human, interrogation of what is our actual experience of the birth of the flesh. And from this we arrive, in the guise of a believer's interpretation this time, at the theological dimension of that other experience, of the resurrection of the body, lived through so far (at least according to Catholic dogma) by Christ and by Mary his mother" (*MF*, 6). Thus, the inspiration for and guiding idea of the book are said to be taken from a biblical story. While the topic of birth is identified as a purely human event and examined philosophically, the analysis then culminates in a theological treatment that is informed by belief and even dogma. Although different methods can be distinguished according to discipline (*MF*, 28; *NA*, 36–37) and Falque generally identifies what he considers to be a theological reading and what he intends to be a philosophical one, theological "content" can be read phenomenologically (and the reverse) and insights gained from one reading have relevant implications for the other discipline. In this sense, Falque both assumes and demonstrates that religious experience can be subjected to phenomenological analyses and that important insights can be gained from such analysis. It is the very exercise of this reading that grants viability to faith and religious practices, rather than a more abstract theoretical argument about them. Falque argues for the reality and importance of religious experience from *within* and *out of* that experience, wagering that his portrayal and analysis of its phenomenological character will speak for itself. In some sense, then, he merely does so in a more radical fashion than the other thinkers who preceded him and thus opened the path for this kind of exploration.

10

Postmodern Apologetics?

Each of the chapters in this part of the book has identified apologetic elements in the work of the thinkers discussed. Before examining some of their appropriations in the North American context in more detail, it might be worthwhile to consider this apologetic or quasi-apologetic character more fully. Are these projects apologetic ones? Do they "defend" the divine and argue on behalf of faith? Certainly their arguments for God are not arguments in the traditional (modern) sense. They are primarily phenomenological depictions of religious experience in a variety of registers. Their depictions do not always agree, although there are indeed significant areas of overlap, such as an emphasis on abundance and excess (some of these similarities will be explored in more detail in the conclusion to the book). Their method, however, is strikingly similar. They all employ phenomenological descriptions for certain excessive experiences, experiences at the "limit" of human experience. Examining such phenomena carefully gives them credibility, especially if others resonate with the description and find themselves encountering similar phenomena. Verification is possible if there is enough area of overlap, enough agreement that phenomena do indeed appear in this way. And although several of these thinkers argue that we cannot "intend" religious phenomena or cannot "plan" for such an experience in any way, even Marion who maintains this the most strongly is equally emphatic that his phenomenology provides an interpretive grid for how such phenomena usually appear (he even says that they *must* appear in this way). This would show, then, that such an examination of religious phenomenality is not non-sensical, but is indeed meaningful. At the very least, it emerges as a significant area of experience: A sufficient number of people undergo such experiences and can hence communicate about them and attempt to reach some sort of overlap of phenomenal description. Such phenomena are then worth careful investigation and depiction. And is that not, indeed, what apologetics has always done at its best: showing that the experience of faith is coherent and meaningful and a position worth holding?

Another important dimension to these contemporary projects that speak about God makes this even clearer: the hermeneutic dimension. All of the philosophers discussed in this book, including the ones who would not identify themselves as hermeneutic thinkers, but as primarily or even exclusively engaged in phenomenology, do indeed make claims about language and truth. And almost all sustain a very similar argument about language, especially about religious language, in order to be able to employ it for their respective projects. Almost all of the statements made about truth seem grounded in Heidegger's analysis of *aletheia* as unconcealment, even when they do not acknowledge this explicitly. All these thinkers (except maybe Ricoeur who is earlier than most of the others) also have taken license from Lévinas's liberal use of biblical imagery. After Lévinas, it has become acceptable (and possible) to analyze religious phenomena. And yet all of them still justify why and how they can talk about such phenomena.

Ricoeur does so by making an explicit distinction between truths of verification and of manifestation. Religious language is poetic language and thus not about verifying facts about the world, but instead for manifesting a world that we might inhabit and that can transform us. Religious language is true, but it is true because it is meaningful, not because it delivers facts. Marion bases his analysis of religious language on Pascal's distinction of the orders of the mind and the heart, or of certainty and charity. While rational (modern) philosophy engages the mind and delivers truths that are certain because they are factual, revealed theology or the phenomenology of faith delivers phenomena that are meaningful and beautiful to behold, that arouse our love and admiration, that overwhelm us with their abundance. We do not confirm the truth of these phenomena by giving factual accounts for them or reasoning through them, but rather by responding to them in love, by choosing to "see" them and respond to their call. Similarly, Chrétien guides us to hearing the appeal of the phenomena he describes. Although he does not describe the language of certainty in the same way some of the other thinkers do, it is clear that he already operates in the realm of poetry and beauty, where truth touches us instead of reasoning with us. He wants to make us experience the truth of the phenomena he describes. Like Ricoeur he emphasizes the polyphony of this truth and also its vulnerability. Henry, although in a different way than the others but maybe even more rigorously, also makes clear distinctions between two types of truth, that of the world and that of the divine life. Despite the fact that his emphasis on utter immanence is not shared in the same way by all the other thinkers, he also sees truth in affectivity and emotion, will and heart, instead of the pure, rational, and abstract mind. He maybe goes furthest in claiming for this truth a kind of absoluteness and self-justification with which most of the others would probably not feel entirely comfortable (Marion probably comes closest while Ricoeur is possibly furthest; both Chrétien and Lacoste are also at times critical of an exclusive emphasis on emotion or self-affectivity). Lacoste includes extensive reflections on the language and truth of theology, suggesting it, like Marion, as a truth to be known through love instead of pure reason. The postmodern project of speaking for God is indeed concerned with questions of truth, even if this truth is not measured in terms of certainty or factual evidence. Although Falque does not draw the same firm distinctions between different types of truth, he relies throughout on phenomenological description instead of rational verification or correspondence. His analysis might be likened to that of Chrétien inasmuch as he wants his phenomenological description of "theological" phenomena to be convincing via this very depiction. His use of theological sources is "justified" by a kind of Ricoeurian wager: Their phenomenological viability will become obvious through the examination itself.

So how is it then a new apologetics? It is such an apologetics precisely by showing that religious talk is meaningful and true—true, defined in the sense just outlined. Ricoeur contends explicitly that religious language is true and meaningful. It has its own criteria of truth and something is said in it that is not said in other discourses. This is how it is *like* traditional apologetics: These projects show that faith makes sense and that it is not irrational to believe it. And they may also be like earlier projects in the sense that at least some of the thinkers claim a kind of uniqueness or even superiority for Christianity. Very tentatively, Ricoeur occasionally suggests that the language of the Bible is uniquely transformative and challenges other discourses, although he usually qualifies such statements almost immediately. Marion privileges Christian phenomena and although he admits that other religious traditions may also have saturated phenomena, Christ as the icon and Word of God does seem to have a unique and privileged place in his work. Henry is unambivalent about the uniqueness of the Truth of Christianity and, in fact, argues for it as absolutely different from and superior to not just the truth of science but also that of other religions. Chrétien and Lacoste make few specific claims about the uniqueness of the Christian tradition, although they draw from it almost exclusively. Falque relies on the Christian tradition for his sources and examinations far more heavily than the others and even argues explicitly for a mutual transformation of the disciplines of theology and phenomenology via extended dialogue between them. All of them, then, privilege Christianity in particular ways and occasionally even insist on its superiority over other discourses.

Yet these projects are also profoundly *unlike* previous apologetic projects, which is why apologetics must be qualified with "postmodern" or maybe better with "phenomenological." The best way to illustrate this might be to focus on a particular example: their various reflections on Anselm's famous "ontological" proof for God's existence. In the modern age (no claims will be made about what the "proof" may have meant at Anselm's time and whether it was actually intended as a proof, as this is hotly contested) this was read as a straightforward proof for God's existence: God is the most perfect being. It is more perfect for a being to exist than not to exist. Thus, God must exist. *Quod erat demonstrandum.* Full-stop. This is how Descartes presents the proof (naturally phrased in much more sophisticated terms) at the beginning of modernity and this is how Kant reads it at the height of the Enlightenment (and obviously then goes on to refute it). But postmodern thinkers read this proof very differently indeed and, interestingly enough, several of the philosophers just discussed have explicitly reflected on Anselm and his supposed "proof." Let me use these various discussions to show how postmodern arguments differ from modern (or more traditionally "apologetic") ones. John D. Caputo, to whom we will turn in Part III, actually summarizes the essence of this difference well in his own interpretation of the proof:

> While Anselm was certainly offering an argument, the context in which Anselm does so makes it clear that the formal argument plays a completely supporting role in a larger drama, that Anselm is saying to his fellow monks—he was addressing monks, not the American Philosophical Association—that their religious life of prayer and personal sacrifice should be buoyed by the idea that God is a being of such perfection that God is just there, there by his very perfection, irrepressibly, overflowingly there. Anselm was trying to awaken in them the idea that God is first, last, and always; the alpha and omega; above us and within us and around us; before us and after us; inside us and outside us; so much so that it is better to think not that God is in us as that we are in God. In other words, Anselm was

formulating an idea of God that expressed his religious experience of living "through Him, and with Him, and in Him," as the ancient liturgical hymn says, and he did not think this a freestanding argument (= philosophy). In a sense he was saying this is not an argument (in the modern sense) but an effort at conceptualizing or clarifying something that is intuitively obvious to all those people who experience God in their daily lives. In fact, when Anselm said this, he wasn't standing, he was kneeling, and this bit of reasoning was meant to clarify the God of his faith, the God given to him in the life of prayer.[1]

Caputo here interprets Anselm's account as a prayer or a phenomenological description of God's greatness instead of as a proof or verification in the modern (Cartesian) sense.

Ricoeur examines this proof in the context of a trajectory of a kind of thinking that reaches from the biblical sources across Anselm to Kant and Nietzsche and beyond.[2] He suggests that the argument only becomes a proof when it loses its tie with the invocations of the divine that mark it as a prayer. For Anselm, understanding is always grounded in faith. We examine what we already believe. It can only become a proof, Ricoeur suggests, when it is separated from belief and God becomes equated with "Being" instead of being "*as* we believe" and *what* we believe. The understanding of faith realizes that "this passage from someone to something is in some way already the object of faith" (181). Ricoeur also reminds us of the context in which faith (and argument) occurs: that of a prior history of various expressions of faith and also of what constitutes understanding or rationality. He shows how the "fool," who responds to Anselm, separates faith and the discourse about God, which the proof then seeks to reunite: "The argument consists, therefore, in reuniting what was already united for faith, and that the fool's discourse had claimed to dissociate, at the price of an absurdity" (183). After examining the rest of Anselm's text, which deals with desire as much as with thought, Ricoeur returns to this point and claims that the entire argument amounts to denying "that the separation of the invoked God and the predicates that make up the predicative name, united to the divine thou, is thinkable" (184–85). Ricoeur then goes on to show the biblical sources for this thought. In the Scriptures "invocation, naming, and the assertion of existence are in principle inseparable" (185). The same move from calling upon God to naming God to assuming God's existence in faith and reason are made within the Scriptures continually.

Ricoeur proceeds to examine Exodus 3:14, which proves an antecedent for Anselm in the sense that it is often interpreted as an ontological naming of God. While Ricoeur does not completely reject the possibility of an onto-theo-logical interpretation of this text (as other thinkers, such as Marion, do), he wants to open the space of interpretation to a more plurivocal naming that allows for many interpretations. Even in this appellation of the divine name, Ricoeur insists, invocation, naming, and God's existence go together (here confirmed by God's fidelity to the covenant). And such naming, Ricoeur points out, is always in the context of God's relation with the people: "God allows himself to be apprehended only as the God of his people, and these people are known to God only as the people of God" (194). Yet due to this openness to the human response, rebellion and rejection are just as possible as affirmation and faith. Ricoeur suggests that this dimension of human freedom (expressed biblically in lamentation or even rebellion) in regard to God actually allows for the later development of proofs for God's existence. God allows humans to argue with and challenge the divine precepts (for example, Abraham or Job; 24). Ricoeur concludes by bringing these biblical antecedents back to Anselm:

> The Anselmian argument may thus be interpreted as an attempt to reopen on a theoretical and speculative plane the debate that Wisdom—at least that expressed in the book of Job—seems to have led to a dead end. But the price to pay for this audacious enterprise seems to be the following. For the relational conception of God, with all its dramatic implications is substituted an abstract concept, in which the predicates of supereminence, which are alone retained from the predicative naming of God, find themselves dissociated from the counterpoint of a perhaps incomplete creation, or in any case from a creation marked by the persistence of evil. An inconclusive dialectic, scanned by the alternation of praise and lamentation, thus finds itself broken in the excess of the cry: "how long, Jahweh, will you forget me? To what end?" (Psalm 13:2)—an excess that exceeds itself in the words of the fool: "No more God!" (Psalm 14:1). (201–2)

Thus, Anselm attempts to name God as the biblical texts do or even to address God directly as is done in praise or lament, yet he ends up enclosing this name in a rational discourse inadequate to the more relational speech that precedes and fuels it. Anselm wants to speak directly to God in a philosophical mode but ultimately fails because his speech becomes too abstract.

Marion deals with the Anselmic "proof" the most directly. He mentions Anselm occasionally in his work on Descartes, but devotes a whole chapter to the proof itself and its appropriation by Descartes, asking even in the title: "Is the Argument Ontological?"[3] He points out that the argument was actually not qualified as "ontological" until Kant—given that the term "ontology" itself only arises at the time of Descartes—and wonders whether this argument truly depends on metaphysics (as defined by Heidegger) despite its use of the term "being." He reviews the modern (Kantian) ontological interpretation, arguing that "a proof of the existence of God becomes an 'ontological argument' only when it rests first upon a concept of God," as is true of Descartes who thinks of the idea of God as an innate concept available to the human mind (*CQ*, 141).[4] The rest of modernity assumes this possible reduction of the divine to a concept, although it is only Malebranche who finally equates the idea of God's essence with the idea of God's existence or "Being" and Leibniz who identifies it with the idea of a necessary Being. This is the version of the idea that Kant and Schelling refute. Marion contends that the Anselmian version neither relies on a concept of the divine essence nor identifies this essence with Being in general. Rather, Anselm relies on faith and actually affirms God's inaccessibility to thought. "The argument never supposes any concept at all, since it rests precisely on the acknowledged impossibility of any concept for God" (*CQ*, 146). Anselm instead thinks of God as excessive, as "greater than any thought," as transcending thought: "God begins when the concept ends" (*CQ*, 147).[5]

Marion thinks that any objection to the proof merely highlights the fact that God is beyond the limits of the thinkable. The argument itself actually affirms this in his view by acknowledging that God cannot be only in the understanding. Marion refers to a much later text in the *Proslogion* where God is said to be much greater than any thought and explains: "If it is a question of God only from the moment when thought reaches its maximum (the transcendental limit of its power to know), God is thus actually experienced only when thought acknowledges, without conquering it, the transcendent that surpasses this limit—when thought thinks that it cannot think what it cannot think and what it cannot think surpasses it by being not only outside its understanding but beyond what it will ever understand" (*CQ*, 149). Similarly, God surpasses essence and being in Anselm, as absolute transcendence is more associated with the supreme good than with supreme being. Consequently, "if it is a question of knowing God as *melius* and supreme good, thought must not lean on the impossible concept of an inaccessible essence, but rather on its own desire, and thus, deprived of any other recourse, on its love" (*CQ*, 154). Marion concludes his examination of Anselm by inscribing Anselm in a theological instead of a metaphysical tradition: "God is not defined by means of any concept of essence, and his presumed essence is not regulated by the *ousia*, but on the contrary can only be thought as it offers itself—beyond

Being, in the horizon of the good" (*CQ*, 156). Marion thus contends that God is known in love and not by metaphysical reason.[6] In no way is Anselm attempting to prove God's existence through any sort of abstract and purely rational parameters, but instead this becomes an example of the kind of knowledge that seeks God through love.

Henry also has interesting comments on the Anselmic proof. Unlike the other thinkers, he does see Anselm as the first step on the modern project to give proofs for God's existence. But like them he utterly disapproves of this project (he just does not reinterpret or exonerate Anselm from it quite as fully as the others). And he does see in Anselm the possibility of access to God within oneself. Unfortunately, in Henry's view, Anselm closes down this possibility too quickly: "Instead of seeking to elucidate this crucial paradox, which lies really at the heart of Christianity, that is, that the essence of God is such that it may be present without anyone seeing it, Saint Anselm confines himself to a hasty borrowing of Scripture . . . Here, then, the condition of access to God is suddenly ruined, since the light in which it resides, meaning access to God, is precisely inaccessible" (*IT*, 154). Henry interprets the proof as the sad reduction of a genuine possibility:

> Our access to God is now reduced to this. It is no longer a question of a revelation of God, of a revelation revealing God and produced by God himself, a revelation made to Beings capable of receiving it, which ultimately means Beings consubstantial with this self-revelation of God—in short, a revelation of itself that Life makes to livings. It is also not a question of Faith understood in its specificity, as Faith and certitude of life in itself, as we have suggested. Access to God is reduced to a conception of the understanding (of our understanding), which consists of what we henceforth are calling Saint Anselm's proof. (*IT*, 155)

He goes on to outline the proof in the traditional way in which modern thinkers (from Descartes to Kant) understood it: Anselm supposedly tries to prove God's existence by claiming that a really existing God is "more perfect" and more real than a God who is merely a figment of our imagination (i.e. who exists only in our understanding). Henry then demonstrates the "massive contradiction implied in this reduction of access to God to a proof of his existence delivered by the understanding" (*IT*, 155). He indicates that for phenomenology such proofs are utterly absurd: "If God could be shown in this way, it would be a rational truth and any reasonable person ought to affirm his existence. There would be a place for a rational theology and for a gradual development of this theology, as for any other rational knowledge" (*IT*, 156). Such "rational theology" suffers from utter confusion about the reality of the divine. It would make God subject to the truth of the world, which Henry has shown to be fundamentally untruthful and completely ignorant of real life or passion. The project of submitting God to truth criteria is completely absurd. God does not appear before the gaze of consciousness because the divine is already experienced deeply within it. And God is not manifested by visible evidence in the exterior of the world because no real Truth can, in fact, ever appear there. Henry rejects all philosophies (including Heidegger's) that try to subordinate God in this way to something foreign to the divine.[7] God is experienced directly and immediately and cannot be proven through the kind of rational discourse that relies on truth criteria or verification.

Lacoste actually explicitly responds to a "modern" (although contemporary) way of interpreting (and ultimately rejecting) the proof by analytic philosopher John Findlay who tries to show the incoherence of proofs for God's existence by refuting Plantinga's interpretation of Anselm. Lacoste suggests that this God whom Findlay defines as a "speculative monster" is "not the God of whom we are speaking, who solicits free consent while performing his own unveiling" (*EA*, 204). His actual article responding to the paper is found in *Présence et parousie*. Lacoste disagrees with the fundamental point that Anselm assumes God's existence as "a matter of fact" and tries to prove it through reason (*PP*, 223). He shows that the religious tradition has never been "sure" of God or assumed God's existence as a matter of fact. Also, religious experience is not identical to theological reasoning about God. Reason often only follows upon conversion or faith. Lacoste explains that there are many "worlds" (the Heideggerian being one of them) where God does not exist or make sense and there are also worlds in which God appears rather differently than via reason or proof. Faith (not belief) is voluntary and thus cannot be proven. We are "possible citizens" in many "possible worlds" (*PP*, 229). God's existence is an opening of possibility, not a restriction. Lacoste submits that it is a cause for rejoicing that the God Findlay defines is dead, because it is Sartrean god whom it is good to abandon. Rational proofs appeal only to reason, but religious existence is in a world much larger than it. In another discussion he points out, like Caputo above, that the proof occurs in the context of a prayer (*PD*, 79). Here Lacoste employs Barth's interpretation of Anselm in order to argue that God's phenomenality is irreducible (*PD*, 80, 84). In fact, he argues that he draws his definition of "knowing God by loving God" from Anselm: "Anselm speaks of God to God" (*PD*, 110). The God praised by Anselm in prayer is precisely the reason why theological language has coherence.[8] Lacoste thus joins Ricoeur and Marion in thinking that Anselm was not actually attempting to provide any sort of abstract proof for God's existence but that he rather serves as an example of someone turned to God in prayer and love.

While Chrétien does not treat the Anselmic proof explicitly, he does occasionally reject the general idea of "proofs" for God:

> The world itself is heavy with speech, it calls on speech and on our speech in response, and it calls only by responding itself, already, to the Speech that created it. How could it be foreign to the word, when it subsists, through faith, only by the Word? It is not a matter first and foremost of knowing if nature "proves" or "does not prove" the existence of God, but of being able to listen to its silence as a "visible voice," as St. Augustine did. (*AS*, 129)

He occasionally mentions Anselm in other contexts and once in a parenthetical remark says that Anselm's work is not limited to the proof "problematically called 'ontological.'"[9] Later in the same book he cites from the *Proslogion* to illustrate the interpretation of a passage that stresses the great joy of God's undeserved love.[10]

Falque focuses, in particular, on the sources Anselm might have employed for his discussion.[11] While trying to decide whether Anselm qualifies as the last of the Fathers or the first of the Scholastics, he also provides brief reviews of many other interpretations of the so-called ontological argument. He suggests that it is false to assimilate Anselm completely either to the Patristic or the Scholastic age, to see him either only as a theologian uninterested in philosophical argument or exclusively engaged in a philosophical proof. Besides being anachronistic, this kind of bifurcation disregards Anselm's particular Benedictine context and his personal experience (as a young man) of God's grandeur. The argument, then, is a "translation" of Anselm's experience of elevating himself toward the divine (97). Falque points out that Anselm draws on both Augustine and Boethius, but also on such "pagan" sources as Cicero and Seneca in his formulation. At the same time, however, Anselm transforms these sources in order to give rational expression to his experience. Anselm is hence not engaged in a metaphysical or purely scholastic argument, nor is he merely devoted to a prayer that has no philosophical relevance. Instead, Anselm fuses the philosophical and theological admirably in a phenomenological fashion: "Whether one makes sense of it or not, the proof of the argument is and will always remain the place of an experience: that certainly of an encounter with God (theological reading), but also that of a demonstration of a concept which is valid in itself and independently of any confession of faith (philosophical, or better, phenomenological reading)" (107). Falque concludes that this calls for a new interpretation of the argument (which he does not pursue any further in this context). In some sense, then, Falque employs Anselm here to overcome the artificial and arbitrary separation of philosophy and theology that he has critiqued in much of his work.

The overall thrust of these analyses is clear: Whether Anselm is interpreted as giving a rational proof (by Henry and to some extent Ricoeur) or whether he is exonerated and re-interpreted (by Ricoeur, Marion, Falque, and Lacoste), the very idea of a rational proof for God's existence is consistently rejected as futile, unhelpful, or even blasphemous. To speak of God with the language of certainty and verification is to succumb to the idea that science has the only access to truth and that truth is only about facts. Such a belief (and it is indeed a "belief") reduces humanity and everything that really matters to it to data or excludes it from discussion altogether. It excludes not only the divine or religious experience, but all meaning and values, all art and creativity, anything that cannot be demonstrated in a lab. This is not the path arguments about God take today. The coherence and maybe even validity of the idea of God is shown in a very different manner: through a phenomenology of religious experience that "verifies" such experience by closely and carefully depicting the many manifestations it takes in the lives of religious believers.

Contemporary philosophical projects, then, are apologetic in a sense of that term that comes much closer to the apologetic defenses of the early Christian communities. They "defend" Christian faith (or faith in God) as coherent and meaningful. As the early Christians argued that their belief in God was genuine and not merely wishful thinking and that it had a real impact on how they lived their lives, so these contemporary projects show that religious experience can be expressed phenomenologically in meaningful and coherent ways that are deeply connected to how we experience the world and live our lives. They do not compel belief through forceful or totalitarian measures (as apologetics at its worst has occasionally done), but rather they present religious experience or an experience of the divine in a manner that leaves it to the choice of the reader how to respond to the divine appeal: on the one hand, the choice about whether to believe in God and what sort of God to believe in and, on the other hand, choices about ourselves, about who we are and how we are to live. And genuine apologetics at all times has left that choice open.

PART III

Appropriations

11

Merold Westphal: Postmodern Faith

Merold Westphal, recently retired as Distinguished Professor of Philosophy at Fordham University, is one of the most significant figures to have appropriated French thought about the divine and religious experience for an American audience, focusing especially on the dimensions of faith. Most of his works circle around the coherence and viability of Christian faith, seeking to show that postmodernity and faith are not as incompatible as they might seem. Deeply influenced by the work of Søren Kierkegaard to whom several of his writings are devoted, he has continually sought to translate postmodern philosophy for a Christian audience. He shows that postmodern thought need not constitute a threat to Christianity, but can indeed provide fruitful criticism and insight for thinking constructively about one's faith and embracing it in an increasingly nihilistic world. His earliest work focused on phenomenology of religion (*God, Guilt and Death* began as a course in phenomenology of religion), but there is also an important hermeneutic dimension to his work. Two of his most recent works, *Overcoming Onto-Theology: Toward a Postmodern Christian Faith* and *Whose Community? Which Interpretation?: Philosophical Hermeneutics for the Church*, are both heavily hermeneutic in focus. Westphal has also been a frequent and beloved presence at countless conferences and has given many addresses on the possibility of fruitful dialogue between postmodern philosophy and Christian thought. He is one of the most significant American figures in explicit Christian appropriation of the French thinkers treated in this book (and, indeed, of other thinkers not treated here, such as Hans-Georg Gadamer).

Westphal is particularly interested in questions of the postmodern self, especially what might be called the "believing soul," and of the possibility of faith in a postmodern world. This project for him has important epistemological dimensions, which he makes more explicit than many other thinkers. *Suspicion and Faith*, an early work on Freud, Marx, and Nietzsche, displays this dimension most explicitly, but it is present also in his other works, especially when he speaks of hermeneutics. Beginning with Hegel and Kierkegaard (though never leaving them), he has increasingly moved to interact with French thinkers, especially Lévinas, Derrida, and Marion. B. Keith Putt has edited a collection of articles reflecting on Westphal's work, which also highlights the hermeneutic and epistemological dimensions of his work: *Gazing Through a Prism Darkly: Reflections on Merold Westphal's Hermeneutical Epistemology*.[1] In his helpful introduction, Putt comments on Westphal's "prophetically critical voice" and argues that Westphal attempts to strike a balance between (and critique of) various types of philosophy of religion (more traditional "apologetic" approaches connected to natural theology and more contemporary phenomenology of religion) as well as between confessional theology and more agnostic philosophical stances. He defines Westphal's thought as focused on questions of knowledge in regard to religious belief while always highlighting the finitude and fallibility of all human knowledge in regard to the divine. Putt shows how Westphal has been consistently critical of religious complacency and yet firmly committed to a confessional stance (calling his philosophy of religion a kind of "apo/paralogetics"). In the same vein, I here interpret Westphal's work as a kind of postmodern hermeneutics of faith. The chapter provides an overview of Westphal's thought by considering three important dimensions of his work: the viability of Christian faith in a postmodern world, the shape of a believing self in this world, and the possibility of depicting God or a notion of transcendence that would not succumb to onto-theology.[2]

Christian Faith in a Postmodern World

In much of his work, Westphal seeks to convince his predominantly Christian audience that postmodern philosophy is not pure nihilism or relativism and is not as threatening to faith as it is often perceived to be. Rather, he interprets it as providing important resources for Christian faith. The faith Westphal defends is a fairly traditional Protestant conception of faith with an important apophatic dimension. He often insists that postmodernity can help us realize that we have no absolute certainty about God or faith, that we gaze as through a mirror or dark glass, recalling 1. Cor. 13:12 and evoked also in the title of Putt's edited collection mentioned previously. This is particularly evident in Westphal's 1993 book *Suspicion and Faith: The Religious Uses of Modern Atheism*, in which he shows how "modern atheism," as represented by Freud, Marx, and Nietzsche, can help introduce the important role of suspicion into religious faith, a dimension he already sees heavily employed by Kierkegaard. In fact, it is precisely Kierkegaard's proximity to many postmodern thinkers and ideas that he often invokes to show that faith and postmodernity are not incompatible. *Overcoming Onto-Theology* (2001) carries this further by engaging also Schleiermacher, Heidegger, Barth, Gadamer, and Derrida, as well as John Caputo's interpretation of some of these thinkers.[3] In the chapters collected in this work, Westphal highlights the role of hermeneutics in Heidegger and Derrida and especially its important role in Christian faith. There is no faith without interpretation and without admitting an important dimension of non-knowledge. It is impossible to have full knowledge when speaking of God because having full knowledge or control would eliminate God's transcendence (this point is also strongly emphasized in *Transcendence and Self-Transcendence*). Westphal argues for finitude and humility as important dimensions of faith that can be learned from postmodern philosophy. Onto-theology, as in Heidegger, denotes the modern attempt at erasure of human finitude and the enclosure of the divine into the human system of knowledge. It does so through its use of abstract and impersonal categories and (as in Leibniz) the principle of sufficient reason. These categories seek to make the divine comprehensible and therefore exclude the mystery essential to religious faith. Westphal suggests that although there may well be onto-theological dimensions in the works of such thinkers as Aquinas and Augustine, they are not truly onto-theological, as they always acknowledge that God is far beyond anything we can grasp or comprehend. Thus, they do not subject the divine to ontology, as is so central to Heidegger's definition. (Westphal points out repeatedly in this context that Heidegger's definitions and criticisms are primarily directed at Hegel and Leibniz, not at Augustine or Aquinas.[4])

Suspicion and Faith explores the value of a "hermeneutics of suspicion." It draws on the thought of Freud, Marx, and Nietzsche, arguing (as the preface says) that their atheism "should be taken seriously as a stimulus to self-examination rather than refuted as an error" (*SF*, x). He contends that these three thinkers can serve as prophets in disguise because their critique of religion "seems to be all too true all too much of the time" (*SF*, x, 16). Believers can learn important lessons from their critique of faith. All too often piety hides self-righteousness and defense of our privileges. The three "prophets" of suspicion can help us see our self-delusions and hypocrisy.

More specifically, Freud uncovers the ways in which religion "makes unwarranted truth claims in the search for happiness" (*SF*, 41). Religion is a disguised way to fulfill our hidden and often suppressed wishes. Westphal's concern, however, is not to refute Freud (for example, for his scientism or various other unfounded presuppositions) or to justify the religious position, but to hear what is valid and useful in Freud's critiques of religion. For example, Freud points out how religion often takes on a useful "demonic function" that helps believers to divest themselves of blame: "To the degree that I am able to project my own deeds and desires onto a deity, I carry out a teleological suspension of the ethical that frees me from all moral accountability. I may not live free from pain, but I can live free from guilt and shame. It isn't all bad to be a victim" (*SF*, 71). Similarly, religion can serve as a way to blame one's own aggression on others and to justify injustice in religious terms in quasi-redemptive fashion, because God is "on our side" (*SF*, 76). Westphal thus calls Freud a "theologian of original sin" who recognizes the human proclivities to cruelty and greed (and especially to repress the guilt of sin, particularly evident in religious ceremonies). The "hermeneutics of suspicion" in regard to Freud has a dual function: "On the one hand it must expose the piety of compromise formations and One-Way Covenants for what it is, while on the other it must make it clear that God cannot be snookered into accepting the bribes offered by such pseudo-piety . . . prophetic consciousness hopes that it [the hermeneutics of suspicion discovered in Freud] will lead to the collapse of irreligion posing as religion, creating a space wherein true faith might flourish" (*SF*, 118–19). Freud's writings thus can be read with profit by believers and guide them to question themselves and believe more authentically.

Marx attacks less the individual believing soul than the communal function of religion as ideology to justify unjust social organizations and a social and political structure of oppression of the disadvantaged. Westphal shows how Marx both appropriates and criticizes Feuerbach's critique of religion as "false consciousness" and displaced desire for power (*SF*, 123). Marx turns this into a political critique of religion's role in legitimizing the social structures and institutions of a given society. In his treatment, Westphal also frequently points to the similarity of some of Freud's and Marx's criticisms. Westphal aligns Marx with the Hebrew prophets (such as Amos) who are highly critical of social injustice and the kind of piety that serves to hide and even justify it. Like Freud, Marx deserves to be taken seriously by religious believers:

When Marx accuses religion of being the Illusion of Overcoming the World, he is not asking whether God is real in some other world, be it future or inward and private, but whether God's presence in the public world of here and now is as an enemy or ally of injustice, oppression, and domination. If any religion says that the world can go to hell while it pursues some future or inward happiness, Marx feels entitled to tell that religion to do the same, since in the world where children suffer it does the work of Satan. (*SF*, 153)

Marx should be refuted by Christians with concrete proof of just social behavior. Merely to cite Christianity's "social principles" is insufficient (in both Marx's and Westphal's view) if these principles are not put into practice (*SF*, 167). Christian ideas have been (mis-)used to justify all sorts of violence and injustice.[5] Westphal criticizes both concrete interpretations of the Bible that wed a particular interpretation to the "overt espousal" of a particular social position and interpretations of "vague generality" that refuse to make any application to specific situations or draw concrete implications from the Scriptures:

> The risk of being wrong and the risk of becoming uncritically and absolutely attached to our historical choices are serious risks. But the apparently safer task is even riskier. To remain safely at the level of Vague Generality is to condemn Evil in the abstract while "enduring," both in theory and practice, the concrete evils from which our sisters and brothers, especially the children, daily suffer and die. By making faith "compatible with" these evils, we confirm the Marxian charge that religion is the opium of the people. (*SF*, 185)

In this context Westphal also condemns what he calls a "dualistic hermeneutics," which disconnects spirituality entirely from any sort of social practice. In all these ways religion can become idolatry that worships the status quo instead of God. Marx, then, helps us notice what the Hebrew prophets are saying when they condemn social injustice (*SF*, 213). He concludes his examination of Marx: "Marx's challenge to the churches is a hermeneutical challenge. It dares us to recognize in some of our most widespread rules of reading the ground of the ideological function and idolatrous substance of our faith. And it defies us to develop a hermeneutics of justice and compassion, one that seeks to hear rather than to hide what the Bible says about the widows and the orphans, the women and children in single-parent families" (*SF*, 216). Faith must be expressed in concrete action on behalf of the poor, oppressed, and suffering.

Westphal interprets Nietzsche as carrying Freud's and Marx's criticism of religion even further. While Freud is suspicious of the way individuals use religion to justify their behavior and Marx is suspicious of the way the ruling minority uses religion to justify its behavior, Nietzsche raises suspicions about the way in which the victims themselves can employ religion to justify their hatred and guilt. Nietzsche, according to Westphal, shows that even the poor, weak, and powerless are riddled by original sin (especially in the form of self-righteousness). Nietzsche is also more radical than Marx and Freud who still subscribe to Enlightenment assumptions about the high value of reason, because he is critical even of the Enlightenment's faith in rationality. Westphal portrays Nietzsche as fundamentally committed to honesty and intellectual integrity, virtues he believes religious people should emulate (*SF*, 237). Nietzsche can help believers to be wary of turning impotence into a virtue and to beware of religious fanaticisms of any sort, especially ones that rejoice in the demonization of the enemy under the guise of a crusade for justice. Westphal suggests that we must strive for a kind of compassion that is not "paternalistic pity" and a generosity that avoids the hypocrisy of moral superiority. Freud, Marx, and Nietzsche tell us the truth about our own pernicious religious practices and thus can help us to be continually suspicious of our motives and to move toward repentance and a more authentic faith. Westphal concludes:

> In calling Freud, Marx, and Nietzsche the great secular theologians of original sin I have suggested that the hermeneutics of suspicion belongs to our understanding of human sinfulness. The self-deceptions they seek to expose, like those exposed by Jesus and the prophets, are sins and signs of our fallenness. If we are to deepen our understanding of our sinfulness with their help, we need to remember at the same time the larger theological context in which the doctrine of the fall is properly placed, between the doctrines of creation and redemption . . . Suspicion can be a kind of spirituality. Its goal, like that of every spirituality, is to hold together a deep sense of our sinfulness with an equally deep sense of the gracious love of God. (*SF*, 288)

Instead of destroying our faith, all three thinkers can help us to move toward more authentic faith if we take their criticisms seriously. By taking the truth in their criticisms of belief to heart, our faith will emerge stronger and in a more purified form.

Westphal's early book on Kierkegaard similarly interprets Kierkegaard as a prophet who exercises a penetrating criticism of Danish society. Philosophy of religion must have a prophetic function that enables us to live our Christian faith more authentically and more inclusively. Phenomenology of religion can be precisely such a prophetic philosophy (*KC*, 3). This seems to serve also as preview or summary of much of Westphal's own writings in the phenomenology of religion, which consistently employ the postmodern thinkers to criticize faith and certain conceptions of God and self with the view of strengthening and deepening faith. Westphal wonders what would happen if contemporary philosophy of religion took Kierkegaard as a model:

> Now let us suppose that philosophers of religion, bringing to bear all of their special training and skills, were to address their contemporaries in this personal, untimely, political, and eschatological manner. It is difficult to predict the result, and even harder to tell whether there would be any healing in it. Clearly it would be a bitter pill, and hard to swallow, but then medicine comes in that form. Perhaps there would be some healing in the kind of philosophy that took Amos and Jeremiah as models rather than Galileo and Newton. (*KC*, 18)

The rest of the book presents Kierkegaard as precisely such a prophetic philosopher. Westphal's own concerns in this analysis become clear repeatedly in comments such as the following after analyzing Kierkegaard's account of Abraham: "And it remains puzzling to me how philosophy can afford the luxury of a contemplation divorced from repentance and exhortation" (*KC*, 84). Westphal shows how Kierkegaard's critique of reason enables a faith that is an act of obedience and trust. Furthermore, "Kierkegaard's logic of the insanity of faith, far from denying this circular character of theological proofs, calls our attention to it in opposition to the insane logic of both the orthodox apologetics and their free-thinking opponents. It directs our attention to the necessity of choice and the inescapability of the leap. It reminds us that theological affirmation is grounded in presuppositions that are chosen, not proven" (*KC*, 94). Here Westphal clearly rejects apologetic endeavors that attempt to prove God's existence and opts instead for affirmations that are rooted in religious choices unsupported by rational constructions but not therefore unreasonable. Westphal concludes his analysis of Kierkegaard by reminding us that "we would do well to remember that Socrates and the early Christians were accused of atheism because they did not worship at the shrines of the self-absolutizing cultures in which they lived" (*KC*, 125). Through his analysis of Kierkegaard Westphal calls his Christian readers to a more radical faith, a faith that is lived against a self-indulgent culture.

Westphal's most recent book, *Whose Community? Which Interpretation? Philosophical Hermeneutics for the Church* (2009), makes this claim about the value of postmodern thought for Christian faith the most explicitly as it is addressed directly to a Christian audience (it appeared in the series "Postmodernism for the Church" edited by James K. A. Smith for a predominantly evangelical Protestant audience). The book is essentially an exposition of Gadamer's philosophy and an argument that such hermeneutics is useful and indeed essential for Christian faith.[6] As he had done in other works (see later discussions of *Overcoming Onto-Theology* and *Transcendence and Self-Transcendence*), Westphal also argues again that Gadamer's hermeneutic extension of Heidegger is just as radical in its own way as that of Derrida. Throughout the book Westphal challenges the conception that assumes that we could have an "immediate" reading of the Scriptures that requires or involves no interpretation whatsoever. All reading is already interpretative and happens within particular contexts. There is no such thing as presuppositionless understanding. The attempt to avoid interpretation arises out of the fear of relativism but tries to hide the desire to make one's own interpretation absolute. Westphal reiterates that hermeneutics is not the position that all interpretations are equally valid and that there is no such thing as a wrong interpretation (*WW*, 26). He also again stresses the need for humility and a recognition that we do not know God absolutely and certainly do not have the divine in our grasp. Hermeneutics precisely recognizes this insight about human finitude and divine transcendence. He emphasizes again and again that "we are creatures, not the Creator" (*WW*, 66).[7] Flowing naturally out of his earlier calls for social action by believers, Westphal criticizes a "consumerist" model of the church, which sees faith only as a way to "feel good" and heal my "hurts" (usually in individualistic terms). Instead, the churches should come together in a community of dialogue. In this context, Westphal explores the recent conversations between Protestants and Roman Catholics as an illustration of the fruitfulness of such dialogue. Hermeneutics can inspire the humility that allows us to listen to each other openly.

Westphal makes the same argument to a maybe less explicitly Christian audience in *Overcoming Onto-Theology: Toward a Postmodern Christian Faith*.[8] This book collects various essays written between 1993 and 2001 on such thinkers as Heidegger, Schleiermacher, Gadamer, Derrida, Hegel, and Nietzsche, but with a heavily hermeneutic emphasis, including an essay on "Hermeneutics as Epistemology" and one on "Positive Postmodernism As Radical Hermeneutics." The theme of faith, expressed in the subtitle of the book, is evident throughout these essays. Again Westphal shows that the likes of Heidegger, Gadamer, and Derrida must not be perceived as threatening to faith, but can indeed provide valuable insights for a "postmodern faith." He reiterates his argument that postmodernism does not equate with relativism or even nihilism, as is often assumed by many Christians. Conversely, he also argues that Christian faith is not necessarily the meta-narrative it is often assumed to be by its postmodern critics. The content of its faith is kerygmatic, not apologetic (*OO*, xiii). Westphal clarifies his reading of hermeneutics in the introduction: "Hermeneutical philosophy, as I understand it, consists of two major branches, the hermeneutics of finitude and the hermeneutics of suspicion. My argument for a Christian appropriation of these, even when developed by postmodern philosophers with no love for Christianity, is theological. The hermeneutics of finitude is a meditation on the meaning of human createdness, and the hermeneutics of suspicion is a meditation on the meaning of human fallenness" (*OO*, xx).[9] This particular volume focuses more on the hermeneutics of finitude, since *Suspicion and Faith* focused primarily on the hermeneutics of suspicion.

Westphal interprets this hermeneutics of finitude as "a reflection on the nature and limits of human knowledge; for it is no longer limited to the interpretation of texts but interprets all cognition as interpretation" (*OO*, 49). He shows how both Gadamer and Derrida carry further and radicalize Heidegger's hermeneutic insights, arguing that they are both equally radical although in a different fashion. While Derrida stresses what Westphal calls the "glass half-empty" position, namely that there is much we cannot know and that all interpretation is radically contextual, Gadamer emphasizes the "glass half-full," focusing more positively on the insights we can gain in conversation and dialogue. This is not so much fundamental disagreement as a different emphasis and in Westphal's view both ultimately agree that reason cannot be self-sufficient in any sense and that interpretation goes "all the way down" (*OO*, 70).

Westphal's desire to "appropriate postmodernism" is again very evident in an essay under that title. He interprets such appropriation as seeking "a middle way between the total rejection of the refusenik and the equally uncritical jumping on the bandwagon of this month's politically correct fad" (*OO*, 76). In this essay especially, he stresses the fundamental postmodern insight that calls for humility and recognition of our finitude. We cannot reach any sort of absolute Truth and yet Westphal contends that this does not imply that there is no truth (or that the divine might not have access to Truth).[10] He clarifies: "In saying that we do not have access to the Truth, I am claiming that we do not possess it, that we do not preside over it, that our knowledge fails to embody the ideals of adequation and correspondence in terms of which Truth has traditionally been defined. But this does not entail that the Truth has no access to us, or that we should abandon the attempt to determine how best to think about what there is" (*OO*, 87). Westphal reinforces this argument in the later chapter on postmodernism as "radical hermeneutics." He reiterates his conviction that Gadamer and Derrida are equally radical in their appropriation of Heidegger and critique of modernity. In this context, however, he insists that a recognition of finitude and the practices of suspicion are not sufficient because they do not satisfy "spiritual hunger" (*OO*, 141). Kierkegaard is the most radical postmodern thinker because he goes beyond suspicion to encounter with the (human and divine) other: "Kierkegaard, who knows as well as Nietzsche how easily professed virtues are really splendid vices, does not give up on compassion and neighbor love but seeks to show how their true form is essential to human flourishing . . . like the Hebrew prophets before him and Levinas after him, Kierkegaard is a philosopher of *shalom* rather than of *polemos*" (*OO*, 146). Throughout the book Westphal interprets postmodernism in general or deconstruction in particular as useful for faith. At one point he defines deconstruction as "*the denial that we are divine*" (*OO*, 189).[11] This brings us to his reflections on the believer, the believing soul, or the postmodern but Christian self.

The "Believing Soul" of the Postmodern Self

Much of Westphal's work has focused on postmodern notions of the self. After the early study of Kierkegaard examined previously, he turned to an exposition of Kierkegaard's *Concluding Unscientific Postscript* under the title *Becoming a Self* (1996). His more recent work, *Transcendence and Self-Transcendence: On God and the Soul* (2004), again focuses on this question of the self in detail. This is also a theme in many of his other works, even when it is not the most explicit focus of the treatment (about half of *Levinas and Kierkegaard in Dialogue* is concerned with questions of subjectivity and intersubjectivity). His early work *God, Guilt and Death* (1984) also tries to examine the phenomenology of the "believing soul,"[12] in a kind of phenomenological examination of existential religious experience, using Merleau-Ponty's phenomenology as a guideline. In all these texts, Westphal presents the self as a self in progress, on the way to becoming and finding identity. Already in *Suspicion and Faith* Westphal had applauded Freud, Marx, and Nietzsche for uncovering the "pious fraud," which hides self-love under supposed "love of God and neighbor" (*SF*, 9, 13). Much of the book is a more detailed examination of the thought of these thinkers to highlight precisely this point and to show how their critique can lead us out of complacency and to a more authentic personal faith. One only finds true identity in response to others, in relation with others.

His earlier book *God, Guilt, and Death*, which he calls "an existential phenomenology of religion," is a broad examination of experiences of guilt and death in many religious traditions. It draws widely on non-Christian texts and experiences, including many Asian and American indigenous scriptures and traditions, moving with ease between Krishna and Augustine. In that sense, it is by far the most inclusive of any of the contemporary texts. (Kearney's most recent book comes closest, but it focuses primarily on the Abrahamic traditions.) The study follows Ricoeur's inspiration in *The Symbolism of Evil* in its examination of the experiences of guilt and death and the way in which they are mediated by various religious practices and rites. Westphal employs a phenomenological method to illustrate these experiences, but it is their concrete examination that forms the bulk of the book; the method is employed and explicitly laid out only in the first chapter. This chapter articulates phenomenology as an alternative to the way philosophy of religion has generally been conducted. It seeks to describe our experiences of guilt and death in order to lead to greater understanding of them instead of explaining them exhaustively or indeed proving anything about them. Religious experience is taken seriously on its own terms without trying to validate its "truth." He depicts this as follows: "The idea that philosophy consists in getting acquainted with the familiar is closely related to the idea that philosophical method can consist in imitating the painter, the actress, and the good listener. For the skill of the painter, actor, and good listener consists in large part of noticing and making explicit what is there to be seen by all but is for the most part overlooked" (*GGD*, 13).[13] Phenomenology helps describe the experiences of faith and thus allows the "believing soul" to emerge in all its complexity.

Westphal begins by describing the recognition of one's own inadequacy, of human fragility and finitude, faced with the ineffable divine mystery. In this context, Westphal both appropriates and criticizes Otto's account of the holy. He does recognize the same ambivalence to the divine (fascinating and repelling) that Otto had already highlighted, depicting it as an "existential pathos" (*GGD*, 49). It also gives rise to resentment. Contra Freud, faith is not always a comfortable position. In being confronted with the overwhelming divinity, the self recognizes its own finitude and is put in question. No certainty remains for the believing self but it is unsettled and displaced. Westphal warns that "only by seeing from the outset that the blessings of the religious life are themselves a threat to the human, all too human, self each of us is, can we hope to avoid reducing the religious life to its attractive dimension, the only one which gets acknowledged by some of its critics and by those of its devotees who have themselves lost touch with the Holy" (*GGD*, 69). He goes on to show that religion has both instrumental and intrinsic value for the believing soul, stressing that it is important to recognize also the instrumental value of dealing with death and guilt instead of focusing only on the more disinterested approach to faith. Religion both addresses deep existential concerns as well as serving as a tool for meeting immediate needs.

Guilt and death are among the most problematic existential experiences for the individual. Religious ritual is a means for coping with these deeply distressing experiences:

> If guilt, then, is an experience, especially conducive to the manifestation of the Sacred as the *mysterium tremendum*, its meaning as *fascinans* will come to light as it helps us deal with guilt in all three of its dimensions. We remain with ambivalence. Religion will be repelling as it gives focus and new intensity to human guilt. But it will be attractive just to the degree that it (1) helps us to avoid the punishment we would otherwise be liable to, (2) gives us sufficient assurance of this to free us from the fear of punishment, and (3) heals the wounded self-consciousness which can only approve the other's disapproval, which knows how vastly its desire for happiness exceeds its worthiness. (*GGD*, 89)

The experience of death is closely linked to that of guilt; indeed, the awareness of impending death can often include a realization of one's self-deceptions and guilt vis-à-vis others. Death reaffirms our finitude and the limitations placed on our freedom. It questions whether we have fulfilled "the task of becoming a self" (*GGD*, 101). Westphal shows how a variety of religious traditions deal with the fear of death and especially the sense of guilt that anticipates punishment and torture after death. Religious ritual is thought to provide some relief from these fears. And yet "the believing soul knows (or learns) that the motivation of the religious life transcends that calculation of benefits that social scientists curiously insist upon calling rational behavior" (*GGD*, 129). Religion also includes an important dimension of disinterestedness. In this context Westphal also examines the practices of prayer and sacrifice that are so central to religion. These practices allow the self to face the transcendent other and lead to thanks and adoration, even imitation, of the divine (*GGD*, 159). Thus the self is faced with its own finitude and fragility in both the traumatic experiences of fear, death, or guilt and the more positive responses of prayer, praise, and sacrifice.

In order to compare various religious responses Westphal distinguishes between three types: exilic (anti-worldly), mimetic (stories about the renewal of life in the ancient Near East and hence life-affirming), and covenantal (also world-affirming but in a different sense than the mimetic) traditions. He considers most of the Eastern traditions as exilic (but he includes in this category also what he calls "Orphic-Pythagorean" and the Gnostic traditions in the West) and describes the Jewish and Christian traditions (along with some others) as affirmative of the world (world designating both nature and history). Exilic religions reassure the soul that it can escape suffering and alienation by awakening to another reality, while covenantal religions cope with guilt and death in the here and now. Westphal stresses that this is not an evaluative distinction (one that judges one religion as better than another) and that there are transitions and hybrids between the three types. The central element in all these traditions is hope (for forgiveness and redemption). Westphal concludes his study of religious phenomenology by affirming that "guilt and death are a central and essentially single concern of the religious life, not only in the biblical tradition, but in religious traditions very different from the former and often thought to differ precisely by the lack of such a concern . . . the form that this concern takes, and thus what we might call the form of salvation, varies from one context to another." And, yet, he affirms, "these variations stand in a meaningful correlation with the basic attitudes toward human being in the world which provide the key to the religious typology developed here" (*GGD*, 251). Indeed he suggests that these two variables (affirmation/negation vs. guilt/death) are closely connected and perhaps even flip-sides of the same issue. The various religious typologies can help us in personal spirituality toward existential self-understanding. Westphal hopes that this will enable us to "live our lives with greater integrity" (*GGD*, 252). Our faith is deepened as we move into greater self-understanding.

Becoming a Self is a close reading of Kierkegaard's *Concluding Unscientific Postscript* and argues that despite all the emphasis on subjectivity and individuality, Kierkegaard sees the self as "essentially relational, first to God and then to neighbor, and that isolation from the crowd is not an end (as if human nature were atomic) but a means to the self's proper relationships, once again first to God and then to other human selves."[14] Furthermore, he interprets Kierkegaard's arguments against rationality as a call to recognize human finitude and against the human desire to deify itself by reaching full intelligibility (as in Hegel). As this work is a very close reading of Kierkegaard's text (including a long section from the *Postscript* as an appendix), the book will not be summarized here. Suffice it to say that the issue of how to become a self before God is central to Westphal's explication of Kierkegaard. Throughout his commentary, Westphal also points out resonances in Kierkegaard's work to postmodern concerns with frequent references to contemporary thinkers. Truth is subjectivity in the sense that it calls us to live our lives authentically instead of escaping to a divine point of view of absolute reason. This selfhood that we are to develop is not an irresponsible individualism but always a call to respond to the divine and the neighbor in love. Again Westphal stresses the essential ambivalence of the religious life, which is neither easy nor necessarily pleasant. Although Kierkegaard's text places the choice of the life of faith before us, the manner of his writing (including the pseudonymous aspects) leave us alone with that choice and do not make it for us.

Transcendence and Self-Transcendence suggests that the kind of self-transcendence discovered by examining the Christian tradition reveals a decentered self that is very similar to postmodern philosophical proposals: "Long before either modernity or postmodernity, the believing soul has understood the God relation as a call to abandon the project of being the alpha and omega of its own existence. But since the decentered self is a central theme of postmodern philosophy, there will be something surprisingly postmodern about the life of the faith that lives out this spirituality" (*TS*, 5). Westphal considers the human soul again in light of Kierkegaard and here also of Lévinas. It previews the arguments spelled out in more detail in *Levinas and Kierkegaard in Dialogue*. In both books, Westphal articulates the need for the self to become a self through relation but aligns Lévinas with love of neighbor and Kierkegaard with love of God. In fact, he sees this as the fundamental difference between the two thinkers, arguing that the rest of their philosophy agrees for the most part (and does so far more profoundly than usually recognized). Westphal is quite critical of what he perceives as Lévinas's exclusive emphasis on the neighbor. He seeks to show that one can also become a self through response to the divine, that the divine partner constitutes a real person in relation, who can similarly serve to individuate the self. He employs Kierkegaard heavily in this context, especially the late text *Works of Love*, which shows Kierkegaard—self-avowed individual—at his most concerned for relations with others. It is clear in both treatments that Westphal prefers Kierkegaard's version: We love the neighbor through God and because we love God. Love of God is the origin and ground for love of neighbor. Yet the two types of love are actually always deeply connected. Westphal affirms as a central message of the Christian tradition: "Our highest duty is obedience to God and our highest good is loving union with God. This union is always on God's terms, not on ours, and this love has its origin in God and not in ourselves" (*TS*, 178). We become a self as we expose ourselves in love to God who loves us first.

God After (and Before) Onto-Theology

When speaking of faith, one must obviously also speak of the one to whom faith is directed: God. Westphal writes often and frequently about the divine but tries to hinder us from turning God into an "object." He employs the postmodern thinkers precisely in order to preserve God's transcendence, to surround the divine with a protective cloud of unknowing. Faith is not sight. Suspicion can be an important and helpful dimension of faith. This is a constant theme in his writings, most succinctly expressed through the criticism of onto-theology: both as exposition of its problematic nature and as refutation of the application of this term and concept to many traditional Christian writers, foremost among them Augustine and Aquinas.[15] All of Westphal's books, but especially the most recent ones, focus to some extent on the question of the divine. In *Transcendence and Self-Transcendence* he describes his position as follows: "I write as a Christian theist engaged in a personal journey of faith seeking understanding and growth in faithfulness. My hope is that my shared reflections will help both believers and unbelievers avoid misunderstandings that theism is heir to and thus to think more clearly about the God they affirm or deny. Thus, the same analysis has an apologetic intention for readers who do not believe and a pastoral intention for readers who do" (*TS*, 2). This work thus moves significantly beyond *God, Guilt and Death*, in which Westphal's main task was merely to describe religious experience from a variety of traditions and he disavowed any sort of apologetic intent. It also shows the close connection between thinking about God and thinking about faith. Preserving God's transcendence in an acknowledgement of the limitations of our knowledge of the divine is an important (if not the central) aspect of the postmodern faith for which he argues.

Already in *Suspicion and Faith*, Westphal had suggested that "we need to see Marx, Nietzsche, and Freud, along with Luther and Barth, as expressing a Promethean protest against all the Zeuses of *instrumental religion, the piety that reduces God to a means or instrument for achieving our human purposes with professedly divine power and sanction*" (*SF*, 6). He carries this argument further in much of his later work where he tries to show that the Christian God (or "the God of Abraham, Isaac, and Jacob," the God of faith) cannot be equated with onto-theological notions of the divine. The chapter on "Overcoming Onto-Theology" that gives the title to the whole volume attempts to clarify what Heidegger actually means by that term. Westphal contends that it is far too often employed merely as a means to silence one's opponent (by accusing him or her of the sin of onto-theology). He suggests that "perhaps onto-theology consists in the pride that refuses to accept the limits of human knowledge," especially in regard to the divine (*OO*, 7). He argues in this and the following chapter that Heidegger's atheism is methodological and not substantive and thus ultimately neutral about questions of faith (which are in the posterior ontic realm rather than the prior ontological one with which Heidegger is concerned). Westphal acknowledges that his "project is to appropriate Heidegger's critique of onto-theology for theistic theology, for religiously significant discourse about the personal Creator, Lawgiver, and Merciful Savior of Jewish, or Christian, or Muslim monotheism" (*OO*, 21). We must learn to speak of God non–onto-theologically precisely because onto-theological language belongs to "the arrogant humanism" that pretends to put the divine at our disposal (*OO*, 24). He concludes that "one way to see how far we have overcome onto-theology is to ask how strongly we are inspired by our theology to sing songs of praise to the God who triumphed over political, economic, and cultural oppression when 'Pharaoh's army got drownded'" (*OO*, 28). A final essay near the end of the book explores the God who may "come after" onto-theology as "divine excess" (*OO*, 256ff.). Here, Westphal shows how Heidegger, Lévinas, and Marion can lead us to the following insights: "We must think God as the mystery that exceeds the wisdom of the Greeks. We must think God as the voice that exceeds vision so as to establish a relation irreducible to comprehension. We must think God as the gift of love who exceeds not merely the images but also the concepts with which we aim at God" (*OO*, 270). These postmodern thinkers can thus help us to combat philosophical and theological arrogance and idolatry. God is ineffable mystery and calls us beyond ourselves.[16]

Transcendence and Self-Transcendence: On God and the Soul is Westphal's most thorough contribution to the question of God and onto-theology (although the more recent study of Lévinas and Kierkegaard also raises the question). He begins by again outlining Heidegger's concept of onto-theology and illustrating it by a more extensive examination of Spinoza and Hegel. Then he goes on to show how the religious tradition has indeed spoken of the divine as mystery in a way that is not onto-theological by focusing specifically on Pseudo-Dionysius, Augustine, Aquinas, and Karl Barth. The approach of negative theology and the notions of analogy found in these thinkers are attempts to recognize and preserve God's transcendence, although they realize that the divine cannot ultimately be known by the human mind. Indeed, even the final section on the call of the soul to responsibility is ultimately still about divine transcendence insofar as this call proceeds from a divine imperative (this is made clear also by the title of Part 3, "Ethical and Religious Transcendence: The Divine Imperative"). Westphal thus illustrates what he calls "the essential link between theology and ethics, or, if you prefer, metaphysics and spirituality" (*TS*, 1). In all these cases Westphal shows that God is never at our disposal and that an important dimension of unknowability remains in our approach to the divine (and must necessarily remain to preserve God's transcendence). Whether via negative theology or through the concept of analogy, the tradition recognizes that the divine mystery cannot finally be known.

Westphal begins the book with a discussion of Heidegger. He outlines what Heidegger means by onto-theology in order to argue that Spinoza and Hegel exemplify such an onto-theological metaphysical system, while Augustine and Aquinas do not. As in earlier works, he points to the elimination of mystery as one of the most important characteristics of onto-theology. It seeks to make God completely comprehensible: "The task of God [for metaphysics] is to make science possible, and metaphysics will treat any God who shirks this responsibility as an illegal immigrant in the brave new world of modernity" (*TS*, 21). Onto-theology is characterized by calculative and representational thinking that eliminates God's transcendence, puts the divine at the disposal of human knowledge, and consequently also threatens human self-transcendence and genuinely ethical action. Onto-theology hence always has both epistemic and ethical implications.

Westphal goes on to show more specifically how Spinoza's and Hegel's philosophies are indeed onto-theological in the sense he has outlined in the first chapter. In this context, he argues for more careful definitions of theism, atheism, and pantheism (*TS*, 43). While Spinoza and Hegel both do indeed speak of God (and hence are not atheists in that sense), neither affirms this God to be personal or to be related to the world in a transcendental sense as its creator (and in that sense they are a-theists). Westphal again points to the important implications of Spinoza's pantheism: "On the epistemic front, the impersonal character of God undermines the notions of divine mystery and divine revelation associated with biblical theism. On the ethical front, it undermines the theistic understanding of God as a moral lawgiver. In each case, the elimination or minimizing of divine transcendence is the elimination or minimizing of a significant mode of human self-transcendence" (*TS*, 53). Consequently, humans become the sole reference point for knowing and acting. Spinoza rejects divine mystery and thus any possibility of knowledge that extends beyond human capacity (*TS*, 60). This means that ethics "is reduced to looking out for Number One" and "the widow, orphan, and stranger disappear from view" (*TS*, 63, 65). Like Spinoza, Hegel denies that God could exist independently of the world. There is no personal relationship possible with Hegel's God. For

Hegel also, human beings remain "at the top of the totem pole both epistemically and ethically" (*TS*, 80). Although Hegel appropriates many central Christian doctrines, such as the incarnation, his system remains essentially onto-theological: "God can enter philosophy's discourse only on the latter's terms and in the service of its project" (*TS*, 85).

In the second part of the book, Westphal turns to show that an emphasis on God's epistemic transcendence and mystery allows escape from onto-theological thinking. Apophatic theology, which stresses the divine mystery, breaks with the onto-theological project in both Augustine and Pseudo-Dionysius and can hence renew "our sense of the otherness of God" (*TS*, 93). Westphal insists again that while onto-theology is concerned with a "Highest Being" that serves as "the First Principle of all reality," genuine theology instead emphasizes God's ineffability or incomprehensibility and maintains that "our conceptual systems are inadequate to the divine reality, too weak to grasp it and too dull to mirror it" (*TS*, 94). While onto-theology renders God completely intelligible, genuine theology stresses the divine mystery. Westphal shows how such preservation of the divine mystery and transcendence is true of Augustine, Pseudo-Dionysius, Aquinas, and Karl Barth. Augustine maintains a permanent ontological and epistemic disparity between Creator and creatures (*TS*, 98). Dionysius develops a method (negative theology) for speaking of the divine in such a way that God's transcendence and essential mystery are preserved. Dionysius escapes a metaphysics of presence precisely by not rendering the divine reality completely intelligible to human knowing. In this context, Westphal interacts with deconstruction (as laid out by Derrida and Caputo) and shows that while it has much in common with negative theology, it must remain essentially agnostic about the possibility of religious experience (*TS*, 108). He concludes that for Dionysius "we speak most appropriately about God when we fully realize and acknowledge the inadequacy of whatever we say" (*TS*, 114). Throughout, he emphasizes consistently how this discourse (or silence) about God has profound ethical implications of care for the neighbor and stranger.

In regard to Aquinas, Westphal stresses the doctrine of the analogy of being and emphasizes the parallels between Aquinas and Dionysius. He also shows how Aquinas articulates God's independence from the world, which does not imply God's indifference to creation but rather a real difference between Creator and creature that enables genuine relationship and freedom. Although for Aquinas created intellects can indeed "see" God's essence (the beatific vision), Westphal asserts that this never means that we "comprehend" the divine. God always exceeds our grasp even in the life to come (*TS*, 133, 140). Westphal then turns to Barth's theology as a twentieth-century example of theological thinking that is not onto-theological. Barth is responding both to liberal Protestant theology and to Roman Catholic theology (pre–Vatican II). Westphal shows how Barth explicitly rejects onto-theology and denies "the notion of a way, a method by which *we* can establish a genuine knowledge of God" (*TS*, 146). Barth opposes any attempt to make the divine dependent upon human knowledge or subjectivity. This is grounded both in human fallenness and in our essential finitude. Westphal concludes of Barth what he has stressed more generally: "In this context to attempt to dissolve the divine mystery is to deface God and to silence God's voice. The God who resists every such project is one who refuses to enter human discourse on philosophy's terms . . . but who *ipso facto* gives Godself to human prayer and worship, singing and (perhaps even) dancing" (*TS*, 161). God is mystery, all knowledge of the divine proceeds from divine revelation and grace, and this implies our utter and permanent dependence on the divine. In the final two chapters, Westphal applies the insights gained about God's transcendence to human self-transcendence, especially in regard to ethical comportment, by returning to his arguments about Lévinas and Kierkegaard, already outlined at the end of the previous section of this chapter.

Westphal, then, seeks to make viable Christian faith and practice in today's world, which is essentially a postmodern world. He assures us that postmodern thinkers are not dangerous atheists out to destroy our faith, but can prove an important resource for a robust, yet also humbler, faith. To acknowledge that we do not have access to absolute Truth, that we do not hold God in our grasp, that we must construct ourselves, and that even reading the Scriptures always remains a matter of interpretation, does not deny that all these activities—searching for Truth, approaching God, becoming a self, shaping community in light of careful reading of Scripture—are important and valuable, but indeed give us new impetus for pursuing them as faithfully and responsibly as possible. He reads the postmodern thinkers in the same way that he reads the masters of suspicion: Reading and appreciating their arguments can deepen and strengthen our faith.

John Caputo: Postmodern Hope

John D. Caputo, recently retired as Thomas J. Watson Professor of Religion and Humanities at Syracuse University and David R. Cook Professor Emeritus of philosophy at Villanova University where he taught for many years, is most well-known for his friendship with Derrida and for highlighting the religious dimension of Derrida's thought. Caputo's work is perhaps best understood as a form of postmodern hope (especially in contrast to Westphal's emphasis on faith and Kearney's concern with charity). Despite being associated so firmly with Derrida, Caputo's earliest work was on Heidegger, tracing what he called the "mystical dimension" of Heidegger's thought and even associating Heidegger with Aquinas (or, maybe more to the point, associating Aquinas with Heidegger). It was only in his work on "radical hermeneutics" that he turned increasingly from Heidegger to Derrida. At first, Caputo seemed to want to find a middle path between Heidegger and Derrida, but he became more and more an expositor of certain dimensions of Derrida's work. Caputo is particularly interested in the structure of religious hope and desire and thoroughly disenchanted with (and often very critical of) particular religious traditions or commitments. All this is driven also by a concern for justice and hospitality, which is expressed primarily in terms of openness and affirmation (Derrida's "oui, oui" is a phrase Caputo employs often and indeed sees as a summary or "nutshell" of deconstruction[1]). Most recently, Caputo has engaged more explicitly in theology by formulating what he calls a "theology of the event," which is an attempt to articulate a notion of God in the face of radical evil and the apparent insignificance of human life in the history of the cosmos. It is in this work that the dimension of hope is most clearly articulated as the central feature of Caputo's thought, although it is present already in his expositions of Derrida. In *The Weakness of God*, he expresses the event precisely in terms of hope:

> The name of God is powerful because it is the name of our hope in the contract Elohim makes with things when he calls them "good," when he calls them *to* the good, when he breathes the life of the good over them. The name of God is a name of an event, the event of our faith in the transformability of things, in the most improbable and impossible things, so that life is never closed in, the future never closed off, the horizon never finite and confining. The name of God opens what is closed, breathes life where there is desolation, and gives hope where everything is hopeless. (*WG*, 88)

Yet this is not a hope for a powerful God to strike and remove the evil ones, but rather a weaker, more fragile hope that calls us toward justice and commitment to the good.[2]

At least as influential as his writings has been Caputo's organizing of countless events, interviews, and roundtables highlighting and celebrating postmodern thought, especially that of Derrida. He has been instrumental in getting such thinkers as Marion, Chrétien, Lacoste, and others translated and known in the American world. The biannual conferences on "Religion and Postmodernism" at Villanova and the Syracuse conferences on "Postmodernism, Culture, and Religion" have been central events at which important debates (beginning with the one where Derrida and Marion debated about the gift) served as impetus for further thinking and have contributed immensely to popularize the work of the philosophers discussed in this book. Caputo has also trained and inspired a steady stream of students, especially at Villanova (the book *Deconstruction in a Nutshell* grew out of the inauguration of the Ph.D. program in philosophy at Villanova University in 1994). While Caputo's original background is Roman Catholic, overall he is much more critical of traditional versions of faith (especially of Christian faith) than Westphal and advocates instead a "religion without religion" inspired by Derrida. While Westphal sees much of his work done in service to the Christian community, Caputo's work is mostly conceived as a criticism of a variety of fundamentalisms and religious authority.

Heidegger

Caputo's earliest work focused on Heidegger. *The Mystical Element in Heidegger's Thought* traces the conversation with Meister Eckhart, which is present in or behind much of Heidegger's thought. This book is a careful exposition of Heidegger's use of Eckhart and the mystical elements that consequently arise in his work. Caputo continues this examination of Heidegger in his book *Heidegger and Aquinas* where he examines Heidegger's reading of scholasticism and draws some parallels between the works of the two thinkers especially in regard to the question of being. He explicitly disavows drawing "connections" between the two thinkers but instead confronts them over the ways in which they describe the nature and content of metaphysics. Caputo argues that, in the final analysis, Aquinas does not escape Heidegger's critique of metaphysics as onto-theology but actually constitutes a good example of it. Nevertheless Caputo highlights a "mystical dimension" to St. Thomas's thought missed by many of his commentators who try to defend him from the Heideggerian charge. A deeper interpretation of his thought might allow us to detect a tendency to "deconstruction" even in Aquinas himself. Aquinas and Heidegger share a common insight of a deeper, quasi-mystical dimension to thought, which can unsettle and deconstruct purely rational metaphysics.

After his first volume on *Radical Hermeneutics*, Caputo becomes increasingly more critical of Heidegger. *Demythologizing Heidegger* shows this particularly clearly. Here Caputo uncovers and criticizes a strong mythologizing tendency in Heidegger's thought, which is obsessed with the early Greeks and which Caputo suggests is closely linked to Heidegger's involvement in Nazism. He argues that "the privileged status of the early Greeks forms the core of a vast, overarching, and—it is now plain—highly dangerous metanarrative, a sweeping myth about Being's fabulous movements through Western history" (*DH*, 2). This metanarrative that holds Heidegger's thinking "captive" is "a myth of monogenesis, a monomaniac preoccupation with a single deep source, with an originary, unitary beginning, which he thought must be kept pure and uncontaminated, like a pure spring" (*DH*, 4). The "myth of Being" excludes "everything that is not Greek" and constitutes a fatal silencing of other traditions, such as the Jewish one (*DH*, 6). Caputo reads various parts of Heidegger's work in subsequent chapters and shows how Heidegger privileged certain elitists and even violent images over concerns with justice and multiplicity. Instead Caputo argues for more "liberating, empowering myths," which he sees instantiated in Derrida, Lyotard, and Lévinas (*DH*, 3).

Caputo begins by demonstrating that Heidegger articulates a critique of the history of metaphysics in *Being and Time* to which he himself becomes unfaithful in his subsequent writings, which privilege particular expressions of Being and provide a more unified (and considerably less critical) view. Caputo suggests that Heidegger's early work thus provides an important critique to his later grand narratives. Heidegger's mythologizing tendency begins here: "Instead of seeing in *a-letheia* the essential delimitation of any historical manifestation of Being, Heidegger engages in a hypervalorization of *aletheia* as a Greek experience, an experience in which the German and the Greek are tied together in a fateful Being-historical way" (*DH*, 21). Caputo finds that Heidegger imposes this particular interpretation of *aletheia* onto the Greeks in order to allow him to write a mythical story of power and exclusion. The problem for Caputo is not that Heidegger tells stories, but which myths he privileges and the ways in which he does so: "It is never a question of thinking in absolutely demythologizing terms, but of opposing good myths to bad ones, salutary and emancipatory myths to totalizing and dangerous ones, of multiplying small myths and *petits récits* to offset the *grand récits* that threaten us all" (*DH*, 38).

Caputo is particularly critical of the ways in which Heidegger privileges violent themes in his thought, which align his writing more explicitly with his political choices. Already in Heidegger's very early writings on the hermeneutics of facticity, themes of violent struggle are prevalent and explicitly linked to the question of Being. Caputo suggests that Heidegger's move away from Kierkegaard, Pascal, and Aristotle in favor of Nietzsche, Jünger, and Hölderlin is fateful in its mytho-poetic language of *Geist* and *Volk*, which portrays the members of the German nation as the true carriers of the Greek spirit. Heidegger speaks of care in terms of struggle and success instead of the healing of suffering. He misses the language of the heart of a more biblical hermeneutics of facticity. Heidegger is not open to feelings of vulnerability and fleshly needs: "He was very responsive to the *Sorge*, the care for one's being-in-the-world, but he entirely missed the *cura*, the healings, the caring for the flesh of the other, the *kardia*. For *cura* also means healing the flesh of the other, tending to the other's pain and afflicted flesh" (*DH*, 72). Caputo argues that there is an "essentializing tendency" in Heidegger's work "that transcends the concrete and suffering subjects of actual history" (*DH*, 73). Heidegger writes responsibility entirely in terms of a call of being, which grounds the vocation to greatness of a people (orchestrated by fate) instead of an appeal from the suffering other calling the self to the responsibility of a response in Lévinas's sense.

And yet Caputo insists again that there are dimensions in Heidegger's thought that allow for another way of reading that can be posited against Heidegger himself in favor of "a profoundly pluralistic, decentered openness to the other" (*DH*, 99). Heidegger's continual call for greater questioning and his emphasis on "unknowing" and "the nothing" unsettles his own unified image of historical fate. Yet instead of pursuing this line of questioning in his post-war writings, Heidegger instead turned to a more essentializing thinking of Being. Heidegger outlines a privileged position of human beings, which separates them from animals and aligns them with Being as such. Again in Caputo's view Heidegger excludes concrete suffering and vulnerable bodies (*DH*, 128). This reaches its height in his scandalous comparison of the modern food industry to the gas chambers. Caputo shows that this is not an isolated comment but fits in with Heidegger's overall insensitivity to concrete human suffering and misery. Heidegger's dazzling myth of Being ignores the victim: "The victim has no voice in the call of Being, cannot speak, cannot be heard . . . Victims have been robbed of their voice, do not have the means to register a protest on their own behalf about the damage that has been done to them. Victims do not make their appearance on the register of Being" (*DH*, 144–45).

Caputo concludes his study by investigating Heidegger's "poets" and his "gods," which make such prominent appearance in his final works. Caputo argues that although Heidegger frequently refers to poets and poetry, his work actually functions to separate thinking from poetry and thus limits poetry's more unsettling effects. His readings of Trakl and others are essentializing and reduce their poetry to a commentary on Being, which ignores concrete historicity. Similarly, Heidegger excludes religious and biblical themes from his work despite his early interest in theology. Caputo interprets Heidegger's exclusion of these approaches as central to his lack of dealing with questions of justice and his silence on concrete suffering. He examines Heidegger's early Catholic writings on the medieval tradition and his move to Protestantism with a focus on Paul, Augustine, Pascal, Luther, and Kierkegaard. His early writings on factical life are grounded in his readings of early Christian life and Caputo suggests that to some extent *Being and Time* constitutes an attempt to "formalize" these structures of religious life in a more general fashion (*DH*, 172–73). Yet, increasingly, Heidegger moves to exclude any theological or religious concerns from philosophy and his work even becomes "openly antagonistic to Christianity" (*DH*, 175). Caputo contends, however, that this is still a mythical, religious thought that introduces new "Greek gods": first a Promethean god of war and finally "a new mythopoetic meditation upon the Holy and the gods" (*DH*, 179). Caputo sees hopeful aspects in Heidegger's later mythologizing tendencies inasmuch as they have useful ecological implications. He still finds, however, that "the difficulty with Heidegger is that his myth of world and thing, of the Fourfold, his sacralizing of the earth is tied to a geophilosophical myth of Being's history, of its favorite sons and favored languages and chosen lands." At the same time, Heidegger "omits and even preempts a myth of justice," which is the "Hebraic myth of the Holy, of the call of the Other One, of the other person" (*DH*, 183). He concludes that Heidegger's thinking ultimately excludes the Jewish and Christian concerns for the poor and marginalized in favor of a poetic neopaganism. Caputo, therefore, in a final chapter highlights the thought of Lévinas and Derrida as a "jewgreek" myth, which allows an alternative vision attentive to justice and compassion. This is also a myth, a call for the "impossible," but it is the impossibility of a "hyperbolic-prophetic justice" that "is a wail, a call for mercy and compassion, a cry against injustice" (*DH*, 208). Caputo sees Derrida as more committed to these concrete questions of justice, including a certain Jewish, even biblical, dimension despite its apparent "atheism."

Derrida and Deconstruction

Caputo's work on Derrida has interesting parallels to his work on Heidegger. In both cases, he tries to highlight the religious or mystical dimensions of their work, in often rather provocative fashion, challenging more traditional (i.e. atheistic or anti-religious) interpretations of their work. This is true both of his early work on Heidegger, which highlights its religious roots and affinities, and the more recent work just examined, which interprets the exclusion of the religious as key for the problematic elements in Heidegger's work. Caputo's central argument in *The Prayers and Tears of Jacques Derrida* is that religious themes inform Derrida's work throughout, culminating with *Circumfession* where they become most explicit.[3] The subtitle of *The Prayers and Tears* serves also as a good summary of Caputo's interpretation of Derrida: "religion without religion." This has become a standard phrase for many commentators who align themselves with Caputo's version of Derrida.[4] In *The Prayers and Tears*, Caputo highlights various quasi-religious dimensions of Derrida's work, which he calls the apophatic, the apocalyptic, and the Messianic, as well as examining Derrida's writings on the gift, on circumcision, and on confession, especially as evident in *Circumfession*. In *Deconstruction in a Nutshell*, he expands this examination to other dimensions of Derrida's thought, although his treatment here is more strictly expository in nature. He interprets Derrida's thought as most fundamentally affirmative, focusing on the "Oui. Oui. Yes. Yes" as the least "bad" summary of deconstruction. Derrida's thought is a philosophy of welcome and hospitality.

Caputo begins by tracing deconstruction's ambivalent relationship with negative theology: "Deconstruction desires what negative theology desires and it shares the passion of negative theology—for the impossible" (*PTD*, 3). He shows both the structural parallels between the two and the ways in which deconstruction is *not* a form of negative theology, especially in its alignment with the emptiness of *khora* instead of the "good beyond being."[5] Yet instead of attacking faith, deconstruction actually serves a positive function of saving and protecting God's name against efforts to constrict or control it:

> To lend a Derridian ear to negative theology is, in my view, to be led to the doors of *faith*, which negative theology tends to leave at the door. Faith is a certain resolve to hold on by one's teeth, to put one's hand to the plow, to push on in the midst of the grammatological flux, to repeat forward, to say *oui* today knowing that this must be repeated later on tonight, and then again tomorrow morning, again and again, *oui, oui*. (*PTD*, 12)

While deconstruction clearly condemns the more totalizing forms of theology, it also criticizes all other forms of totalizing discourse, including ones that want to exclude languages of faith. Examining Derrida's two explicit essays on negative theology ("How to Avoid Speaking" and *Sauf le nom*), Caputo highlights a certain "generalized apophatics" that is the mark of a deeper desire for the impossible, for the coming of the *tout autre* (every other or the wholly other). This is a dream that appears in various guises in Derrida's work, such as the "democracy to come," which is "a completely open-ended, negative, undetermined structure" (*PTD*, 56). Deconstruction itself is a kind of faith "miming and repeating the structure of faith in a faith without dogma" (*PTD*, 57). Caputo thus uncovers what he sees as an "apocalyptic" dimension of Derrida's thought, namely as a welcome of what is always to come, a structural dimension of hospitality, which always says "come" to the unforeseeable and unpredictable: "*Viens* is not a matter of counting, but of watching, staying awake in messianic time. *Viens* is a certain structural wakefulness or openness to an impossible breach of the present, shattering the conditions of possibility, by which we are presently circumscribed" (*PTD*, 96). He interprets this dimension as a criticism of power and authority. The secret to which we never have access is the condition for what is to come. The secret has apophatic quality and yet is not theology. The wholly other, then, has many names besides that of "God." Indeed, God is the impossible; the term functions as a name for the other.[6]

Caputo especially emphasizes the messianic character of Derrida's work. The messianic is the most explicit convergence between deconstruction and the religious. Yet this is an examination of a messianic *structure* not a messianic content. Derrida is critical of various religious fundamentalisms and of a Christian political version of Europe. Thus Derrida advocates not any particular messianism but a certain messianicity. Yet here Caputo admits that Derrida's work can be read as a kind of messianism of its own, a charge he generally does not continue to make in his later writings on Derrida. He points out that "the difficulty is not so much that we do not know what the messianic *means*, since Derrida is clear enough, even quite eloquent, about 'the "yes" to the *arrivant(e)*, the "come" to the future that cannot be anticipated.'" Rather, the "difficulty is that we are at a loss to describe the *status* of this undeterminability, this indeterminable messianic, without specific content, which cannot be a true or conventional or garden variety universal" (*PTD*, 139). In Caputo's view (at least here), there can be no "general" or universal messianic, but only particular messianisms, of which Derrida's is one among many (*PTD*, 142). The coming of a Messiah then haunts deconstruction, although this coming is always infinitely deferred. Thus,

> deconstruction takes the form of a certain re-ligious re-sponsibility to what is coming, to what does not exist. Deconstruction turns on a certain pledging of itself to the future, on a certain *religio* that religiously observes its covenant with the *revenant* and the *arrivant*, to what is coming back from the past, and to what is arriving from the past as the future. Deconstruction is, in that sense, a messianic religion within the limits of reason alone, that is, it is inhabited and structured in a messianic-religious way. (*PTD*, 149–50)

Later, Caputo will generally speak of Derrida as indicating only the *structure* of the messianic and not giving it any content.

In the second part of the book, Caputo examines the notions of the gift and of circumcision more particularly. The gift displays the same character of the impossible that has already been evident in the apocalyptic and the messianic. Caputo explicates Derrida's reading of Kierkegaard's account of Abraham's sacrifice of Isaac and Derrida's critique of Patočka's religious vision of Europe (as set forth especially in Derrida's *The Gift of Death*). Caputo claims again in light of this reading that Derrida helps to think "the structural possibility of the religious, of a certain radical messianic structure, without the dangerous liaisons of the particular religions, without the dogma, without the determinate messianic faiths that divide humanity into warring parties" (*PTD*, 195). While the concrete messianisms push us to war, the more general messianic is concerned with peace. Caputo shows how Derrida's commitment to the other is "structurally religious" in Kierkegaard's sense inasmuch as it is willing to abandon the terminology of the ethical so prominent in Lévinas's work (*PTD*, 206). Caputo reads Derrida's interpretation of the hyperbolic economy in Matthew as a commentary on the abundant for-givenness of the kingdom, which is not about vengeance or reciprocity but a "mad economy" "without principle," a wildly asymmetrical "measure of love" (*PTD*, 228–29).

Caputo then goes on to examine the possibly "Jewish" nature of Derrida's work in a section on circumcision. He points out that even Derrida's concern with *écriture* might be read as an interest in "Scripture" and not merely in writing per se.[7] Already, Derrida's early reading of Hegel in *Glas* is characterized by an attention to the way in which the Jewish has been systematically silenced by Hegel in favor of the Christian. Caputo claims that "Derrida's prophetic passion and distrust of incarnation is also very close to Jesus the Jew. For Jesus showed the same prophetic distrust of long robes and religious power, and the same—shall we say divine?—predilection for the disempowered and displaced, the outsider and the marginalized" (*PTD*, 247). Caputo consistently reads Derrida as a similar attack on power and authority in favor of the marginalized and the suffering, which he contends is an eminently Jewish reading, although it is of course also always deeply philosophical ("jewgreek"). Employing Derrida's reading of Yerushalmi's reading of Freud, which focuses on the theme of hope as particularly Jewish and which Derrida unsettles in his treatment, Caputo argues that it is not possible to figure out whether deconstruction is a "Jewish science" for structural and systematic reasons, as any such claim would need to be deconstructed immediately. There is no privileged view, not even the autobiographical one.

Caputo's analysis culminates in the final part of the book where he examines *Circumfession* in the most detail, although the text is behind the whole work. He shows how Derrida is continually in search of a "certain God," "a God whose name he is constantly seeking" (*PTD*, 286). This search is not a theology but a kind of prayer. For Derrida, the name of God "is the name of the absolute secret, a placeholder for the secret that there is no secret truth, the blank truth in virtue of which we are always already exposed to multiple interpretations . . . The name of God is the most powerfully deconstructive name we can invoke, for it is the name that destroys the earthly towers to truth we are all the time building" (*PTD*, 289–90). Caputo brings together many of the themes he has already explicated throughout the book. They culminate in the "circumcised confession" of *Circumfession*. God, the gift, the mother, the cut of circumcision, the hope for coming and forgiveness, even death, are all assimilated and even conflated with each other in an undecidable fashion. Thus, Derrida's destiny is "to keep the cut open, to keep de-circumcision and a-destination alive, to be impassioned by the cut, for that is the condition of keeping the future open, of letting the unforeseeable and unanticipatable come, of letting events happen. His destiny is to let the unimaginable come, to call for it to come, to invoke and provoke events, to heave and sigh for the incoming, the invention, of the other, to dream the dream of the impossible" (*PTD*, 306). Caputo ends with a reflection on blindness, moving from the exhibition that inspired *Memoirs for the Blind* to the blinding tears of *Circumfession*. This dimension of blindness is central to Derrida's work, always haunting and unsettling any in-"sight." Caputo concludes with what will remain the theme for most of his work:

> Faith is a passion for something to come, for something I know not what, with an unknowing, non-savoir, sans savoir, which is such that I cannot say what is a translation of what. I cannot say whether God is a translation of "justice," so that whenever I pray and weep over justice I am praying and weeping over God, dreaming and desiring God, with a deep and abiding passion for God. Or whether everything I mean by the passion for God, by loving God, by the desire for God, by "my God," is a way of dreaming of justice. (*PTD*, 338)

Caputo will consistently emphasize this desire and passion for God that is not grounded in any sort of knowledge about the divine and is rooted more in the *name* of God than in any assurance about the being of God. The name of God stands for the hope of justice.

Radical Hermeneutics

Caputo's two books on hermeneutics, *Radical Hermeneutics* and *More Radical Hermeneutics*, frame his more explicit works on Derrida. *Radical Hermeneutics* was published in 1987 and to some extent marks the beginning of Caputo's engagement with Derrida's thought. In this book, he interprets deconstruction as a radicalizing of Heidegger's hermeneutic project (while criticizing Gadamer as a romanticizing form of Heidegger). Caputo posits himself between Heidegger and Derrida in this particular work, trying to show how they can interact productively.[8] Here he calls Derrida's a "cold hermeneutics" (a term he employs positively). After *Radical Hermeneutics*, he increasingly moves to the Derridian side of things and identifies almost exclusively with Derrida. This is particularly obvious in the sequel *More Radical Hermeneutics*, published in 2000, which focuses much more heavily on Derrida and develops what Caputo calls a "devilish hermeneutics," which unsettles the more "holy" or divine hermeneutics of the particular religions. Yet in both works, Caputo always also highlights the implications of this work for ethics, politics, and the engagement with contemporary science and technology, something evident also in his 1993 work *Against Ethics*, which already is deeply informed by deconstruction.[9]

Caputo claims that "radical hermeneutics" "pushes itself to the brink and writes philosophy from the edge" (*RH*, 3). He contends that Derrida does not overthrow hermeneutics but "drives it into its most extreme and radical formulation, pushes it to its limits" (*RH*, 4). Deconstruction is an attempt to be faithful to the flux of experience, which is eventually shut down in most other versions of hermeneutics. It is in *Radical Hermeneutics* that Caputo is most critical of Gadamer for not going far enough and for having tamed down and domesticated Heidegger's more radical project (this is the claim Westphal rejects as discussed in the previous chapter). Caputo begins the book with a reflection on Kierkegaard, especially of his book *Repetition*, which he interprets as central to Kierkegaard's exploration of the authentic self. Repetition "on the ethical level is the constancy and continuity of choice by which the self constitutes itself as a self, by which it returns again and again to its own innermost resolution and establishes its moral identity" (*RH*, 30). Caputo interprets this in terms of an "end to metaphysics," which he contends deeply influenced Heidegger's own desire to "overcome metaphysics." Kierkegaard's project "proceeds by way of a religious delimitation of onto-theo-logic, a religious way out of philosophy and metaphysics, and hence belongs essentially to the project of the deconstruction or overcoming of metaphysics" (*RH*, 34). He argues that Kierkegaard's existential hermeneutics of shaping a self is one prong inspiring the hermeneutic project. The other is Husserlian phenomenology to which the second chapter is devoted. Caputo here summarizes his definition of hermeneutics in terms of flux: "For hermeneutics in the broadest sense means for me coping with the flux, tracing out a pattern in a world in slippage. Hermeneutics is the latest form of the philosophy of becoming, the latest response to the Heraclitean challenge" (*RH*, 37). Husserl's "anticipatory doctrine of constitution" contributes an important part to this, especially in terms of its desire to make sense of the flux of experience. He argues that "intending" for Husserl really is already a form of interpreting (*RH*, 41). At the same time, he is critical of Husserl for continuing a Cartesian project of gaining certainty in terms of "objective" evidence. Caputo also explicates Derrida's "genetic" interpretation of

Husserl according to which intentionality functions in a way very similar to Heidegger's conception of understanding, both "laying out the implicit fore-structures which make explicit experience possible" (*RH*, 53). In Husserl, this is a kind of proto-hermeneutics because he does end up returning to a more traditional metaphysical position in Caputo's view. The third chapter goes on to outline Heidegger's hermeneutics in *Being and Time*. He explicates the circular structure of understanding in *Being and Time* and stresses Heidegger's (usually unacknowledged) dependence on Kierkegaard in his exploration of the authentic being of Dasein. In this context, he also suggests (a claim he elaborates in a later chapter) that Heidegger does provide an implicit ethics. Caputo argues that in all three thinkers (Kierkegaard, Husserl, Heidegger) "repetition functions as a way of establishing identity and of coping with the flux, not as a way of denying it" (*RH*, 92).

The second part of the book establishes the conversation between Heidegger and Derrida more explicitly. Caputo traces the development of Heidegger's hermeneutics in Heidegger's own later work (which he calls a "deeper repetition of hermeneutics") and in Gadamer's and Derrida's appropriation of it, which he sees as a "conservative" and a "deconstructive" hermeneutics respectively. He contends that Gadamer domesticates the project of *Being and Time* by turning it into a "philosophy of unchanging truth" (*RH*, 111). Gadamer is not comfortable with the "flux" of hermeneutics and instead presents "the most liberal version of a fundamentally conservative idea" (*RH*, 115). Derrida conversely challenges the "sacred" provenance of hermeneutics and instead advocates a "free play of signs" by rejecting the idea of some "originary truth" we might discover (*RH*, 118). Caputo carries this further by focusing primarily on Derrida for the rest of the book. He first explores Derrida's reading of Husserl, which interprets reduction as a "critical power" of undoing (*RH*, 121). Both object and subjects are products of the flux. In Derrida's view, the "opposition between presence and representation" has to be displaced and signs have to be liberated (*RH*, 123). Language is thus always necessary, even at the very origin and heart of transcendental life. Derrida challenges the semantic priority of meaning in Husserl and shows the continual need for repetition and dissemination. Caputo then explicates Derrida's reading of Heidegger, which claims that Heidegger is still beholden to a metaphysics of presence. Derrida deconstructs and demythologizes Heidegger's "eschatology" (*RH*, 155). Derrida condemns the teleological thrust of Heidegger's work. Caputo points out, however, that there are more radical possibilities in Heidegger than Derrida is willing to acknowledge.

The final section of the book tries to articulate the "cold hermeneutics" that comes out of this conversation between Derrida and Heidegger:

> Cold hermeneutics does not believe in "Truth"—it renounces all such capitalization—something hidden by and stored up in a tradition which is groaning to deliver it to us. It has lost its innocence about that and is tossed about by the flux, by the play, by the slippage. It understands that meaning is an effect. This is not a hermeneutic we seek but one which is visited upon us against our will, against our *vouloir-dire*, which we would just as soon do without. It catches us off guard, in an unsuspecting moment, just when we were beginning to think all was well and the tremors had passed. (*RH*, 189)

Radical hermeneutics, then, tries to preserve the flux of experience and unsettles all our certainties and beliefs about reality. He stresses Derrida's criticism of authority and his focus on continual questioning. Yet this is not anarchy "but free and open debate" that takes place in the marketplace and shows the "contingency of every discourse and every practice" (*RH*, 196–97). In light of this "cold hermeneutics" inspired by both Heidegger and Derrida, Caputo wonders about the implications of this demise of metaphysics and certainty for science and ethics. In response, he suggests that we require a new rationality that is one of openness, a movement of creativity and thus a kind of poetics.[10] Caputo also uses this term of poetics to depict an alternative "ethics" in his *Against Ethics* and continues to employ it even in his most recent work on the "theo-poetics of the kingdom," which stresses a similar commitment to the poor without access to any notion of absolute truth. In *Radical Hermeneutics*, he relies on Kuhn for a critique of science that realizes that paradigms shift and that there is no objective view from nowhere, that there are competing versions of rationality: "any adequate account of scientific rationality must see that in its finest hour—in moments of crisis and discovery, of revolution and progress—reason requires a moment of free play and intellectual legroom. We do not destroy the reputation of reason with this talk of play; we just tell a more reasonable story about it" (*RH*, 222). We must free reason from the constant danger of institutionalizing and controlling it. Caputo here is particularly critical of the hegemony and logic of technology.

Just as reason requires "free play," so Caputo suggests that we must have a more fluid version of ethics, namely one that originates in fear and trembling instead of a certainty about absolute Truth. Radical hermeneutics fosters an ethics of humility. (This is the call to obligation explored in more detail in *Against Ethics*.) There is no clear guidance, no ultimate principles or absolute foundation. Instead, it is characterized by compassion and respect for others. Not only ethics, but indeed faith must be freed from dogmatism and instead find its way in fear and trembling. This new version of the religious, which operates from "below" not from "above," admits God's absence and sees suffering as outrage. It is the *name* or the *idea* of God that speaks of hope for and empathy with those who suffer.[11] This "freer" faith gives no assurance of salvation but instead calls for justice and encapsulates the hope that this call will be heard and elicit a response. Ethics and religion are then closely linked here. Religion articulates the structure of hope, which inspires compassion and obligation for the poor and suffering.

More Radical Hermeneutics tries to radicalize this notion of hermeneutics further, emphasizing even more strongly that "we don't know who we are," as expressed in the subtitle and a phrase Caputo reiterates often throughout the book. This book is even more deeply marked by Derrida whose work he puts in conversation with that of Foucault, Gadamer, Nietzsche, Rorty, and Drucilla Cornell. Here also, Caputo reflects on the status of science and the possibility of ethics after "the end of ethics." He is slightly more positive about Gadamer, yet still insists that "the difference between Gadamer and Derrida . . . is that deconstruction, in virtue of its more radical anti-essentialism, provides for a more radical conception of friendship and hospitality, of putting oneself at risk, and if hermeneutics means putting one's own meanings at risk, as Gadamer has so beautifully written, then deconstruction also effects a more radical hermeneutics" (*MRH*, 58). Caputo repeatedly stresses the themes of friendship and hospitality in Derrida's work, including in Derrida's writings on politics. Derrida wants to displace autonomy and autarky and instead offers hospitality to the stranger "in the name of God," which coincides with God's withdrawal (*MRH*, 81–82). Against Rorty, Caputo argues for the importance of the political dimension of Derrida's thought.[12] Rorty, in Caputo's view, is just a little too American, and defines groups and communities a bit too clearly. Instead, Caputo wants to advocate a Derridian "democracy *to come*" instead of one already present and identifiable (*MRH*, 124).

In Part 2 of *More Radical Hermeneutics*, Caputo focuses on questions of gender, science, and ethics. He suggests that Derrida cannot be read as a sort of "messianic feminism" (*MRH*, 139), although deconstruction can certainly be useful for feminism. Deconstruction goes beyond gender distinctions to welcoming a multiplicity of differences. The chapter on science returns to Heidegger and suggests that *Being and Time* does not denigrate science but shows its derivative nature. Caputo is more critical of Heidegger's later writings, which he suggests tend to lapse into essentialism. He concludes in a way that previews some of his most recent work:

> We are better served by leaving Reality, Great Greeks, God, and the Devil out of the argument and taking natural science for what it is, an astonishingly successful and insightful way to conceptualize natural processes and to get a handle on them, one that unquestionably gets at things in a more disciplined and incisive way than do common sense or uncommon philosophical explanations like matter and form or a priori forms of intuition. But science need not, for all its success, be elevated to the status of some sort of Secret seizing upon the essence of Reality, and it need not suffer the fatal inflation of capitalization. (*MRH*, 170)

There is no point in rejecting science entirely or denying its success. This is a theme that Caputo has pursued much more fully in his most recent lectures and a forthcoming book where he strongly insists on the need to take science seriously.[13]

Picking up on many of the themes already explored in *Radical Hermeneutics* and *Against Ethics*, Caputo focuses again on Derrida's phrase "*tout autre est tout autre*" ["every other is wholly other"] in order to articulate an ethics after the end of ethics. The other is absolutely singular and unforeseeable. Ethics is a gift of love not of duty, about the surplus not payment. Rules thus must always remain provisional. He concludes that ethics is much more profoundly about honestly confessing our disorientation and dislocation. All ethical rules are provisional and universals are no longer available. We must instead find our way today without such assurances. This is very similar to the "ethics of obligation" already articulated in *Against Ethics* and many of the same themes are reiterated in his more recent *What Would Jesus Deconstruct?* and *The Weakness of God*.

The final part of the book defends "devilish hermeneutics" by contrasting it to "holy hermeneutics." It is not based on revelation and there is no "heavenly hook" to "bail us out" (*MRH*, 193). The empty tomb and its silence teach us how to speak. Deconstruction is an affirmation of discontinuity and the unforeseeable. In this context, Caputo is very critical of Marion's eucharistic hermeneutics. There is no absolute hermeneutics, but always only perspectives. We can have no unmediated gift or text or revelation, but always only translations. This is why humility is necessary. Devilish hermeneutics saves us "from worship of idols and false pretenders of sanctity" (*MRH*, 213). Only thus can we preserve the divine transcendence, which is marked by discontinuity and alterity. Similarly, God's address is always characterized by silence and undecidability. This should not be closed down in any sort of reductionism. Caputo engages here with the kingdom of God theology in Sheehan and Schillebeechx but argues for an even more radical undecidability. The story of the resurrection is not to be taken literally but rather must be interpreted as faith in the "impossibility of murder, of the inextinguishability of innocence, of the triumph of love over death" (*MRH*, 239). Caputo ends by focusing again on prayer and tears: "We are not praying for The Secret, but praying and weeping all the more because we are *in the secret*, deprived of secret access, which is the occasion of more and more prayers. The absolute secret does not leave us disconsolate and without a prayer, but, on the contrary, it leaves us on our knees, praying like mad, praying like hell, praying like the devil" (*MRH*, 249). Mystical discourse is always self-effacing, always marked by tears and the language of desire. It is thus similar to deconstruction, but they are not identical. Deconstruction teaches us the desire for the impossible, an indeterminable prayer, a devilish prayer.

Postmodern "Theology" of Hope

In his most recent work, Caputo engages more traditionally theological questions (though still in fairly untraditional fashion). His *The Weakness of God* posits itself as a theology and indeed interacts with such traditional theological questions as creation, God's power, the question of theodicy, and holy living. In some ways, this book follows on his brief book *On Religion*, written for a popular audience, in which he defines religion primarily as a passion of love and desire, framing it in terms of the Augustinian question "What do I love when I love my God?" He suggests that the structure of passionate desire and devoted love is an essentially religious structure. He again employs Derrida's emphasis on affirmation to support this. In this book, he argues that our supposedly secular world is becoming increasingly more obsessed with notions of the spiritual, using the popular series *Star Wars* and the prevalence of various sorts of fundamentalism to illustrate this. He articulates postmodern faith as a desire for the impossible, which is "the very quality that also defines religion . . . there is a fundamentally religious quality to human experience itself" (*OR*, 109). Employing again Derrida's notion of "religion without religion," he rejects the idea of one true religion, but argues that each of the particular religions are "so many different ways to love God" (*OR*, 110).[14] Caputo consistently stresses love over knowledge in this book: "Religious truth, the love of God, does not have to do with approved propositions" (*OR*, 112). True religion is the virtue of truly loving God. Religion without religion means that "*we do not know what we believe or to whom we are praying*"

(*OR*, 129). The question "what do I love when I love my God?" cannot ultimately be answered. Caputo argues that "the distinction between theism and atheism, religion and unreligion, is beset by a certain confusion and subject to the holy undecidability that I have been analyzing. For religion is the love of God, which is living and life-transforming when justice rolls down like waters, which is also denied when justice is denied" (*OR*, 136). Thus, "the *meaning* of God is enacted in an openness to a future that I can neither master nor see coming, in an exposure to possibilities that are impossible for me, which surpass my powers, which overpower me, which drive me to the limits of the possible, which draw me out to God, *à Dieu*. With whom nothing is impossible" (*OR*, 139). Religion is hope and desire for the impossible. God is the "name" of the impossible event that drives me to the doing of justice.

Caputo makes a similar argument in a brief exposition of the history of interaction between philosophy and theology. He argues that in medieval times theology governed and dominated philosophy while this relation was reversed in the modern age with philosophy governing over and determining theology. In postmodernity we now have a chance for a new and more equal conversation between the two disciplines. Caputo stresses again the inherently hermeneutic nature of all our talk, which we always speak and write and understand from within particular perspectives and can never get to a view "from nowhere." Thus, even philosophy and science include elements of faith and are situated in certain ways. The distinction between faith and reason is no longer an absolute or even very firm one: "The distinction between philosophy and theology is not what we thought it was all along; it is not what has been classically described as the distinction between faith and reason, where reason sees and faith does not quite see. Rather, *the distinction between philosophy and theology is drawn between two kinds of faith*, by which I mean two kinds of 'seeing as'" (*PT*, 57). Near the end of the book Caputo employs what he calls the "atheistic Augustinianism of Jacques Derrida" in order to illustrate this role of faith in postmodern philosophy. Derrida speaks of God, faith, and prayer while "rightly passing for an atheist." Derrida advocates a "pure messianic, by which he means the pure form of hope and expectation," which is marked by "open-endedness and unforeseeableness" (*PT*, 65). Caputo concludes that "there is something irreducibly religious and prayerful, faithful and hopeful about Derrida, every bit as much as there is about Augustine" (*PT*, 66). They represent two different kinds of faith, hope, and expectation.

In *The Weakness of God*, Caputo for the first time writes an explicitly theological book while continuing to express his ambivalence about theology. He calls the book a "poetics" by which he means "a non-literalizing description of the event that tries to depict its dynamics, to trace its style, and to cope with its fortuitous forces by means of felicitous tropes." He seeks "to impede the closure of these names, to block their literalization or ontologization, however sacred these names may be. The more sacred, the better, for their sacredness does not merely tolerate but demands deliteralization, and this in virtue of the event they shelter" (WG, 4). By "theology," he means the following:

> To say that theology is the logos of the name of God means to say that it is the hermeneutics of the event that is astir in that name, for the event is what that name "means." By a "meaning" I do not mean a semantic content but what a name is getting at; what it promises; what it calls up, sighs and longs for, stirs with, or tries to recall; what we are praying for. The event of theology is the theology of the event. By the same token, the event of theology could also be called a deconstruction of the name of God, insofar as deconstruction is the deconstruction of the conditioned name in order to release the unconditional event that is sheltered in the name. (WG, 6)

The book as a whole defies the traditional alignment between God and power, including the heavy emphasis on God's "existence" and thereby on ontology. The kingdom itself is a kind of "unsettling shock," what he calls a "disturbance in being."[15] Instead he re-reads the notion of the kingdom of God in terms of the "weak forces" of patience, peace, and forgiveness. Thus, this notion of the kingdom holds open the promise of the impossible, which Caputo has already consistently emphasized in his work on Derrida.

In the first chapter, he outlines his vision of a God without power and who does not "stir up expectations of power" (WG, 23). In this context, he draws heavily on his prior explications of Derrida and deconstruction as a critique of sovereignty, authority, and any sort of omnipotence. God is not to be thought of as transcendent in the traditional sense that turns the divine into remote omnipotent power, but a God of *khora*. This is an appeal that lays a claim on us and calls us beyond ourselves. To live before such a God is "to live on call, under the call, always already solicited, called upon, pressed by the weak force of the call, called by the call to let the kingdom come, which is what is called *for*" (WG, 39). Caputo rejects any notion of absolute omnipotence and tries to re-read various aspects of the tradition that have insisted on this notion, associating his weaker interpretation of God with the Pauline theology of the cross, which is one of weakness and humility, not hidden power. A central piece of his discussion is a rejection of the traditional doctrine of creation *ex nihilo* [out of nothing], in favor of creation *ex amore* [out of love]. Following Catherine Keller's arguments, he suggests that *ex nihilo* is connected to Greek philosophical conceptions of omnipotence that reject chaos, *khora*, and the feminine in favor of a patriarchal, removed, powerful deity. He contrasts the affirmative (and more balanced) late priestly creation account, which refers to God as Elohim with the earlier account of the "Yahwist," which he judges a far more ambivalent, more pessimistic, and also more patriarchal narrative.[16] Instead of focusing on power, the creation narratives are instead about "a primordial benediction." This benediction is about God's hope for creation in the form of "a gentle breeze blowing out of Paradise that bears the word 'good' across the ages, the event of a word. In them, the name of God harbors the event of a yes, while their authors make no effort to conceal that there is a dicey dimension to this thing called creation, and we hope it works" (*WG*, 82–83).

Throughout this work, Caputo takes a strong position against any theology that "defends" the divine power in the face of evil. Any association of the divine with murder is false. It is blasphemy to employ the name of God in order to give a "rationality" to evil and suffering.[17] Caputo claims that the event of God cannot be known or identified, that this recognition, in fact, is "*constitutive* of it" (*WG*, 97). God's weakness is expressed in this call to the good, not in any powerful imposition of justice. We are called to instantiate justice by listening and responding to the call. This is also the theme of a "hermeneutic interlude" where Caputo articulates more fully what he calls a "poetics of the kingdom." This hermeneutics seeks to explicate the name of God, which stands for our passion for justice and our hope in the event.[18] He employs deconstruction to emphasize the characteristics of justice and hospitality, including the impossible possibility of the gift beyond economy. He speaks of this as a "hyper-realism" that is excessive, but comes from below, that celebrates what is "unforeseeable, unimaginable, uncontainable, undeconstructible" (*WG*, 123).

The final part of the book explicates this poetics of the kingdom further in terms of its real impact on everyday life. Employing the parables, Caputo shows that "Jesus was a healer of souls and a mender of bodies, of the two together, offering freedom from the shackles both of the mind and the body, proffering both a teaching, a didactics or kerygmatics, and a therapeutics" (*WG*, 130). He insists that Jesus's concern was with the poor, vulnerable, and outcast of society, especially the vulnerability of flesh, in a continual undermining of the authorities. The ethics of the kingdom consist in what Caputo calls a "sacred anarchy" of the "weak force of justice." Forgiveness is absolutely central to this. Caputo also emphasizes what he calls the "quotidianism" of the "every-day." Here he moves very close to some of Richard Kearney's expositions on religion as concern with "the least of these" and micro-eschatological engagement with the everyday and the quotidian (see the next chapter). We are to live like the "lilies of the field" without concern for the morrow: "God says 'yes,' calls 'yes' to us from afar, from across an infinite distance. To say 'yes' in turn, to countersign the signature that God has sprawled across the surface of the world, is not to count upon some kind of divine intervention from on high to straighten out things here below. It is to affirm, or re-affirm." This affirmation is closely linked to the name of God: "To say 'yes' to God, to invoke the name of God . . . is not to sign on to a belief in a magical suspension of natural laws in order to allow for a divine averting of natural disasters, or the divine advocacy of particular historical causes, of a particular nation, political party, religion, race, or gender in order to see that in the end one historical cause will win out over another" (*WG*, 178). Instead, God gives us hope in the face of evil. Here Caputo includes a chapter on eschatology that envisions the future as hope for the impossible instead of Peter Damian's desire to change the past, before going on to consider the topics of forgiveness, resurrection, and hospitality. He argues that the story of Lazarus is not about a literal raising from the dead, but instead about the event of hope in the face of death. Again, he stresses the theme of hope in this context: "Hope is not hope if you can see what you are hoping for on the horizon. We need hope when we cannot see the way out. Hope requires blindness. Hence, the work of the historian is the impossible one of giving comfort to the dead by way of memory and hope for the coming of the messianic time" (*WG*, 256). Caputo's examination culminates with a consideration of the topic of the *à-Dieu* in Lévinas and Derrida. He interprets this theme as encapsulating concern for and welcome of the stranger. He closes by stressing again the dimension of hope:

> Were I—never fear—to resort to politics to keep prayer and desire alive, I would tour the country giving a stump speech in which I would say "The only thing in which we have to hope is hope itself." We are saved more by hope itself than by *what* we hope in, which differs from time to time and place to place and is at best a temporary placeholder for something, I know not what, for some more elemental quality of our lives. There is no single and exclusive, no sustainably determinate "what" in hope, no fixed object of hope; for once something is fixed in place, it collapses under the weight of more hope. So just as FDR campaigned on the premise that the only thing we have to fear is fear itself, I will run a more Derridean campaign and proclaim that the only thing in which we always and everywhere have to hope is hope itself, which is not deconstructible. Whatever determinate and identifiable something we hope in, whatever that turns out

to be, is and ever will be deconstructible; but hope itself, if there is such a thing, is not deconstructible. (*WG*, 297)[19]

This undecidability always attempts to keep tension alive and gaps open. It is defined by passion and desire, fueled by undecidability and unknowability. We pray to "we know not what" but do so passionately and unceasingly. He ends this book, like several of his others, with the affirmation "Viens, oui, oui [Come, yes, yes]" (*WG*, 299).

Caputo's most recent book *What Would Jesus Deconstruct?*, written for the same series as Westphal's *Whose Community? Which Interpretation?*, is perhaps the most explicitly religious of his works. He employs Sheldon's popular novel *What Would Jesus Do?* and its important call to social justice as a foil for reflecting on what he calls the "theo-poetics of the kingdom," which interprets Jesus's message in the Gospels in terms of a strong commitment to "the least of these." As usual Caputo is rather critical of any version of fundamentalism or religious authority. Throughout, he contrasts the fundamentalists' assumption that they *know* the Truth or are in possession of it with a *doing* of the truth, a dangerous truth that asks us to change our lives. Caputo suggests that Jesus would deconstruct most of our conceptions about faith and church. He reiterates that we cannot know the Truth, that there is not only one (official and authorized) interpretation, but that all decisions must be made in faith and hope, which means precisely faith in what seems incredible, hope in what appears utterly hopeless (*WWJD*, 45). Caputo claims that deconstruction and the kingdom of God both "are marked by a common love of paradox and aporia and by a common appreciation of the path, not as a well-paved, well-marked superhighway but as an obstructed path, a step/not, a movement of the beyond, of excess, and ultimately of the madness of love" (*WWJD*, 46). Relying on the Gospel narratives, he shows that Jesus consistently sided with the vulnerable and powerless, those who were rejected and pushed aside by society. He insists that this weakness is not simply powerlessness, but that "the God of forgiveness, mercy, and compassion shines like a white light on the hypocrisy of those who, under the cover of God, oppress the most defenseless people in society" (*WWJD*, 83). Jesus's ministry is not that of a powerful superhero, but instead a kind of madness that subverts all our expectations. Jesus's message is not one of moderation but of excess, of "love without measure" (*WWJD*, 86). Caputo insists that this politics of the kingdom is about forgiveness and hospitality, which imagines God not in terms of omnipotence but as hope for a new theological paradigm of compassion for the weak.[20] Hermeneutics is what allows us to put this into practice. It designates "our responsibility to breathe with the spirit of Jesus, to implement, to invent, to convert this poetics into a praxis, which means to make the political order resonate with the radicality of someone whose vision was not precisely political" (*WWJD*, 95). Caputo argues strongly for a radical vision of social justice, non-violence, and inclusiveness for various marginalized groups. Such a vision unsettles the easy embrace of capitalism, war, and patriarchy of many so-called Christians. Caputo concludes by giving two examples of churches acting out Jesus's vision in some way: one a Roman Catholic priest in North Philadelphia working among the poor and the other the alternative "liturgy" of the "emerging church" movement (focusing on one group called *Ikon*). He concludes his book with a tentative answer to the question: "But, what, then, is the kingdom of God? Where is it found?" His answer is about hospitality and justice: "It is found every time an offense is forgiven, every time a stranger is made welcome, every time an enemy is embraced, every time the least among us is lifted up, every time the law is made to serve justice, every time a prophetic voice is raised against injustice, every time the law and the prophets are summed up by love" (*WWJD*, 138).

Poetics of Hope

Caputo's work, then, while not exactly religious in any traditional sense of the term (especially in regard to any links with particular confessions) continually circles around the question of religion and certainly does so from a Christian—or rather, post-Christian—perspective. One might say that while Westphal seeks to appropriate postmodern thought for the sake of religious faith, Caputo appropriates religious hope for postmodern thought and highlights the quasi-religious dimensions of supposedly a-religious thinkers such as Heidegger and Derrida. He is more interested in the *structure* of religion than in any particular confession or its concrete content. Yet much of his work has profoundly influenced the ways in which postmodernism and the thinkers associated with it have been read in religious (predominantly Christian) circles in the United States.

Most appropriately, Caputo's response to a conference on his *Prayers and Tears* that resulted in *Religion with/out Religion: The Prayers and Tears of John D. Caputo* is entitled "Hoping in hope, hoping against hope." The article precedes most of Caputo's later work, but it already emphasizes the important element of hope in his thought. He responds in his usual tongue-in-cheek way to the papers in the volume and then concludes:

> For *khora/différance*, makes the word of faith possible and impossible, makes it possible, even as it destabilizes it, leaving it, and us, to

take what Levinas calls *un beau risque*, a good risk, a good bet, a bet on the good, but without any assurance that the deck is stacked in our favor. For even if I say that the Good who called all things from the abyss and saw that they were good, that this Good has stacked the deck, I would insist that that too is part of the bet. Hope is always hope in hope, hope against hope, hoping like hell.[21]

While Caputo consistently refuses to give any sort of determinate content to this hope and, in fact, would interpret any such content as an attempt to limit or close down the absolute hospitality and promise of the event, the structural desire for the divine characterizes all of his work. This is not a *faith* in any particular God, but it is about the *name* of God, a very important distinction for Caputo. This is why it is about hope and not primarily about faith: The name of God does not give us any confidence or certainty or any sort of content, but it fuels our hope for the good, for life, for justice. It is the name of a promise, the structure of an incoming event for which we hope but which we cannot control and which has no determinative content. The Messiah will never come; the notion of literal resurrection is futile. Yet the passionate hope for the Messiah and the (albeit empty) promise of resurrection drives us to affirm and work for life and justice and against suffering, death, and injustice. "Hope is always hope in hope, hope against hope, hoping like hell."

Richard Kearney: Postmodern Charity

Richard Kearney currently holds the Charles B. Seelig Chair in philosophy at Boston College and is visiting professor at University College Dublin. Originally from Ireland, Kearney worked closely with Ricoeur, Lévinas, and Derrida in France (he received his doctorate there under Ricoeur's direction) and has taught in the United States for several decades. Over the years, he has labored vigorously to establish communication and conversation between many of the thinkers treated in this book (in various interviews, roundtable discussions, and other venues), but has himself also contributed significantly to the discussion of religious phenomenology and hermeneutics. His most recent publications *The God Who May Be: A Hermeneutics of Religion*; *Strangers, Gods and Monsters*; and *Anatheism: Returning to God After God* make that very clear. Indeed, Merold Westphal, John Caputo, and Richard Kearney are good friends and often appear together at conferences. All three have worked closely together in many circumstances and often comment on each other's work. Yet there are also important differences and emphases in their respective projects, despite the fact that they are all three deeply influenced and shaped by Heidegger, Derrida, Lévinas, and to some extent Ricoeur, and are in conversation with Marion and, to a lesser degree, Henry, Chrétien, and Lacoste.[1]

Kearney is deeply steeped in a Ricoeurian-Aristotelian hermeneutic approach but also profoundly influenced by Lévinas's ethics of alterity. He converses frequently with Marion and Derrida, although he also criticizes them at times and tries to find a more mediating position. Recently, he has called this position a "fourth reduction," employing Marion's description of his own work as a "third reduction" of givenness beyond Husserl's first and Heidegger's second reductions.[2] The themes of ethics, welcome, and hospitality are central to Kearney's writing, as are those of possibility and promise. As is true of the other thinkers, his discussion of the divine also implies very much a rethinking of what it means to be authentically human or what it might mean to live in faith, to live before God (or maybe even to live as God). For Kearney, we "help" God be God (he often refers to Etty Hillesum in this context[3]), we help God "become" God, we make real God's possibilities by "sharing a cup of cold water." Our acts of charity are ways of instantiating the divine. It is not that Kearney's God is "impotent," a weakling who needs our support, but rather that Kearney rethinks traditional notions of omnipotence/*potentia* in order to open the divine (or perhaps better, our notions of the divine) to possibility and transformation. Although he pursues similar themes as Caputo does in his work, he is often also quite critical of Caputo whom he associates closely with Derrida.

Unlike some of the other thinkers discussed, Kearney does not merely employ religious notions as a given but justifies their use more explicitly. He also draws from significantly more diverse Christian sources than most of the French thinkers and at times even from other religious traditions. Kearney actively seeks to re-conceive a notion of God and argues for the need for this re-thinking and re-imagining. Kearney is also much less clear in the way in which he communicates his own religious commitments. That is not to say that he does not have such commitments, but he is more open to and more cognizant of other faiths. That does not imply that the French thinkers are intolerant or close-minded, but they rarely acknowledge the plurality of religious faith as much. Here is how Kearney expresses his hermeneutic stance at the beginning of *The God Who May Be*:

> So how would I respond to the standard hermeneutic question: Where do you speak from? . . . How do I identify my own position? Philosophically, I would say that I am speaking from a phenomenological perspective, endeavoring as far as possible to offer a descriptive account of such phenomena as persona, transfiguration, and desire, before crossing over into hermeneutic readings. In this domain my primary intellectual mentors are Husserl, Heidegger, Levinas, Ricoeur, and Derrida. Religiously, I would say that if I hail from a Catholic tradition, it is with this proviso: where Catholicism offends love and justice, I prefer to call myself a Judeo-Christian theist; and where this tradition so offends, I prefer to call myself re-

ligious in the sense of seeking God in a way that neither excludes other religions nor purports to possess the final truth. And where the religious so offends, I would call myself a seeker of love and justice *tout court*. (*GMB*, 6)

Strangers, Gods, and Monsters is even less explicitly Christian, although *After God* and *Anatheism* do rely predominantly on the Abrahamic faiths.[4]

Dialogue and Imagination

Kearney's early work is deeply imbued with the spirit of dialogue and conversation. Indeed, to many people he is known primarily for the ways in which he has facilitated conversation and dialogue. He was the moderator for the discussion between Derrida and Marion at the first Villanova conference on the gift and has often served as the facilitator of such dialogues at conferences and even in social and political life. (He was, for example, involved in fostering dialogue between Protestants and Catholics during the peace process in Northern Ireland.) He has also conducted countless interviews with other thinkers and has special talent for drawing them out to speak of their work. David Tracy speaks of Kearney as a "remarkable interviewer": "He asks questions in order to really understand what someone is thinking, and thus is able to draw them out and get them to say things that perhaps they wouldn't otherwise. As a result, his interviews are very important" (in *AG*, 340). Many of these interviews are collected in *Dialogues with Contemporary Thinkers: The Phenomenological Heritage* and *Debates in Continental Philosophy: Conversations with Contemporary Thinkers*.[5] This spirit of dialogue and generous welcome to the other also characterizes his writings about God and religion.

An important role in fostering such dialogue and even in fertilizing thought about the divine is played by narrative and imagination. Kearney's first two books were on imagination: *Wake of Imagination* and *Poetics of the Possible*, as is a recent book entitled *Traversing the Imaginary*.[6] He is also author of several novels and has written extensively on literature.[7] In these earlier works, Kearney is already interested in the way phenomenology might be employed hermeneutically and might help us to listen to each other through narrative imagination. He carries this argument further in *On Stories* where he argues about the important function of narrative in allowing us to welcome others instead of fearing or destroying them. Kearney expresses these sentiments even more clearly in *Strangers, Gods, and Monsters* which focuses specifically on the question of otherness and where he contends that "the key is to let the other be other so that the self may be itself again" through a kind of "narrative understanding: a working-through of loss and fear by means of cathartic imagination and mindful acknowledgement" (*SGM*, 8). Kearney chides the kind of postmodern philosophies that exalt alterity and the sublime to an extreme degree making any communication or negotiation impossible. He insists that "the attempt to build hermeneutic bridges between us and 'others' (human, divine, or whatever) should not, I will argue, be denounced as ontology, onto-theology or logocentrism—that is to say, as some form of totalizing reduction bordering on violence" (*SGM*, 9). Kearney suggests that this emphasis on radical alterity must be tempered by a more balanced way that seeks to find connections and build bridges between extremes. Philosophy can make such mediation possible.[8] Kearney tries to find a middle way between these extremes of total rejection of otherness and unlimited openness to it, showing that we must discern where hospitality is required and where real danger lurks. He always insists on the importance of "imagining, narrativing or interpreting alterity," which emphasizes the need for "phenomenological and hermeneutic inquiry" (*SGM*, 11).

Kearney also speaks much more explicitly of postmodernism in his work. Like Westphal and Caputo, he is far more comfortable with this term than the French thinkers, although he is also critical of some of its interpretations or applications. Postmodernism is not a celebration of total relativism or nihilism for its own sake. Instead, Kearney attempts to find a middle way between "vertiginous heights and abyssal depths" by drawing on (and criticizing) many contemporary thinkers, including Kristeva, Derrida, Lyotard, Lévinas, Gadamer, Ricoeur, and others. Kearney argues that we need "symbolic imagination" and "hermeneutic translation" for this task of building bridges between extremes. He calls this a "diacritical hermeneutics," which is neither "romantic" (assuming one could ultimately come to complete understanding of or even become one with the other, as advocated by Schleiermacher, Dilthey, and Gadamer) nor "radical" (rejecting any kind of appropriation or mediation in favor of irreducible dissymmetry between self and other, as advocated by Caputo, Lyotard, and Derrida). Kearney tries to prevent both of these extremes: "Obviating both the congenial communion of fused horizons and the apocalyptic rupture of non-communion, I will endeavor to explore possibilities of intercommunion between distinct but not incomparable selves" (*SGM*, 18). This is not a Hegelian fusion but a constant conversation that does not close down differences in an all-embracing synthesis but holds open plurality and multiplicity. "The basic aim of diacritical hermeneutics" is, according to Kearney, "to make us more hospitable to strangers, gods and monsters without succumbing to mystique or madness" (*SGM*, 18). Kearney will bring this same mediating desire to his thought about God, attempting to mediate between what he perceives as excesses in most of the available positions. Although *Strangers, Gods and Monsters* was written after *The God Who May Be*, I will examine it first here, as it deals with the question of the divine in more general (and less explicitly Christian) terms.

Hospitality to the Stranger

In *Strangers, Gods and Monsters*, Kearney examines some of the ways that the Western tradition has dealt with what is foreign, strange, or "other." He shows how we establish self-identity and self-consciousness by distinguishing ourselves from what is "strange" or "monstrous" by locating it somewhere outside and far away from us instead of admitting the "strangeness" within ourselves. Already in much of his earlier work Kearney had been concerned with the role of the imagination and that of narrative in shaping identity and dealing with what troubles us about ourselves. In this context, he examines not just the ways in which foreigners have served as scapegoats and the ways in which we are fascinated by aliens (even as we are repulsed by them), but also investigates the role "God" might play in these various instances of otherness.[9] He defines the role of "gods" in this context as follows:

> Gods are the names given by most mythologies and religions to those beings whose numinous power and mystery exceed our grasp and bid us kneel and worship. Sometimes they are benign, at other times cruel and capricious. But whatever their character they refuse to be reduced to the bidding of mortals. Transcending laws of time and space, they readily take on immortal or protean status. Gods' ways are not our ways. They bedazzle and surprise us. It is not ours to reason why. But where monsters arise from underworlds, and strangers intrude from hinterworlds, gods generally reside in otherworlds beyond us. Whether it be Jehovah, Zeus, or Jupiter, deities inhabit sublime heights. We look up to them, if we dare look at all. (*SGM*, 4)

Clearly, Kearney's interest here is much wider than a traditional Christian version of God. He is writing about the very notion of "gods" or "deities," not of a particular manifestation of "God." Kearney interprets these phenomena of otherness as repressed parts of the human psyche that are projected upon others or the outside instead of being affirmed within ourselves. He proposes that we must find new ways of embracing the otherness within ourselves today "in an age crippled by crises of identity and legitimation" (*SGM*, 5). Kearney suggests that philosophy might help us in our approach to the other or the monstrous by advocating "a certain kind of understanding" (*SGM*, 7). He sees this philosophy in dialogue with other disciplines (other ways of coping with strangeness), especially art, religion, and psychoanalysis.

While Kearney cites several examples of Christian hospitality to strangers and redemption from otherness and monstrosity, he is also hesitant to accept Girard's contention "that a single confessional theology has the remedy to the enigma of otherness." He does not want to believe that "all *non* Judaeo-Christian religious myths are necessarily scapegoating" and wonders: "Are there not at least some which might *not* be so, that is, which might not be based on the need to project false accusations onto innocent victims? Might not certain Buddhist, Taoist or native American myths, for example, also express a genuinely open impulse to imagine other possibilities of existence which challenge the status quo and embrace peace and justice over dualist agonistics?" (*SGM*, 41). Girard's account of Christian escape from scapegoating practices is too exclusively focused on the Christian solution and disregards the potential for hospitality in other traditions. This is a question to which Kearney returns often in his work. He concludes in an appendix to this chapter, where he examines Girard's theory of myth in more detail, that religious traditions need to learn from each other:

> In short, if Western monotheism has much to teach us about the virtues of ethical judgement (when it comes to sacrifice and scapegoating), Eastern wisdom traditions are there to remind us that judgement must be ever wary of lapsing into judgementalism. For if Jerusalem is indeed one way to peace, it is not the only one. The religions of Abraham have much to give *and* to receive in dialogue with the religions of Tao and the Buddha (and others). Interbeing is the way between. (*SGM*, 46)

Kearney indicates that his future work will be dealing with some of these questions (especially that of inter-religious dialogue) in far more detail, although these themes already become increasingly stronger in his most recent writings.

Kearney argues that hermeneutics must play a central role in a more informed and more hospitable approach to alterity. Hermeneutics enables us to discern and to judge as we welcome the other, so that we need not indiscriminately approach friend and foe in exactly the same way without precluding the possibility that what may seem strange and threatening may actually require our welcome.[10] Kearney argues that justice requires "unconditional hospitality to the alien" even beyond the law (*SGM*, 68). Yet, against Derrida who argues for complete and unlimited hospitality that may transform the host into a hostage, Kearney advocates a more discriminating hospitality. Kearney insists that ethics itself requires discrimination between "benign and malignant strangers, between saints and psychopaths" (*SGM*, 70). He suggests that "deconstructive non-judgementalism needs to be supplemented . . . with a hermeneutics of practical wisdom which might help us better discern between justice and injustice. For if we need a logic of undecidability to keep us tolerant—preventing us from setting ourselves up as Chief High Executioners—we need an ethics of judgement to commit us, as much as possible, to right action" (*SGM*, 72). Kearney argues that a diacritical hermeneutics of judgment would be able to discern between kinds of otherness.[11] Such a hermeneutics also insists on the importance of narrative memory to preserve the stories of those others who have been treated unjustly and whose stories deserve to be heard to grant them at least some measure of justice. Kearney thus argues for a pluralism and a polysemy of alterity that would be able to listen to all sorts of alterity without welcoming all kinds equally uncritically and which also considers the self instead of eliminating it entirely as seems to happen in some of the contemporary accounts.

In the context of an analysis of the Scriptural account of evil as both a force outside of us and our own choices and activities, he criticizes again the "postmodern teratology of the sublime" that seems to exalt evil and horror because of their very difference and monstrosity: "By this account, horror is just as 'ineffable' as the vertical transcendence of God (invoked by Levinas and the negative theologians). There is, in short, an apophasis of the monstrous analogous to an apophasis of the divine" (*SGM*, 88). Such thinking can go to the extremes of regarding the Holocaust as a sacred event that is so ineffable that it cannot be represented. Kearney strongly censures such a view and criticizes Kristeva, Žižek, Lyotard and other thinkers who would seem to advocate extreme versions of the sublime that can no longer be distinguished from the horrible or the monstrous. In the face of this postmodern tendency of glorifying the monstrous, Kearney advocates a critical hermeneutic position that would encourage "practical understanding (*phronesis-praxis*); working-through (*catharsis-Durcharbeitung*); and pardon" (*SGM*, 100). Examining each in turn, he points out how pardon is only possible with narrative understanding, but may ultimately approach a religious hermeneutics (*SGM*, 106). As in *On Stories* where he addresses the question of narrative about the Shoah in more detail, Kearney advocates narrative as an important tool for forging understanding, gaining wisdom for action, and remembering for the sake of justice. This criticism of Derrida, to whom Kearney is in many ways quite close, serves to highlight in what ways he does self-identify as a religious thinker.[12] The disagreement with Derrida is almost exclusively over this issue of discrimination and Kearney's more positive imagery that avoids the terror of *khora* is almost invariably drawn from religious sources, most commonly Christian ones.[13] Thus, even this critique of contemporary thinkers shows Kearney's own conviction that language, narratives, and imagery for hospitality, justice, and compassion can more fruitfully be drawn from Christian (or other religious) traditions.

The final two chapters of *Strangers, Gods and Monsters* are devoted more specifically to the topic of God. Kearney analyzes the notion of *khora*, which has a certain likeness to God, especially in Derrida's reflection on *différance* (although Derrida is emphatic that they are not the same). Kearney does not think of Derrida as a new desert Father or a kind of Kierkegaard (as he claims Caputo does), as in Derrida undecidability never gives way to praise or affirmation of God. He insists that the difference between *khora* and God matters:

> It is not inconceivable that *khora* could inspire its own kind of belief (an-*khora*-itic albeit not theistic). It might well trigger its own kind of leap of faith (albeit not towards God). It might even be that God and *khora* are two different ways of approaching the same indescribable experience of the abyss. But the choice between the two is not insignificant. Which direction you leap in surely matters. For while the theistic leap construes our experience in the desert as "a dark night of the soul" *on the way towards* God, the latter sees it as a night without end, a place where religious prayer, promise and praise are *not* applicable. Not, I imagine, a place the desert fathers would want to hang around for very long . . . . There is a genuine difference between anchorite fathers and deconstructive sons. A healthy difference to be sure. But one that can't be magicked away in a soft-shoe shuffle of undecidability. (*SGM*, 202–3)

Kearney expresses his discomfort with the extreme version of deconstruction in two respects: On the one hand, there does seem to be a commitment for *khora* over against God. On the other hand, the very nature of *khora* is so undecideable that it might as well be the monstrous itself. Giving many examples of what *khora* might mean concretely, Kearney concludes: "Who would deny the *reality* of these kinds of *khora*-esque experience? They may well be the *most* 'real' (at least in Lacan's sense) of human experiences, the most unspeakably traumatic 'limit experiences' of things that exceed our understanding. The most sublime of horrors. But again I have to say I would find it hard to make a preferential option for them, or counsel others to do likewise" (*SGM*, 205). While both *khora* and the divine are important, they should not be equated with each other, and both experiences call for discernment.

Against what he takes to be the position of deconstruction, Kearney claims that there is an important difference in searching for the divine or for *khora* and that they should not be conflated with each other. The emptiness and desolation of the desert is not what is valuable in and of itself, but it is the means of focusing on the divine.[14] Kearney criticizes Caputo for setting deconstruction up as an alternative to theology, as a better version of the divine that does not succumb to the supposedly totalitarian and hierarchical ecclesiology of the Christian tradition. Kearney insists that this is a caricature and that "not every notion of the Trinitarian God—not to mention Yahweh or Allah—is a fetish of presence or hyperessence" (*SGM*, 207). He concludes:

> To avoid such polarizing gestures, we might remind ourselves that there are many degrees of latitude between the North Pole of God (qua pure hyperessence) and the South Pole of *khora* (qua anonymous abyss). My short list above—ranging from Eckhart to *perichoresis*— not to mention other approximations sketched in this volume, signal tentative, probing paths toward a "between" way. There are, I am suggesting, more than just two options. And the third option I am adumbrating here would, I wager, liberate a space of chiasmic play between *khora* and *hyperousia*. A space for what . . . I call the possible God. (*SGM*, 208)

He returns to this important difference and the need for discrimination again and again in his work. For example, in a later interview he says in regard to Derrida and Caputo: "We're not all desperate Desert Fathers waiting for Godot as the apocalyptic dusk descends! It need not be that angst-ridden or melodramatic. The world is a place of light and dark: we always have a bit of both" (*AG*, 378).

In his final chapter, "Last God and Final Things: Faith and Philosophy," Kearney describes the divine as a limit-experience, evidenced by the many disagreements about how to name God. He argues that "faith" and "reason" are not such extreme opposites as they have often been presented to be in the tradition. Reflecting on Heidegger's early essay on phenomenology and theology and others of Heidegger's writings, he argues that the distinction between "Being" and "God" is neither particularly clear nor as simple as Heidegger pretends (especially as he later moves increasingly toward a poetic kind of God or notion of the holy). Kearney engages in an analysis of Heidegger's "last God" and shows that it has very little to do with the Christian (or any kind of religious) God. He claims that "Heidegger's Last God inhabits a zone of unsayable indigence and distress. And it seems to me that such a space is far removed from eschatological hope in a God of eternal promise, kenotic giving or theophanic redemption . . . it certainly has very little to do with the God who declares love and promises justice" (*SGM*, 219). His criticism of Heidegger, then, is very similar indeed to those of Derrida and Caputo: "My difficulty with the divinity proposed by Heidegger is, however, its curiously non-personal and non-ethical character. By completely bypassing, for example, the Judaeo-Christian ethic of pardon and hospitality to the stranger . . . Heidegger espoused a certain nostalgia for primordial fusion and bedazzlement." This, Kearney insists, "runs the risk of blurring our capacity to discern in matters of moral responsibility and political justice" (*SGM*, 221). Kearney thus recognizes important parallels between Heidegger's "distressing" divine and the monstrous deconstructive *khora* discussed earlier.

By seeing what version of the divine Kearney rejects (Derridian *khora*, Heidegger's "last God"), one already receives a good sense of the kind of God Kearney will favor, namely a God of love, justice, hospitality, and compassion. Kearney advocates a "loving possible" in light of these other proposals.[15] He does admit that Heidegger's emphasis on possibility over actuality can contribute something positive to a new theology of God as loving possibility. For Kearney this is an eschatological hope that is ethical and calls for justice. It is concerned with the most vulnerable and responds to them in responsibility.[16] He concludes by calling for a religious pluralism that enables us to be open to many different kinds of otherness, including different beliefs about the divine.[17] Kearney's work as a whole seeks to recover such a plurality of images for the divine that avoids absolutism and injustice. And it is this version of a divine Other as loving possible that he proposes in *The God Who May Be*.

The Loving Possible

In *The God Who May Be: A Hermeneutics of Religion*, Kearney first and most fully lays out his argument for divine possibility. He explores the famous passage in Exodus 3:14, where God is revealed to Moses in the burning bush and responds to Moses's request for God's name. Kearney tries to find a middle way between an "ontological" or "onto-theological" reading, in which God is simply identified with being, and an "anti-ontological" reading, which is that of "negative theology," which Kearney judges too transcendent (he puts both Marion and Derrida in this camp), by favoring what he calls an "eschatological" reading of the text, where God reveals Godself as the one who promises, who comes, or who "may be." There is a "dynamism" in God's coming that is different from the traditional interpretations of *potentia* as power. God is not the immutable, all-powerful, completed perfection Christianity has often worshipped. Rather, God gives Godself in loving vulnerability. God is faithful to the causes of love and justice, but does not impose rules by divine fiat. God calls us to fulfill God's promises. This presumes an open-ended view of history and a different response to the problem of suffering.

Kearney supports this by engaging in hermeneutic readings of several biblical narratives and texts. He examines what he calls the "eschatological legacy" of the transfiguration. Christ's glory is interpreted as an unsettling of the disciples' assumptions about Christ's identity and expected actions (the historical Christ becomes a "fetish of presence" in Peter's desire to hold him). Kearney draws on his analysis of *persona* in the first chapter where he had argued, in the wake of Lévinas, that a person is a "face" and not a fixed entity. Christ's persona is similarly unstable and uncontainable. Christ calls us toward transformation, not fixation (*GMB*, 44). Here, Kearney articulates what will become a major theme in his most recent work (although it has always been present to some extent), namely the notion that the kingdom is primarily for the "little people":

> The post-paschal stories of the transfiguring persona remind us that the Kingdom is given to hapless fisherman and spurned women, to those lost and wandering on the road from Jerusalem to nowhere, to the wounded and weak and hungry, to those who lack and do not despair of their lack, to little people "poor in spirit." The narratives of the transfigured-resurrected Christ testify that after the long night of fasting and waiting and darkness and need—afloat on a wilderness of sea—breakfast is always ready. The transfiguring persona signals the ultimate solidarity, indeed dissociability, of spirit and flesh. (*GMB*, 51)

God, for Kearney, if the notion is to be credible today, is always a God of love expressed in mercy, compassion, and justice. Only a loving God (as opposed to an all-powerful one) is still believable today. Hence while this analysis of God as the "possible" certainly speaks of hope for the future, Kearney's primary emphasis is on "charity": on acts of compassion and justice, on care for the "littlest" and most downtrodden.

The second biblical text Kearney examines is the *Song of Songs* and its portrayal of God as "desiring," again uncovering the eschatological dimensions of the text. He draws on Rabbinic interpretations, as well as some of

Kristeva's and Ricoeur's insights, emphasizing that the poem "confronts us with a desire that desires beyond desire while remaining desire" (*GMB*, 60). Again, he contrasts an onto-theological with an eschatological reading. He analyzes Lévinas's phenomenology of eros where desire moves us away from "totality" and toward "infinity" and goes beyond voluptuosity toward fecundity and paternity (*GMB*, 67). While appropriating Lévinas's emphasis on asymmetry, vigilance, and eschatology, Kearney does not follow him all the way. Instead, he moves to more deconstructive readings, which he finds in Derrida and Caputo who celebrate "desire as such" and where the Messiah can never actually come because the messianic always remains expected. Even as he appropriates this work to some extent, he also again criticizes the extreme emphasis on indeterminacy in Derrida for whom faith is so completely blind that no ethical choices can be made and that the term "God" becomes completely evacuated of any content. Despite his consistent emphasis on plurality and polysemy, Kearney does argue for a particular version of God (namely as loving), one certainly more determinate than Derrida's messianic faith in utter indeterminacy, which he criticizes throughout. Kearney asks: "Can we draw a line in the sand between deconstruction as desertification of God and desertion of God? Can we dance and sing before the God of deconstruction? Can we desire God without *some* recourse to narrative imagination? Without some appeal to tradition(s)? Without some guide for the perplexed?" (*GMB*, 77). Here emerges again one of the fundamental questions Kearney consistently seeks to address in his work: "So my final question is: how do we read in the dark?" (*GMB*, 79). His answer is a hermeneutic one: look at the stories.

The final biblical story Kearney evokes is that of the possibility of entry into the kingdom, where Christ insists that "with God all things are possible" (*GMB*, 80). Kearney draws on Husserl, Bloch, Heidegger, and Derrida to explore what he calls "post-metaphysical readings of the possible." This notion of the "possible" is "radically transcendent"; it is "possible" in terms of the "faith in the promise of advent"; it calls and solicits us, and it is "eschatological" as "always a surprise and never without grace" (*GMB*, 100). Kearney concludes that we can thus speak of God in terms of possibility, drawing on Western mystical notions of "God-play" and Eastern notions of *perichoresis* as divine dance. Kearney insists that this is not a return to dualism but an invitation to participate in the play of creation:

> To respond to the song of the Creator is to hear the Word which promises a possible world to come, a second creation or recreation of justice and peace, a world which the divine *posse* is always ready to offer but which can come about only when humanity says yes

by joining the dance, entering the play of ongoing genesis, trans-figuring the earth. God cannot become fully God, nor the Word fully flesh, until creation becomes a "new heaven and a new earth." (*GMB*, 110)

This is the God "who may be" of the title of the work, the loving possible who invites us to loving response. He summarizes this again in *After God*, where he interprets this "I am who may be" as "God is saying something like this: I will show up as promised, but I cannot be in time and history, I cannot become fully embodied in the flesh of the world, unless you show up and answer my call 'Where are you?' with the response 'Here I am.'" (*AG*, 43). He really does mean that we "help" God "be" or "become" God with all the risky implications of such a notion, as he clarifies in an interview: "God helps us to be more fully human; we help God to be more fully God—or we don't. If we don't we can blow up the world and that's the end of humanity, and that's the end of God qua Kingdom on earth because there's nobody here anymore to fulfill the promise" (*AG*, 372). There is a synergy at play here where divine and human work together, each enriching the other by the mutual relationship. And yet like all love this encounter or relationship involves tremendous risk.

Kearney does wonder repeatedly about what it would mean if we were to destroy the world. If God is really dependent upon our response, our willingness to embody the divine, what would happen to God if we were to refuse to do so and finally annihilate ourselves? He insists that we can-not take this possibility lightly, that indeed it would be like "a flowering seed arrested before it could come to full flourishing and fruition on the earth . . . the divine advent would be deprived of a historical, human fu-ture" (*AG*, 50). Our choices make a real difference to God. Yet if God is truly the "loving possible," then God would endure as faithful in spite of our denial. God would keep every moment of mercy and justice eternally in the divine memory. And God would not be prevented from starting over, from trying again. He describes the persistent welcome of the king-dom and its God in the imagery of the feast:

The great thing about this promise of an eschatological banquet is that no one is excluded. The Post-God of *posse* knocks not just twice but a thousand times—nay, infinitely, ceaselessly—until there is no door unopened, no creature, however small or inconsequential, left out in the cold, hungry, thirsty, uncared for, unloved, unredeemed. The Post-God keeps knocking and calling and delivering the word until we open ourselves to the message and the letter becomes spirit, and the word, flesh. And what is this message? An invitation to the

Kingdom. And what is the Kingdom? The Kingdom is a cup of cold water given to the least of these, it is bread and fish and wine given to the famished and unhoused, a good meal and (we are promised) one hell of a good time lasting into the early hours of the morning. A morning that never ends. (*AG*, 54)

Much of Kearney's writing gives us vivid narrative images of this invitation to the kingdom.

Micro-Eschatology

Kearney develops his own position further in *After God* where he defines it as a fourth reduction or a "micro-eschatology." The fourth reduction comes after the first reduction to objects by Husserl, the second to Being by Heidegger, and the third to givenness or love by Marion. Kearney suggests that such a fourth reduction would be a return to the "everyday," namely to the most common and the "littlest" things. Such a return to the little things challenges the power and authority of traditional notions of omnipotence. Kearney wants to highlight what he calls "theophanies of the simple and familiar": "Transcendence in a thornbush. The Eucharist in a morsel of madeleine. The kingdom in a cup of cold water. San Marco in a cobblestone. God in a street cry" or Gerald Manley Hopkins's "speckled, dappled things" (*AG*, 3). Kearney suggests that such close attention to the little things will embody and enflesh our vision of God and also humble it.

Such a return, Kearney contends, involves an eschatological move. The fourth reduction is an eschatological one—not an eschaton beyond and far away, but a foretaste of the kingdom in the humblest here and now. It is a "revisiting of the least of things, in order to retrieve the voice and visage of highest in the lowest" (*AG*, 5). This eschatological retrieval is kenotic in character. It gives of the self in order to make space for the other.[18] This retrieval of the least is thus not in contrast to his prior work on otherness. Rather, the stranger is often precisely the "least." We encounter the other or the stranger in the vulnerability of his or her face. To pay attention to the least and lowly is precisely to be attuned to their vulnerability and to offer hospitality and welcome to them. Kearney also contends that such attentiveness allows for more particularity and specificity than is the case, for example, in Lévinas. He says that "the eyes of the other *do* have color," contra Lévinas, and "they are embodied as particular, living, sensible flesh" (*AG*, 6). To notice the little and the insignificant is to look at it closely and see it as valuable in its very individuality. It is to be attentive to the particular way it is embodied and to its own peculiar beauty. This is indeed how the divine or the kingdom comes to us, embodied in the particular and the finite, the meek and the vulnerable. And this includes, as Kearney has discussed earlier, the specificity given by narrative identity. It involves hearing the other's story, taking the time to listen to the twists and the turns of this particular narrative.

Kearney also insists that this will allow us to return to God "after God": "The fourth reduction might thus be said to move from meta-physics to ana-physics: that is, back to the most concretely enfleshed phenomenon of the *prosopon* in its infinite *capacity to be*. In other words, there is nothing at all new about the *prosopon* in itself. All that is new is our way of *seeing* and *hearing* it. But it was always already there, summoning us, from the start" (*AG*, 7). Kearney is very emphatic about the importance of this hermeneutic retrieval. He worries about phenomenological proposals that refuse to engage in hermeneutics or at least to be aware of their hermeneutic commitments. A hermeneutic retrieval is not exclusive or triumphalist. It refuses both absolutism and relativism. The hermeneutic emphasis necessarily highlights its interpretive and plural character. If this is an interpretation, then other interpretations are possible. This does not mean, again, that all interpretations are equal and that one could not distinguish between them. Judgment and discernment are clearly required for Kearney and he returns to that need for discernment again and again. Yet it is far more dangerous to refuse to recognize when one is providing an interpretation (as any depiction of God must necessarily be as we are not God) and to proclaim it as the Absolute Truth. Such a proclamation will quickly wipe out any alternative voices, especially if they are weak and vulnerable ones. Ultimately, Kearney desires an "interconfessional hospitality," which he thinks hermeneutics enables. This will make possible fruitful dialogue: "At this critical juncture, we find intuition [phenomenology] recovering interpretation [hermeneutics]. We see the *eschaton* selving itself in various ways, featuring itself in multiple faces, singing itself in many voices. A polyphony of call and response. A banquet of translation" (*AG*, 11).

Already in this book, Kearney has called this an "anatheistic retrieval," which he associates with other "retrievals" (ana-esthetic, ana-dynamic, ana-phatic, ana-physical, ana-ethical, ana-choral, ana-erotic) and which is spelled out in more detail in his more recent work.[19] He thinks of it as a retrieval because it does not seek to supercede any of the other reductions prior to it, but rather to return through them to the everyday. It recalls even these more extreme versions from their occasional flights into utter transcendence. He suggests that "we are not obliged to become sightless and speechless (*apo-phasis*) before the sublimity of God. No. What we seek, with the fourth reduction, is a 'repetition' of speech (*ana-phasis*), a retrieval of saying beyond silence" (*AG*, 12). This is a sacramental, embodied recovery, which draws also on poetics or imagination (and thus Kearney's own early work on these topics). Kearney calls for an understanding of the heart that finds illumination in poetry, narrative, and other concrete manifestations of insight.

Kearney actually stresses in this context that this is not an apologetic project (so, of course, do many of the other thinkers discussed here).[20] He claims that it is not apologetic because it is not dogmatic but rather hermeneutic, the assumption being that all apologetics is dogmatic in character. He interprets his work as postmodern in the sense that it is willing to entertain discussion with other narratives and alternative interpretations. At best, so he contends, "the eschatological reduction carves out an agora where philosophy and theology may confront one another anew in 'loving combat'" (*AG*, 14). Yet Kearney certainly is providing an argument for the "possible God," even if he is doing so hermeneutically. He does suggest that this vision of God is coherent, convincing, and meaningful and his rejection of other, more extreme alternatives, as problematic and condoning injustice, supports this. It is actually precisely his emphasis on hermeneutics that makes it possible for him to show that his interpretation of the Christian narrative is meaningful and coherent. Like Ricoeur, he engages in a wager that the interpretation he explores will bear fruit and that new insight will be gained from it that will allow us to ascertain to what extent it is meaningful and "true." And Kearney addresses questions of suffering, religious multiplicity, and other aspects of postmodernism (including popular culture) in much more explicit fashion than most of the French thinkers who operate primarily in a more homogenous culturally Catholic (if functionally agnostic) environment. His imagery and styles draw on a much wider range of religious traditions, literary and poetic metaphors and images, and even other genres (such as film).[21] In some sense, then, he actually engages in a much greater effort to establish common ground with his audience.

Anatheism

In his most recent work, Kearney describes his concern as "anatheistic": neither "theistic" nor "atheistic." Anatheism means a retrieval of the divine at the boundary where sacred and secular meet. Like his previous work, it draws on poetic and narrative sources of various kinds. It is also even more explicitly inter-religious than his other writings, which already gesture in that direction but do not necessarily bring them into full conversation yet. In this book, Kearney especially engages the three Abrahamic traditions, but he previews his project as explicitly and necessarily inter-religious in that it will be followed by two further books pursuing this angle specifically (projected as *Interreligious Imagination* and *Traversing the Heart*). He defines as his thesis: "My wager throughout this volume is that it is only if one concedes that one knows virtually nothing about God that one can begin to recover the presence of holiness in the flesh of ordinary existence" (*A*, 5). Anatheism is not a new version of religion, but rather a "reopening of that space where we are free to choose between faith or nonfaith. As such, anatheism is about the *option* of retrieved belief. It operates *before* as well as *after* the division between theism and atheism, and it makes both possible. Anatheism, in short, is an invitation to revisit what might be termed a primary scene of religion: the encounter with a radical Stranger who we choose, or don't choose, to call God" (*A*, 7). Anatheism is neither the atheist militant refusal of God nor the theist dogmatic affirmation of God beyond doubt. Instead it draws from both but also precedes them.[22] Again, Kearney draws on various literary sources for the retrieval of this experience and this space: Scripture, poetry, philosophy, mystical writings, tragedy, art. All these sources give evidence of anatheistic moments.

The first and to some extent central theme in *Anatheism*, and maybe in all of Kearney's work, is hospitality (loving welcome). Like Derrida and Ricoeur, he emphasizes the ambivalence of that notion. The stranger may be welcomed with hospitality or greeted in fear and hostility. This is true also of our response to the divine. Kearney employs several biblical stories shared by all three Abrahamic faiths to show various ways of responding to the stranger and the darkness of unknowing in which this encounter occurs. Abraham's response to the three strangers whom he welcomes and feeds is one that must be made over and over throughout the tradition. There is no once-and-for-all welcome. To practice hospitality instead of hostility is to be open to the face of the other, to choose justice, mercy, and peace over war, violence, and destruction. Kearney shows how the stranger is associated with the name of God and yet also with the most vulnerable and defenseless (widow, orphan, and foreigner). Often, the human stranger is later recognized to have been the divine and yet, when this recognition occurs, usually God has already left. The divine is recognized in the trace left within the human. This is true, Kearney contends, even of Christ. Over and over again Christ has to respond to his disciples' fear and terror with compassion. Not even his family recognizes him. And Christ himself challenges us to recognize him "in the least of these" in the parable of the last judgment (*A*, 28–29). Kearney traces this ambivalent tension between hospitality and hostility through all three Abrahamic traditions. All three call for hospitality to the stranger in light of the tendency to war and violence. Both choices of love and violence are always possible. Hence we must consistently choose hospitality over hostility.

Kearney outlines his project as a five-fold wager, which is characterized by imagination, humor (closely linked to humility), commitment, discernment and hospitality. Together they form a "hermeneutic arc" that enables what he calls "interreligious translation" (*A*, 48–52). Translation does not mean an elimination of difference, but rather an opening to the stranger: "In sum, I am wagering here on the possibility of a spiritual acoustics capable of reinterpreting the oldest cries of the religious heart in both our sacred and secular worlds" (*A*, 52). Such openness does involve a rejection of traditional notions of divine sovereignty as superiority over all alternative visions. He appeals here again to God's powerlessness or kenosis (self-emptying), the "realization that God is a promise, a call, a desire to love and be loved which can not *be* at all, unless we allow God to be God" (*A*, 53). Theodicy makes rational arguments for God's existence incoherent and unconvincing. In order for genuine religious experience to become possible, we must acknowledge that we do not know. Doubt is not a threat to faith, because there can be no faith without it. There is a "fertile tension" between theism and atheism: "The bracing oscillation between doubt and faith, withdrawal and consent is the aperture that precedes and follows each wager. It is the guarantee of human freedom before the summons of the stranger. The choice to believe or not believe is indispensable to the anatheist wager. And it is a choice made over and over, never once and for all" (*A*, 56).

In his third chapter Kearney argues forcefully that in light of the Shoah, theodicy has become impossible. Any "justification" of the divine in the face of evil is no longer credible. The powerful name of "God" died at Auschwitz and Dachau, certainly including any notion of a sovereign, all-good, all-powerful divine. Reflecting on Hillesum, Arendt, and Greenberg, Kearney insists that we must choose a God of love, life, and justice instead of "a Moloch of murder and death." He agrees with Elie Wiesel "that it would be a 'moral monster' that could have come to save those burning children and did not," concluding that "the only Messiah still credible after the death camps would be one who wanted to come but could not because humans failed to invite the sacred stranger into existence" (*A*, 61). Kearney discusses various Jewish thinkers' responses to this question, such as Arendt, Lévinas, and even Derrida. While he embraces Derrida's exposition in *Sauf le nom*, he is here again critical of the lack of discernment and commitment in the Derridian "religion without religion."[23] Kearney also examines Christian responses to this question, in particular that of Bonhoeffer and Ricoeur. He suggests that Bonhoeffer's post-religious Christianity constitutes a rejection of a sovereign God in favor of a suffering God. Such a faith also makes us more committed to the world and returns us to the fullness of life. Anatheism, however, is always an option and not a necessity. There is no *obligation* to retrieve an anatheistic faith after the death of God. Ricoeur, in Kearney's view, presents such a retrieval of aspects of traditional religion for a post-theistic or post-religious faith. Ricoeur took the hermeneutics of suspicion in Freud and Nietzsche seriously and yet goes beyond them in his work by imagining the possibilities of new beginning. While the divine cannot be possessed, there can be a retrieval of the symbols of life in the Scriptures where God can be received as a gift of faith (*A*, 76).

In this book, Kearney also engages in a sacramental retrieval. He is not necessarily speaking of ecclesial sacraments in the standard sense of the term, but rather "those special awakenings of the divine within the bread and wine of quotidian existence" (*A*, 86). Here Kearney focuses in particular on a phenomenology of the flesh, as explicated by Maurice Merleau-Ponty and Julia Kristeva. Kearney retrieves eucharistic imagery for the body in Merleau-Ponty who finds the sacramental in the most basic experience of the human flesh. And, in fact, Merleau-Ponty extends this beyond the human body to nature. Kearney finds Merleau-Ponty's account particularly useful also because he is clearly not a confessional writer, but committed to methodological agnosticism in phenomenology. A period of unknowing or suspension of belief is necessary for true belief to emerge or become possible. Kearney finds a similar suspension of belief and yet careful attention to the sacramental in the concrete and secular in Kristeva's writings.

Kearney also attempts a literary retrieval through the works of Joyce, Proust, and Woolf. He contends that although they do not advance any theist positions, their modernist fiction highlights the anatheistic moment well. In their work, "the eucharistic imagination, described by Merleau-Ponty and Kristeva in the last chapter, is no longer the exclusive preserve of High Church liturgies, but is generously extended to acts of quotidian experience where the infinite traverses the infinitesimal" (*A*, 102). Sacred and secular, art and religion come together here. Kearney analyzes several of their writings in order to show how eucharistic moments give weight and significance to the seemingly insignificant and everyday. In Joyce, Kearney suggests, there is a certain "eucharistic comedy" at work where the sacred becomes visible in everyday experience. In Joyce, "the scatological and the eschatological rub shoulders. As do Greek and Jew, man and woman, life and death. And they do so, I submit, without ever succumbing to some totalizing synthesis." He suggests that "Joyce keeps the dialectic on its toes to the end, refusing the temptation of metaphysical closure. The eucharistic transformation of death and rebirth is carried out on earth. Word is always made flesh of our flesh" (*A*, 108). Kearney goes on to retrieve and interpret eucharistic moments and imagery in Marcel Proust, again using Kristeva as a guide. Finally he reflects on Virginia Woolf's *To the Lighthouse*, arguing that despite Woolf's openly avowed atheism she is able to retrieve an "epiphany of the ordinary" where "the renunciation of inappropriate expectations allows for the unexpected return of the sacred" (*A*, 127, 126). Instead of an omnipotent God, the main character embraces a mysticism attuned to the invisible in the visible. He concludes: "This mysticism after God, is, I suggest, an affirmation of a Eucharist of the everyday, of a sacrament of common 'reality,' of an epiphany of 'It/it' residing at the core of Woolf's vision." This is a "world at once itself and yet simultaneously transfigured . . . a world poised on a razor's edge where opposites balance without collapsing into sameness. A world of anatheism" (*A*, 127). All three novelists, then, regardless of their particular commitments, enable a movement between self and other, sacramental and everyday, and hospitality to the stranger. They make possible a eucharistic return, even a kind of resurrection.

In the final part ("Postlude"), Kearney explores what all this may mean in practical terms. What might anatheism mean in our secular age and how can we choose between "a God of fear and a God of hospitality"? (*A*, 139). He emphasizes again especially the kenotic character of anatheistic faith, its weakness and concern for the vulnerable. Sacred and secular must come together and inform each other. If the sacred can be in relation to the secular, instead of seeking to dominate or erase it, then it can enable a genuine hospitality to many views. And this must also include openness to non-Abrahamic faiths. At their deepest level, Kearney suggests, most religious and wisdom traditions exhort to compassion and care for the other. This makes possible "fraternal praxis and mystical communion," because, as Kearney insists again: "anatheistic hospitality toward the stranger is, as noted, not just the recognition of the other *as the same as ourselves* (though this is crucial to any global ethic of peace). It also entails recognizing the other *as different to ourselves*, as radically strange and irreducible to our familiar horizons" (*A*, 150). In a final chapter, he explores the lives of Dorothy Day, Jean Vanier, and Mahatma Ghandi as examples of how to live such practical hospitality. All three bore sacramental witness to care for the vulnerable and practiced peace and compassion.[24] Anatheism, then, Kearney concludes "does not say the sacred *is* the secular; it says it is *in* the secular, *through* the secular, *toward* the secular" (*A*, 166). These figures embody exactly the kind of faith Kearney advocates.

And finally for him this is again about discernment, about hermeneutic choosing between love and hate, justice and injustice, good and evil, hospitality and hostility. Kearney does not advocate syncretism, however. He is not suggesting that all the great religions really say "the same thing." Hospitality is as much about openness to the strangeness and difference of the other and *not* reducing it to a tame and manageable version more compatible with one's own beliefs. Rather, we must speak from within our own traditions and be honest about differences:

> So, rather than too rapidly renouncing our respective convictions—in the name of one global religion or morality—might it not be wise to acknowledge what differentiates us? For in thus recognizing the existence of otherness in each other we may mutually attest to a *surplus of meaning* that exceeds all our different beliefs. A surplus that is Other than every other. More strange than every stranger. This something "more" is what enables humans to do the impossible, to break with conditioned patterns of thinking and behavior. . . . This discovery of something "different," "ulterior," "more," is stronger, I suggest, when it is made from *inside* each conviction than when imposed from *outside* by some abstract God's-eye view. (*A*, 178)

Kearney does not ask us to leave our own traditions, but rather to examine them rigorously and critically from within, informed and enriched by our encounter with the other. Such critique and examination then enables us to be more open and hospitable to the stranger, which might lead to further discovery and self-examination:

> Anatheism is not about a facile consensus that ignores the reality of conflicting convictions. It is an effort to retrieve a unique hospitality toward the Stranger at the inaugural scene of each belief. In thus exposing ourselves to the Gods of other traditions we take the risk of dying unto our own. And in such instants of kenotic hospitality, where we exchange our God with others—sometimes not-knowing for a moment which one is true—we open ourselves to the gracious possibility of receiving our own God back again; but this time as a gift from the other, as a God of life beyond death. In losing our faith, we may gain it back again, as a God of life beyond death. In losing our faith, we may gain it back again: first faith ceding to second faith in the name of the stranger. That is the wager of anatheism. And the risk. For in surrendering our own God to a stranger God no God may come back again. Or the God who comes back may come back in ways that surprise us. (*A*, 181)

True hospitality takes this anatheistic risk of openness.

Kearney provides us, then, with the kind of vision of God that he finds convincing in a contemporary world: a loving God who calls us to real acts of charity: to practice hospitality, compassion, and justice. This is not an omnipotent God. We can no longer believe in such a God after all the atrocities of the past century. Rather, it is a God who requires our collaboration, who asks us to keep the faith and express it in concrete loving actions of kindness to the most weak and vulnerable, to the outcast and the stranger. Kearney argues for this kind of God in hermeneutic terms, drawing on narratives from a variety of religious traditions. These religious images and metaphors can provide the language and insight required for knowing how we are to live and how we are to approach the other.

Conclusion

This book has suggested that several contemporary French thinkers (namely those examined in Part II of this text) sustain a quasi-apologetic argument in their respective works. I have also argued in Part I that Heidegger, Lévinas, and Derrida are not religiously motivated and do not have such an apologetic project, but that their philosophies provide the context for, and to some extent enable, these more explicitly religious projects. Finally, Part III has explored some of the ways in which the French thinkers and their respective ideas are appropriated in the English-speaking discussion of their work, especially in North American Continental philosophy of religion. If, then, the French philosophical projects examined in Part II and to some extent their English-speaking appropriations in Part III can be considered "apologetic," what sort of *apologia* is this? Does their defense of religion have anything in common? What does it mean to defend an experience of the divine today? Is it possible to identify any common characteristics in contemporary Continental philosophy of religion? While a variety of answers could be given to this question, let me focus on just one particularly striking characteristic.

What stands out in almost all of these projects—from Lévinas to Caputo—is their emphasis on excess and hyperbole. The one thing almost all of these ways of speaking about the divine and religious experience have in common is that such experience is always depicted in superlative terms. It seems that a defense of faith or even a mere use of religious imagery automatically pushes language to the very limit. Religious experience is tantamount to excessive and exceptional experience. At times excess seems to be employed in order to show something about God (especially in Marion and Lacoste) while often the reverse is true: Religious imagery is employed to say something about the impossible or the excessive (as in Lévinas, Derrida, and Caputo). Whether religion is affirmed or rejected, it is consistently associated with the excessive, extreme, and hyperbolic.

Already Lévinas's work is characterized by heavily hyperbolic speech. Consistently, he refers to absolute alterity, complete otherness, the radical, diachronous other to whom we are completely responsible in utter passivity to the point of becoming hostages. To be sure, he employs such superlative language not just of the divine but especially about the human other. And yet he stresses that the infinite is even further removed, other than the other, other to the point of absence. As I have tried to show, it seems to be precisely this radical divine alterity that continues to hold open human alterity for Lévinas and continually reminds us of our absolute responsibility for the human other. Despite Lévinas's almost exclusive devotion to the *human* other, to some extent he inaugurates the focus on excess and superlatives.

Derrida employs hyperbolic language in a very different register. Much of his project is about undercutting all sorts of authorities and excessive hegemonies, whether religiously grounded or not. Yet much of his later writings on the gift, on hospitality, on justice, and on forgiveness increasingly take on a Lévinassian tenor. He speaks of all of these in terms of the impossible, consistently pointing to their radical and excessive character, contrasting the "pure" and radical meanings of forgiveness, hospitality, or the gift with their particular and always compromised versions in our economies, politics, and religions. While he is suspicious of a hyperbolic good (in Lévinas's or even more in Marion's terms), the utter emptiness of khōra and the insistence on the non-deconstructibility of the realities of justice, hospitality, and forgiveness are in many ways equally extreme even if they are not excessively "full" but may be instead "excessively empty" (this is, of course, more true of khōra than of hospitality).

Marion's language is especially characterized by excess. His entire project is about affirming absolute givenness and making it phenomenologically viable. Language of purity, primacy, and radicality pervades his works. The most obvious example of this is the saturated phenomenon that is so excessive that it overwhelms all our faculties, renders us utterly unable to grasp it, blinds and bedazzles us. A phenomenon of revelation is paradoxical to a second degree, doubly saturated, even far more overwhelming than other saturated phenomena. Saturated phenomena blow us away, render all our concepts insufficient and even meaningless. The saturated phenomenon gives itself entirely from its own initiative; it is characterized by radical purity and otherworldly strangeness, unseen and invisible.

Chrétien's phenomenological analyses, although they seldom use language as excessive as that of Marion, intentionally focus on showing the extraordinary in the ordinary. Although his depictions are careful and minute and often about the "every-day," they consistently emphasize what is special and extraordinary about it. His analyses of art and beauty, of the voice and speech, focus on the breaking-points and paradoxes in these experiences. Although his language is more tempered than Marion's, almost all the experiences he describes and analyzes are indeed limit-experiences or in some way excessive. This is also the case for Falque, who does not necessarily employ very hyperbolic language in his work, but does focus on excessive experiences, such as death, resurrection, and suffering.

Something similar is true of Lacoste, whose language is much more careful than Marion's, even when the content is not. The very titles of his books imply excess: Experience and the *Absolute*, Presence and *Parousia*, Being *in Danger*. Religious or liturgical experience for him is defined by liminality, by radical abnegation and kenosis. He consistently describes it in extreme terms, whether speaking of the all-night vigil, which suspends our normal relations with time, or of the desert, which undoes our usual relation to space. All his characters are hyperbolic: the saint, the ascetic, the pilgrim who leaves everything familiar, the holy fool (or even lunatic). Religious experience is experience at the very limit or at the very core of human experience. It goes further than general human being-in-the-world, shows something more fundamental about who we are, pushes our experience to the extreme.

Although Ricoeur is generally far more balanced in his overall philosophy, he also associates religious language with excess. Biblical language is characterized by a logic of superabundance that undoes the logic of equivalence characteristic of everyday experience. Biblical "poetry" is excessive, calls us beyond ourselves, undoes our common perceptions of reality, and challenges our coherent sense of self, unsettling and displacing us. Many biblical genres, such as the parables and proverbs, contain limit-expressions, which depict experience at the limit but also push the reader to similarly excessive experience. Overall, as we have seen, Ricoeur consistently grounds his hope that the good will ultimately triumph in his religious convictions. Thus, despite his usual reluctance to speak of this more fully, religious belief seems to be about what calls us beyond ourselves to the good.

Michel Henry is perhaps the most excessive of the French writers. Although his excess is wholly immanent and he refuses any notions of transcendence, his language about Christianity is almost entirely in absolute terms. He contrasts the lying and deceptive truth of science with the radical and incomparable Truth of Christianity. Christianity *alone* gives access to absolute Life, it alone has a truly phenomenological understanding of "man" as absolute Son of God, as generated out of the divine Life. And this experience of the divine Life is complete, radical, and utter immediacy, inseparably immanent in our self-affected flesh. Our most passionate and intense feelings and experiences of suffering and joy are direct and immediate indicators of the divine Life from which no separation is possible short of death.

This excess is continued to some extent in the English-speaking appropriations in Part III (with the possible exception of Kearney who is, at points, rather critical of the excess in the contemporary discussion). Although his language is not anywhere as radical as that of other thinkers, Westphal describes phenomenology of religion as dealing with existential limit situations of guilt and death. He consistently affirms divine unknowability and speaks of the believing self in kenotic and self-abnegating terms. Westphal calls us to a more radical faith that defies the self-indulgence of contemporary culture. Religious experiences decenter us and challenge us to move beyond ourselves toward the holy other.

The commitment to excess is particularly evident in John Caputo's writings, which exalt in superlatives. Although he certainly distances himself from the excess of saturation in Marion or the utter immediacy of Henry, his language throughout is intensely hyperbolic. The passion for God is the passion for the impossible. This is absolute passion without limit. Most of the excessive language circulates around the notion of the impossible, whether speaking of the gift, hospitality, forgiveness, love, or God. The question "What do I love when I love my God?" is consistently interpreted as a question about absolute passion. At the same time, Caputo stresses the complete non-knowledge and infinite undecidability and deferral of questions about the divine: I cannot know; God remains absolutely unknowable. God, for Caputo, "is the name of a limit-state, an extremity, a name in which we are driven to an extreme, our faculties stretched beyond themselves, beyond the possible to the impossible. The people of God are, for better or worse, impossible people, people with a taste for the impossible, with a taste for the worst violence and the most radical peace."[1] Religion is without religion, "hope without hope, against hope, hoping like mad." Prayer is fueled to its most excessive extremes precisely because of this insecurity and unknowability. Although for Marion the excess is filled and for Caputo it is empty, Kearney is right to point out that they are equally excessive.

In contrast to these, Kearney is much more tempered and, indeed, his project is precisely to formulate a spirituality of the ordinary and everyday. He is occasionally quite critical of the excessive nature of much of contemporary thinking and argues for a more mediating position, often contrasting the two sides of excess (fullness and emptiness, God and khōra, the good above and the empty or even demonic beneath) to each other and rejecting both as too extreme. Yet his own writing is often also characterized by a focus on limit experiences or extreme encounters. His series is entitled "Philosophy at the Limit" and seeks to explore "experiences of extremity which bring us to the edge" (*SGM*, 3). Throughout the book, he examines such extremes, as he points out at times: "Once again in this chapter, as in several others in this volume, we find ourselves confronting a limit experience on the edge of the sayable; a no man's land of dread where fantasies—strangers, gods and monsters—proliferate" (*SGM*, 166). At times his examples also tend to be excessive. *Anatheism* explores Dorothy Day and Gandhi as examples of the religious life, arguably moral saints who stand out precisely because of their passionate and absolute commitment. Kearney's examinations of the anatheistic versions of hospitality and welcome to the stranger are about the mysterious divine appearances to Abraham at the oak of Mamre, to Mary in the annunciation, and to Mohammed. Surely not your average religious experience. Similarly, the eschatological dimension is strongly stressed in the articulation of the "God who may be."

What is particularly interesting is that this excessive language about the divine is often linked to a depiction of other experiences of excess. In Lévinas, the divine and the human alterity are closely linked to the point that some have considered them indistinguishable (both Marion and Derrida occasionally make this claim). In Derrida, the impossibility of the gift, of hospitality, of forgiveness, of justice, of the democracy to come all share structural similarities that are themselves similar to the "messianic" even if this does not function in any way as a determinate religion and is certainly not explicitly connected to a particular tradition (although Derrida does acknowledge the religious provenance and connotations of some of the words he uses). Marion insists on the "banality" of saturated phenomena. They depict not only religious experiences but the excess of historical and cultural events, of art and music, of one's own flesh and the face of the other. Similarly, in Chrétien, artistic, poetic, and religious experience seem closely linked and at times become almost indistinguishable. All his accounts move smoothly between discussions of poetry or artistic representations and religious texts or experiences. Religious and narrative texts carry great structural similarities also for Ricoeur. They are all (in some way or another) "poetry," as they open a world to the reader and challenge us to envision ourselves differently within it. The experience of the divine life pulsating in the immediacy of the flesh is, for Henry, an experience of pathos, of suffering and joy. Simultaneously, that experience is about everything that matters: everything that is not of the "world" but is immediately experienced in the flesh. The strong critique of technology links more authentic creativity with the Truth of Life instead of the truth of the world, which reduces and excludes life and any authentic human existence. For Falque, also, religiously inspired notions of resurrection and sacramentality speak of our experiences of life and death and concern our fleshly "animality." Lacoste's experience of the Absolute, which he describes as an experience at the limit, although it focuses on our "being-before-God," is not strictly speaking purely religious experience but also seeks to reach a deep level of human experience more generally (and again finds certain parallels in art). One might contend that even in Heidegger religious and poetic sensibilities are closely associated. The creative and the holy dwell in intimate proximity. This is just as true for Caputo and Kearney. Caputo repeatedly stresses the replaceability of God, passion, love, hope, event, and so forth. He often says that he is not sure whether love is a term for God or God a term for love. God becomes the name of an excessive event that calls us beyond ourselves, but it is not at all clear that this has to be a distinctly religious experience. Excess itself seems quite sufficient. Even for Kearney, despite or maybe even through his attempt to mediate some of the superlative language of other thinkers, the roles of imagination, art, literature, and religion are closely connected. Even his most fully "theologically" oriented works include literary reflections, and he explores explicitly the quasi-eucharistic imagery of such literary figures as James Joyce and Virginia Woolf. The theophanies of the everyday and the "holy in a cup of tea" can be discovered for him not only in religious but also in poetic and artistic depictions. At times, they become almost indistinguishable.

One might say, then, that what most characterizes the "apologetic" character of contemporary philosophical (predominantly phenomenological) thinking is that it identifies human boundary experiences in religious terms. Religious experience is excessive and deeply passionate. While the claim that God is infinite or excessive, beyond anything we can control or even comprehend, is certainly not new or particularly startling (the apophatic tradition, after all, has a long and deep history), this consistent association of excessive experience with religious experience and the quasi-equation of religion with poetry or other artistic expression evident in many contemporary thinkers does present a shift in thought. The medieval tradition both East and West, even in its most apophatic moments, had always been fairly critical of passion, which was often associated with lack of control or even demonic possession. The modern period insisted far more strongly on God's rational character than on divine incomprehensibility or ineffability. The name of God has taken on various connotations at different times and in different traditions. The contemporary discourse is definitely not "religion within the limits of reason alone," nor is God equated with morality or absolutely self-conscious spirit, as in Kant and Hegel respectively. Rather, the contemporary proposals seem to equate the divine with excessive experience. Of course they do not all do so in the same way or to the same extent, nor do all agree to what extent excessive experiences of art or literature can be identified as or equated with religious experiences. Yet there does seem to be substantial agreement that human boundary experience has a religious character and that religious experience is best described in terms of hyperbole and excess. Postmodern apologetics, if there is such a thing (*s'il y en a*, as Derrida would say), is a defense of experiences of radical excess as originating in some fashion in or at least as closely associated with the divine, a defense of passion at the very limit of human experience as a *religious* phenomenon.

Notes

Introduction: The "Death of God" and the Demise of Natural Theology

1. See Chapters 8–12 of Minucius Felix's *Octavius* for a statement of these particular accusations, and Chapters 28–31 for his response. The whole work is an apologetic for Christian faith, including an extended argument about providence.

2. Many of the most well-known early Fathers, such as Irenaeus of Lyon or Justin Martyr, were such apologists, although even later thinkers in a predominantly Christian environment still tried to convince the "pagans," such as Athanasius's famous *Contra Gentes* and *De Incarnatione*. Irenaeus defended the Christian faith primarily in response to Gnostic groups, while Justin confronted Judaism (especially in his "Dialogue with Trypho"). The debate with Judaism is a particularly difficult case, as it often degenerated into what is today called "supercessionism" (i.e., the conviction that Christianity is far superior to Judaism and has come to complete it or even replace it), an argument that can be found to some extent already in Paul's letters. The first Christian communities were all Jewish and met in the synagogues, but often they would run into conflict with the non-Christian Jews. As the Christian faith spread and increasingly admitted non-Jewish members, it became more and more separated from the Jewish communities in which it had arisen. And, as often happens when groups split who share many of the same views, the contentions became more and more hostile, especially as Christianity gained in influence and anti-Semitism was a strong current in the larger culture even then.

3. Clement of Alexandria was one of the earliest thinkers to try to reconcile faith and reason and to appropriate philosophical thought into the Christian faith.

His *Stromata* is essentially a very learned refutation of many aspects of "pagan" thought, while it also appropriates much of it and is clearly imbued with its spirit.

4. This is particularly evident in writings on the spiritual life, but also obvious in more philosophical treatises, such as Gregory of Nyssa's *On the Immortality of the Soul* (both here and in his *Life of St. Macrina* he refers to his sister Macrina repeatedly as a philosopher).

5. See Boethius, *The Consolation of Philosophy*.

6. See Nemesius of Emesa, *On the Nature of Man*, trans. R. W. Sharples and P. J. van der Eijk (Liverpool: Liverpool University Press, 2008). There are many such early treatises on human nature, most of which make heavy use of Platonic, Aristotelian, and Stoic philosophical concepts.

7. See S. A. Wallace-Hadrill, *The Greek Patristic View of Nature* (Manchester, UK: Manchester University Press, 1968).

8. It is completely false to portray the Middle Ages as "dark"; it would be more correct to speak of a time of preparation, germination, and growth that culminated in great cultural change, such as that of the Renaissance, Humanism, and the Scientific Revolution.

9. Chapter 10 will discuss several contemporary interpretations of the Anselmic "proof" given by the thinkers treated in Part II of this book.

10. See the first few questions of the *Summa Theologiae*, which involve questions of method and ask whether theology is a science and whether it is possible to have knowledge of God. See also his *The Division and Methods of the Sciences*, trans. Armand Maurer (Toronto: Pontifical Institute of Mediaeval Studies, 1953).

11. For Newton's Arianism and the way in which it influenced his scientific research (he was also very interested in alchemy and in biblical interpretation), see Betty Jo Teeter Dobbs, *The Janus Faces of Genius: The Role of Alchemy in Newton's Thought* (Cambridge: Cambridge University Press, 1991). For a briefer review of Newton, see Richard S. Westfall, "Isaac Newton," in Gary B. Ferngren, *Science and Religion: A Historical Introduction* (Baltimore: Johns Hopkins University Press, 2002).

12. See Ernan McMullin, "Galileo on Science and Scripture," in *The Cambridge Companion to Galileo*, ed. Peter Machamer (Cambridge: Cambridge University Press, 1998), 271–307. See also Arthur Koestler, *The Sleepwalkers: A History of Man's Changing Relation to the Universe* (New York: Macmillan, 1968).

13. See David Lindberg, *The Beginnings of Western Science: The European Scientific Tradition in Philosophical, Religious, and Institutional Context* (Chicago: University of Chicago Press, 1992); Gary B. Ferngren, *Science and Religion: A Historical Introduction* (Baltimore: Johns Hopkins University Press, 2002); Alistair C. Crombie, *Augustine to Galileo*, vol. 2 of *Science in the Later Middle Ages and Early Modern Times: 13th to 17th Centuries* (Harmondsworth, U.K.: Penguin Books, 1959); Pierre Duhem, *Medieval Cosmology: Theories of Infinity, Place, Time, Void, and the Plurality of Worlds*, trans. Roger Ariew (Chicago: University of Chicago Press, 1985).

14. See David Hume, *Dialogues on Natural Religion*.

15. Marion argues that Descartes actually opposes this movement and insists on the creation of the eternal truths against Mersenne, Kepler, and Galileo (see Chapter 5 on Marion).

16. As put forth especially in Kant's famous essay "An Answer to the Question 'What is Enlightenment?'" Kant's answer, provided in the first two sentences of the essay, is: "*Enlightenment is man's emergence from his self-imposed immaturity. Immaturity* is the inability to use one's understanding without the guidance from another." Cited from: *Perpetual Peace and Other Essays*, trans. Ted Humphrey (Indianapolis: Hackett, 1983), 41.

17. *Religion within the Limits of Reason Alone* is the title of one of his most important works, outlining a new rational religion as the foundation of morality and universal peace. The title describes his thrust precisely. Kant is rather dismissive of what he calls *Schwärmerei*, religious enthusiasm (such as the Pietist or Methodist movements), based on feeling instead of reason.

18. These constitute the "antinomies" at the end of his most important (and most difficult) work, *The Critique of Pure Reason*.

19. This is the argument put forth in Kant's *Critique of Practical Reason*, which outlines the *practical* analysis of the will, while *The Critique of Pure Reason* examines the *theoretical* uses of the understanding (*Verstand*). "Reason" translates *Vernunft*, which includes both *Verstand* (understanding) and will. The *Critique of Judgment* tries to bring these two uses of reason together through an examination of the faculty of the imagination.

20. It is important to note that it was not Darwin's goal to "demolish" natural theology or even to attack religion in any form. Yet his elucidation of the way life (including that of human beings) evolved on the planet and especially his careful description of the processes of selection and adaptation did for many people dispense with the need for a belief in God as guiding the process of creation or even as being particularly involved in it.

21. All this is, of course, a very sweeping summary that harshly oversimplifies the ideas and theories of all these important thinkers. They are far more complex than can possibly be explicated here.

22. The most well-known versions of this are the four kinds of interpretations of texts that many thinkers in the Middle Ages and especially in the Christian East assumed: literal, allegorical, moral, and analogical. The East also often spoke of a typological interpretation.

23. Friedrich Nietzsche, *The Joyful Wisdom*, Section 283. Citation taken from Walter Kauffman, *Existentialism from Dostoevsky to Sartre* (New York: Meridian, 1956), 126.

24. He explicates this in his early lectures on Christianity, as well as in many other places in his work. The notion of *ressentiment* is associated with Christianity especially in *The Genealogy of Morals*. Nietzsche is a very complex thinker whose relationship to Christianity as well as his critique of it are not at all straightforward. I am here merely summarizing the effect some of his claims had on the larger intellectual culture.

25. This conviction is carried to its height in Sartre's existentialism, which he insists must, by definition, be atheistic (see especially his address "Existentialism is a Humanism"). He depicts the difficulty and even despair associated with finding one's own values and not being able to ground them in some higher belief system in vivid language (for example in, *Nausea* and many plays such as *No Exit*). He is joined in this attitude by many other early twentieth-century French thinkers, such as André Gide and Albert Camus.

26. See his *The Postmodern Condition: A Report on Knowledge* (Minneapolis: University of Minnesota Press, 1984).

27. John D. Caputo, *Philosophy and Theology* (Nashville: Abingdon Press, 2006), 48–49. The book as a whole is a readable (and entertaining) introduction to the history of the relationship between philosophy and theology (focusing especially on the "and" between them) and an introduction to what Caputo sees as Derrida's contribution to a new and different relationship between the two.

28. Ibid., 50.

29. This is still extremely evident in popular science writing, such as that of Carl Sagan, Richard Dawkins, Daniel Dennett, and others.

30. Alvin Plantinga and Richard Swinburne are probably the most well-known representatives of this tradition, although there are many others.

31. The "intelligent design" movement is one particular example of this and on a more basic—and more conservative—level actually most versions of creationism specifically, and Christian fundamentalism more generally, are as well: They all attempt to employ the Enlightenment assumptions about the clarity and goodness of reason for their own purposes. They are thus essentially modern projects.

32. His address was translated as "The Theological Turn in French Phenomenology" and is published together with articles by several of the people he accused of such a turn as *Phenomenology and the "Theological Turn": The French Debate* (New York: Fordham University Press, 2000).

33. In Husserl's work there are several such reductions, most importantly a phenomenological and an eidetic one. Most of the thinkers that follow will refer primarily to the phenomenological reduction and be less interested in an eidetic reduction to essences.

1. Martin Heidegger and Onto-theo-logy

1. Janicaud relies on Courtine's study of Heidegger's "phenomenology of the unapparent" and claims that "without Heidegger's *Kehre*, there would be no theological turn." He later proposes returning to Heidegger's strict delineation between phenomenology and theology in Dominique Janicaud et al., *Phenomenology and the "Theological Turn": The French Debate* (New York: Fordham University Press, 2000), 31 and 100–1, respectively.

2. For example, Marion will argue (in *On Descartes' Metaphysical Prism*) that, in Descartes, the ego cogito functions as such a "supreme being," grounding the being of all other beings.

3. *Zürich Seminar, Gesamtausgabe* 15 (Frankfurt: Klostermann, 1986), 436–37.

4. Ibid.

5. The lectures were first printed in German as volume 60 of the *Gesamtausgabe* of Heidegger's works in 1995.

6. *Being and Time*, Section 44. Translations of "On the Essence of Truth" and "The End of Philosophy and the Task of Thinking" are included in David Krell's edited collection *Basic Writings*, 111–38 and 427–49, respectively.

7. In "The Origin of the Work of Art" Heidegger clarifies: "The proposition 'the essence of truth is un-truth' is not, however, intended to state that truth is at bottom falsehood. Nor does it mean that truth is never itself but, viewed dialectically, is also its opposite" (*BW*, 180). He explains in more detail later: "Truth is un-truth, insofar as there belongs to it the reservoir of the non-yet-revealed, the un-uncovered, in the sense of concealment. In unconcealment, as truth, there occurs also the other 'un-' of a double restraint or refusal. Truth essentially occurs as such in the opposition of clearing and double concealing" (*BW*, 185).

8. The clearest exposition of this is found in his "Memorial Address," given to a lay audience on the occasion of the 150th birthday of composer Konradin Kreutzer who was born in the same town as Heidegger. A translation of the address is included in *Discourse on Thinking*, 43–57.

9. Marion will be very critical of this inclusion of the divinities within the fourfold and it becomes a large part of his critique of Heidegger in *God Without Being*. He suggests that this is a concrete instance (the subordination of theology as a discipline to phenomenology in the early essay is a more general one) of Heidegger's desire to subject God to Being, despite all his claims that being and God have nothing to do with each other. (See Chapter 5 on Marion.)

10. *Der Spiegel*, May 31, 1976. Translated as "Only a God Can Save Us: Der Spiegel's Interview with Martin Heidegger," *Philosophy Today* 20 (1976): 267–84.

11. Richard Kearney, *Strangers, Gods, and Monsters* (London: Routledge, 2003), 215–20.

12. Idem, *The God Who May Be* (Bloomington: Indiana University Press, 2001), 92–93.

13. Idem, *Strangers*, 219.

14. John D. Caputo, *Demythologizing Heidegger* (Bloomington: Indiana University Press, 1993), 184. See the fuller discussion in Chapter 12 on Caputo's work.

15. Ben Vedder, *Heidegger's Philosophy of Religion: From God to the Gods* (Pittsburgh: Duquesne University Press, 2007), 217. All references within the next few paragraphs refer to this text.

16. Benjamin D. Crowe, *Heidegger's Phenomenology of Religion: Realism and Cultural Criticism* (Bloomington: Indiana University Press, 2008). All references within the next paragraph refer to this text. I also want to acknowledge here the very helpful comments of my colleague Duane Armitage who has just completed a dissertation on Heidegger's phenomenology of religion and sees far

more continuity in Heidegger's position on religion than is usually acknowledged (especially by Caputo and Kearney). He contends that in his larger phenomenological work, Heidegger seeks to generalize his early phenomenological insights about the life of faith (in a heavily Lutheran register).

2. Emmanuel Lévinas and the Infinite

1. *Ethics and Infinity*, trans. Richard Cohen (Pittsburgh: Duquesne University Press, 1985), 27. See also Lévinas's comments in the interview with Richard Kearney in 1984: Richard Kearney, *Debates in Continental Philosophy: Conversations with Contemporary Thinkers* (New York: Fordham, 2004), 67.

2. The full dedication to *Otherwise Than Being* reads: "To the memory of those who were closest among the six million assassinated by the National Socialists, and of the millions on millions of all confessions and all nations, victims of the same hatred of the other man, the same anti-semitism."

3. In the interview with Kearney he says: "I always make a clear distinction, in what I write, between philosophical and confessional texts. I do not deny that they may ultimately have a common source of inspiration. I simply state that it is necessary to draw a line of demarcation between them as distinct methods of exegesis, as separate languages. I would never, for example, introduce a Talmudic or biblical verse into one of my philosophical texts to try to prove or justify a phenomenological argument" (*Debates*, 70).

4. With this terminology, Lévinas evokes Heidegger's "es gibt," which is also translated as "there is." German uses the auxiliary verb "to give" for this expression, whereas French uses "to have" and English "to be." In his analysis of the *il y a*, Lévinas explicitly opposes the connotations of generosity and giving in Heidegger's expression and analysis.

5. Richard Kearney explores this in much more detail in his *Strangers, Gods, and Monsters*. Julia Kristeva traces a general history of how "the stranger" was treated in Europe from antiquity to the present in *Strangers to Ourselves*.

6. He uses this phrase frequently, especially in interviews. It is also the title of one of his final lectures.

7. While Heidegger "destructs" and criticizes "metaphysics" and instead attempts to recover "ontology," Lévinas condemns "ontology" but often employs the term "metaphysics" in a quite neutral fashion.

8. This is first explicated in the section on "Exteriority and the Face" in *Totality and Infinity*, but the term is so central to his work that it shows up in all his subsequent writings.

9. Lévinas was quite critical of Buber. See especially several of his essays in *Difficult Freedom*.

10. This is also a phrase Lévinas uses frequently. See, for example, *GDT*, 190. It also appears repeatedly in *Otherwise Than Being*.

11. Jacques Derrida, *Writing and Difference*, trans. Alan Bass (Chicago: University of Chicago Press, 1978). All page numbers within the next paragraph refer to this text.

12. Derrida claims that "by making the origin of language, meaning, and difference the relation to the infinitely other, Levinas is resigned to betraying his own intentions in his philosophical discourse. The latter is understood, and instructs, only by first permitting the same and Being to circulate within it" (Ibid., 151).

13. As the title indicates, he also is much more concerned in this book with freeing this account from the language of ontology, something he will also pursue in later lectures and writings.

14. Dominique Janicaud et al., *Phenomenology and the "Theological Turn": The French Debate* (New York: Fordham University Press, 2000), 43.

15. Ibid., 49. "The Swerve" is the title of Chapter 2, which is primarily a critique of Lévinas.

16. In this section of the chapter, I am to some extent reusing (in revised form) and expanding on parts of my article "The Neighbor and the Infinite: Marion and Levinas on the Encounter between Self, Human Other, and God," *Continental Philosophy Review* 40 (2007): 231–49.

17. Emmanuel Levinas, *Humanism of the Other*, trans. Nidra Poller (Urbana and Chicago: University of Illinois Press, 2006), 39.

18. Ibid., 40 and 44, respectively (trans. modified).

19. "God and Philosophy," *BPW*, 129–48.

20. "The Infinite transcends itself in the finite, it *passes* the finite, in that it directs the neighbor to me without exposing itself to me" (*BPW*, 146).

21. "God and Philosophy," *BPW*, 136 and 139, respectively.

22. This third is not the same thing as the third in the relation of justice referred to previously. Lévinas does not distinguish these "thirds" from each other explicitly, but it is quite clear that they do not refer to the same experience. "The infinite which signifies itself in the witness is not in front of its witness and one cannot speak of it as of a name. It is attested in its excess in the accusative of the '*me voici!*' which responds to its call. The order which orders me does not leave me any possibility to climb back up toward the infinite as toward a name which is placed within a theme. In this way God escapes objectivation and is not even found in the I-thou relationship, is not the thou of an I, is not dialogue or within dialogue. But he/it is also not separable from the responsibility for the neighbor who (the neighbor) is a thou for a self. God is thus the third person or illeity" (*GDT*, 203).

23. *Debates*, 76. Interestingly enough, in the very next sentence Lévinas suggests that such a call might also proceed from other religious traditions.

24. Marion's book *God Without Being* appeared at about the time of Lévinas's final lectures and he refers to the book a couple of times. His engagement with the language of ontology, of course, goes back to some of his earliest writings and is particularly evident in *Otherwise Than Being*.

3. Jacques Derrida and "Religion Without Religion"

1. Kevin Hart, *The Trespass of the Sign: Deconstruction, Theology and Philosophy* (New York: Fordham University Press, 2000; originally published by Cambridge University Press in 1989).

2. Hent de Vries, *Philosophy and the Turn to Religion* (Baltimore: Johns Hopkins University Press, 1999).

3. For a fuller examination of this text, see the chapter on Caputo in Part III of this book.

4. Derrida's contributions are most prominent in the roundtable discussions for the first three conferences. He also gave the keynote lecture (on forgiveness) for the second conference and responded briefly to each paper in the first conference. See John D. Caputo and Michael J. Scanlon, eds., *God, the Gift, and Postmodernism* (Bloomington: Indiana University Press, 1999) and John D. Caputo, Mark Dooley, and Michael J. Scanlon, eds., *Questioning God* (Bloomington: Indiana University Press, 2001).

5. This emphasis on the "yes" is evident in Derrida's work from an extensive note (note 5 to Chapter IX) in the comparatively early text *Of Spirit: Heidegger and the Question*, trans. Geoffrey Bennington and Rachel Bowlby (Chicago: University of Chicago Press, 1987), 129–36, where he discusses various aspects of this "yes" in relation to Heidegger's notion of "*Zusage*," to a 2003 seminar on the event, translated as "A Certain Impossible Possibility of Saying the Event," in *The Late Derrida*, ed. W. J. T Mitchell and Arnold I. Davidson (Chicago: University of Chicago Press, 2007), 235, where Derrida stresses the necessary repetition of the "yes" of welcome.

6. *Speech and Phenomena And Other Essays on Husserl's Theory of Signs* (Evanston, Ill.: Northwestern University Press, 1973), 129–60. All page references in the next paragraph are to this text.

7. Harold Coward and Toby Foshay, eds., *Derrida and Negative Theology* (Albany, N.Y.: SUNY Press, 1992).

8. Derrida examines the status of the narrative voice in John's text where John is citing Jesus who is "dictating" the letters to the churches in Asia. John functions as messenger of this voice conveyed by an angelic messenger, but also as its testimony. Thus what appears at first as straightforward communication actually emerges as multiple "sendings" and deferred testimonies. Derrida claims that a similar (unacknowledged) deferral and referral to previous voices takes place in more recent apocalyptic speaking. The author of the message cannot be clearly determined and its cryptic tone and secretive message often comes with heavy political implications. Derrida also briefly reflects on the invitation of the "come," which ends John's Apocalypse, and identifies it as the event preceding the event. "Come" does not designate a place but a gesture of speaking, an invitation or an imperative (*DNT*, 65).

9. For more on his Jewish/Abrahamic background, see his essay "Abraham, the Other" in *Judeities: Questions for Jacques Derrida*, eds. Bettina Bergo, Joseph Cohen, and Raphael Zagury-Orly, trans. Bettina Bergo and Michael B. Smith (New York: Fordham University Press, 2007), 1–35.

10. Derrida argues that negative theology does not defer sufficiently. While denying certain aspects of the divine or refusing to attribute certain properties to God in the name of divine transcendence or human unknowing, it does not go

far enough because it continues to posit the divine and make claims about it. Its denial and unnaming remain insufficient. This is the claim to which Marion responds in his presentation to the Villanova conference on the gift by arguing that mystical theology moved beyond both positive and negative descriptive moves to a purely performative speech of prayer or praise. Derrida refers repeatedly to Marion in the footnotes, although he does not discuss him in the text itself.

11. This essay and the larger conversation about negative theology in which it is situated become the context for the early reception especially of Marion's work and for much of the first conversations about it. The first three works that seriously consider Marion's work (Thomas Carlson's *Indiscretion: Finitude and the Naming of God*, Robyn Horner's *Rethinking God as Gift*, and Bruce Ellis Benson's *Modern Idolatry*) all set him in explicit conversation with Derrida (and all three clearly prefer Derridean undecidability over Marion's more overt religious commitments).

12. Derrida also takes the question of the name up again briefly in the context of the work of translation in his "Des Tours de Babel" (written in 1980, included in *Acts of Religion*). Most of the essay is an examination of Benjamin's essay on the task of the translator, but repeatedly refers to the translatability of the divine name.

13. See the final two chapters of *Strangers, Gods and Monsters* where this is articulated in the most detail. I provide a summary of his argument in Chapter 13, which treats Kearney's work.

14. The "fifty-nine periods and periphrases" of "Circumfession" were written between January 1989 and April 1990. *Sauf le nom* dates to August 1991.

15. "Abraham, the Other," 13.

16. For a more detailed exposition, see Chapter 12 on Caputo's work.

17. "The account of Isaac's sacrifice can be read as a narrative development of the paradox constituting the concept of duty and absolute responsibility. This concept puts us into relation (but without relating to it, in a double secret) with the absolute other, with the absolute singularity of the other, whose name here is God. Whether one believes the biblical story or not, whether one gives it credence, doubts it, or transposes it, it could still be said that there is a moral to this story, even if we take it to be a fable" (*GD*, 66).

18. I am employing the English translation of the introductory lecture used as keynote address for the Postmodernism and Religion 2 conference "Questioning God" in Caputo, *Questioning God*. All page references in the next paragraph are to this text. For a shorter version of this, see the essay "On Forgiveness" in *Cosmopolitanism and Forgiveness* (London/New York: Routledge, 2001).

19. This is especially evident in the lectures reprinted as "Hostipitality" in *Acts of Religion* of which one is entirely devoted to the topic of forgiveness and the gift is frequently mentioned.

20. It also evokes texts by Hegel and Bergson, as Michael Naas points out in his thorough treatment of this difficult essay in *Miracle and Machine: Jacques Derrida and the Two Sources of Religion, Science, and the Media* (New York: Fordham

University Press, 2012), 40–41. As this text was published when the manuscript of this book was already in production, I do not draw on it explicitly in my summary of Derrida's essay, but Naas's treatment provides a much fuller engagement with the text and is deeply grounded in his thorough knowledge of Derrida's oeuvre and long-standing engagement with it. Naas not only provides context and background for Derrida's address, but also juxtaposes it with DeLillo's novel *Underworld*, written at roughly the same time as Derrida's essay.

21. Naas also points out that "if the theme of faith will have thus been of interest to Derrida from the beginning, it will have never been reducible to religion. To understand Derrida's skepticism with regard to the so-called return *to* religion or return *of* religion in 1990s, we will have to bear this crucial distinction in mind" (*Miracle and Machine*, 33).

22. Naas explains this "ineluctable and autoimmune relationship between religion and science" as follows: "Derrida's hypothesis is that, when confronted with all these forces of abstraction (disincarnation, deracination, delocalization, universalizing schematization, telecommunication, and so on) 'religion' is at once in 'reactive antagonism' to these forces and in constant reaffirmation of them, not simply appropriating them in a minimal way but actually upping the ante of them through what Derrida calls a *surenchère réaffirmatrice*. In other words, religion reacts against the movements of abstraction, deracination, delocalization, and universalization as they are deployed in teletechnoscience and telecommunication by appropriating these same movements so as to return to all those things threatened by them" (*Miracle and Machine*, 53). See also especially Naas's discussion in Chapters 3 and 5 of *Miracle and Machine*.

23. For a full discussion of this latter part of Derrida's essay, see especially Chapter 6 of *Miracle and Machine*.

24. *Impossible God: Derrida's Theology* (Hants: Ashgate, 2003), 163.

4. Paul Ricoeur: A God of Poetry and Superabundance

1. See Kearney's introduction to Ricoeur's *On Translation* (London/New York: Routledge, 2006), vii–xx. He also provides a useful brief introduction to Ricoeur's life and philosophical career.

2. Unlike most of the other thinkers treated in Part II of this book, Ricoeur was Protestant. France is a predominantly Roman Catholic country (although it is mainly secular now).

3. Janicaud recognizes this in his *Theological Turn* where he explicitly excludes Ricoeur from his condemnations of contemporary "theological" thinkers. Yet Ricoeur participated in the symposium of thinkers responding to Janicaud, which also included Marion, Henry, and Chrétien. Lévinas had already died.

4. Although no previously published material is explicitly reused in this chapter, many of the general ideas and summaries I present here have also been articulated in some of my previous publications on Ricoeur, especially the following two articles: "Our Responsibility for Universal Evil: Rethinking Fallenness in

Ecological Terms," in *I more than Others*, ed. Eric Severson (Cambridge Scholars Publishing, 2010) [for Ricoeur's work on symbolism] and "Ricoeur's Hermeneutic of God: A Symbol That Gives Rise to Thought," *Philosophy and Theology* 13 (2001): 287–309 [for his work on biblical hermeneutics].

5. "Such is the wager. Only he can object to this mode of thought who thinks that philosophy, to begin from itself, must be a philosophy without presuppositions. A philosophy that starts from the fullness of language is a philosophy with presuppositions. To be honest, it must make its presuppositions explicit, state them as beliefs, wager on the beliefs, and try to make the wager pay off in understanding . . . Only a philosophy first nourished on the fullness of language can subsequently be indifferent to the modes of approach to its problems and to the conditions of its activity, and remain constantly concerned with thematizing the universal and rational structure of its adherence" (*SE*, 257).

6. He articulates these levels (and argues against theology) in many different texts. See, for example, "Philosophy and Religious Language" (*FS*, 35–47) and "Hermeneutic of the Idea of Revelation," in *Essays on Biblical Interpretation*, ed. Lewis S. Mudge (Philadelphia: Fortress Press, 1980).

7. In other places, he also distinguishes between what he calls a phenomenology of manifestation (the more general religious sense of the "sacred") and a "hermeneutics of proclamation" (the biblical, which is often critical of the "sacred"). See "Manifestation and Proclamation" (*FS*, 48–67).

8. Ricoeur first introduced this notion in his lecture "Hermeneutic of the Idea of Revelation." Poetry "points to the obliterating of the ordinary referential function" and "turns back on itself." He insists: "My deepest conviction is that poetic language alone restores to us that participation-in or belonging-to an order of things which precedes our capacity to oppose ourselves to things taken as objects opposed to a subject. Hence one function of poetic discourse is to bring about this emergence of a depth-structure of belonging-to amid the ruins of descriptive discourse" (9). See also the much later analysis of biblical discourse as poetic in section III of "Naming God," (*FS*, 221–23).

9. See especially the article "Naming God" (*FS*, 217–35). Ricoeur is not always entirely consistent in his lists of the various biblical genres. At times, New Testament texts seem to fall into the genres he identifies in the Hebrew Scriptures; at times they seem to contain their own distinctive genres (for example, parables, letters, eschatological literature). See also "Hermeneutic of the Idea of Revelation," "Manifestation and Proclamation" (*FS*, 55–61), "The Bible and the Imagination" (*FS*, 144–66), and "Biblical Time" (*FS*, 167–80).

10. In a reflection on biblical hermeneutics he says: "The referent 'God' is at once the coordination of these diverse discourses and the vanishing point, the index of incompletion, of these partial discourses" (*TA*, 97).

11. See "The Logic of Jesus, the Logic of God" (*FS*, 279–83).

12. See "Love and Justice" (*FS*, 314–29).

13. These are usually referred to as mimesis$_1$ (prefiguration), mimesis$_2$ (configuration), and mimesis$_3$ (refiguration or transfiguration). Mimesis refers to the

originally Greek (especially Aristotelian) conception of tragedy or narrative as a "mirror" or "imitation" of life.

14. Ricoeur examines this relation between philosophy and biblical hermeneutics in an article included in *From Text to Action* with the title "Philosophical Hermeneutics and Biblical Hermeneutics" (*TA*, 89–101). He acknowledges that biblical hermeneutics is a *regional* hermeneutics, a specific case of the more general philosophical hermeneutics. Yet that does not mean a subordination of the biblical to the theological. Rather, "theological hermeneutics presents features that are so original that the relation is gradually inverted, and theological hermeneutics finally subordinates philosophical hermeneutics to itself as its own organon" (*TA*, 90).

15. See the epilogue "Difficult Forgiveness" in *Memory, History, Forgetting*, trans. Kathleen Blamey and David Pellauer (Chicago: University of Chicago Press, 2004), 457–506.

16. *The Just*, trans. David Pellauer (Chicago: University of Chicago Press, 2000), 144.

17. Simone Ricoeur died on January 7, 1998 of a lingering illness that lasted from about 1996 to 1998. Catherine Goldenstein dates the first manuscript "Up to Death" to 1995 (*LD*, 91–93).

18. Jean Greisch, "Le même, l'autre, le soi: Paul Ricoeur à la recherche d'une herméneutique du soi," *Cahiers Parisiens/Parisian Notebooks*, vol. 3, ed. Robert Morrissey (Paris: Beaudoin, 2007), 26. See also Maureen Junker-Kenny and Peter Kenny, eds., *Memory, Narrativity, Self and the Challenge to Think God: The Reception within Theology of the Recent Work of Paul Ricoeur* (Munster: LIT Verlag, 2004). While this latter text is primarily written by theologians responding to and appropriating Ricoeur's work for theology, several of the contributing authors do indeed challenge some of the demarcating lines Ricoeur draws in his work between the two discourses.

19. In his essay "Conviction, Critique and Christian Theology" Peter Kenny divides Ricoeur's thinking about the relation between the two discourses into three distinct periods, relating to the extent to which Ricoeur felt free to engage in more faith-based concerns (early period of mixed writings, middle period more strictly philosophical in response to criticism, late period after his retirement when he no longer needed to establish his credentials). He helpfully examines many of Ricoeur's own statements about the relation between the two discourses. *Memory, Narrativity, Self,* 92–102.

20. *History and Truth*, trans. Charles A. Kelbley (Evanston, Ill.: Northwestern University Press, 1965, reprinted 2007), 94.

21. The lecture was originally given at the 334th University Conference of All Learning on November 29, 2000.

22. Richard Kearney has developed some of these implications further in *The God Who May Be*.

23. "Hermeneutic of the Idea of Revelation," 1.

5. Jean-Luc Marion: A God of Gift and Charity

1. Dominique Janicaud, *Phenomenology "Wide Open": After the French Debate*, trans. Charles N. Cabral (New York: Fordham University Press, 2005).

2. This is the fundamental argument of my *Reading Jean-Luc Marion: Exceeding Metaphysics*. Although I do not reuse any previously published material in this chapter, much of my presentation here overlaps with arguments I have made in various publications on Marion's work.

3. These remain untranslated to date. (Although a translation of *Ontologie grise* has been announced repeatedly it has so far failed to appear). The titles are explained in the first section of this chapter.

4. See especially his essay on Aquinas ("Aquinas and Onto-theo-logy") and his more recent work *Au Lieu de Soi* [*In the Self's Place*].

5. In the preface to the English translation of *God Without Being*, he replies to the question whether the title "was insinuating that the God 'without being' is not, or does not exist?" He answers: "Let me repeat now the answer I gave then: no, definitely no. God is, exists, and that is the least of things. At issue here is not the possibility of God's attaining to Being, but, quite the opposite, the possibility of Being's attaining to God. With respect to God, is it self-evident that the first question comes down to asking: before anything else, whether he is? . . . with respect to Being, does God have to behave like Hamlet?" (*GWB*, xix–xx).

6. "The Image and the Prototype," *The Crossing of the Visible*, translated by James K. A. Smith (Stanford, Calif.: Stanford University Press, 2004).

7. See, for example, the essay "Metaphysics and Phenomenology: A Relief for Theology" (retranslated as Chapter 3 in *The Visible and the Revealed*).

8. This argument is made especially in *God Without Being*, 40–41, 70–71, and 103–5.

9. See, for example, Ruud Welten, "Saturation and Disappointment: Marion according to Husserl," *International Journal in Philosophy and Theology* 65.1 (2004): 79–96. Janicaud has also argued this repeatedly. More recently, Shane Mackinlay provides a fairly extensive critique of Marion's use of Husserl in his recent book on Marion. See Shane Mackinlay, *Interpreting Excess: Jean-Luc Marion, Saturated Phenomena, and Hermeneutics* (New York: Fordham University Press, 2010), especially Chapter 3.

10. He first outlines the four types of phenomena in this way in *Being Given*. He develops them in much more detail by devoting a separate chapter to each type of saturated phenomenon in *In Excess*.

11. Marion has written extensively on painting and on aesthetics in general. See the first two studies in *The Crossing of the Visible*, the chapter on the idol in *In Excess*, and his more recent article "What Shows Itself" in *Idol Anxiety*, ed. Aaron Tugendhaft (Stanford, Calif.: Stanford University Press, 2011).

12. See especially Chapter 7, "The Banality of Saturation," in *The Visible and the Revealed*.

13. For this, see especially "What Cannot Be Said," retranslated as Chapter 6 in *The Visible and the Revealed*.

14. For a detailed review of the various criticisms, see my *Reading Jean-Luc Marion*.

15. He presented this in detail about many early phenomenological thinkers in his keynote address at the 2009 Steubenville conference on his work: "The Phenomenological Origins of the Concept of Givenness," *Quaestiones Disputatae* 1.1 (2010): 3–18.

16. For the strongest statement see John Caputo's "God is Wholly Other— Almost: Difference and the Hyperbolic Alterity of God," in *The Otherness of God*, ed. Orrin F. Summerrell (Charlottesville: University of Virginia Press, 1998). This is also essentially the line taken by many of Marion's translators, such as Thomas Carlson, Robyn Horner, and James K. A. Smith.

17. See especially his argument in *The God Who May Be*.

18. See especially Chapter 2 of his *Interpreting Excess*. Jean Greisch and Jean Grondin had already criticized Marion's lack of hermeneutics repeatedly in French articles.

19. See Marlène Zarader, "Phenomenality and Transcendence," in James E. Faulconer, ed. *Transcendence in Philosophy and Religion* (Bloomington: Indiana University Press, 2003).

20. I employ these three in particular because they have already been translated in other places and are thus more accessible to the English-speaking audience. The references will indicate the English translations instead of referring to the French originals.

21. "The Phenomenality of the Sacrament—Being and Givenness," in *Words of Life: New Theological Turns in French Phenomenology*, eds. Bruce Ellis Benson and Norman Wirzba (New York: Fordham University Press, 2010), 89–102.

22. "The Invisibility of the Saint," *Critical Inquiry* 35.3 (Spring 2009): 703–10.

23. Most of these articles can be found in *The Visible and the Revealed*, although the article "What Love Knows," which was added as the final chapter to the English translation of *Prolegomena to Charity*, is also important in this context. Marion makes very similar arguments in his most recent work *Le croire pour le voir*. One of the reasons for the reluctance of many of the thinkers discussed to employ the term "Christian philosophy" is the fact that it has a very particular connotation in France, referring to the Thomistic philosophy of such thinkers as Etienne Gilson and others (a tradition with which neither Ricoeur nor Marion want to be linked).

24. He explored this idea in the most detail in the final section of *On Descartes' Metaphysical Prism*, but he refers to it quite often in other texts as well. He makes a similar argument in regard to Augustine in *Au lieu de Soi*.

25. "How to Distinguish Philosophy and Theology Today," Address at the Silverman Lectures, Duquesne University, April 29, 2009; revised as "On the Foundation of the Distinction Between Theology and Philosophy" in *Phenomenology and the Theological Turn: The Twenty-Seventh Annual Symposium of The Simon Silverman Phenomenology Center*, ed. Jeffrey McCurry and Angelle Pryor (Pittsburgh: The Simon Silverman Phenomenology Center, 2012), 48–71.

26. Conclusion of the original Silverman lecture; this passage is not found in the printed text.

27. See especially the final chapter ("What Love Knows") in *Prolegomena to Charity*.

6. Michel Henry: A God of Truth and Life

1. Ruud Welton argues, in fact, that there is an interesting connection between the Marxist and the Christian themes in Henry's writings. See his article "From Marx to Christianity, and Back: Michel Henry's Philosophy of Reality," *International Journal in Philosophy and Theology* 66 (2005): 415–31.

2. Michel Henry, "Quatre principes de la phénoménologie," *Revue de Métaphysique et de morale* 96.1 (1991): 3–26. Page references within the paragraph refer to this text.

3. "Schematically, we have just spoken about what it is to be living and consequently about the nature of the relations between the living in a community inasmuch as the nature of their relations is equally their own nature. These relations are not situated primarily in the world and its representation, putting the laws of this representation and the laws of consciousness into play. Instead, these relations are situated in life, putting the laws of life and its nature into play. In the first place, these are the affects and the forces that life produces. Hence, we can say that every community is essentially affective and based on drives. This holds not only for the fundamental communities of society—the couple and the family—but also for every community in general, whatever its interests and explicit motivation may be" (*MP*, 130–31).

4. "If one must say a word here about the experience of the other, how is each one of the members of the community related to the others in life, prior to being related in a world? This primal experience is barely conceivable, because it escapes every thought. Here the living being is neither for itself nor for the other; it is only a pure experience, without a subject, without a horizon, without a meaning, and without an object. It experiences both itself—the basis (*fond*) of life—and the other, inasmuch as the other likewise has this basis. It thus does experience the other in itself but on this basis, in terms of the other's own experience of this basis. Both the self and the other have a basis in this experience. But neither the self nor the other represents it to themselves. The community is a subterranean affective layer. Each one drinks the same water from this source and this wellspring, which it itself is. But, each one does so without knowledge and without distinguishing between the self, the other, and the basis" (*MP*, 133).

5. See, for example, the introduction to *I Am the Truth* (3–11), especially his discussion of history and texts.

6. For example: "The implementation of that kind of technology carries consequences that are visible everywhere today, to the point that you could say that the modern world is its billboard. Such consequences are necessary to the extent that they merely repeat the presuppositions of a system that extends its reign to the whole planet, sowing desolation and ruin everywhere" (*IT*, 271). I will explore

this criticism in more detail at the end of this chapter. His critique of technology is articulated much more fully in his work *Barbarism*.

7. The book is replete with quotations from the biblical text. Again, Henry basically ignores contemporary biblical scholarship, as he is not really involved in an exegesis of these texts per se. Rather, he employs the texts in order to gain phenomenological insight from them. It is not clear that their theological import or historical accuracy matter to him in any significant fashion. These issues are clearly not what is at stake in his discussion.

8. Henry's work on the artist Kandinsky in his book *Seeing the Invisible* is also significant here and prepares this analysis.

9. This is especially true of his repeated insistence that access to Life and reality is only possible through a "new birth," a conversion-type experience. See, for example: *IT*, 152–70. One should be very careful, however, not simply to identify or conflate Henry's claims about Christ, Christianity, sin, and salvation with traditional Christian understandings of those terms. Henry's interpretation of the Scriptures and of Christian claims more generally is a radically phenomenological reading. He mines the biblical (almost exclusively New Testament) sources for the support of his understanding of phenomenological immediacy and not the other way around. When Henry speaks of the Christian insights as unique and of Christianity as the only path to salvation, it is salvation understood in *his* terms, which are not always necessarily the common theological interpretations of these terms. The most significant aspect of this appropriation is Henry's insistence on radical immediacy. In no sense of the term (at least as generally employed) is God or Christian Life "transcendent" for Henry. Incarnation means complete and utter immanence to the point that, especially in the earlier texts, it becomes difficult for him to articulate any clear distinction between Christ and us. Ultimately, the divine life is radical self-affection and thus at times seems equated with our very feelings and sensations. And yet this is not pantheism, as some commentators have worried. Pantheism identifies God with the world and, for Henry, the distinction between God and the world could not be starker. In some sense, Henry reverses the playing field entirely: It is the world that becomes transcendent and God who becomes immanent. We are separated from the world but totally intimate with God (although we need to realize it). We are alienated from ourselves—lose ourselves—in the lies of the world. We find ourselves, become ourselves, when we live in the truth of God or Life. *Words of Christ* articulates the distinctions between Christ as Arch-Son and Word of Life and us as sons of life much more clearly and more successfully than *I Am the Truth*. For a critique of Henry's notion of incarnation and its theological implications (especially the lack of distinction between individuals and between the divine and the human), see Antonio Calcagno, "The Incarnation, Michel Henry, and the Possibility of an Husserlian-Inspired Transcendental Life," *Heythrop Journal* 45.3 (2004): 290–304.

10. See, for example: *WC*, 117–18.

11. Janicaud was probably the first to launch an extensive and explicit critique of Henry's phenomenology of Life because of its Christian connotations. Janicaud rejects Henry's proposal along with that of Marion in his *Theological Turn* and his *Phenomenology "Wide Open."* In fact, his criticism of Henry increases significantly in the second work (probably because more of Henry's explicitly Christian works had been published at that point, as was true also of Marion). Janicaud accuses both of them of engaging in a maximalist phenomenology that is obsessed with the unapparent and the invisible. This is not what ought to be phenomenology's primary concern. Instead, phenomenology must focus on observable phenomena (which is, of course, exactly what constitutes Henry's most fundamental critique of phenomenology). Several other works, both engaging and criticizing Henry's "Christian" phenomenology, have appeared in France, although none of them are yet translated: Sébastien Laoureux, *L'Immanence à la limite: Recherches sur la phénoménologie de Michel Henry* (Paris: Éditions du Cerf, 2005) and Philippe Capelle, ed. *Phénoménologie et christianisme chez Michel Henry* (Paris: Éditions du Cerf, 2004). The most useful English criticism so far has appeared in the Spring 2009 volume of the *International Journal of Philosophy*, which is devoted to Henry's work, and an edited volume by Jeffrey Hanson and Michael R. Kelly, *Michel Henry: The Affects of Thought* (London: Continuum, 2012).

7. Jean-Louis Chrétien: A God of Speech and Beauty

1. These are the titles of his works that are so far untranslated: *Lueur du secret* [Glow of the Secret] (Herne, 1985); *L'effroi du beau* [The Shock of Beauty] (Cerf, 1987); *L'antiphonaire de la nuit* [The Antiphonary of the Night] (Heren, 1989); *Traversée de l'imminence* [Traversal of Immanence] (Herne, 1989); *La voix nue: Phénoménologie de la promesse* [The Naked Voice: Phenomenology of Promise] (Minuit, 1990); *Loin des premiers fleuves* [Far from the First Rivers] (Différence, 1990); *Parmi les eaux violentes* [Among the Violent Waters] (Mercure de France, 1993); *Effractions brèves* [Short Inbreaking] (Obsidiane, 1995); *De la Fatigue* [About Fatigue] (Minuit, 1996); *Entre flèche et cri* [Between Arrow and Cry/Shout] (Obsidiane, 1998); *Le regard de l'amour* [The Gaze of Love] (Brouwer, 2000); *Joies escarpées* [Steep Joys] (Obsidiane, 2001); *Marthe et Marie* [Martha and Mary] (Brouwer, 2002); *Saint Augustine et les actes de parole* [Saint Augustine and the Acts of Speech] (PUF, 2002); *L'intelligence du feu* [The Knowledge of Fire] (Bayard, 2003); *Promesses furtives* [Furtive Promises] (Minuit, 2004); *Symbolique du Corps* [Symbolism of the Body] (PUF, 2005); *La joie spacieuse* [Spacious Joy] (Minuit, 2007); *Répondre: Figures de la réponse et de la responsabilité* [Responding: Figures of Response and Responsibility] (PUF, 2007); *Sous le regard de la Bible* [Under the Gaze of the Bible; a translation of this work is forthcoming from Fordham University Press] (Bayard, 2008); *Pour reprendre et perdre haleine* [Catching and Losing One's Breath] (Bayard, 2009); *Reconnaissances philosophiques* [Philosophical Acknowledgments; reconnaissance can also mean "recognition" or "gratitude"] (Cerf, 2010).

2. See also somewhat later in the text where he emphasizes this again: "My voice starts by translating. Alterity inhabits it in some irreducible way, including throughout the motion that allows my voice to become its own. In order to incorporate anything at all, one must have a body: not only does voice presuppose this body, it puts it to its proper use as a human body" (*CR*, 78).

3. This link between promise and vulnerability is evident also in other places. It appears frequently in Chrétien's reflections on art and beauty, but also in his more explicitly religious writings. The final chapter of his *Pour reprendre et perdre haleine* focuses specifically on the "wounding" (*blessure*) and vulnerability that are characteristic of the spiritual life. The earlier *Promesses furtives* also reflects on the fragility of promise and speech (including a chapter on "the humanity of tears" and one on the way in which speech is incarnated in the flesh).

4. These pieces were originally given as six lectures at the *Institut catholique* in honor of Etienne Gilson.

5. There are interesting parallels here to an earlier article where he speaks of immortality as something particular to humans. As God cannot be mortal, the notion of immortality makes no sense in relation to God. See Chapter 8 of *Le regard de l'amour*.

6. At the end of the essay, he directs criticism at Michel Henry (without explicitly mentioning him) by rejecting Henry's blanket condemnation of contemporary culture as "barbaric" and insensitive to great works of art. He suggests that rather than dismissing young people as "uncultured," we must carry the promise of art into "the open air" instead of relegating "dead art" to museums. *Reconnaissances philosophiques* (Paris: Cerf, 2010), 204–5.

7. Chrétien examines the relationship between beauty and nature also in an essay on Kant in *Reconnaissances philosophiques* (Chapter 12 of that book).

8. "Wounded, too, is this speech because it attempts to give voice to all the voices that are silent, excluded as they are from prayer by the hollow echoing effect created when they address their individual or collective idols, or by the atrocious plight of the destiny they endure, whose despair does not even become a cry in which they could voice their complaint to God, which itself may be a way of praying" (*AS*, 37).

9. "What is decisive here, in this beauty that we hear and that we welcome within ourselves without seeing, is its character as an event and an advent. Anyone who sees this beauty does not remain untouched by it but is radically transformed and renewed by it. And the very act whereby he discovers this beauty against all appearance is inseparable from the act whereby he himself, against all expectation, becomes beautiful. It starts to give him a form and to reform him wherever he has welcomed its form into himself. What we have here is a beauty that does not keep itself to itself, but gives itself: it is impossible to distinguish in time between the moment when it is grasped and the moment when it gives itself, in other words embellishes us. This is its way of saying adieu" (*AS*, 106).

10. While Marion certainly also speaks of the flesh and of corporeality, he primarily adopts Henry's account and does not connect it as explicitly to the voice or to the language of praise.

11. "There is nothing at all contentious in what the same author writes of philosophy *and* theology, which is the case here" (*UU*, 128).

8. Jean-Yves Lacoste: A God of Liturgy and Parousia

1. A special case of liturgical experience is mystical experience. Not all mystical experience is liturgical, but this experience, in particular, challenges the assumption that philosophical experience is the paradigm for all other experience (*PP*, Chapter 8). Mystical experience goes beyond the basic experience of the world and thus challenges the assumption that experience is only possible in the world and is limited to the present. Lacoste relies on medieval descriptions of mystical experience and other such accounts in the tradition, arguing that they present enough detail about the experience to allow for a phenomenological analysis. This mystical experience is an experience lived "in the mode of beginning" (*PP*, 209). Mystical experience speaks of a type of knowledge that bears witness to the reality of a mystical life in a parallel fashion to the way philosophical experience bears witness to the philosophical life. They are thus not ultimately completely disconnected.

2. In "Presence and Affection," the first article included in *Présence et parousie*, Lacoste analyzes presence as an event linked to the gift, grounding this analysis in the mystery of the Eucharist, which literally means thanksgiving. It is a gift where humans act: "Presence is as such in the act of gift, but in the dramatic proper to that gift, in its liturgy, the human being is always already taken and never spectator" (*PP*, 26). Although liturgy is about things (like bread and wine) and about mortals (the ones who receive), it is neither about objects nor about anything that could be objectively perceived. Presence is about liturgy and gives rise to liturgy. "The time of liturgy is that of a spectacle without spectator" (*PP*, 27). God is also said to be "present" in creation, but even in that liturgy is always present: "In any place where humans want to face God, the gestures of the liturgy (of the *esse coram Deo*) can be posited/posed, and how could one not say that this is also an event of presence?" (*PP*, 27–28). In the final chapter, he again emphasizes that presence has a place in theology, especially in the theology of the Eucharist: "The theology of the Eucharist speaks of presence, but this presence is under the species of absence. The Word speaks today, but it comes to us from yesterday and the 'event of the word' is also an event of remembering, anamnesis" (*PP*, 327).

3. Liturgy is a "remarkable regional experience in which we do not simply engage one characteristic of our being-in-the-world, but its reality in its entirety. It is the symbolic space of definitive existence in the margins of the world, and the subversive space of its inchoation. Of even greater importance, liturgy is the experience that reveals to us most exactly how far away from the eschaton we actually exist . . . One exists liturgically from one's absolute future onward" (*EA*, 72).

4. "Whoever takes the risk of praying does not ask God to bring to perfection a world already nearing completion: the liturgical vigil is not an offertory for the good we have done; it allows us to raise up nothing but empty hands at the hour of the evening sacrifice . . . the first request that must be made of God . . . is for forgiveness. . . . What we are is thus constituted by a twofold distance: a distance in relation to the origin and a distance in relation to the beginning. This twofold distance is what liturgy enables us to traverse" (*EA*, 92–95).

5. "We pray, of course, in order to praise—it is in praise that the prayer manifests its essence in its purity—and praise can pass for the historical image or inchoation of an eschatological practice. But we always pray in the knowledge of the inescapable reality of the world and in the knowledge that it interposes itself between us and a God" (*EA*, 43).

6. Lacoste puts this somewhat humorously: "Because doctors of philosophy have no monopoly over abnegation, those who decide not to exist in the mode of the subject are obviously not required to know the theoretical stakes in their act. But because this gesture is thinkable, doctors of philosophy should not fail to recognize its importance. Abnegation therefore accepts that the Absolute, once man is liturgically turned toward it, takes away its right to embody the figure of humanity afforded him in modernity" (*EA*, 162).

7. "The freely made choice not to possess, or at least to possess less, is more revealing still. It proves that there is no equivocation between the ontological and the economic senses of poverty, that fundamental ontology can be translated into ways of being, into an ethos, and into concrete gestures that break with every kind of divertissement. It thus proves that nonpossession defines man more primitively than does his participation in the play of appropriation. And it proves—in particular—that this more primitive determination can govern the experience we have of ourselves and of the world" (*EA*, 175).

8. "On the other hand, it is not as pure case of *Mitmenschlichkeit* that the liturgical assembly proposes itself, but as image or anticipation of a 'with' which overflows the modest requests inscribed in the 'fact' of the coexistence and the concern for the other considerably. This overflowing can maybe be described in three rubrics: that of a reconciled existence, that of a word liberated from chatter [idle-speaking], that of a community which remains or in any case of its promise" (*PP*, 52).

9. "The Jewish or Christian experience, let's say the biblical experience, is lived in the horizon of public acts of speech; and these acts postulate the affirmability of the true" (*PP*, 95).

10. He relates this to Wittgenstein's theory of language games.

11. *PP*, 137. Similarly, he says in *Experience and the Absolute*: "What is to be thought is given by God, but he first gives us to think that the work of the logos will lead to misunderstandings if it does not enable us to encounter God. Liturgy requires knowledge. But knowledge calls for liturgy" (*EA*, 183).

12. "Returned from the word to silence, from theory to praxis, any equilibrium of fundamental theology is in play here. The question of evil, in fact, is not

that of a region of experience, of an experience that some make and which others do not have, it is rather the obstacle which can forbid any theological discourse, that is to say, to empty it of all credibility. We have certainly no desire to attribute an apologetic function to him who heals rather than speaking—'the works of mercy' do not have as their goal to make a word credibly that the facts perpetually seem to refute. But accomplished from all necessity (we speak of a theology 'reduced to silence' more than a theology deciding to keep silent), they manifest that the only licit theological speech is on the lips of the one who gives more than true words" (*PP*, 175).

9. Emmanuel Falque: A God of Suffering and Resurrection

1. He has made this argument especially in regard to Marion's work. See, for example, his essay "*Lavartus pro Deo*: Jean-Luc Marion's Phenomenology and Theology," in Hart's *Counter-Experiences: Reading Jean-Luc Marion*.

2. *Saint Bonaventure et l'entrée de Dieu en théologie* (Paris: Vrin, 2001). As this is a detailed exploration of Bonaventure, some of which reappears in *Dieu, la chair, et l'autre*, this early work will not be summarized in detail here.

3. For explanation of the curious title, see the discussion of the work in the section on suffering and finitude.

4. He also points out repeatedly that Heidegger's own phenomenological project is deeply grounded in his interactions with medieval texts. See especially *DCA*, 27–30 and 477–78.

5. He previews in a footnote that his next book will be on precisely this topic.

6. He claims that searching for onto-theo-logy in a thinker is like searching for a truly kindred spirit: "the more one looks for it the less one finds it" (*DCA*, 43).

7. Falque is assuming a familiarity with all kinds of theological ideas and doctrines. "Intelligible ideas" refer to the theological assertion that God created the world through his divine Word and that it has a certain rationality because of its grounding in Christ. In fact, much scientific research was driven precisely by a desire to discover these divine ideas, which are the patterns of rationality in the universe and thus at the same time such research is a way of knowing God's mind or design for the world.

8. *Décès* is literally "deceasing" but usually translated as death. Falque is making a distinction between our fear of annihilation and our experience of death. *Angoisse* can mean both anxiety and anguish.

9. Falque does acknowledge in his most recent book that the experience of the flesh was still taken too lightly in the earlier treatment (*NA*, 25). He therefore proposes a deeper and more radical reading in the new treatment (see the full discussion of the book in the section on flesh and animality).

10. These were the three topics discussed in the first three chapters comprising Part I. In general, Falque's books tend to be highly structured with parallel numbers of chapters in parts and frequent relationships between chapters. He does make the reader sufficiently aware of these relationships by providing frequent previews and summaries.

11. The French term *jouissance*, which means enjoyment, has sexual connotations and also denotes the moment of orgasm. It appears fairly prominently in many French thinkers' discussions.

12. Like some of the other French thinkers (for example, Henry and Marion), Falque draws a very firm distinction between humans and all other animals. From an ecological and biological viewpoint, these distinctions seem far too absolute, but unfortunately that is not a criticism that can be explored any further in this context.

13. Falque reiterates this over and over again; he seems very concerned that his account of human animality would not be read as reducing or equating humans to animals because to do so would be "pagan." He seeks to ground this both theologically and philosophically.

14. He examines the kind of language employed for the sacrament of the Eucharist, especially that for transforming the bread into the body of Christ. Again, word and flesh are united.

15. This does not necessarily mean that it succeeds in all points—for example, he claims that the biblical injunction for wives to be submissive to their husbands has no connotation of domination (*NA*, 242). Yet despite some of the problems remaining in his account, he is more or less the only one of the French thinkers discussed here who addresses the issue of gender or sexual difference. Even Marion's account of eros contains no explicit reference to gender or discussion of sexual difference in any form.

16. One should probably point out in this context that Falque's treatment is decidedly heterosexual and seems to make homosexuality impossible, or at least deeply problematic. While he does not explicitly condemn homosexuality, any consideration of it is entirely excluded from his account. It is also interesting (and perhaps problematic) that for him an account of sexual difference can be so self-evidently modeled on Trinitarian relations, although the divine persons are presumably not gendered.

17. In a couple of articles, he has explicitly addressed the question of the relationship between philosophy and theology and suggests that they should not only engage in dialogue, but must influence and transform each other. They cover the same ground and deal with similar topics, but they do so in different ways. Trying to keep them entirely separate is to make each ultimately sterile. See "Philosophie et théologie: nouvelles frontières," *Études* (2006): 201–10 and "Tuilage et conversion de la philosophie par la théologie," in *Philosophie et théologie en dialogue, 1996–2006*, eds. E. Falque and A. Zielinski (Paris: Harmattan, 2005), 45–56.

10. Postmodern Apologetics?

1. John D. Caputo, *Philosophy and Theology* (Nashville: Abingdon Press, 2006), 15.

2. "Fides Quaerens Intellectum: Biblical Antecedents," trans. David Pellauer, in *The Honeycomb of the Word: Interpreting the Primary Testament with André*

LaCocque, ed. W. Dow Edgerton (Chicago: Exploration Press, 2001), 179–208. All page numbers in the next two paragraphs refer to this article.

3. It is the final chapter of *Cartesian Questions: Method and Metaphysics*.

4. Marion has recently returned to this Kantian refutation in much more detail in his "The Question of the Unconditioned" presented as the Greeley Inaugural Lecture at the University of Chicago on November 3, 2011, forthcoming in the January 2013 issue of the *Journal of Religion*. Besides a detailed reading and critique of Kant, Marion suggests that Anselm thinks of God as the "unconditioned." He concludes the lecture by interpreting this notion of the unconditioned as "more intimate to us than we are ourselves and . . . more highly elevated than our greatest excess."

5. More fully: "For 'that than which a greater cannot be thought' (*id quo majus cogitari nequit*) does not define God, even negatively. It does not pretend to grant access to a transcendent term (or being); it simply designates the limit that will be encountered by any possible *cogitatio* when it attempts to think God—in other words, when it attempts to think beyond the maximum limit of the thinkable for a finite thought. Before exposing itself to God, and in order to do so, thought that reaches 'that than which a greater cannot be thought' reaches the limit of its own capacity to know" (*CQ*, 147).

6. "Indeed, God must be: yet this is not an objective or a glory, only a means, which enables one to pray to Him with the full realization that He is the transcendent good and, in this sense, the sovereign good. To be sure, one must know that God is, but only in order to use intelligibly the horizon that, in advance, He has always already opened to the listening mind. The question, even when setting out to demonstrate that the sovereign good exists, does not primarily consist in thinking it in terms of the two alternatives of being or not being; for being does not define or exhaust God's essence, nor can it reach the eminence of the good. Being offers a path, a humbly indispensable path, to the overeminent good of a God who must be loved. Although the question of being also concerns God, God is never circumscribed within the 'question of being,' as a horizon that would precede or predetermine Him. God is, in order simply to give Himself and to receive praise" (*CQ*, 159–60).

7. In regard to Heidegger, he asks: "The absurd subordination of God to Being is the subordination of Life's Truth to the world's. Even worse is the misrecognition of the former as the latter and its exclusive reign. Whether one simply denies it or carries ignorance of Truth to the extreme of absurdly subordinating it to the world's truth is actually of secondary importance. What good is citing the 'sacred,' 'god,' or gods, when one has totally lost the divine essence in its proper and irreducible phenomenality?" (*IT*, 157).

8. Lacoste here contrasts Anselm to the rationality of Scholasticism that excludes praise and prayer from theological discourse (*PD*, 208–9).

9. *Le regard de l'amour* (Paris: Brouwer, 2000), 158.

10. Ibid., 226. There are a couple of other very brief references to Anselm in Chrétien's work, usually to illustrate something he has just said about love

or beauty. To date, Chrétien has not devoted a separate longer treatment to Anselm.

11. Emmanuel Falque, "Anselme de Cantorbéry: Dernier des pères ou premier des scolastiques? Les sources de l'argument," *Revue des sciences philosophiques et théologiques* 91 (2007): 93–108. All page numbers in this paragraph refer to this article.

11. Merold Westphal: Postmodern Faith

1. B. Keith Putt, ed., *Gazing Through a Prism Darkly: Reflections on Merold Westphal's Hermeneutical Epistemology* (New York: Fordham University Press, 2009). See also his enlightening comparison between Westphal's and Caputo's work, "Friends and Strangers / Poets and Rabbis: Negotiating a 'Capuphalian' Philosophy of Religion," presented at the fourth Postmodernism, Culture, and Religion Conference at Syracuse University in April 2011 (and forthcoming in the volume based on that conference). He begins by calling Caputo a "poet" and "friend" and Westphal a "rabbi" and "stranger," but then turns the tables by showing how both also have elements of the other.

2. Westphal consistently spells onto-theology with only one hyphen; hence, this will be the spelling used in this and the following chapter.

3. On this issue, he takes a critical distance from Caputo's interpretations. Westphal often challenges Caputo's condemnation of Gadamer as not sufficiently radical. (For Caputo's position, see the next chapter.)

4. For the fullest articulation of his interpretation of onto-theology, see Chapter 1 (devoted to Heidegger) of *Transcendence and Self-Transcendence*.

5. Westphal is particularly critical of South African apartheid in this book, published before the political change in South Africa. He also draws heavily on liberation theology in the sections on Marx.

6. As with Westphal's expositions of Kierkegaard, I will not summarize his summary of Gadamer's philosophy, but instead highlight the ways in which he appropriates Gadamer's thought.

7. In the conclusion, he makes this point in the following fashion: "To speak of the divine nature of Scripture and of the church as a community built on the foundation of Scripture is to speak of revelation, and to speak of revelation is to speak of divine transcendence. The divine voice is not reducible to the human voices that give us Scripture either by writing it or interpreting it" (*WW*, 149). He concludes that this will enable us to "hear the very voice of God in our finite and fallen interpretations" (*WW*, 156).

8. More exactly, he claims that his audience is two-fold: "my postmodern friends who do not share my faith and my Christian friends who are allergic or even a bit apoplectic when it comes to postmodern philosophy" (*OO*, xxi).

9. In a later essay in the volume, he examines the possibility "that a hermeneutics of finitude will illumine the epistemic meaning of creaturehood, and that a hermeneutics of suspicion will illumine the epistemic significance of sin,

even if developed by those who do not speak the language of Creation and Fall" (*OO*, 178).

10. "It seems to me that the postmodern arguments are about the limits of human understanding and that they support the claim that we do not have access to Truth. But that is different from the claim that there is no Truth, which would be true only if there were no other subject or subjects capable of Truth. But one looks in vain for an argument, even a bad argument, for the claim that the conditions for human understanding are the conditions for any understanding whatever" (*OO*, 86). Westphal stresses human finitude also in his essay on Schleiermacher's hermeneutics.

11. "The deconstructive theory of textuality is, perhaps above all else, an attempt to point toward an overcoming of nihilism that is willing to remain human. To that end it seeks to articulate the coexistence of relativity and critique. In terms of its own critique of finality it can hardly expect to be or be taken to be the last word on this problem. But it is not a theory that Christian cultural theory needs to fear and to demonize" (*OO*, 196).

12. He is clear that calling this the believing *soul* is merely a short-hand way of speaking of human existence, not a denial of embodiment (*GGD*, 90).

13. In many ways, the book's power comes precisely from its descriptive accounts and thus trying to reduce these to a few summative statements necessarily loses much of its message.

14. *Becoming a Self: A Reading of Kierkegaard's* Concluding Unscientific Postscript (West Lafayette, Ind.: Purdue University Press, 1996), ix.

15. Augustine is a favorite thinker for many contemporary writers, possibly due to Derrida's use of him in *Circumfession* and Caputo's heavy extrapolation of this connection.

16. In fact, his early study on *God, Guilt and Death* already illustrated this sense of the ineffable by describing its presence in many religious traditions (especially Chapter 2 of the work).

12. John Caputo: Postmodern Hope

1. See especially the closing pages of *Deconstruction in a Nutshell*. Caputo reiterates this "summary" of deconstruction in many interviews and several other publications.

2. He continues the preceding passage by defining what he means by God's power: "The name of God is powerful, not with the power of brute strength, but with the power of an event. It opens up like an abyss, like a word of abyssal power—which means a groundless ground, not a grounding and foundational one—by means of which it shatters every horizon of representation or imagination, of foreseeability or programmability. But I do not mean this in the fantastic sense, as if God were a super-hero who arrives in the nick of time to save us from the brink of danger by steering the hurricane out to sea and away from populated areas, or by turning back the advancing army of our enemy, or by resuscitating those who are dead" (*WG*, 88).

3. I will provide a fairly thorough summary of this book here as it played an important role in "religious" discussions of Derrida's work and is still Caputo's most well-known work.

4. Of course there are also less religiously inclined commentators of Derrida who find this interpretation unconvincing despite Derrida's apparent endorsement of it.

5. In his work, Caputo typically italicizes *khora* and does not include the diacritical mark. In discussing Caputo and his work in this chapter, I have maintained Caputo's presentation of *khora*.

6. "God is not the possible but the impossible, not the eternal but the futural. To call upon God, to call God's name, to pray and weep and have a passion for God, is to call for the *tout autre*, for something that breaks up the ho-hum homogeneity of the same and all but knocks us dead. The name of God is a name that calls for the other, that calls from the other, the name that the other calls, that calls upon us like Elijah at the door, and that calls for something new" (*PTD*, 113).

7. He acknowledges that this has already been highlighted by several other commentators on Derrida's early work (*PTD*, 232).

8. The following gives a good feel for the (Derridian) tenor of the book: "'Radical hermeneutics' operates a shuttle between Paris and the Black Forest, a delivery service whose function is not to insure an accurate and faithful delivery of messages, like a good metaphysical postmaster (it has its doubts about masters of the post and masters of any sort). Rather, it engages in a creative rereading of the postcards each sends the other, in a repetition that produces something new" (*RH*, 5).

9. *Against Ethics: Contributions to a Poetics of Obligation with Constant Reference to Deconstruction* (Bloomington: Indiana University Press, 1993). I do not examine this book separately as it contains many of the same themes and arguments as some chapters of *Radical Hermeneutics* and *More Radical Hermeneutics* (and indeed others of Caputo's works) and also because it does not address religious questions as explicitly. The book does, however, draw heavily on Kierkegaard, both in style and content. In fact, there is a sense in which the work constitutes a Kierkegaardian reading of Derrida (or maybe a Derridian reading of Kierkegaard). Caputo advocates a "minimalist" ethics of obligation, one characterized by the "anarchy" of the cross instead of metaphysical purity. The book also previews some of his later concern with the event: "Obligations spring up in a void, like grass in the cracks of sidewalks . . . Personal events happen. *Es gibt / il y a /* it gives persons—they, you, we, I—for the while that it gives them, because it gives them, without why . . . Obligation is an operation introduced by life to mend its wounds, to let the links of life form their own spontaneous combinations . . . Flesh flickering under a starless sky; the exultations of flourishing flesh; the cries of joy; the calm cadences of quiet conversations among friends; the quiet repose of solitary thought; the laughter of lovers fading into dark, starless nights. Those are all the stars we have, all the stellar direction we are likely to come upon" (238).

10. This is "a notion of 'reason' which begins by acknowledging the uncircumventable futility involved in trying to nail things down. In the end, I want to say, science, action, art, and religious belief make their way by a free and creative movement whose dynamics baffle the various discourses on method. But I do not treat that as a negative start, as a kind of despair in reason, but as the only really sensible, or reasonable, view of reason. The problem with reason today is that it has become an instrument of discipline, not a mark of freedom, and that, when it is put to work, it is taken out of play" (*RH*, 211).

11. "Religion, accordingly, is fundamentally a defiant gesture. It speaks in the name of life and against the powers that demean and degrade life. It does not arise negatively, from a rejection, but affirmatively, from an affirmation of life, from the momentum and energy of life itself. In this framework, the very idea of 'God' means He who stands always and necessarily on the side of those who suffer, He who intervenes on behalf of the sufferer. Religion has both a fiduciary quality, a certain trust in a loving hand which supports those who suffer, and a defiant quality, which is neither passive nor acceptive of suffering. In the face of suffering, the believer is compelled to think, as one who believes in life and refuses to allow it to be wasted, that God stands with those who suffer, that that indeed is what it means for there to be a God" (*RH*, 280).

12. "But Derrida, who takes a more radical view of democracy, is much more intolerant of this suffering than Fukuyama, intolerant with a prophetic intolerance for *anything* short of letting justice flow like water over the land. *As long as one of the least among us* is homeless or unfed, unjustly imprisoned or exiled, without a school to attend or a home to come home to, there is injustice, and that injustice is intolerable, 'absolutely' or 'infinitely' intolerable, and 'we' are absolutely or 'infinitely responsible,' *here and now*, just in virtue of the justice or democracy to come. That is why Derrida insists that his ideas of singularity and the secret are anything but private, that they are meant to have public and political consequences, consequences for justice, by keeping the political field open, antitotalitarian, and protective of the singular" (*MRH*, 120).

13. For the fullest formulation of this, see his keynote lecture at the fourth Syracuse Postmodernism, Culture and Religion Conference on "The Future of Continental Philosophy of Religion" (April 7–9, 2011) and his forthcoming book *The Insistence of God: A Theology of "Perhaps"* (Bloomington: Indiana University Press, 2013). In this work, he examines the writings of Malabou, Milbank, Žižek, and a new group of critics called "speculative realists" and responds to them. He also carries further his proposal for a theo-poetics in which the name of God stands for the event that calls for our response with its "insistence" (instead of being concerned with God's "existence"). He previews this argument in a response to a piece reflecting on *The Weakness of God*: "I am not saying that God exists but is weaker than we thought. The question of the existence of God for me is the question of the extent to which we are able to make God exist in the world, to make God actual in the world, to make the world a place that has been touched by God, touched by the event that stirs within the name of God. The name of

God is a summons to make God live in the world. The 'death of God' for me would mean that we have entirely failed in this regard, that every trace of God has been erased from the world. One might say that the event belongs to the 'insistence' of God in the world, where we ourselves are called upon to supply God's existence (ex-sistence). We are called upon to supply what is missing in God, to provide the actualization of God in the world, to carry out the translation of the event harbored in his name into actuality. I do not say that God exists but that God insists. I do not say that God is but that God calls. Existence is our responsibility, which is also to say that it is by responding that God exists." *Cross and Khōra: Deconstruction and Christianity in the Work of John D. Caputo*, eds. Marko Zlomislić and Neal DeRoo (Eugene, Oreg.: Pickwick Publications, 2010), 322.

14. In a different context, he also clarifies: "I do not think of this 'pure' faith or 'religion without religion' as a faith that somebody believes, or a religion that somebody can inhabit, or a position that somebody takes, or as a proposition that somebody can propose. I am not an advocate of religious abstractionism or an abstractionist religion. I take this pure *foi* as a ghost, a specter, that haunts us in the sorts of concrete positions—philosophical, political, and religious—that we take, the displacing place (*khōra*) in which they are situated. A religion without religion is not an abstract religion that anyone actually holds . . . but a specter that disturbs the hold our various faiths have on us. . . . That I recommend we not 'leave' the love of God to the theologians and religions now means—here is its spooky sense—do not leave them alone (the theologians and religions), do not let up on them, give them no rest, no leave" (*Cross and Khōra*, 114).

15. "Indeed, were I coerced by the police of orthodoxy into coughing up an argument for the existence of God, I would offer, not a teleological argument, but an ateleological one. I would point to all the disturbances in being and ask, What is the anarchic arche at the heart of all this disorder? And instead of asking whether some intelligent being must not have designed it, I will ask whether something amorous must not have loved it!" (*WG*, 14)

16. "God is the source of good and its warrant. That is the stamp or the seal that God puts on creation; that is God's covenant with us. But God is not the power supply for everything that happens. In the beginning, they are there, and then God made good; that is, God fashioned them and started them out well, but who knows how it will turn out! On the contrary, he very frequently vents his anger at just how many things go wrong and how little influence he has in the world" (*WG*, 73).

17. "When religion becomes a strong force, it becomes consummately dangerous. If you think of God in terms of power, you will be regularly, systematically confounded by—let us say, to put it politely—the unevenness of God's record on behalf of the poor and the oppressed, the irregularity of the help that God gives when my enemy oppresses me. Beyond obfuscation and mystification, it is in the end an outright blasphemy to say that God has some mysterious divine purpose when an innocent child is abducted, raped, and murdered. That is not a mystery but a misconception about God and about the power of God. God's power is

invocative, provocative, and evocative, seductive and educative, luring and allur-
ing, because it is the power of a call, of a word/Word, of an affirmation or promise. That murder is not part of a long-term good, a more mysterious good that we
just can't understand. The murder is a violation of the 'good,' a contradiction of
God's benediction, which strains and stresses God's word, puts it to the test, puts
us to the test. God is not testing us like Job with this murder, but we are all of
us—Job and God, God and God's word, 'good . . . very good'—being put to the
test" (*WG*, 91).

18. He explains the hermeneutical dimension of his project as follows: "Theology is the logos of our passion for God, with or without religion or the churches
or what is ordinarily called theology, the name of God being too important to
leave to the special interest groups. The theological work undertaken here may be
described as a hermeneutics of the name of God, the explication (*Auslegung*) of
what is unfolding in the event of this name, or as a deconstruction, which means
to release the event that is trapped in the name" (*WG*, 101).

19. He links this again to the "passion" for the divine: "My ultimate passion
is the passion of nonknowing, the passion that does not know what stirs its passion, the passion for God, for the unknown God, a prayer for the event that is
harbored in the name of God, which means the passion for God knows what,
the strong passion of weak theology, for which I live unreservedly, for which I
pray day and night" (*WG*, 297).

20. "A politics of the kingdom would be marked by madness of forgiveness,
generosity, mercy, and hospitality . . . the crucified body of Jesus proposes not
that we keep theology out of politics but that we think theology otherwise, by
way of another paradigm, another theology, requiring us to think God otherwise, as a power of powerlessness, as opposed to the theology of omnipotence
that underlies sovereignty" (*WWJD*, 88).

21. James H. Olthuis, ed., *Religion With/Out Religion: The Prayers and Tears of
John D. Caputo* (London/New York: Routledge, 2002), 148.

13. Richard Kearney: Postmodern Charity

1. For some of the differences between Caputo and Kearney, see "Richard
Kearney Scholar Session" in *Philosophy Today* 55 (2011): 56–85, which includes
an article by Caputo on Kearney and a response by Kearney to this piece.

2. Marion actually uses the term ambiguously, sometimes associating the first
reduction with Descartes and the second with phenomenology in general, sometimes calling his own a fourth instead of a third reduction and presenting Lévinas as a third after Husserl and Heidegger.

3. The full quote from Hillesum, which he employs quite often, is: "You
[God] cannot help us, but we must help you and defend Your dwelling place in-
side us to the last." From: Etty Hillesum, *An Interrupted Life* (New York: Owl
Books, 1996), 176. [Reference taken from *GMB*, 2 and 113, note 1.]

4. *After God* is primarily a collection of essays on Kearney's work and responses
to him. Yet it also includes two of Kearney's own articles and an interview with

him about his work in the context of contemporary Continental thought on religion.

5. *Dialogues with Contemporary Thinkers: The Phenomenological Heritage* (Manchester, U.K.: Manchester University Press, 1984). *Debates in Continental Philosophy: Conversations with Contemporary Thinkers* (New York: Fordham University Press, 2004). This latter book includes all of the interviews published in the earlier one, which is now out of print. *After God* also contains several interviews.

6. For example, his *Postnationalist Ireland: Politics, Literature, Philosophy* (London: Routledge, 1996).

7. His novels include *Sam's Fall* and *Angel of Patrick's Hill*. He has also published a volume of poetry entitled *Walking at Sea Level*.

8. The conflation between the extremes of "high" and "low" (divine and monster) must "be addressed by a critical hermeneutics of self-and-other. This, I will argue, calls for a practice of narrative interpretation capable of tracing interconnections between the poles of sameness and strangeness. Faced with the postmodern fixation with inaccessible alterity we need to build paths between the worlds of *autos* and *heteros*. We need to chart a course between the extremes of tautology and heterology. For in this way philosophy might help us to discover the other in our self and our self in the other—without abjuring either" (*SGM*, 10).

9. He outlines his project as follows: "Strangers, gods, and monsters are the central characters of my story. Their favourite haunts are those phantasmal boundaries where maps run out, ships slip moorings and navigators click their compasses shut. No man's land. Land's end. Out there, as the story goes 'where the wild things are.' These figures of Otherness occupy the frontier zone where reason falters and fantasies flourish. Strangers, gods and monsters represent experiences of extremity which bring us to the edge" (*SGM*, 3).

10. "I will argue that what is needed—if we are to engage properly with the human obsession with strangers and enemies—is a critical hermeneutic capable of addressing the dialectic of others and aliens. Such a hermeneutic would have the task of soliciting ethical decisions without rushing to judgement, that is, without succumbing to overhasty acts of binary exclusion. In short, I am suggesting that we need to be able to critically discriminate between different kinds of otherness, while remaining alert to the deconstructive resistance to black and white judgements of Us versus Them. We need, at crucial moments, to discern the other in the alien and the alien in the other" (*SGM*, 67).

11. "Hermeneutics suggests that the other is neither absolutely transcendent nor absolutely immanent, but somewhere between the two. It suggests that, for the most part, others are intimately bound up with selves in ways which constitute ethical relations in their own right. Human discourse involves *someone saying something to someone about something*. It is a matter of one self communicating to another self, recognizing that if there is no perfect symmetry between the two, this does not necessarily mark a total dissymmetry. Not all selves are irreparably sundered or shattered" (*SGM*, 79).

12. At a conference session reviewing and discussing the recent publication of *The God Who May Be*, Kearney said in response to John Caputo: "While Derrida rightly passes for an atheist, I rightly pass for a theist" (Society for Phenomenology and Existential Philosophy, 41st Annual Conference, held in Chicago in October 2002).

13. Like Caputo, Kearney generally does not add the diacritical marks on *khora*. Although his interpretation of *khora* arguably differs from that of Caputo and Derrida, such difference is independent of any distinction in spelling.

14. "Anchorite monks went to the desert to find God, not *khora*. They didn't make a mystery of loss or a virtue of the void. And if it is indeed true that they traversed emptiness and destitution it was *faute de mieux*. An unavoidable detour on the way to grace" (*SGM*, 206).

15. As this notion of the "possible" God suggests, the theme of hope is also very important in Kearney's writings. Yet this is always hope for compassion and justice focused on "the least of these." This is why I suggest that "postmodern charity" is an even more appropriate way to appreciate Kearney's work. (Similarly, Westphal's and Caputo's works also display a commitment to justice and charity, although the themes of faith and hope respectively seem even more central to their writings.)

16. "There is an ethical urgency to eschatological expectation. There is an awareness that if the 'possible advent' indeed comes as unpredictable surprise, like a thief in the night, it always comes through the face of the most vulnerable— the cry of 'the smallest of these,' the widow, the orphaned, the anguished, the hungry, those who ask: 'Where are you?' To reply to this ethical call, it is crucial to be able to say *I am* here. And this *being present* here and now before the summons of the fragile other, requires that the *eschaton* still-to-come already intersects, however enigmatically and epiphanically, with the ontological order of being as loving possible" (*SGM*, 228).

17. "Belief in God as a transcendent alterity does not have to deny that the divine Other may take the form of different others. For just as Being, in Aristotle's formula, manifests itself in diverse ways, is this not also true for God? Faith in an Absolute might best avoid the trap of absolutism—source of so many wars and injustices—by embracing a hermeneutics of religious pluralism. For thus might we endeavour to judge between different kinds of selves and different kinds of others, while avoiding the twin temptations of judgementalism and (its opposite) relativism. A diacritical hermeneutics of discernment, committed to the dialogue of self-and-other, wagers that it is still possible for us to struggle for a greater philosophical understanding of Others and, in so doing, do them more justice" (*SGM*, 232).

18. "For the eschaton is a creative and loving emptying (*kenosis*) which gives space to beings. It is the gap in God incarnate in the littlest of things. The infinitesimal infinite" (*AG*, 9).

19. He defines them very briefly as follows: "*Ana-esthetic* = retrieval of radiance after abjection; *ana-dynamic* = retrieval of the possible after the impossible; *ana-phatic* = retrieval of speech after silence; *ana-physical* = retrieval of the natural after

the supernatural; *ana-ethical*= retrieval of the good after normativity; *ana-choral*= retrieval of divine chora after the abyss; *ana-erotic*= retrieval of desire after desirelessness" (*AG*, 8).

20. In contrast, he thinks that Marion is very much engaged in apologetics, but won't own up to it (*AG*, 366).

21. He calls them "all poetic testimonies to the possible that becomes incarnate in all these little moments of eschatological enfleshment" (*AG*, 374).

22. "Anatheism differs from dogmatic atheism in that it resists absolutist positions *against* the divine, just as it differs from the absolutist positions of dogmatic theism *for* the divine . . . Anatheism is a freedom of belief that precedes the choice between theism and atheism as much as it follows in its wake. The choice of faith is never taken once and for all. It needs to be repeated again and again—every time we speak in the name of God or ask God why he has abandoned us. Anatheism performs a drama of decision whenever humans encounter the stranger who, like Rilke's statue, whispers: 'Change your life!' And every moment is a portal through which this stranger may enter" (*A*, 16).

23. "In the name of a universal openness to any other at all . . . Derrida's 'religion without religion' seems to have no visage to speak of, no embodied presence in space and time . . . here messianicity becomes, arguably, so devoid of any kind of concrete faith in a person or presence (human or divine) that it loses any claim to historical reality. Which leaves me with this question: does deconstructive 'faith' not risk becoming so empty that it loses faith in the here and now altogether?" (*A*, 64, 65).

24. In Kearney's view these "three exemplars of the sacramental" "shared the option for a God of hospitality over a God of power. . . . They each restored, in specific ways, the bond between the sacred and the secular, challenging the tendency to oppose inner and outer, private and public, human and divine. These pioneers did not, I submit, deny a difference between the two poles but lived the productive tension embedded in between. Their lives bore testimony to the incarnation of divinity in the flesh of the world. And, so doing, they resisted God as sovereign in favor of God as guest. For Day this guest was the oppressed urban poor, for Vanier the disabled and wounded, for Gandhi the struggling multitudes of India" (*A*, 165).

Conclusion

1. John D. Caputo, "Hospitality and the Trouble with God," in *Phenomenologies of the Stranger: Between Hostility and Hospitality*, eds. Richard Kearney and Kascha Semonovitch (New York: Fordham University Press, 2011), 83.

For Further Reading

Please note that this is a list (especially designed for students) suggesting further readings in light of the discussions in the chapters and is not meant to serve as a bibliography. (For this reason also only sources in English are listed.)

Introduction: The "Death of God" and the Demise of Natural Theology

Caputo, John. *Philosophy and Theology*. Nashville: Abingdon Press, 2006.

Goodchild, Philip, ed. *Rethinking Philosophy of Religion: Approaches From Continental Philosophy*. New York: Fordham University Press, 2002.

Hart, Kevin. *The Trespass of the Sign: Deconstruction, Theology and Philosophy*. New York: Fordham University Press, 2000 (originally published 1989).

Janicaud, Dominique et al. *Phenomenology and the "Theological Turn": The French Debate*. New York: Fordham University Press, 2000.

Tarnas, Richard. *The Passion of the Western Mind: Understanding the Ideas That Have Shaped Our World View*. New York: Ballantine, 1991.

Vries, Hent de. *Philosophy and the Turn to Religion*. Baltimore: Johns Hopkins University Press, 1999.

1. Martin Heidegger and Onto-theo-logy

Primary Sources

Heidegger, Martin. *Phenomenology of Religious Life*. Translated by Matthias Fritsch and Jennifer Anna Goscetti-Ferencei. Bloomington: Indiana University Press, 2004.

————. *Pathmarks*. Edited by William McNeill. New York: Cambridge University Press, 1998.

————. *Being and Time*. Translated by Joan Stambaugh. Albany, N.Y.: SUNY Press, 1996.

————. *Basic Writings*. Edited by David Farrell Krell. San Francisco: Harper-Collins, 1993.

————. "Only a God Can Save Us: Der Spiegel's Interview with Martin Heidegger." *Philosophy Today* 20 (1976): 267–84.

————. *Identity and Difference*. Translated by Joan Stambaugh. New York: Harper & Row, 1969.

————. *Discourse on Thinking*. Translated by John M. Anderson and E. Hans Freund. New York: Harper & Row, 1966.

Secondary Sources

Caputo, John D. *The Mystical Element in Heidegger's Thought*. New York: Fordham University Press, 1982.

————. "Heidegger's Gods." In *Demythologizing Heidegger*. Bloomington: Indiana University Press, 1993.

Crowe, Benjamin. *Heidegger's Phenomenology of Religion: Realism and Cultural Criticism*. Bloomington: Indiana University Press, 2008.

Crownfield, David R. "The Question of God: Thinking After Heidegger." *Philosophy Today* 40.1 (1996): 47–54.

Gall, Robert S. *Beyond Theism and Atheism: Heidegger's Significance for Religious Thinking*. Dordrecht: Martinus Nijhoff Publishers, 1987.

Godzieba, Anthony J. "Prolegomena to a Catholic Theology of God between Heidegger and Postmodernity." *Heythrop Journal* 40 (1999): 319–39.

Hemming, Laurence Paul. "Heidegger's God." *The Thomist* 62 (1998): 373–418.

Ionescu, Cristina. "The Concept of the Last God in Heidegger's *Beiträge*: Hints towards an Understanding of the Gift of *Sein*." *Studia Phenomenologica* II.1–2 (2002): 59–95.

Kovac, George. *The Question of God in Heidegger's Phenomenology*. Evanston, Ill.: Northwestern University Press, 1990.

Law, David R. "Negative Theology in Heidegger's *Beiträge zur Philosophie*." *International Journal for Philosophy of Religion* 48 (2000): 139–56.

Robbins, Jeffrey W. "The Problem of Ontotheology: Complicating the Divide Between Philosophy and Theology." *Heythrop Journal* (2002): 139–51.

Thomson, Iain. "Ontotheology? Understanding Heidegger's Destruktion of Metaphysics." *International Journal of Philosophical Studies* 8.3 (2000): 297–327.

Vedder, Ben. *Heidegger's Philosophy of Religion: From God to the Gods*. Pittsburgh: Duquesne University Press, 2007.

Vycinas, Vincent. *Earth and God: An Introduction to the Philosophy of Martin Heidegger*. The Hague: Martinus Nijhoff, 1961.

Welte, Bernhard. "God in Heidegger's Thought." *Philosophy Today* 26.1 (1982): 85–100.

2. Emmanuel Lévinas and the Infinite

Primary Sources

Lévinas, Emmanuel. *Humanism of the Other*. Translated by Nidra Poller. Urbana and Chicago: University of Illinois Press, 2006.

———. *God, Death, and Time*. Translated by Bettina Bergo. Stanford, Calif.: Stanford University Press, 2000.

———. *Entre-nous: On Thinking-of-the-Other*. Translated by Michael B. Smith and Barbara Harshav. New York: Columbia University Press, 1998.

———. *Basic Philosophical Writings*. Bloomington: Indiana University Press, 1996.

———. *Time and the Other*. Translated by Richard Cohen. Pittsburgh: Duquesne University Press, 1987.

———. *Ethics and Infinity*. Translated by Richard Cohen. Pittsburgh: Duquesne University Press, 1985.

———. *Otherwise Than Being or Beyond Essence*. Translated by Alphonso Lingis. Pittsburgh: Duquesne University Press, 1981.

———. *Existence and Existents*. Translated by Alphonso Lingis. Pittsburgh: Duquesne University Press, 1978.

———. *Totality and Infinity: An Essay in Exteriority*. Translated by Alphonso Lingis. Pittsburgh: Duquesne University Press, 1969.

Secondary Sources

Bloechl, Jeffrey. *Liturgy of the Neighbor: Emmanuel Levinas and the Religion of Responsibility*. Pittsburgh: Duquesne University Press, 2000.

Bloechl, Jeffrey, ed. *The Face of the Other and the Trace of God: Essays on the Philosophy of Emmanuel Levinas*. New York: Fordham University Press, 2000.

Cohen, Richard A. *Elevations: The Height of the Good in Rosenzweig and Levinas*. Chicago: University of Chicago Press, 1994.

Cohen, Richard A., ed. *Face to Face with Levinas*. Albany, N.Y.: SUNY Press, 1986.

Dudiak, Jeffrey. *The Intrigue of Ethics: A Reading of the Idea of Discourse in the Thought of Emmanuel Levinas*. New York: Fordham University Press, 2001.

Kosky, Jeffrey. *Levinas and the Philosophy of Religion*. Bloomington: Indiana University Press, 2001.

Peperzak, Adriaan, ed. *Ethics as First Philosophy: The Significance of Emmanuel Levinas for Philosophy, Literature and Religion*. New York: Routledge, 1995.

Perpich, Diane. *The Ethics of Emmanuel Levinas*. Stanford, Calif.: Stanford University Press, 2008.

3. Jacques Derrida and "Religion Without Religion"

Primary Sources

Derrida, Jacques. *Acts of Religion*. Edited by Gil Anidjar. London/New York: Routledge, 2002.

———. *On Cosmopolitanism and Forgiveness*. London/New York: Routledge, 2001.

———. *Of Hospitality*. Stanford, Calif.: Stanford University Press, 2000.

———. *Adieu: To Emmanuel Levinas*. Translated by Pascale-Anne Brault and Michael Naas. Stanford, Calif.: Stanford University Press, 1997.

———. *The Gift of Death*. Translated by David Willis. Chicago: University of Chicago Press, 1995.

———. *On the Name*. Edited by Thomas Dutoit. Stanford, Calif.: Stanford University Press, 1995.

———. *Circumfession*. In *Jacques Derrida*, edited by Geoffrey Bennington. Chicago: University of Chicago Press, 1993.

Secondary Sources

Bergo, Bettina, Joseph Cohen, and Raphael Zagury-Orly, eds. *Judeities: Questions for Jacques Derrida*. New York: Fordham University Press, 2007.

Caputo, John D. *The Prayers and Tears of Jacques Derrida*. Bloomington: Indiana University Press, 1997.

Cixous, Hélène. *Derrida as a Young Jewish Saint*. Translated by Beverley Bie Brahic. New York: Columbia University Press, 2004.

Coward, Harold and Toby Foshay, eds. *Derrida and Negative Theology*. Albany, N.Y.: SUNY Press, 1992.

Hart, Kevin. *The Trespass of the Sign: Deconstruction, Theology, and Philosophy*. New York: Fordham University Press, 1989, 2000.

Llewelyn, John. *Margins of Religion: Between Kierkegaard and Derrida*. Bloomington: Indiana University Press, 2009.

Naas, Michael. *Derrida From Now On*. New York: Fordham University Press, 2008 (especially Chapters 1, 3, and 7).

———. *Miracle and Machine: Jacques Derrida and the Two Sources of Religion, Science, and the Media*. New York: Fordham University Press, 2012.

Ofrat, Gideon. *The Jewish Derrida*. Translated by Peretz Kidron. Syracuse: Syracuse University Press, 2001.

Rayment-Pickard, Hugh. *Impossible God: Derrida's Theology*. Burlington, Vt.: Ashgate, 2003.

Saghafi, Kas. *Apparitions—Of Derrida's Other*. New York: Fordham University Press, 2010 (especially Chapters 1–3).

Vries, Hent de. *Philosophy and the Turn to Religion*. Baltimore: Johns Hopkins University Press, 1999.

4. Paul Ricoeur: A God of Poetry and Superabundance

Primary Sources

Ricoeur, Paul. *Living Up to Death*. Translated by David Pellauer. Chicago: University of Chicago Press 2009.

———. *History and Truth*. Translated by Charles Kebley. Evanston, Ill.: Northwestern University Press, 1965, 2007.

———. *Reflections on the Just*. Translated by David Pellauer. Chicago: University of Chicago Press, 2007.

———. *On Translation.* Translated by Eileen Brennan. London/New York: Routledge, 2006.

———. *The Course of Recognition.* Translated by David Pellauer. Chicago: University of Chicago Press, 2005.

———. *Memory, History, Forgetting.* Translated by Kathleen Blamey and David Pellauer. Chicago: University of Chicago Press, 2004.

———. *Thinking Biblically: Exegetical and Hermeneutical Studies* (with André LaCocque). Translated by David Pellauer. Chicago: University of Chicago Press, 1998.

———. *Figuring the Sacred: Religion, Narrative and Imagination.* Edited by Mark I. Wallace. Translated by David Pellauer. Minneapolis: Fortress Press, 1997.

———. *Oneself as Another.* Translated by Kathleen Blamey. Chicago: University of Chicago Press, 1993.

———. *From Text to Action: Essays in Hermeneutics II.* Translated by Kathleen Blamey and John B. Thompson. Evanston, Ill.: Northwestern University Press, 1991.

———. *Critique and Conviction: Conversations with François Azouvi and Marc de Launay.* Translated by Kathleen Blamey. New York: Columbia University Press, 1988.

———. *Fallible Man.* Translated by Charles Kebley. New York: Fordham University Press, 1986.

———. *Time and Narrative.* 3 vols. Translated by Kathleen Blamey and David Pellauer. Chicago: University of Chicago Press, 1984–88.

———. *Essays on Biblical Interpretation.* Edited by Lewis S. Mudge. Philadelphia: Fortress Press, 1980.

———. *Interpretation Theory: Discourse and the Surplus of Meaning.* Fort Worth: Texas Christian University Press, 1976.

———. *The Conflict of Interpretations: Essays in Hermeneutics.* Evanston, Ill.: Northwestern University Press, 1974.

———. *Freud and Philosophy: An Essay on Interpretation.* Translated by Denis Savage. New Haven: Yale University Press, 1970.

———. *The Symbolism of Evil.* Translated by Emerson Buchanan. New York: Harper & Row, 1967.

———. *Freedom and Nature: The Voluntary and the Involuntary.* Translated by Erazim V. Kohak. Evanston, Ill.: Northwestern University Press, 1966.

Secondary Sources

Blundell, Boyd. *Paul Ricoeur between Theology and Philosophy: Detour and Return.* Bloomington: Indiana University Press, 2010.

Evans, Jeanne. *Paul Ricoeur's Hermeneutics of the Imagination.* New York: Peter Lang, 1995.

Fodor, James. *Christian Hermeneutics: Paul Ricoeur and the Refiguring of Theology.* Oxford: Clarendon Press, 1995.

Hahn, Lewis Edwin, ed. *The Philosophy of Paul Ricoeur*. Chicago: Open Court, 1995.

Ihde, Don. *Hermeneutic Phenomenology: The Philosophy of Paul Ricoeur*. Evanston, Ill.: Northwestern University Press, 1971.

Joy, Morny, ed. *Paul Ricoeur and Narrative: Context and Contestation*. Calgary: University of Calgary Press, 1997.

Junker-Kenny, Maureen and Peter Kenny, eds. *Memory, Narrativity, Self and the Challenge to Think God: The Reception within Theology of the Recent Work of Paul Ricoeur*. Münster: LIT Verlag, 2004.

Kaplan, David M., ed. *Reading Ricoeur*. Albany, N.Y.: SUNY Press, 2008.

Kearney, Richard. *On Paul Ricoeur: The Owl of Minerva*. London: Ashgate, 2004.

Pellauer, David. *Ricoeur: A Guide for the Perplexed*. London: Continuum, 2007.

Stiver, Dan R. *Theology After Ricoeur: New Directions in Hermeneutical Theology*. Louisville: Westminster John Knox Press, 2001.

Treanor, Brian and Henry I. Venema, eds. *A Passion for the Possible: Thinking with Paul Ricoeur*. New York: Fordham University Press, 2010.

Vanhoozer, Kevin J. *Biblical Narrative in the Philosophy of Paul Ricoeur: A Study in Hermeneutics and Theology*. Cambridge: Cambridge University Press, 1990.

Van Leeuwen, T. M. *The Surplus of Meaning: Ontology and Eschatology in the Thought of Paul Ricoeur*. Amsterdam: Rodopi, 1981.

Wood, David, ed. *On Paul Ricoeur: Narrative and Interpretation*. London: Routledge, 1991.

5. Jean-Luc Marion: A God of Gift and Charity

Primary Sources

Marion, Jean-Luc. *In the Self's Place: The Approach of Saint Augustine*. Translated by Jeffrey L. Kosky. Stanford, Calif.: Stanford University Press, forthcoming in 2013.

————. *Essential Writings*. Edited by Kevin Hart. New York: Fordham University Press, forthcoming in 2013.

————. *Descartes's Grey Ontology: Cartesian Science and Aristotelian Thought in the Regulae*. Translated by S. Donahue. St. Augustine's Press, 2012.

————. *The Reason of the Gift*. Translated by Stephen E. Lewis. Charlottesville: University of Virginia Press, 2011.

————. "The Phenomenality of the Sacrament." In *The Phenomenological Turn in French Philosophy*. Edited by Bruce Benson and Norman Wirzba. New York: Fordham University Press, 2010.

————. "The Invisibility of the Saint." *Critical Inquiry* 35.3 (2009): 703–10.

————. *The Visible and The Revealed*. Translated by Christina M. Gschwandtner and others. New York: Fordham University Press, 2008.

————. *On the Ego and on God: Further Cartesian Questions*. Translated by Christina M. Gschwandtner. New York: Fordham University Press, 2007.

———. *The Erotic Phenomenon*. Translated by Stephen E. Lewis. Chicago: University of Chicago Press, 2007.

———. "The Impossible for Man—God." In *Transcendence—And Beyond*. Edited by John D. Caputo and Michael S. Scanlon. Bloomington: Indiana University Press, 2007. [Revised version included in *Certitudes négatives*]

———. *The Crossing of the Visible*. Translated by James K. A. Smith. Stanford, Calif.: Stanford University Press, 2004.

———. "Saint Thomas Aquinas and Onto-theo-logy." In *Mystic: Presence and Aporia*. Edited by M. Kessler and C. Sheppard. Chicago: University of Chicago Press, 2003.

———. *In Excess: Studies of Saturated Phenomena*. Translated by Robyn Horner and Vincent Berraud. New York: Fordham University Press, 2002.

———. *Being Given: Toward a Phenomenology of Givenness*. Translated by Jeffrey L. Kosky. Stanford, Calif.: Stanford University Press, 2002.

———. *Prolegomena to Charity*. Translated by Stephen E. Lewis. New York: Fordham University Press, 2002.

———. *The Idol and Distance: Five Studies*. Translated by Thomas A. Carlson. New York: Fordham University Press, 2001.

———. *Cartesian Questions: Method and Metaphysics*. Chicago: University of Chicago Press, 1999.

———. *On Descartes' Metaphysical Prism: The Constitution and the Limits of Onto-theo-logy in Cartesian Thought*. Translated by Jeffrey L. Kosky. Chicago: University of Chicago Press, 1999.

———. *Reduction and Givenness*. Translated by Thomas A. Carlson. Evanston, Ill.: Northwestern University Press, 1998.

———. *God Without Being*. Translated by Thomas A. Carlson. Chicago: University of Chicago Press, 1991.

Secondary Sources

Caputo, John D. "God Is Wholly Other—Almost: 'Difference' and the Hyperbolic Alterity of God." In *The Otherness of God*. Edited by Orrin F. Summerell. Charlottesville: University Press of Virginia, 1998.

———. "How to Avoid Speaking of God: The Violence of Natural Theology." In *Prospects for Natural Theology*. Edited by Eugene Thomas Long. Washington: The Catholic University of America Press, 1992.

———. "The Poetics of the Impossible and the Kingdom of God." In *Rethinking Philosophy of Religion: Approaches from Continental Philosophy*. Edited by Philip Goodchild. New York: Fordham University Press, 2002.

Gschwandtner, Christina M. *Reading Jean-Luc Marion: Exceeding Metaphysics*. Bloomington: Indiana University Press, 2007.

Han, Beatrice. "Transcendence and the Hermeneutic Circle: Some Thoughts on Marion and Heidegger." In *Transcendence in Philosophy and Religion*. Edited by James Faulconer. Bloomington: Indiana University Press, 2003.

Hart, Kevin, ed. *Counter-Experiences: Reading Jean-Luc Marion*. South Bend, Ind.: Notre Dame University Press, 2007.

Horner, Robyn. *Jean-Luc Marion: A Theo-logical Introduction*. Hants: Ashgate, 2005.

———. "The Betrayal of Transcendence." In *Transcendence: Philosophy, Literature, and Theology Approach the Beyond*. Edited by Regina Schwartz. New York/London: Routledge, 2004.

———. *Rethinking God as Gift: Derrida, Marion, and the Limits of Phenomenology*. New York: Fordham University Press, 2001.

Janicaud, Dominique. *Phenomenology "Wide Open": After the French Debate*. Translated by Charles N. Cabral. New York: Fordham University Press, 2005.

Janicaud, Dominique, Jean-François Courtine, Jean-Louis Chrétien, Michel Henry, Jean-Luc Marion, and Paul Ricœur. *Phenomenology and the "Theological Turn": The French Debate*. New York: Fordham University Press, 2000.

Jones, Tamsin. *A Genealogy of Marion's Philosophy of Religion: Apparent Darkness*. Bloomington: Indiana University Press, 2011.

Kosky, Jeffrey L. "Philosophy of Religion and Return to Phenomenology in Jean-Luc Marion: From *God without Being* to *Being Given*." *American Catholic Philosophical Quarterly* 78.4 (2004): 629–47.

Leask, Ian and Eoin Cassidy, eds. *Givenness and God: Questions of Jean-Luc Marion*. New York: Fordham University Press, 2005.

Mackinlay, Shane. *Interpreting Excess: Jean-Luc Marion, Saturated Phenomena, and Hermeneutics*. New York: Fordham University Press, 2010.

Morrow, Derek J. "The Love 'without Being' That Opens (To) Distance, Part One: Exploring the Givenness of the Erotic Phenomenon with Jean-Luc Marion." *Heythrop Journal* 46.3 (2005): 281–98.

———. "The Love 'without Being' That Opens (To) Distance, Part Two: From the Icon of Distance to the Distance of the Icon in Marion's Phenomenology of Love." *Heythrop Journal* 46.4 (2005): 493–511.

Welten, Ruud. "The Paradox of God's Appearance: On Jean-Luc Marion." In *God in France: Eight Contemporary French Thinkers on God*. Edited by Peter Jonkers and Ruud Welten. Leuven: Peeters, 2005.

———. "Saturation and Disappointment: Marion According to Husserl." *Tijdschrift voor Filosofie en Theologie/International Journal in Philosophy and Theology* 65.1 (2004): 79–96.

White, John R., ed. *Selected Papers on the Thought of Jean-Luc Marion. Quaestiones Disputatae* 1.1 (2010).

Zarader, Marlène. "Phenomenality and Transcendence." In *Transcendence in Philosophy and Religion*. Edited by James Faulconer. Bloomington: Indiana University Press, 2003.

6. Michel Henry: A God of Truth and Life
Primary Sources

Henry, Michel. *Words of Christ*. Translated by Christina M. Gschwandtner. Grand Rapids, Mich.: William B. Eerdmans Publishing Company, 2012.

———. *Barbarism*. Translated by Scott Davidson. London: Continuum, 2012.

———. *Material Phenomenology*. Translated by Scott Davidson. New York: Fordham University Press, 2008.

———. *I Am the Truth: Toward a Philosophy of Christianity*. Translated by Susan Emanuel. Stanford, Calif.: Stanford University Press, 2003.

———. "Material Phenomenology and language (or, pathos and language)." *Continental Philosophy Review* 32 (1999): 343–65.

———. *The Essence of Manifestation*. Translated by Girard Etzkorn. The Hague: Nijhoff, 1973.

Secondary Sources

Benson, Bruce Ellis and Norman Wirzba, eds. *Words of Life: New Theological Turns in French Phenomenology*. New York: Fordham University Press, 2010, Part III.

Calcagno, Antonio. "The Incarnation, Michel Henry, and the Possibility of an Husserlian-Inspired Transcendental Life," *Heythrop Journal* 45.3 (2004): 290–304.

Hanson, Jeffrey and Michael R. Kelley, eds. *Michel Henry: The Affects of Thought*. London: Continuum, 2012.

Hart, James G. "Michel Henry's Phenomenological Theology of Life: A Husserlian Reading of *C'est moi, la verité*," *Husserl Studies* 15 (1999): 183–230.

Janicaud, Dominique. *Phenomenology "Wide Open."* New York: Fordham University Press, 2005.

Smith, Jeremy H. "Michel Henry's Phenomenology of Aesthetic Experience and Husserlian Intentionality," *International Journal of Philosophical Studies* 14.2 (2006): 191–219.

Steinbock, Anthony J. "The Problem of Forgetfulness in Michel Henry," *Continental Philosophy Review* 32 (1999): 271–302.

Welten, Ruud. "From Marx to Christianity, and Back: Michel Henry's Philosophy of Reality," *International Journal in Philosophy and Theology* 66 (2005): 415–31.

Zahavi, Dan. "Michel Henry and the phenomenology of the invisible," *Continental Philosophy Review* 32.3 (1999): 223–40.

International Journal of Philosophical Studies 17.1 (2009). [The entire issue is devoted to Michel Henry's work.]

7. Jean-Louis Chrétien: A God of Speech and Beauty
Primary Sources

Chrétien, Jean-Louis. *Under the Gaze of the Bible*. New York: Fordham University Press, forthcoming.

————. *The Ark of Speech*. Translated by Andrew Brown. London: Routledge, 2004.

————. *The Call and the Response*. Translated by Anne A. Davenport. New York: Fordham University Press, 2004.

————. *Hand to Hand: Listening to the Work of Art*. Translated by Stephen E. Lewis. New York: Fordham University Press, 2003.

————. The *Unforgettable and the Unhoped For*. Translated by Jeffrey Bloechl. New York: Fordham University Press, 2002.

Secondary Sources

Benson, Bruce Ellis, and Norman Wirzba, eds. *Words of Life: New Theological Turns in French Phenomenology*. New York: Fordham University Press, 2010, Part IV.

Wirzba, Norman. "The Touch of Humility: An Invitation to Creatureliness." *Modern Theology* 24.2 (2008): 225–44.

8. Jean-Yves Lacoste: A God of Liturgy and Parousia

Primary Sources

Lacoste, Jean-Yves. "The Appearing of the Revealed." In John Milbank and Graham Ward, eds. *Illumination: Essays on Light*. Oxford: Blackwell, forthcoming.

————. "The Appearing and the Irreducible." In *Words of Life: New Theological Turns in French Phenomenology*. Edited by Bruce Ellis Benson and Norman Wirzba. New York: Fordham University Press, 2010: 42–67.

————. "The Phenomenality of Anticipation." In *Not Yet in the Now: Phenomenology and Eschatology*. Edited by Neil DeRoo and John Panteleimon Manoussakis. Farnham, U.K.: Ashgate, 2009.

————. "Perception, Transcendence, and the Experience of God." In *Transcendence and Phenomenology*. Edited by Conor Cunningham and Peter M. Candler Jr. London: SCM Press, 2007: 1–20.

————. *Experience and the Absolute: Disputed Questions on the Humanity of Man*. Translated by Mark Raftery-Skeban. New York: Fordham University Press, 2004.

————. "The Work and the Complement of Appearing." In *Religious Experience and the End of Metaphysics*. Edited by Jeffrey Bloechl. Bloomington: Indiana University Press, 2003: 68–93.

————. "Presence and Affection." In *Sacramental Presence in a Postmodern Context*. Edited by L. Boeve and L. Leijssen. Leuven: Leuven University Press, 2001: 212–31.

————. "Presence and Parousia." In *The Blackwell Companion to Postmodern Theology*. Edited by Graham Ward. Oxford: Oxford University Press, 2001: 394–98.

————. "Liturgy and Coaffection." In *The Experience of God: A Postmodern Response*. Edited by Kevin Hart and Bruce E. Wall. New York: Fordham University Press, 2000: 93–103.

Secondary Sources
Schrijvers, Joeri. *An Introduction to Jean-Yves Lacoste.* Hants: Ashgate, 2012.
————. *Ontotheological Turnings? The Decentering of the Modern Subject in Recent French Phenomenology.* Albany, N.Y.: SUNY, 2012.
————. "Jean-Yves Lacoste: A Phenomenology of Liturgy." *Heythrop Journal* 46 (2005): 314–33.

9. Emmanuel Falque: A God of Suffering and Resurrection
Primary Sources
Falque, Emmanuel. *The Nuptials of the Lamb: A Philosophical Essay on the Body and the Eucharist.* Translated by George Hughes. New York: Fordham University Press, forthcoming.
————. *The Metamorphosis of Finitude: An Essay on Birth and Resurrection.* Translated by George Hughes. New York: Fordham University Press, 2012.
————. "*Lavartus pro Deo*: Jean-Luc Marion's Phenomenology and Theology." In *Counter-Experiences: Reading Jean-Luc Marion.* Edited by Kevin Hart. Notre Dame, Ind.: Notre Dame University Press, 2007.

11. Merold Westphal: Postmodern Faith
Primary Sources
Westphal, Merold. *Whose Community? Which Interpretation? Philosophical Hermeneutics for the Church.* Grand Rapids, Mich.: Baker Academic, 2009.
————. *Levinas and Kierkegaard in Dialogue.* Bloomington: Indiana University Press, 2008.
————. *Transcendence and Self-Transcendence: On God and the Soul.* Bloomington: Indiana University Press, 2004.
————. *Overcoming Onto-Theology: Toward a Postmodern Christian Faith.* New York: Fordham University Press, 2001.
————. *Suspicion and Faith: The Religious Uses of Modern Atheism.* New York: Fordham University Press, 1998.
————. *Becoming a Self: A Reading of Kierkegaard's* Concluding Unscientific Postscript. West Lafayette, Ind.: Purdue University Press, 1996.
————. *Kierkegaard's Critique of Reason and Society.* Macon, Ga.: Mercer University Press, 1987.
————. *God, Guilt, and Death: An Existential Phenomenology of Religion.* Bloomington: Indiana University Press, 1984.

Secondary Sources
Putt, B. Keith, ed. *Gazing Through a Prism Darkly: Reflections on Merold Westphal's Hermeneutical Epistemology.* New York: Fordham University Press, 2009.

12. John Caputo: Postmodern Hope

Primary Sources

Caputo, John D. *What Would Jesus Deconstruct? The Good News of Postmodernism for the Church.* Grand Rapids, Mich.: Baker Academic, 2007.

———. *Philosophy and Theology.* Nashville: Abingdon Press, 2006.

———. *The Weakness of God: A Theology of the Event.* Bloomington: Indiana University Press, 2006.

———. *On Religion.* London/New York: Routledge, 2001.

———. *More Radical Hermeneutics: On Not Knowing Who We Are.* Bloomington: Indiana University Press, 2000.

———. *Deconstruction in a Nutshell: A Conversation with Jacques Derrida.* New York: Fordham University Press, 1997.

———. *The Prayers and Tears of Jacques Derrida: Religion Without Religion.* Bloomington: Indiana University Press, 1997.

———. *Against Ethics: Contributions to a Poetics of Obligation with Constant Reference to Deconstruction.* Bloomington: Indiana University Press, 1993.

———. *Demythologizing Heidegger.* Bloomington: Indiana University Press, 1993.

———. *Radical Hermeneutics: Repetition, Deconstruction, and the Hermeneutic Project.* Bloomington: Indiana University Press, 1987.

———. *Heidegger and Aquinas: An Essay on Overcoming Metaphysics.* New York: Fordham University Press, 1982.

———. *The Mystical Element in Heidegger's Thought.* Athens, Ohio: Ohio University Press, 1978.

Secondary Sources

Martinez, Roy, ed. *The Very Idea of Radical Hermeneutics.* New Jersey: Humanities Press, 1997.

Olthuis, James H., ed. *Religion With/Out Religion: The Prayers and Tears of John D. Caputo.* London/New York: Routledge, 2002.

Simpson, Christopher Ben. *Religion, Metaphysics, and the Postmodern: William Desmond and John D. Caputo.* Bloomington: Indiana University Press, 2009.

Zlomislić, Marko and Neil DeRoo, eds. *Cross and Khōra: Deconstruction and Christianity in the Work of John D. Caputo.* Eugene, Oreg.: Pickwick Publications, 2010.

13. Richard Kearney: Postmodern Charity

Primary Sources

Kearney, Richard. *Anatheism: Returning to God After God.* New York: Columbia University Press, 2010.

———. *Dialogues with Contemporary Thinkers: The Phenomenological Heritage.* Manchester, U.K.: Manchester University Press, 1984. Reprinted with other texts in *Debates in Continental Philosophy: Conversations with Contemporary Thinkers.* New York: Fordham University Press, 2004.

————. *Strangers, Gods and Monsters: Interpreting Otherness*. London: Routledge, 2003.

————. *The God Who May Be: A Hermeneutics of Religion*. Bloomington: Indiana University Press, 2001.

————. *On Stories*. London: Routledge, 1999.

————. *Poetics of Imagining: Modern to Post-Modern*. New York: Fordham University Press, 1998.

————. *The Wake of Imagination*. London: Routledge, 1998.

Secondary Sources

Burke, Patrick. "Kearney's Other: The Shadow." *Philosophy Today* 55 (2011): 65–74.

Caputo, John D. "God, Perhaps: The Diacritical Hermeneutics of God in the Work of Richard Kearney." *Philosophy Today* 55 (2011): 56–64.

Manoussakis, John Panteleimon, ed. *After God: Richard Kearney and the Religious Turn in Continental Philosophy*. New York: Fordham University Press, 2006.

————. "From Exodus to Eschaton: On the God Who May Be." *Modern Theology* 18.1 (2002): 95–107.

Index

beauty (cont.)
156; of painting, 143, 145, 160; of universe, 8; of the visible, 157; of the world, 147, 157. *See also* aesthetic *and* art

Being, xix, 19–21, 27, 28, 29, 30, 31, 32, 36, 41, 51, 52, 53, 57, 61, 62–63, 89, 92, 107, 111, 115, 126, 150, 163, 164, 175, 183, 192, 206, 213, 215, 216, 244–47, 269, 273, 278, 301n12, 307n5, 317n6, 317n7, 325n17; as such, 21, 22, 28, 112, 115, 246; at-the-limit, 174; before-God, xxi, 24, 163, 165, 167–68, 171, 177, 180, 183, 292; being-present, 60; of beings, 21, 27, 28, 29, 34, 87, 107, 108, 298n2; call of, 149, 245; disclosure of, 32, 57; ethics better than, 43, 55; forgetting of, 27, 204; God not contaminated by, 50, 57; God without, 63, 105, 106, 109–11, 115, 119, 188, 215, 299n9, 301n24, 307n5; good beyond, 55, 57, 61–63, 78, 248; ground of, 29–30, 107, 134; human, 12, 20, 22, 31, 32, 34, 35, 37, 42, 56, 57, 100, 108, 131, 136, 139, 147, 163, 170, 175, 176, 180, 191, 192, 194, 195, 198, 200, 203, 204, 207, 235, 240, 246, 289, 297n20, 313n2; in-the-world, xxi, 22, 26, 31, 38, 89, 91, 131, 132, 134, 163, 167, 169, 171, 173, 175, 176, 177, 178, 186, 199, 245, 289, 313n3; language of, 110; liturgical, 168–69, 171, 173, 174, 178, 181; meaning of, 20; meditative, 32–33; mode of, 20, 21, 22, 24, 163, 167, 171, 173, 178, 188, 196, 314n7; mystery of, 33; myth of, 244, 246; phenomenality of, 115; question of, 30, 34, 57, 244–45, 317n6; region of, 23; supreme, 3, 20, 21, 27, 28, 29, 34, 35, 60, 107, 110–11, 212, 215, 240, 298n2; thinking of, 37, 246; toward death, 26, 69, 171, 172–73, 175, 177, 192; truth of, 34; with-others, 177–78, 190. *See also* Dasein
beingness, 27, 113. *See also* Being
belief, xvii, 2, 5, 10, 12, 50, 78, 87, 88, 100–1, 141, 199, 207, 213, 217, 219, 261, 272, 281, 283, 285, 305n5; blind, 139; Christian, xix, xxiii, 8, 12; criticism of, 228; in democracy, 80; freedom of, 326n22; in God, 5, 10, 54, 197, 219, 274, 297n20, 325n17; Jewish, xix; about reality, 254; religious, xx, 2, 8, 38, 54, 100, 101, 141, 183, 224, 289, 321n10; suspension of, 197, 283; system, 12, 298n25. *See also* faith
Bible, 9, 88, 93, 102, 147, 211, 227, 305n9, 311n1
birth, 56, 98, 132, 134, 196, 199, 200, 207; as finitude, 203; of the flesh, 207; of God, 189; joy of, 199; new, 131, 196, 199, 310n9; physical, 132, 196; second, 135. *See also* rebirth
body, xxi, 44, 119, 126, 128, 131–33, 143, 145, 148, 150, 154–55, 170, 176, 178, 179, 191, 195, 197, 199–206, 260, 311n1, 312n2; of

Christ, 133, 138–39, 150, 154, 176, 190, 199, 202–6, 316n14; crucified, 323n20; ecclesial, 190, 199; eucharistic, 202–6, 283; experience of the, 170, 195, 204; flesh and, 160, 199, 201, 205–6; human, 5, 14, 176, 283, 312n2; laboring, 127; materiality of the, 131, 154, 202, 204–5; mystical, 133–34, 139, 150, 154, 206; resurrected, 197, 207; self-affection of the, 140; and soul, 149, 155, 161, 167, 177, 201; symbolism of the, 154; and touch, 154
Boethius, 2, 218, 296n5
Bonaventure, 184, 189, 199, 200–1, 315n2
breath, 67, 146, 311n1; of the body, 204; of space, 9

call, xxi, 24, 44, 51, 68, 81, 91, 143, 144; 145–54, 155–59, 210, 218, 236, 238, 246, 255, 259–60, 277, 279, 282, 289, 301n22, 301n23, 320n6, 321n13, 323n17; of beauty, 149, 156–57; of being, 245–46; of Christ, 91, 275; of conscience, 73; for discernment, 65, 273; and election, 56; of God, 149, 156, 175, 286; for the impossible, 247; for justice, 68, 243, 255, 260, 262, 274; of the other, 45, 47, 54, 58, 160, 162, 247, 320n6; for peace, 80; to responsibility, 49, 52, 149, 238, 254, 325n16; for universality, 80. *See also* appeal *and* response
Caputo, John D., xxii, xxv, 11, 36, 37, 59, 60, 65, 66, 67, 68, 82, 117, 136, 212, 213, 217, 225, 240, 242–64, 265, 266, 268, 272–76, 287, 288, 290, 292, 298n27, 299n14, 300n16, 302n3, 302n4, 303n16, 303n18, 308n16, 316n1, 318n1, 318n3, 319n15, 319n1–323n21, 323n1, 325n12, 325n13, 325n15, 326n1
Cartesian, 39, 51, 105, 106–8, 115–16, 117–18, 122, 127, 161, 191, 213, 252, 317n3. *See also* Descartes, René
Catholic, 4, 75, 103, 105, 117, 202, 206, 207, 230, 241, 243, 246, 263, 266, 267, 280, 304n2
causa sui, 20, 28–30, 107, 109
certainty, 12, 69, 72, 107, 116, 181, 210, 225, 233, 252, 254, 264; of existence, 116; language of, 210, 219; negative, 106, 116, 118; of the sciences, 122; truth as, 101–2, 211, 254
charity, xxii, 44, 105, 121, 122, 210, 242, 265, 266, 275, 286, 325n15. *See also* love
Chrétien, Jean-Louis, xxi, 24, 32, 33, 35, 40, 58, 60, 82, 136, 143–62, 163, 177, 184, 201, 202, 210, 211, 212, 218, 243, 265, 289, 291, 304n3, 311n1–313n11, 318n10
Christ, xx, 2, 9, 91, 95, 119, 120, 128–31, 132–35, 141, 145, 150, 152, 190–98, 200, 202, 204, 205, 207, 211, 275, 276, 281, 310n9, 315n7; body of, 154, 176, 190, 199,

202–6, 316n14; flesh of, 190, 198, 200–1, 204; hands of, 153; words of, 136–39, 142. *See also* Jesus

Christian, xviii, xix, xxii, xxiii, 1–10, 12, 20, 22–28, 36–38, 40, 44, 61, 62, 64, 67, 70, 73, 77, 82, 85, 86, 88, 91–95, 98, 100, 104, 117, 122, 125, 128, 133, 136, 139–41, 143, 147, 152, 153, 154, 160, 162, 189, 192, 196, 197, 200, 201, 219, 223, 227, 229–31, 237, 238, 246, 247, 249, 250, 263, 266, 267, 269, 270, 272, 280, 282, 295n2, 297n22, 309n1, 310n9, 311n11, 318n8, 319n11; domesticity, 79; eschatology, 193; ethic, 135, 274; experience, 25–27, 122, 129, 139, 160, 161, 162, 179, 314n9; faith, xviii, xxii, 1, 2–6, 12, 28, 36, 38, 40, 79, 98, 118, 121, 122, 123, 145, 162, 186, 207, 219, 223, 224–25, 229, 230, 241, 243, 295n1, 295n2, 295n3; fundamentalism, 298n31; God, 237, 274; hope, 194; hospitality, 270; imagery, 143, 162; mysticism, 143; phenomenology, 128, 211; philosophy, 23, 62, 95, 121, 123, 308n23; revelation, 153; self, 232; theology, 128, 240, 306n19; tradition, 98, 154, 160, 163, 175, 212, 235, 236, 272, 273; truth, 129–30. *See also* Christ *and* Christianity

Christianity, xvii, xviii, xx, xxiii, 2, 10, 33, 37, 68–70, 73, 78, 81, 85, 86, 93, 104, 121, 122, 125, 128–31, 135–37, 139–42, 197, 206, 211–12, 216, 223, 227, 231, 246, 275, 283, 289, 290, 295n2, 297n24, 310n9. *See also* Christian

Christianness, 22

circumcision, 66, 247–51

communion, 110, 178, 195, 268; mystical, 284; of saints, 190, 199. *See also* Eucharist

community, 65, 80, 88, 95, 97, 100, 101, 102, 119, 128, 176, 180, 181, 191, 230, 241, 309n3, 309n4, 314n8, 318n7; of animals, 204; of bodies, 205; Christian, 243; of faith, 88, 90; Jewish, 40; phenomenology of, 127–28, 188–92; religious, 14, 24, 92, 98, 154

compassion, 48, 77, 94, 99, 148, 181, 190, 198, 227, 228, 232, 247, 255, 262, 272, 274, 275, 281, 284, 286, 325n15

confession, 66–67, 101, 116, 173, 181, 190, 224, 247, 250, 270; of faith, 218; religious, 68, 263, 300n2, 300n3

consciousness, 11, 13, 14, 16, 41–43, 56–57, 112–13, 126–27, 131, 132, 138, 164–65, 174, 177, 178, 180, 191, 193, 195, 198, 203–4, 217, 226, 234, 269, 309n3

conviction, 93, 95–98, 101, 285, 289

corporeality, xxi, 24, 144, 151, 154, 162, 170, 176, 184, 189, 190, 195, 197, 199, 313n10; angelic, 191; Christ's, 206. *See also* body *and* flesh

correspondence, 31, 141, 211, 231; truth as, 31, 101

creativity, 32, 33, 204, 219, 254, 292. *See also* art

cross, 110, 119, 153, 194, 196; anarchy of the, 320n9; theology of the, 259

Dasein, 20, 22, 23, 25, 26, 31, 34, 35, 38, 40, 45, 57, 62, 69, 126, 131, 163, 167, 172, 173, 177, 190, 197, 253

death, 31, 41, 47, 63, 66, 67, 68, 69, 70, 76, 80, 94–95, 99, 100, 104, 120, 140, 172–73, 175, 177, 184, 189, 192–96, 199, 200, 203, 234, 251, 257, 261, 264, 282, 283, 284, 289, 290, 292, 315n8; being toward, 26, 69, 171–73, 175, 177, 192; gift of, 69–71, 80–81; of God, 1, 9, 30, 34, 78, 110–11, 197, 283, 322n13; guilt and, 233–35, 290; life beyond, 285; of the other, 47, 94, 193

deconstruction, xviii, 10, 30, 59, 63, 81, 232, 240, 242, 244, 247–50, 251, 252, 255–57, 259–60, 262, 272, 273, 276, 319n1, 323n18

deferral, 60, 61, 63, 65, 68, 290, 302n8. See also *différance*

democracy, 65, 68, 78–80, 81, 291, 321n12; to come, 248, 255. *See also* globalatinization

demonic, 63, 68–69, 226, 291, 292

Derrida, Jacques, xix–xx, xxii, xxiii, xxv, 10, 13, 14, 37, 40, 46–47, 56, 59–82, 85, 95, 111, 115, 136, 189, 203, 224, 225, 230–32, 240, 242–44, 247–59, 261, 263, 265, 266, 267, 268, 271, 272–73, 274, 276, 281, 282, 287, 288, 291, 293, 298n27, 300n11, 301n12, 301n1–304n24, 319n15, 320n3–320n9, 321n12, 325n12, 325n13, 326n23

Descartes, René, 6, 10, 45, 52, 53, 105–9, 115, 116, 133, 137, 212, 214–15, 216, 297n15, 298n2, 323n2. *See also* Cartesian

desire, 8, 51, 54–55, 65, 68, 93, 94, 116, 130, 137, 140, 141, 172, 176, 177, 186, 205, 213, 215, 226, 230, 235, 242, 261, 262, 266, 276, 282, 326n19; for communion, 178; for the divine, 63, 168, 251, 257, 264; erotic, 205, 257; for happiness, 234; for the impossible, 248, 257, 258; for the infinite, 51–52; for the parousia, 170, 172; for the secret, 73. *See also* passion

detachment, 188–89

diachrony, 43, 53, 172, 288

différance, xx, 60–61, 65, 263, 272

Dionysius, 3, 9, 62, 108, 111, 187, 238, 240

discernment, 65, 273, 279, 282, 285, 325n17

divine, xvii, xx, xxii, xxiii, 5, 6, 7, 8, 12, 15, 22, 24, 28, 30, 34, 35, 38, 49, 50–55, 58, 62, 63–65, 68, 69, 70, 81, 82, 92, 104, 109, 110, 111, 114, 115, 116, 117, 120, 123, 126, 135, 136, 141, 143, 151, 153, 155, 156, 158, 165, 167, 168, 170, 172, 174, 176, 180–82, 187, 188, 189, 190, 198, 200, 203, 204, 205,

gratitude, 35, 147, 156–57, 311*n*1
ground. *See* grounding
grounding, 20–21, 28–30, 33, 35, 69, 77,
    100, 101, 107, 137–38, 169, 175, 188, 189,
    236, 319*n*2; of being, 28–30, 107, 134,
    298*n*2; in a highest being, 20, 107; in
    revelation, 22; of truth, 10; of values, 10,
    30, 34, 111
guilt, 23, 45, 47, 58, 70, 86, 100, 226, 228,
    233–35, 237, 290

heart, xx, 33, 122, 123, 135, 138, 141, 178,
    210, 211, 245, 280, 282
Hegel, Georg Wilhelm Friedrich, 27, 28, 152,
    168, 224, 225, 230, 235, 238, 239–40, 250,
    268, 293, 303*n*20
Heidegger, Martin, xix, xx, xxi, xxii, xxiii, 14,
    15, 19–38, 39, 40, 41, 45, 47, 56, 57, 61,
    62–63, 69, 70, 105, 106, 107, 111, 112, 113,
    117, 126, 129, 131, 133, 134, 139, 149, 160,
    163, 164, 165, 167, 170, 171–73, 176,
    177–78, 183, 185, 187–89, 190, 191, 192,
    193, 194, 195, 196, 197, 202, 204, 210, 215,
    217, 225, 230, 231, 232, 237, 238, 239, 242,
    244–47, 251, 252, 253–55, 263, 265, 266,
    273–74, 276, 278, 287, 292, 298*n*1–300*n*16,
    300*n*4, 300*n*7, 302*n*5, 315*n*4, 317*n*7, 318*n*4,
    323*n*2
Henry, Michel, xx, 13, 14, 15, 24, 33, 40,
    56, 58, 82, 103, 105, 106, 112, 125–42,
    143, 146, 154, 164, 188, 189, 195, 202,
    204, 211, 216–17, 219, 265, 289, 290, 291,
    304*n*3, 309*n*1–311*n*11, 312*n*6, 313*n*10,
    316*n*11
hermeneutic circle, 15, 38, 87, 88, 97. *See also*
    hermeneutics
hermeneutics, xviii, xix, xxii, xxiii, 9, 13–15,
    25, 31, 33, 65, 77, 85–89, 93, 103, 117, 123,
    172, 182, 210, 223, 224, 225, 227, 230–31,
    252–56, 258, 260, 262, 265–68, 270–71,
    275, 276, 279–80, 282, 285, 286, 306*n*14,
    308*n*18, 319*n*10, 323*n*18, 324*n*8, 324*n*10,
    324*n*11, 325*n*17; absolute, 256; of adhesion,
    99; biblical, 85, 92, 96, 102, 305*n*4, 305*n*10,
    306*n*14; cold, 251, 254; devilish, 252, 256;
    diacritical, 268, 271, 325*n*17; of the
    Eucharist, 119, 256; of the event, 259; of
    facticity, 25, 31, 245; of finitude, 231;
    radical, 232, 242, 251–56, 320*n*8; religious,
    xx; of the self, 96; of suspicion, 102, 225,
    226, 228, 231, 283, 318*n*9. *See also*
    hermeneutic circle
Hölderlin, Friedrich, 37, 111, 245
holiness, 51, 56, 78, 120, 281. *See also* glory
hope, xxi, xxii, 35, 59, 68, 76, 81, 89, 90, 100,
    152–53, 160, 171, 182, 194, 233, 235,
    242–43, 250, 251, 255, 257–64, 274, 275,
    289, 290, 292, 325*n*15; of resurrection, 193.
    See also promise

hospitality, xx, xxii, 64, 65, 68, 71, 74–77, 81,
    82, 98, 101, 144, 146, 148, 159, 162, 177,
    242, 248, 255, 260, 261, 262, 263, 264,
    266, 268, 269–72, 274, 278, 279, 281–82,
    284–86, 288, 290, 291, 323*n*20, 326*n*24
hostage, 45, 48, 51, 52, 58, 74, 75, 76, 271,
    288
hostipitality, 75, 303*n*19. *See also* hospitality
Husserl, Edmund, 13–14, 39, 40–41, 44, 56,
    57, 105, 112–13, 117, 127, 129, 133, 137,
    139, 154, 165, 167, 177, 180, 183, 188, 189,
    190, 191, 195, 201, 252–53, 266, 276, 278,
    298*n*33, 307*n*9, 323*n*2

icon, 88, 106, 109–10, 111, 119, 120, 178, 211
idol, 35, 106, 109–11, 140, 256, 307*n*11,
    312*n*8. *See also* idolatry
idolatry, xx, 73, 88, 109–11, 119, 120, 153,
    227, 238. *See also* idol
il y a, 41, 43, 300*n*4, 320*n*9
illeity, 50, 54, 301*n*22. *See also* third
immanence, xx, 126, 174, 193, 197, 198, 211,
    310*n*9; of the flesh, 154
immemorial, 135, 144, 150, 152
impossible, 54, 64, 73, 74, 75, 76, 81, 116,
    146, 215, 243, 247, 248, 249, 251, 258, 260,
    261, 263, 285, 288, 290, 320*n*6, 325*n*19;
    promise of the, 77, 259; encounter with the,
    157; desire for the, 248, 257, 290
incarnation, xxii, 5, 12, 67, 133, 136, 138, 148,
    153, 154, 160, 185, 186, 187, 188, 189, 191,
    195, 196, 197, 198, 200, 201, 203–4, 205,
    240, 250, 310*n*9, 312*n*3, 325*n*18, 326*n*21,
    326*n*24
individuation, 191–92, 205
infinite, xix, 9, 30, 49–56, 71–74, 76, 79, 98,
    109, 116, 138, 149, 150, 249, 279, 283, 288,
    290, 292, 301*n*20, 301*n*22, 325*n*18; desire
    for the, 52, 140; difference, 43, 261;
    generosity, 48; glory of the, 49, 53; idea of
    the, 51–52, 107; testimony to the, 52, 53,
    149; trace of the, 53
intention, 14, 56, 112, 113, 177, 189. *See also*
    intentionality *and* intuition
intentionality, 14, 41, 44, 58, 127, 128, 189,
    202, 206, 253. *See also* intention
intuition, 14, 41, 56, 112–15, 166, 256, 279
invisible, 29, 32, 72, 73, 109, 117, 119, 120–21,
    122, 126, 127, 130, 131, 132, 135, 137, 166,
    284, 289, 311*n*11. *See also* visible *and* unseen
ipseity, 77, 132, 134, 150. *See also* self
Irenaeus, 133, 189, 199, 200–1, 295*n*2

Janicaud, Dominique, 12–13, 19, 30, 49, 106,
    117, 118, 142, 157, 160, 298*n*1, 304*n*3,
    307*n*9, 311*n*11
Jankélévitch, Vladimir, 73–74
Jesus, 36, 91, 95, 179, 193, 228, 250, 260,
    262–63, 302*n*8, 323*n*20. *See also* Christ

Luther, Martin, 26, 237, 246, 300*n*16
Lyotard, Jean-François, 10, 244, 268, 271

manifestation, 20, 23, 33, 38, 57, 62, 71, 88,
    127–29, 145, 158, 172, 178, 182, 185, 189,
    199, 219, 280, 305*n*7; of Being, 20, 245; of
    the flesh, 200; of God, 51, 182, 188, 269; of
    the Sacred, 234; truth as, xx, 33, 89, 90,
    102, 129, 210. *See also* revelation *and*
    aletheia
Marion, Jean-Luc, xx, xxiii, 13, 21, 24, 30, 30,
    32, 33, 35, 40, 56, 57, 58, 59, 60, 65, 68, 82,
    92, 94, 103, 105–24, 125, 126, 136, 160,
    166, 176, 180, 182, 183, 184, 185, 187, 192,
    195, 197, 199, 201, 202, 203, 204, 205, 209,
    210, 211, 214–16, 217, 219, 224, 238, 243,
    256, 265–66, 267, 274, 278, 288, 289, 290,
    291, 297*n*15, 298*n*2, 299*n*9, 301*n*16,
    301*n*24, 303*n*10, 303*n*11, 304*n*3, 307*n*1–
    309*n*27, 311*n*11, 313*n*10, 315*n*1, 316*n*12,15,
    317*n*4, 323*n*2, 326*n*20
Marx, Karl, 8, 87, 125, 224, 225, 226–28, 232,
    237, 309*n*1, 318*n*5
me voici, 45, 49, 150–51, 301*n*22
memory, xxi, 25, 94, 99, 143, 152–53, 160,
    178, 206, 261, 271, 277, 300*n*2. *See also*
    immemorial
Merleau-Ponty, Maurice, 13, 14, 133, 139, 197,
    198, 201, 232, 283
Messiah, 59, 68, 69, 75, 76, 81, 136, 139, 247,
    248, 249–50, 255, 258, 261, 264, 276, 282,
    291, 326*n*23
messianic. *See* Messiah
messianicity. *See* Messiah
messianism. *See* Messiah
metaphysics, 6, 10, 20, 28–30, 34, 64, 92,
    106–8, 109, 115, 117, 120, 121, 122,
    186–87, 193, 215, 218, 239, 240, 252, 253,
    276, 284, 300*n*7, 320*n*8, 320*n*9; in
    Descartes, 106–8, 115; and God, 37, 111,
    187, 192, 216; history of, 20, 21, 29, 30, 215,
    245; nature of, 20, 28, 244; as onto-theo-
    logy, xix, 20, 22, 27–30, 31, 35, 38, 57,
    107–8, 239, 244; overcoming of, 20, 30, 46,
    106–8, 111, 115, 160, 187, 252, 254; of
    presence, 253; of representation, 127
Moltmann, Jürgen, 198
morality, 7, 10, 48, 56, 71–73, 102, 147, 228,
    239, 252, 274, 282, 291; and accountability,
    226; foundation for, 297*n*17; and God, 110,
    111, 293; religion and, 9, 78, 92, 99, 285.
    See also ethics
mysterium tremendum, 69, 70, 234
mystery, 70, 149, 176, 178, 180, 240,
    269, 322*n*17, 325*n*14; of Being, 33; cult, 2;
    demonic, 69; divine, 233, 238–41; of the
    Eucharist, xxi, 176, 205, 313*n*2; of faith,
    187, 225; of the sacred, 68; of the universe,
    6. *See also* secret

mystic, xxi, 33, 34, 38, 82, 94, 125, 146, 160,
    161, 186, 242, 244, 247, 257, 276, 281, 284,
    313*n*1; and authority, 78; Christian, 62, 143;
    Jewish, 46
mystical. *See* mystic. *See also* body: mystical
    and theology: mystical
mysticism. *See* mystic

name. *See* God: name of
natural theology. *See* theology: natural
neighbor, 44, 50–56, 72, 113, 121, 235–36,
    240, 301*n*20; encounter with, 53; love of,
    232, 236; responsibility for, 51, 53, 54,
    301*n*22
Nietzsche, Friedrich, 8, 9, 10, 30, 34, 87, 110,
    111, 152, 168, 197, 213, 224, 225, 228, 230,
    232, 237, 245, 255, 283, 297*n*24
nihilism, 10, 34, 121, 224, 231, 268, 319*n*11

object, 6, 11, 14, 32, 41, 42, 43, 44, 47, 57, 69,
    76, 112, 114, 115, 116, 117, 123, 126, 130,
    137, 139, 166, 178, 182, 199, 309*n*4, 313*n*2;
    of consciousness, 42, 57, 165; constitution
    of, 56; of faith, 213; God as, 52, 164, 166,
    237, 301*n*22; of hope, 261; metaphysical,
    120; of perception, 127, 167; properties of,
    130; reduction to, 178; subject and, 177,
    178, 253, 305*n*8
objectivity, 50, 52, 102, 113, 123, 137, 170,
    176. *See also* object
ontological difference, 21, 29–30, 107, 111
ontological proof. *See* proof: ontological
ontology, xix, 6, 20, 22, 23, 25, 28–29, 31, 37,
    43, 50–51, 56, 60, 62, 78, 107, 132, 187,
    188, 193, 194, 196, 197, 213, 215, 225, 238,
    240, 259, 268, 274, 300*n*7, 314*n*7, 325*n*16;
    Descartes's grey, 106; history of, 27;
    language of, 55, 57, 108–9, 111, 301*n*13,
    301*n*24
onto-theo-logy, xix, xxii, xxiii, 20–21, 27–30,
    31, 35, 37–38, 49, 57, 60, 99, 107–8, 186,
    214, 224, 225, 237–41, 244, 252, 268, 274,
    276, 315*n*6, 318*n*2, 318*n*4
ontotheology. *See* onto-theo-logy
onto-theology. *See* onto-theo-logy
Origen, 189, 190, 195
other, 30, 40–58, 63, 64, 70, 72–76, 77, 94,
    95, 102, 115, 119, 127, 132, 144, 146–48,
    149–50, 155, 157, 169, 177–79, 183, 184,
    185, 187, 189–92, 198, 232, 234, 247, 250,
    251, 267–70, 279, 284, 286, 288, 301*n*12,
    303*n*17, 309*n*4, 320*n*6, 324*n*10, 324*n*11,
    325*n*16, 325*n*17; alterity of the, 50, 53, 54,
    285; beings, 28, 29, 31, 107–8, 111; call of
    the, 45; care for the, 47, 284; death of the,
    94, 193; divine, 116, 232, 274, 325*n*17;
    encounter with the, 41, 42, 45, 52, 127, 134,
    153, 176, 236, 278, 285, 309*n*4; enigma of
    the, 41; face of the, 51, 52, 281, 291; flesh of

the, 186, 205, 245; hospitality to the, 75, 144, 267, 270; human, xix, xxi, 41, 49, 50, 51, 52, 53, 54, 56, 113, 119, 136, 151, 152, 155, 158, 160, 165, 232, 235, 288; kill the, 44; philosophy of the, 40, 74; proximity of the, 56; reducing the, 42, 43, 45; responsibility for the, 45, 47, 48, 50, 52, 53, 56, 58, 69, 71–72; self and, 105, 196, 268, 284, 324n8, 325n17; share world with, 26; suffering of the, 181, 245; trace of the, 50; transcendence of the, 69, 234; wholly, 38, 54, 70, 71, 72, 248, 256

otherness, xix, 42, 49, 52, 53, 54, 57, 99, 108, 204, 240, 267–71, 274, 278, 285, 288, 324n9, 324n10. See also alterity

Otto, Rudolf, 70, 233. See also mysterium tremendum

pardon, 48, 66, 67, 74, 76, 94, 153, 271, 274. See also forgiveness

parousia, xxi, 26, 170, 171–72, 177. See also eschatology

Pascal, Blaise, 94, 122, 210, 245, 246

passion, 132, 190, 198, 202, 203, 205, 217, 248, 250, 251, 257, 260, 262, 264, 290, 292, 293, 320n6, 323n18, 323n19. See also pathos

pathos, 127, 128, 130, 204, 205; of life, 127; existential, 233; experience of, 292. See also feeling and suffering

Patočka, Jan, 68–70, 249

Paul, 24, 25–27, 37, 70, 91, 134, 135, 161, 194, 197, 246, 259, 295n2

peace, 26, 44, 49, 50, 72, 80, 89, 93, 117, 176, 183, 250, 259, 267, 270, 281, 284, 290, 297n17; ethic of, 284; gift of, 180; justice and, 276

phenomenology, xviii, xix, xx, xxi, xxii, 13–14, 19, 22–25, 40–43, 49, 56, 57, 77, 85, 106, 112–14, 116, 117, 118, 119, 122, 123, 125, 126, 127, 128, 129, 142, 143, 149, 162, 165–67, 170, 174, 180, 183, 185–91, 197–99, 202, 205, 207, 209–10, 216, 232–33, 252, 267, 279, 283, 311n1, 311n11, 323n2; of birth, 199; Christian, 128, 311n11; critique of, 40, 42, 126; of eros, 276; of the flesh, 125, 131, 283; French, 12, 39, 40; of the gift, 120; of givenness, xx, 112, 116, 117, 120; of the human person, 131; of immanence, xx; of life, 130, 131, 311n11; of liturgy, xxi; of manifestation, 305n7; of marriage, 201; material, 125, 127; minimalist, 13, 106; of religion, 37–38, 141, 167, 219, 223–24, 229, 233, 235, 265, 290, 299n16; of response, 151; of the resurrection, 198, 199; and theology, 22, 25, 173, 185, 206, 212, 273, 298n1, 299n9; of touch, 154; of the voice, 145

phenomenon, 7, 13–14, 19, 32, 42–44, 118, 126, 129, 130, 143–45, 162, 165–67, 171, 186–88, 209–11, 266, 279, 311n11; erotic, 115; ontological, 37; of otherness, 269; poor, 112–13; religious, xix, xx, 25–26, 117–18, 120–23, 138, 142, 149, 210, 293; response to the, 151; of revelation, 114, 288; of the sacrament, 119; of sacrifice, 116, 119; saturated, xx, 65, 106, 112–16, 117–18, 123, 205, 211, 288–89, 291, 307n10; of truth, 31; of the voice, 148. See also phenomenology

physicality, xxi, 131, 145, 148, 152; of the body, 154; of the flesh, 200; of the voice, 144, 145, 154. See also corporeality

piety, 29, 226, 237. See also belief

plurivocal, 63, 101, 145, 214

poetry, 37, 38, 89–90, 93, 145, 151, 157, 177, 210, 246, 280, 281, 289, 291, 292, 305n8

postmodern, xvii, xviii, xxii, 1, 10–11, 12, 24, 59, 211, 212, 223, 224, 225, 229, 230, 231, 232, 235, 236, 237, 238, 241, 242, 243, 257–58, 263, 268, 271, 280, 293, 318n8, 319n10, 324n8, 325n15

praise, xxi, 37, 62, 94, 111, 112, 116, 148, 157, 159, 160, 174, 180, 214, 217, 234, 272, 303n10, 314n5, 317n6, 317n8; language of, 63, 111, 160, 180, 313n10; song of, 238; of the world, 148, 159

prayer, xxi, 3, 12, 24, 62–64, 66–68, 90, 110, 111, 119, 146, 149, 157–60, 167, 172–73, 174, 177, 178, 180, 181, 182, 183, 212, 213, 217, 218, 234, 241, 250, 257, 258, 261, 272, 290, 303n10, 312n8, 314n5, 317n8, 323n19

presence, xxi, 35, 41, 42, 52, 71, 144, 151, 155, 164, 166, 170, 171–72, 174, 177–78, 203, 253, 273, 275, 281, 313n2, 326n23; act of, 181; critique of, 170; eschatological, 177; gift of, 194, 204, 206; of God, 174, 175, 188, 227; of liturgy, 171; metaphysics of, 240, 253; real, 205; retrieval of, 170, 199; sacramental, 172

promise, xxii, 26, 49, 62, 73, 76, 77, 81, 137, 143, 145, 151, 153, 160, 166, 168, 172, 173, 175, 177, 259, 264, 266, 272, 274–75, 276–78, 282, 311n1, 312n3, 312n6, 314n8, 323n17

proof, 4, 7, 26, 123, 129, 141–42, 212–19, 227; for God's existence, 4, 12, 99, 108–9, 135, 143, 212–19; of God's presence, 174; of the Infinite, 52; ontological, 212–19, 296n9; theological, 229

Pseudo-Dionysius. See Dionysius

purity, 108, 113, 126, 288, 289, 314n5, 320n9

reality, xxii, 4, 6, 10, 31, 47, 60, 87, 103–4, 125, 127, 129–33, 137, 138, 139, 141, 165, 172, 173, 175, 180, 187, 192, 193, 195, 196, 199, 200, 202, 204, 205, 206, 208, 217, 235,

spirit, 6, 138, 142, 148, 191, 200, 245, 262, 267, 277, 293, 315*n*6; flesh and, 197, 275; Holy, 2, 119, 198, 200; poor in, 275

spiritual. *See* spirituality

spirituality, xxi, 3, 24, 34, 136, 143, 146, 154, 162, 167, 171, 180, 190, 198–99, 200–1, 227, 228, 232, 235–36, 239, 257, 282, 290, 296*n*4, 312*n*3

stranger, 36, 42, 44, 49, 51, 52, 56, 75–76, 81, 239, 240, 263, 269, 271, 278, 281–82, 285–86, 291, 300*n*5, 318*n*1, 324*n*9, 324*n*10, 326*n*22; welcome to the, xxii, 75–76, 255, 261, 268, 270, 274, 281–82, 284–85, 291. *See also* hospitality *and* neighbor

subject, 6, 11, 41, 42, 45, 47, 58, 113, 115–16, 126, 175, 177–78, 189, 245, 253, 305*n*8, 309*n*4, 314*n*6, 319*n*10; Cartesian, 115, 117, 118; consciousness of the, 113; human, 16, 32, 91, 113; as hostage, 52; question of the, 99; self-sufficient, 58, 98, 115; transcendental, 51. *See also* self

subjectivity, 37, 56, 73, 127–28, 130, 133, 161, 175, 179, 202, 232, 235, 241; inter-, 128, 165, 178, 189, 190–91, 232

substitution, 46–47, 51, 76–77, 152

suffering, 10, 24, 36, 47, 52, 54, 94, 126–27, 130, 131–33, 138, 141, 148, 156, 158, 162, 181, 184, 190, 192–96, 198–99, 202, 203, 206, 227, 235, 245–46, 250, 255, 260, 264, 275, 280, 283, 289, 290, 292, 315*n*3, 321*n*11, 321*n*12. See also *pathos*

superabundance, 100, 161; logic of, 91, 93–94, 289

supernatural, 6, 122, 182, 191, 326*n*19

symbol, 86–88, 100, 154, 167, 170, 173, 181, 194, 201, 205, 268, 283, 305*n*4, 313*n*3

theology, xix, 4, 8, 12, 20, 21, 22–25, 28–30, 34, 37–38, 46, 49, 55, 56, 63, 67, 78, 82, 88, 95, 102, 106, 108, 111, 112, 118, 119, 122–23, 128, 156, 161, 166, 182, 184, 185–87, 189, 197, 206–7, 212, 216, 219, 224, 238, 240–41, 246, 248, 250, 257, 258–60, 270, 273, 274, 280, 296*n*10, 298*n*27, 298*n*1, 299*n*9, 305*n*6, 306*n*18, 313*n*11, 313*n*2, 314*n*12, 316*n*17, 323*n*18, 323*n*19, 323*n*20; and ethics, 239; of the event, xxii, 242, 259; language of, 180–82, 211; liberation, 318*n*5; logic of, 200; mystical, 82, 111, 116, 303*n*10; natural, xix, xxi, 4–5, 7–8, 224, 297*n*20; negative, xx, 60–65, 78, 82, 111, 180, 238–39, 240, 248, 274, 302*n*10, 303*n*11; Patristic, 111; revealed, 4–5, 210

third, 48, 54, 115, 189, 301*n*22; order, 94; reduction, 266, 323*n*2; world, 188. *See also* illeity

time, 2, 4, 41–42, 50, 76, 115, 116, 135, 150, 164, 166, 168, 169–74, 180, 183, 191, 194,

197–99, 248, 261, 269, 277, 289, 312*n*9, 313*n*2, 326*n*23. *See also* space

touch, 131, 144, 146, 148, 154–55, 185, 195, 205, 210, 233, 312*n*9, 321*n*13

trace, 44, 50–51, 53–55, 64, 153, 281, 322*n*13

transcendence, xix, 40, 49, 50, 52–55, 57–58, 62, 69, 126, 157–58, 167, 188, 215, 224, 225, 230, 236, 237, 238–41, 256, 271, 278, 279, 289, 302*n*10, 318*n*7

transubstantiation, 203, 205–6

truth, xix, 5, 10, 11, 16, 20, 22, 30–33, 34, 36, 38, 53, 56, 57, 64, 67, 74, 85, 86, 87, 88, 89–90, 93, 100, 101–4, 116, 125, 128–30, 132, 134, 135, 137, 138, 140–42, 153, 154, 164, 179, 182, 188, 195, 207, 210–11, 216–17, 219, 228, 231, 233, 241, 250, 253–54, 262, 267, 290, 292, 299*n*7, 310*n*9, 317*n*7, 319*n*10; absolute, 10, 231, 241, 254, 279; Christian, 4, 290; claims, 89, 102, 226; eternal, 7, 106, 108, 109, 297*n*15; religious, xx, 4, 90, 103, 257; as subjectivity, 235; of science, xxi, 11, 12, 31, 38, 139, 211; as verification, 33, 89, 90, 101–2, 210–11; of the world, xx, 33, 125, 129–30, 217, 292, 317*n*7. *See also* aletheia, correspondence, evidence *and* verification

univocity, xx, 91, 108, 192, 203. *See also* analogy

unseen, 32, 121, 289. *See also* invisible

verification, 12, 33, 89, 90, 101–2, 189, 209, 210, 211, 213, 217, 219. *See also* evidence *and* proof

visible, 32, 43, 72, 73, 85, 119, 120–21, 126, 131, 132, 137, 148, 151, 157, 166, 182, 188, 217, 218, 283, 284. *See also* appearance, evidence *and* unseen

voice, xxi, 11, 36, 53, 63, 65, 89–91, 92, 101, 102, 114, 143–48, 150–52, 154, 156–60, 162, 218, 224, 246, 263, 278, 279, 289, 302*n*8, 312*n*2, 312*n*8, 313*n*10; of God, 56, 238, 241, 318*n*7. *See also* speech *and* word

vulnerability, 47, 123, 144, 145, 150–51, 158–59, 162, 196, 211, 245, 275, 312*n*3; apologetics of, 123; of the face, 278; of the flesh, 260; of the other, 44. *See also* suffering *and* woundedness

wager, 86–87, 88, 90, 185, 186, 208, 211, 273, 280, 281, 282, 285, 305*n*5, 325*n*17

welcome, xxii, 51, 55, 75, 81, 144, 170, 172, 188, 248, 261, 263, 266, 267, 270, 277, 278, 281, 291, 302*n*5, 312*n*9. *See also* hospitality

Westphal, Merold, xxii, xxiii, 38, 136, 223–41, 242, 243, 252, 262, 263, 265, 268, 290, 318*n*1–319*n*16, 325*n*15

will, 33, 116, 122, 175, 297*n*19; of God, 142;
to power, 20, 175

witness, 32, 51, 52, 53, 55, 58, 64, 79, 102,
147, 148, 153, 157, 174, 176, 284, 301*n*22,
313*n*1

word, 49, 50, 55, 61, 64, 95, 119, 144, 146–47,
148, 150, 155, 161, 177, 179, 188, 201, 203,
276–77, 284, 313*n*2, 314*n*8, 314*n*12,
315*n*12, 316*n*14, 323*n*17; biblical, 36, 90; of
Christ, 129, 133, 136–39, 142; eucharistic,
177, 206; event of the, 260, 313*n*2; of faith,
24, 263; of forgiveness, 81; of God, 9, 51,
54–56, 91, 115, 119, 128, 136, 138, 139,
142, 160, 191, 211, 218, 315*n*7, 323*n*17; of
the holy, 37; of hope, 81; human, 159; of life,
137, 138, 310*n*9; liturgical, 176, 177; of the
world, 137. *See also* language *and* voice

world, 9, 11, 14, 15, 19, 26, 31, 38, 41, 46, 48,
54, 71, 75, 79, 89–92, 102–3, 108, 109,
126, 128, 130, 132, 133, 134, 135, 137, 140,
144, 149, 150, 151, 154–62, 164, 167–80,
188, 190, 192, 195–99, 204, 206–7, 210,
217, 218, 223, 227, 235, 239–40, 241, 247,
252, 257, 261, 273, 277, 282–84, 286, 292,
309*n*3, 309*n*4, 309*n*6, 310*n*9, 313*n*3,
314*n*4, 314*n*5, 314*n*7, 315*n*7, 321*n*13,
322*n*16, 324*n*8; of the animal, 204;
anti-Christian, 139; beauty of the, 147,
156–57; being-in-the, xxi, 22, 26, 31, 38,
89, 91, 131, 132, 163, 167, 169, 171, 173–78,
186, 245, 289, 313*n*3; biblical, 89, 103;
communal, 25, 190, 191; creation of the, 5,
132, 138, 147; death to the, 189; entities
within the, 20, 28; experience of the, 14, 26,
45, 167, 219, 313*n*1; of faith, 24; flesh of the,
277, 326*n*24; history, 34; life-, 26, 186; logic
of the, 122; natural, 3, 4, 5, 6; offering of
the, 148, 159; opening of the, 31, 168, 177,
291; order of the, 6; praise of the, 148;
prelinguistic, 11; possible, 276; postmodern,
224, 241; relations with the, 25; response to
the, xxi; reverence for the, 37; shelter for the,
146; symbolic, 87, 88; of the text, 89–90,
93; thrown into the, 31; truth of the, xx,
32–33, 125, 129–30, 211, 217, 292, 317*n*7;
vision of the, 92

woundedness, 144, 156, 158

yes, 59, 150, 151, 155, 157, 159, 248, 249, 260,
261, 262, 267, 278, 302*n*5

Perspectives in Continental Philosophy

John D. Caputo, series editor

Karl Jaspers, *The Question of German Guilt*. Introduction by Joseph W. Koterski, S.J.

Jean-Luc Marion, *The Idol and Distance: Five Studies*. Translated with an introduction by Thomas A. Carlson.

Jeffrey Dudiak, *The Intrigue of Ethics: A Reading of the Idea of Discourse in the Thought of Emmanuel Levinas*.

Robyn Horner, *Rethinking God as Gift: Marion, Derrida, and the Limits of Phenomenology*.

Mark Dooley, *The Politics of Exodus: Søren Keirkegaard's Ethics of Responsibility*.

Merold Westphal, *Overcoming Onto-Theology: Toward a Postmodern Christian Faith*.

Edith Wyschogrod, Jean-Joseph Goux, and Eric Boynton, eds., *The Enigma of Gift and Sacrifice*.

Stanislas Breton, *The Word and the Cross*. Translated with an introduction by Jacquelyn Porter.

Jean-Luc Marion, *Prolegomena to Charity*. Translated by Stephen E. Lewis.

Peter H. Spader, *Scheler's Ethical Personalism: Its Logic, Development, and Promise*.

Jean-Louis Chrétien, *The Unforgettable and the Unhoped For*. Translated by Jeffrey Bloechl.

Don Cupitt, *Is Nothing Sacred? The Non-Realist Philosophy of Religion: Selected Essays*.

Jean-Luc Marion, *In Excess: Studies of Saturated Phenomena*. Translated by Robyn Horner and Vincent Berraud.

Phillip Goodchild, *Rethinking Philosophy of Religion: Approaches from Continental Philosophy*.

William J. Richardson, S.J., *Heidegger: Through Phenomenology to Thought*.

Jeffrey Andrew Barash, *Martin Heidegger and the Problem of Historical Meaning*.

Jean-Louis Chrétien, *Hand to Hand: Listening to the Work of Art*. Translated by Stephen E. Lewis.

Jean-Louis Chrétien, *The Call and the Response*. Translated with an introduction by Anne Davenport.

D. C. Schindler, *Han Urs von Balthasar and the Dramatic Structure of Truth: A Philosophical Investigation*.

Julian Wolfreys, ed., *Thinking Difference: Critics in Conversation*.

Allen Scult, *Being Jewish/Reading Heidegger: An Ontological Encounter*.

Richard Kearney, *Debates in Continental Philosophy: Conversations with Contemporary Thinkers*.

Jennifer Anna Gosetti-Ferencei, *Heidegger, Hölderlin, and the Subject of Poetic Language: Towards a New Poetics of Dasein*.

Jolita Pons, *Stealing a Gift: Kierkegaard's Pseudonyms and the Bible*.

Jean-Yves Lacoste, *Experience and the Absolute: Disputed Questions on the Humanity of Man*. Translated by Mark Raftery-Skehan.

Charles P. Bigger, *Between Chora and the Good: Metaphor's Metaphysical Neighborhood*.

ınique Janicaud, *Phenomenology "Wide Open": After the French Debate.* Translated by Charles N. Cabral.

n Leask and Eoin Cassidy, eds., *Givenness and God: Questions of Jean-Luc Marion.*

Jacques Derrida, *Sovereignties in Question: The Poetics of Paul Celan.* Edited by Thomas Dutoit and Outi Pasanen.

William Desmond, *Is There a Sabbath for Thought? Between Religion and Philosophy.*

Bruce Ellis Benson and Norman Wirzba, eds., *The Phenomenology of Prayer.*

S. Clark Buckner and Matthew Statler, eds., *Styles of Piety: Practicing Philosophy after the Death of God.*

Kevin Hart and Barbara Wall, eds., *The Experience of God: A Postmodern Response.*

John Panteleimon Manoussakis, *After God: Richard Kearney and the Religious Turn in Continental Philosophy.*

John Martis, *Philippe Lacoue-Labarthe: Representation and the Loss of the Subject.*

Jean-Luc Nancy, *The Ground of the Image.*

Edith Wyschogrod, *Crossover Queries: Dwelling with Negatives, Embodying Philosophy's Others.*

Gerald Bruns, *On the Anarchy of Poetry and Philosophy: A Guide for the Unruly.*

Brian Treanor, *Aspects of Alterity: Levinas, Marcel, and the Contemporary Debate.*

Simon Morgan Wortham, *Counter-Institutions: Jacques Derrida and the Question of the University.*

Leonard Lawlor, *The Implications of Immanence: Toward a New Concept of Life.*

Clayton Crockett, *Interstices of the Sublime: Theology and Psychoanalytic Theory.*

Bettina Bergo, Joseph Cohen, and Raphael Zagury-Orly, eds., *Judeities: Questions for Jacques Derrida.* Translated by Bettina Bergo and Michael B. Smith.

Jean-Luc Marion, *On the Ego and on God: Further Cartesian Questions.* Translated by Christina M. Gschwandtner.

Jean-Luc Nancy, *Philosophical Chronicles.* Translated by Franson Manjali.

Jean-Luc Nancy, *Dis-Enclosure: The Deconstruction of Christianity.* Translated by Bettina Bergo, Gabriel Malenfant, and Michael B. Smith.

Andrea Hurst, *Derrida Vis-à-vis Lacan: Interweaving Deconstruction and Psychoanalysis.*

Jean-Luc Nancy, *Noli me tangere: On the Raising of the Body.* Translated by Sarah Clift, Pascale-Anne Brault, and Michael Naas.

Jacques Derrida, *The Animal That Therefore I Am.* Edited by Marie-Louise Mallet, translated by David Wills.

Jean-Luc Marion, *The Visible and the Revealed.* Translated by Christina M. Gschwandtner and others.

Michel Henry, *Material Phenomenology.* Translated by Scott Davidson.

Jean-Luc Nancy, *Corpus.* Translated by Richard A. Rand.

Joshua Kates, *Fielding Derrida.*

Michael Naas, *Derrida From Now On.*

Shannon Sullivan and Dennis J. Schmidt, eds., *Difficulties of Ethical Life.*